ECONOMIC
NATIONALISM
IN A
GLOBALIZING
WORLD

A volume in the series
Cornell Studies in Political Economy
edited by PETER J. KATZENSTEIN

A full list of titles in the series appears at the end of the book.

ECONOMIC NATIONALISM IN A GLOBALIZING WORLD

EDITED BY

Eric Helleiner and Andreas Pickel

Cornell University Press

ITHACA AND LONDON

An earlier version of chapter 5, "Japanese Spirit, Western Economics: The Continuing Salience of Economic Nationalism in Japan," by Derek Hall, appeared in *New Political Economy* 9, no. 1 (March 2004). It is used here with permission.

First published 2005 by Cornell University Press
First printing, Cornell Paperbacks, 2005

Printed in the United States of America

Library of Congress Cataloging-in-Publication Data

Economic nationalism in a globalizing world / edited by Eric Helleiner and
Andreas Pickel.
    p.   cm. — (Cornell studies in political economy)
  "Preliminary drafts of the chapters in this book were first presented at a workshop hosted
by the Trent International Political Economy Centre in August 2002"—Pref.
  Includes bibliographical references and index.
  ISBN 0-8014-4312-1 (cloth : alk. paper) — ISBN 0-8014-8966-0 (pbk. : alk. paper)
  1. Economic policy.   2. Protectionism.   3. Nationalism.   4. Globalization.
I. Helleiner, Eric, 1963–   II. Pickel, Andreas.   III. Series.
  HD87.E257 2005
  337—dc22

                                                                    2004015590

Cloth printing   10 9 8 7 6 5 4 3 2 1
Paperback printing 10 9 8 7 6 5 4 3 2 1

Contents

NA

Preface

This book offers a critique of conventional understandings of economic nationalism. Economic nationalism is frequently portrayed as an outdated phenomenon in this age of globalization. This view, however, rests on an assumption that economic nationalism is best understood as a "protectionist" ideology or a variant of realism. This book highlights how this conventional understanding neglects the nationalist content of economic nationalism. It suggests that the study of economic nationalism should focus instead on how nationalism and national identities shape economic policy and processes. Adopting this approach, the various contributors argue that economic nationalism remains a potent force in the contemporary world. They highlight how nationalism and national identities continue to exert an important influence on economic policy in a wide range of countries and contexts. And in so doing, they contribute to recent critiques of "rationalist" political economy by highlighting the significant role of this ideational factor in economic policymaking.

We are grateful to the contributors to this volume for their participation. Preliminary drafts of the chapters in this book were first presented at a workshop hosted by the Trent International Political Economy Centre in August 2002. For support for this workshop, we are also grateful to Trent University as well as to the Social Sciences and Humanities Research Council of Canada's Aid to Small Universities program and the Canada Research Chair programs. We extend special thanks to Peter Katzenstein and Roger Haydon for their interest in this project and for their very helpful comments. We are also grateful for the detailed comments of one anonymous reviewer.

E.H. and A.P.

Peterborough, Ontario

Notes on Contributors

RAWI ABDELAL is an Assistant Professor at the Harvard Business School.

MAYA EICHLER received a Magistra in Political Science and Russian Language from the University of Vienna. She is currently a doctoral candidate in the Political Science Department at York University in Toronto.

PATRICIA GOFF is Assistant Professor of Political Science at Wilfrid Laurier University.

DEREK HALL is Assistant Professor of International Development Studies and Political Studies at Trent University, Peterborough, Ontario.

ERIC HELLEINER is Canada Research Chair in International Political Economy, Trent University.

KLAUS MÜLLER received his Ph.D. in Economics and Social Sciences in 1993 at the Free University Berlin, where he is teaching sociology.

ANDREAS PICKEL is Professor in the Department of Political Studies, Trent University.

JACQUI TRUE is a Senior Lecturer in the Department of Political Studies, University of Auckland, New Zealand.

ANDREI P. TSYGANKOV is an Assistant Professor in the Departments of International Relations and Political Science, San Francisco State University.

MEREDITH WOO-CUMINGS is Professor of Political Science at the University of Michigan.

ECONOMIC
NATIONALISM
IN A
GLOBALIZING
WORLD

Introduction: False Oppositions ⸮

Recontextualizing Economic Nationalism
in a Globalizing World

Andreas Pickel

Nationalism in general and economic nationalism in particular have gained a reputation as anachronistic ideologies. Their survival in an age of globalizing markets and declining nation-states is widely portrayed as the backlash of misinformed masses and their ill-intentioned leaders against the progress of economic and political liberalization. We consider this reputation undeserved and the source of misleading and inappropriate policy advice. The purpose of this book is to recast discussions about economic nationalism in the context of globalization. We have three central objectives: to offer a critique of the conventional view of economic nationalism; to reorient and broaden the discussion around the relationships between national identities and economic processes; and to contribute to debates about the role of ideas in the literature of international relations (IR) and international political economy (IPE).

While there are large literatures both on nationalism and on the political economy of globalization, neither one has systematically addressed how their objects of study relate to each other. The most recent nonhistorical, book-length scholarly study specifically devoted to economic nationalism, entitled *The New Economic Nationalism,* was published in 1980.[1] That national identity and economics are closely and significantly related, and that globalization processes may in fact reinforce rather than weaken these relationships, are among the major findings of our contributors. One notable implication of this finding is that economic nationalism and neoliberalism are not the necessary opposites they are usually taken to be. Rather, in a

---

1. Hieronymi (1980). Mayall (1990) devotes two chapters to economic nationalism, the second of which is entitled "The New Economic Nationalism." Two excellent articles about economic nationalism are Crane (1998) and Levi-Faur (1997a). New studies by two of our contributors are Abdelal (2001) and Tsygankov (2001). I'm not including recent popular or political treatments of the subject, e.g., Buchanan (1998) and Frank (1999).

1

variety of circumstances from postcommunist transformations to country "rebranding" under globalization, neoliberalism has become one form of economic nationalism. By demonstrating the economic significance of national identities, we undermine the standard narrow conception of economic nationalism. However, we take an additional step by analyzing *how* the national affects the economic. This introductory chapter sets the stage for the subsequent historical-empirical studies.

It is not unusual for social scientists' concepts to be used in other, especially political, discourses. "Democracy," "market economy," and indeed "globalization" are typical examples of such conceptual overlap. There are different strategies one can use to deal with the potential confusion inherent in adopting such "loaded" concepts for social science. Simply ignoring the problem is one. Another is to legislate one's own definition, which, given the absence of a sovereign legislator for such matters, frequently leads to a proliferation of mutually more or less inconsistent definitions. Yet another strategy is to abandon the concept as hopelessly contaminated. None of these responses seems to us satisfactory. We do not want to skirt the issue, add another idiosyncratic definition, or discard the concept as ideology. Economic nationalism can be understood as a specific ideology and policy doctrine, but it is also much more than that, as I will argue below. We take as our point of departure a reconstruction of what the concept of economic nationalism means and implies in current political debates as a way of establishing a context for our discussions. Each of the contributors proceeds to "unpack" this dominant conception by critically examining its claims and assumptions in light of a specific case study, and each contributes a perspective on the significance of national identity for the political economy.

The Conventional View of Economic Nationalism

> There is no doubt that America has been one of the biggest beneficiaries of globalisation. How striking then that globalisation, and trade policy especially, have become increasingly controversial and politically charged.
>
> —*The Economist*, September 28, 2000

In contemporary political and economic discourse, economic nationalism is usually juxtaposed to globalization and its ideological advocate, neoliberalism. This politically neat distinction is in practice difficult to sustain, as the above quotation illustrates. The strength of any political discourse, however, lies in part in its ability to make clear, simple, and stark distinctions between good and bad, friend and foe. Neoliberal discourse treats economic nationalism as a pernicious doctrine, and its proponents as a political enemy. Calling a particular policy approach or action an instance of economic nationalism is thus, in the current context, a way of disqualifying it. The same is true for the appellation "economic nationalist." The underlying dichotomy between "economic nationalist" and "economic liberal" is well established and widely shared—even among scholars. Long before the ascent of neoliberalism, the economist Harry Johnson analyzed economic nationalism as an economic program that "seeks to extend the property owned by nationals so as to gratify the taste for nationalism. . . . Nationalism will tend to direct economic policy toward the production of psychic income in the form of nationalistic satisfaction, at the expense of material income" (Johnson [1965] 1994, 238–39). "An investment in the creation of a middle class, financed by resources extracted from the mass of the population by nationalistic policies, may be the essential preliminary to the construction of a viable national state. This problem, however, belongs in the spheres of history, sociology, and political science rather than economics" (240).

This "economistic" conception of economic nationalism is in one form or another shared by a number of different approaches.[2] Johnson does not deny the potential significance of nationalistic economic policies for such "extra-economic" projects as state building, but he considers their analysis beyond the purview of economics. What economics can say is that such policies are costly in material terms. Even more narrow is the "economism" of mainstream economists, who are largely unaware of or uninterested in the literature on nationalism and its potential implications for economic processes. Much the same holds for the "economism" of rational choice theorists who *are* committed to the study of extra-economic phenomena, including nationalism (Woodruff 2000; Olson 1987), but whose specific brand of methodological individualism gives them no instruments to examine social wholes—such as nations, societies, cultures, and other social systems (Appel 2000; Bunge 1999, chap. 5).[3] The following seem to be basic assumptions in this discourse:

- *Economism:* economic nationalism can be adequately explained in strictly economic terms without taking into account historical, political, cultural, or social factors.

2. As Eric Helleiner (2002) shows, it was not shared by nineteenth-century economic liberals such as Ricardo, Mill, or Cobden, who "saw free trade primarily as a tool to strengthen peaceful cosmopolitan world society."
3. In this view, for example, the state is conceptualized in terms of "rent-seeking" individuals, and cultures are conceptualized as aggregates of individual preferences. It is also the "economism" of neoliberal discourse which theoretically rests on neoclassical or rational-choice foundations. Finally, it is the "economism" of radical left analyses preoccupied with the primacy of class (Panitch and Leys 2001) and dismissive of what one author in the current context has called "progressive nationalism" (Radice 2000).

- *Homogeneity:* economic nationalism, like economic liberalism, refers to essentially the same economic doctrines across time and space.
- *Interests:* nationalist economic doctrines are advanced by, and for, special economic interests disguised as the general interest.
- *Validity:* the validity of such economic doctrines can be decided by modern economics. Unlike economic liberalism, economic nationalism produces economic costs and therefore can claim little scientific support.

Yet as scholars and activists from Friedrich List to Raul Prebisch knew, economic nationalism cannot be examined and assessed as an economic doctrine in an abstract economic framework precisely because it responds to problems situated in particular historical, political, cultural, and social contexts. Invoking "variables" such as "psychic enjoyment" or "taste for nationalism" to account for dimensions of the phenomenon that go beyond such a framework indicate that other approaches may be needed.

The field of international political economy seems to provide just such an approach in what it calls promisingly the "Nationalist perspective" (Gilpin 1987; Balaam and Veseth 2001). However, as both Abdelal and Goff argue in this volume (see also Abdelal 2001), this approach is based on the same narrow distinction between economic liberalism and economic nationalism criticized above. Moreover, it follows the treatment of nationalism in the international relations literature generally, which does not conceptualize the nation as distinct from the state.[4] As a result, economic nationalism in the "Nationalist perspective" is reduced to the doctrine that "economic activities are and should be subordinate to the goal of state building and the interests of the state" (Gilpin 1987, 31). This points us to the nationalism literature, in which the distinction between nation and state is fundamental.

The burgeoning field of nationalism studies has not devoted systematic attention to the ways in which national identity shapes and affects economic processes. Perhaps the main reason for this neglect is that the literature on nationalism is preoccupied with explaining the origins, forms, and manifestations of nationalism rather than its interactions with the economy. Two fundamentally opposed presuppositions in the literature address the relationship between nation and economy directly. On one side, exemplified by Ernest Gellner's (1983) modernist (and materialist) theory of nationalism, the emergence and power of nationalism is explained as a subordinate, albeit highly functional, part of more general processes of socioeconomic transformation. Here, the primary interest is to explain nationalism, rather

---

4. This refers to the realist and liberal approaches in the international relations literature. These have recently been challenged by so-called constructivist approaches that are more open to the concerns of this volume.

than explain how economic processes interact with and are shaped by national identities. In a complete reversal of this explanatory logic, Liah Greenfeld's (2001a) idealist approach attempts to explain the emergence of capitalism as a function of nationalism.[5] Both fundamental presuppositions are too strong and one-sided for an approach to examining the problem of whether, to what extent, and how national identity is implicated in economic processes. As I will suggest in the next section, however, the nationalism literature, even if it has not systematically addressed *economic* nationalism, is nevertheless a rich source of insights for our purposes.

Broadening Our Perspective: A Brief Survey of Other Relevant Scholarly Literatures

> The geographical definition of any economy is given by the area across which business firms maximize profit—that is, across which they search to find the cheapest places to produce and the most profitable places to sell their goods and services. With today's communication and transportation technologies, business firms increasingly search the globe on both of these dimensions. In the process, a global economy is emerging that will in the end dissolve our existing national economies.
>
> —Lester Thurow, "Globalization"

If ours is truly a historical period of globalization rather than nation building, economic nationalism can no longer claim to be a doctrine of progressive development. It would indeed seem to be an ideological anachronism. But neither "national economies" nor "economic nations" are dissolving, while the significance of different national economic cultures is only just being (re)discovered. Globalization discourse has called into question the national as a unit of analysis—whether with respect to economies, states, societies, or cultures. The strongest claims describe a new global economy that has eclipsed national economies and is progressively undermining the relative significance of national states, societies, and cultures. A world economy once made up of national economies is rapidly being transformed into a global economy composed of transnational economic actors, regions, and networks. National states and societies are disintegrating as a result of economic globalization—processes manifested in such divergent social phenomena as emerging global cultures and transnational movements, on the one hand, and cultural and economic marginalization and ethnic violence,

---

5. See, for a critical review, Rutland (2003).

on the other. Plausible and popular as this "economistic" view may be, it is fundamentally flawed. Economic globalization has no such general effect on national states, societies, and economies.[6] In order to gauge the actual effects of current economic changes, we need a more fine-grained conceptual apparatus than is offered by economistic views.

The conventional, economistic view of economic nationalism is based on a "thin" conception of the economy. It is the neoclassical model plus—the "plus" referring to a variety of largely unsupported assumptions about politics, culture, society, and psychology with the help of which economic nationalism is understood. There is of course no reason why unsupported assumptions need to be accepted when various social sciences—such as political economy, socioeconomics, historical sociology, social psychology, and management studies—have produced a range of important and well-supported results on these questions. I will point to some of the major findings from a variety of such scholarly literatures that seem to be particularly relevant for reconceptualizing economic nationalism.

National Economies

If one assumes a geographical definition of national economy, as Thurow does above, national economies do indeed appear to be dissolving, insofar as economic activity, especially finance and trade, is rapidly internationalizing. But economic activity, especially production and consumption, still occurs in particular national social and political contexts, which in turn provide fundamental resources for, and constraints on, such global-level economic activity. Two bodies of literature have made particularly significant contributions to establishing the continuing significance of the national economy. The first is the literature critical of the "new global economy" thesis (see, e.g., Wade 1996a; Zysman 1996; Doremus et al. 1999; Sorge 1999). The second is the "varieties of capitalism" literature, which calls into question the convergence thesis according to which globalization is producing one dominant model of market economy (Hall and Soskice 2001; Berger and Dore 1996; Goricheva 1997; Hollingsworth and Boyer 1997; Streeck and Crouch 1997; Streeck 1992). For the purposes of our discussion, the following results are particularly important.

- Extension of economic activity beyond national boundaries does not equal the end of national economy; the latter, qua political, social, and cultural economy, continues to be the basis for the former.
- Generalizations about *the* national economy, now as in the past, ignore the great diversity of conditions for particular national economies.

6. For a wide-ranging collection of recent analyses on the nature and implications of economic globalization, see Held and McGrew (2000).

National States

Part of the distinctiveness of individual national economies arises from the specific patterns of interaction between state and economy that have evolved. These roles of the state—in many respects nationally specific—are examined in an extensive literature (Boyer and Drache 1996; Garrett 1998; Helleiner 1994; Iverson, Pontusson, and Soskice 2000; Jessop 1999; Weiss 1998). This literature shows why and how, even under the "rule of the global economy," political economies are still governed by states. While economic globalization is a convenient shorthand for referring to changing global economic conditions, the decline or even end of the nation-state is not the other side of this coin. First, economic globalization has been engineered by certain nation-states and continues to be shaped by them. Second, given the continued significance of national economic systems, states remain the central actors in all political economies.

Another literature with a long tradition (Gerschenkron 1962; Bendix 1977) underscores the centrality of nations and cultures in state formation, industrialization, postcommunist transformation, and stability and change (Bönker, Müller, and Pickel 2002; Linz and Stepan 1996; Steinmetz 1999). Two central implications of this literature are:

- The current transformations of national economies in the context of economic globalization are directed, shaped, or strongly influenced by national states and particular groups of states, and *by* the international organizations they dominate.
- Generalizations about *the* national state, now as in the past, ignore the great diversity of types of and conditions for states, in particular their cultural specificity.

Economic Nations

The conventional view of economic nationalism has no conception of economic nationhood, since it is based on a "thin" view of economics that cannot deal with phenomena such as national identity. By contrast, taking the concept of a nation seriously means that it is not just as a synonym for country or state. While the relationship between state and nation is a mainstay of the literature on nationalism, this literature has paid relatively little attention to the relationship between the nation and the economy. In part, this is a result of an unfortunate division of labor between students of nationalism and students of political economy. Yet it is not difficult to translate some of the major results of current scholarly debates on nationalism into relevant insights for the study of economic nationalism. First, the categorical distinction between civic and ethnic nationalism (i.e., between good, Western, liberal patriotism and bad, non-Western, authoritarian nationalism) has been demolished (Billig 1995; Spencer and Wollman 1998). The upshot of this debate is a refocusing of attention on nationalism as a generic phenomenon that is in principle compatible with a variety of ideological content—from liberalism (Miller 1995; Tamir 1993) to fascism. While ideologically sensible, it is theoretically unproductive to reserve the term "nationalism" for any specific type of doctrine, as the conventional view of economic nationalism does. This is a central point in many of the chapters in this book.

A further insight generated by the nationalism literature is that the widespread tendency to conceive of nationalism exclusively as ideology or doctrine misses the all-important concrete context of political interactions—whether contentious or integrative—in which such ideas are developed and deployed (Beissinger 1996; Brubaker 1996; see also Tarrow 1994). Thus economic nationalism should be understood simultaneously as political action in a specific historical context, rather than as economic doctrine in a universal context of ideas.[7] Another fundamental insight of the recent nationalism literature is that both as a symbolic system and as a societal structure, the nation has become a fundamental pattern that is constantly being reproduced globally in a variety of forms (Anderson 1983; Calhoun 1997; Gellner 1983; Kyvelidis 2000; Meyer et al. 1997). As Charles Tilly (1999, 418) has put it:

> As in the cases of citizenship and democracy, nationalism exhibits the paradox of a general process characterized by path-dependent particularism. On one side, classic mechanisms of invention, ramification, emulation, and adaptation recur in the generation of nationalist claims. On the other side, each new assertion of nationalism responds to its immediate historical and cultural context, then modifies conditions for the next assertion of nationalism. Like all culturally constrained social processes, nationalism proceeds in cultural ruts that greatly limit the directions it can go, relies on collective learning, but by its very exercise alters relations—including shared understandings—among parties to its claims."

The following insights from the nationalism literature seem particularly important.

- Nationalism should be understood fundamentally as generic discursive structure rather than any particular substantive doctrine.

7. As Szeleny (1999, 486) has pointed out in the postcommunist transformation context, "despite radically altered contexts of political, legal, and economic incentives, and even where elite circulation has been significant, old political rationalities continue to structure the political agenda and order debate." These "rationalities" are of course nationally specific.

- Nationalism is not just an ideology or doctrine, but also political contention in the context of particular historical conditions.
- Nationalism is a combination of discourse, action, and structure.

National Economic Cultures

Just as individual political nations have developed particular national political cultures (Bendix 1977, 1978; Elias 1978, 1996), economic nations have their own economic cultures. Let us begin by illustrating the general concept with a concrete empirical example, drawn not from an earlier, now largely discredited literature on national character (Lamont 1995, 351), but from contemporary political economy.

> German economic culture is often traditionalist. Savings rates are high, and consumer credit, although increasing, remains low by comparison. Price competition is mitigated by socially established preferences for quality. Markets do not per se confer merit: social status and solidarity interfere, and security is regarded as important. Speculation is not valued. Continuous monitoring of one's short-term balance of economic advantage is not a social norm, encouraging long-term orientations and commitments and supporting, among other things, a redistributive tax system. Professional competence is highly regarded for its own sake; German managers tend to be engineers and authority at the workplace is based on superior technical knowledge. Collectivism and discipline have given way as core cultural values to privacy and autonomy from organisational control and market pressure, as shown by strong cultural support for short working hours, low participation in paid employment, and a qualification-based organisation of work. (Streeck 1997)

The same author (Streeck 1999) has also coined the phrase "competitive solidarity" to underline nationalism's economic potential in global competitiveness. The significance of different national economic cultures is increasingly discussed in the scholarly management literature.[8] As Geert Hofstede, a cultural psychologist influential in management theory, has formulated it:

> Because management is about people, it is part of the culture of the society in which it takes place. Culture is "the collective programming of the mind that distinguishes the members of one group or category of people from another." The core elements in culture are values. Values are "broad tendencies to prefer certain states of affairs over others." They are about what is evil and

---

8. The work of G. Hofstede (e.g., 1991, 1980) has been seminal in this literature, spawning a large number of empirical studies.

what is good, dirty and clean, immoral and moral, irrational and rational. Relationships between people in a society are affected by the values that form part of the collective programming of people's minds in that society. So management is subject to cultural values. Cultural values differ among societies, but within a society they are remarkably stable over time. This is why I claim that management processes, which are embedded in a culture, differ from society to society but within each society show strong continuity. . . . While I argue that management in the 21st century will not be basically different from management in the 20th, I do expect a breakthrough in the development of theories of management, which will become more adapted to national cultural value systems in different parts of the world. (Hofstede 1999, 36, 39)[9]

A similarly critical view of a cultural, thin conceptions of economic society can also be found in recent studies of national legal cultures (Boyle 2000; Chua 1998), public administrative cultures (Kouzmin 1997; Macdonald and Thomas 1997), and national "repertoires of evaluation" (Lamont and Thevenot 2000). The general social and cultural embeddedness of markets is studied by economic sociologists (cf. Granovetter and Swedberg 1992) and economic anthropologists (see, e.g., Hefner 1998). The following points are particularly relevant:

- National economic cultures exist both as symbolic and as social systems, and as such can be mapped.
- Economic cultures have limited variation within a society, but strong variations between societies.
- National economic cultures as values and practices are central constituents of economic nations and make up the concrete historical context for economic nationalism.

National economies and states, as well as economic nations and cultures, have been traditional concerns of the social sciences since at least the nineteenth century. The current challenge is therefore not to reinvent the wheel but to reassemble a new model from the various parts already available. Perhaps the most important part to be reemphasized, especially in light of the globalization debate, is that the national cannot be understood in separation from or contradistinction to the international or global. They are, as

9. Contrast this rich conception of economic culture with the thin conception of the economist L. Thurow (2000): "Traditionally, culture is older people telling younger people what they should believe and how they should act. What is frightening about the new electronic culture is that it is a 'for-sale' culture that jumps right across the generations directly to the young. In contrast to older forms of culture, this culture does not have any specific values that it wants to inculcate. Those who produce this culture provide whatever sells—whatever the young will buy. It is a culture of economics (profits) rather than a culture of values (morals)."

dependency theorists used to put it, two sides of the same coin. The relationships between globalizing and nationalizing processes should therefore not be seen in terms of a zero-sum game (Pickel and True 2002).

An Analytical Framework for the Study of Nation and Economy

Summing up the results of this chapter to this point, a review of the conventional, economistic conception of economic nationalism shows that its underlying approach, based on the distinction between economic liberalism and economic nationalism, is limited and misleading. Other literatures, in particular those of international political economy and nationalism, study either economic processes or national identity but not both, presumably on the assumption that these spheres of social life do not significantly affect each other. We found the two strong positions linking these spheres—that the economic determines the national, and that the national determines the economic—both too reductionist for our purposes. National identities significantly affect economic processes, but generally speaking they do so in indeterminate ways.

This indeterminacy has two major sources. The first results from the causal intervention of typical structural, institutional, and interest variables in economic processes. In other words, national identities matter for the economy, but any adequate explanation of how it does so requires the systematic incorporation of such variables. These variables are stressed particularly in Eichler's chapter. The second is a result of the historically unique and diverse types of relationships between particular national identities and economic processes. This ultimate uniqueness requires that any empirical account exploring the significance of the nation for the economy needs to incorporate a systematic reconstruction of its specific content, history, and international context. Several of the following chapters provide such case-specific reconstructions. A general theory of economic nationalism therefore is ruled out. Not ruled out, however, are limited generalizations about economic nationalism in a globalizing world, though the scope and depth of the generalizations we arrive at, and their value and significance, is for the reader to assess. The concluding chapter summarizes what our collective effort has yielded. It also provides a more detailed discussion of how our project fits into the larger debate in IR and IPE on ideas and interests. The remainder of this introduction will sketch an analytical framework for the study of the relationships between nation and economy, which is then followed by a brief overview of the structure of the volume.

While we do not believe in the possibility of a *general* theory of economic nationalism, we are interested in theorizing typical relationships between national identity and economy. For this purpose, as well as for the following individual historical-empirical accounts, it is useful to have as a common

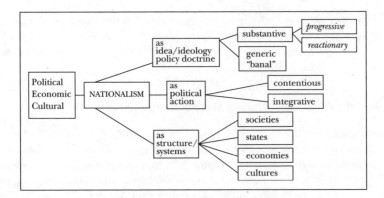

Figure I.1. An analytical framework for the study of economic nationalism

reference point a basic analytical framework for the study of economic nationalism. This framework is schematically represented in the accompanying figure.

We assume that *economic* nationalism, like political or cultural nationalism,
can be understood only if it is analyzed in the context of nation and nationalism in general, rather than as just another economic doctrine or ideology (the conventional economistic view criticized above). This is perhaps
the single most important move in our reconceptualization. It gives us access to the insights generated in the various literatures reviewed above, including the nationalism literature. This allows us to make the fundamental
analytical distinction between three dimensions of (economic) nation and
nationalism: as ideology or policy, as political action, and as structure. Let
us take each in turn.

The conventional view criticized above considers economic nationalism
as a reactionary ideology and policy doctrine. This is at best a partial view.
While economic nationalism appears also as a substantive policy doctrine,
its content, and even more so its political desirability, have always been contested (in debates between economic liberals and economic nationalists, for
example). In our view, the concept of economic nationalism need not be restricted to specific policy doctrines but rather should be viewed more generically. That is, the global significance of the national, as culture and rhetoric,
suggests that whatever the specific content of such policy doctrines, their
conception and legitimation always (and in most cases primarily) occur in
a national context. The most important implication of this conceptual shift
is that it allows us to treat economic liberalism as a particular form of economic nationalism. This shift is not an arbitrary definitional fiat, but a conscious attempt to reconceptualize how we think about the relationship
between national identity and economy.

Seeing economic nationalism exclusively as ideology or policy doctrine, whether substantive or generic, still imposes excessive limits on our analytical scope. Thus while this viewpoint may be convenient for economists who favor a strict division of labor with historians, sociologists, and political scientists (see the quotation from Johnson above), it does not work for a sociologically informed political economy. The latter is interested precisely in the processes linking doctrines and political action, and it therefore requires an analytical framework making room for both. The significance of examining processes of "cultural framing" in a context of political contention has been amply demonstrated in the social movement literature and fruitfully employed in the study of nationalism (e.g., Beissinger 2002; Tilly 1998). It is important to note that these are not instrumentalist reductions in which political interests opportunistically employ whatever doctrine or ideology may suit them; it is, on the contrary, a serious approach designed to explore their interaction.

The "ultimate" source of the continuing power and significance of both nationalist doctrines and politics is structural. That is, notwithstanding processes of internationalization and internal fragmentation, the national in societies, states, economies, and cultures remains fundamental. In all these social systems it is the "nationalizing" mechanisms that we need to take into account in order to make sense of the relationships between national identity and political economy. These nationalizing mechanisms include the political legitimation of states; the reproduction of a repertory of common epistemic and moral orders fundamental for the coordination of political and economic action; a constantly evolving national discourse; and national identities as processes of shared social representations, social practices, and forms of collective action. This broad reconceptualization of economic nationalism as a complex set of relationships between nation and economy marks the outer boundaries within which the theoretical and empirical work presented in this volume is situated. While this framework is ambitious, we do not claim to be taking more than initial steps in illustrating its usefulness.

An Overview

This volume is divided into four parts. The first explores economic nationalism in the post–Soviet Union context. This context has been a rich one for those seeking to reinterpret the meaning and significance of economic nationalism. The three chapters in part 1 explain why: nationalism and national identities have played a significant role in influencing the content and direction of the dramatic changes in economic policy in this region since 1991.

Rawi Abdelal begins with an examination of the different choices made by various post-Soviet governments to either maintain or reduce their close economic ties with Russia. To explain these choices, he argues, one must examine the role played by nationalism and national identities. Throughout the region, nationalists advocated reducing their country's economic dependence on Russia as a way of bolstering national autonomy, despite the short-term economic costs. In countries such as Lithuania, where national identities were coherent and consensual, this argument was very influential in policymaking circles. But in countries where national identities were more contested, fragmented, or ambiguous, such as Belarus and Ukraine, Abdelal shows how government policymakers were more inclined to maintain and even strengthen economic ties with Russia.

Andrei Tsygankov examines how Russian policymakers approached the same question of economic relations within the post-Soviet region. He too contends that Russian foreign economic policymaking cannot be fully understood without an analysis of the role played by national identities. After 1991 Russian policymakers initially saw their country as "Little Russia," an identity that encouraged economic disengagement from the former Soviet region and closer economic ties with the West. By the mid-1990s, their conception of Russia's "geoeconomic identity" had changed in response to both domestic and international developments. As they came to see Russia as more of a "Eurasian" power, Russian elites advocated the rebuilding of closer economic ties with the former Soviet republics.

Did national identities play an important role in influencing the path of *domestic* economic reform in the postcommunist context? Maya Eichler highlights how competing conceptions of national identity were used both to legitimize and to contest specific economic reform strategies in Russia and Ukraine. In the former, the radical economic liberalization of the early 1990s was associated with a pro-Western definition of the national identity, while resistance to "shock therapy" was linked to conceptions of Russia as a Eurasian power. In the case of Ukraine, Eichler argues that the more gradual pace of economic reform after 1991 was legitimized on the nationalist grounds that this strategy aimed at bolstering the country's distinct identity vis-à-vis Russia.

Part 2 examines economic nationalism in the East Asian region. The region is an important one for our purposes because the development strategies of Japan, South Korea, and Taiwan are often described as classic examples of "economic nationalism." What is usually meant by the phrase is that these countries have pursued state-led industrial policies that have departed from liberal economic orthodoxy. This is, of course, precisely the use of the term that we critique, since it ignores the role played by nationalism itself. For this reason, it is important to be able to reinterpret economic nationalism in the region by highlighting the role of nationalism and national identities in the economic policymaking of these three countries.

Our contributors take up this task in two important and distinct ways. Meredith Woo-Cumings analyzes the historical experiences of rapid industrialization in Japan, South Korea, and Taiwan. Her central argument is that nationalism was indeed at the core of the "economic nationalism" of these countries. It played a crucial role in facilitating the mobilization of the domestic populace behind rapid economic development in an uncertain international security environment. In her view, any analysis of these countries' rapid economic growth must recognize how nationalism acted as the central "binding agent" of their development strategies.

Derek Hall examines Japanese economic liberalization in recent years. Some analysts have portrayed this trend as signaling the decline of Japanese "economic nationalism." Hall challenges this interpretation by showing that economic liberalization has often been promoted for nationalist reasons within Japan. He shows that the specific forms of liberalization have also been influenced by perceptions of the Japanese national identity held by those advocating liberalization. For these reasons economic nationalism— understood in the sense employed in this volume—remains a potent force in Japan.

Parts 3 and 4 shift away from a specific regional focus. The theme in part 3 is the role of economic nationalism in the monetary sector. In this age of globalization, policymakers across the world have become increasingly interested in "depoliticizing" monetary policy by allocating its management to an independent central bank (or even a currency board) or by joining larger monetary unions. These initiatives are generally applauded by economic liberals, who see them as a way to insulate the management of money from untrustworthy national politicians. For this same reason, these moves are also often portrayed as an important sign of the erosion of nationalist economic policy in the monetary realm. Our authors question this interpretation.

The all-important case of Germany is examined by Klaus Müller. West Germany played a pioneering role in the postwar period in developing and promoting the idea that monetary policy should be managed by an independent central bank whose prime goal was the maintenance of price stability. Müller highlights how this liberal monetary arrangement—and other liberal economic policies that were associated with the country's rapid postwar growth—also became linked with the West German national identity in the postwar period. Indeed, in the post–Bretton Woods era, Müller shows, the stability of the deutsche mark became a significant source of national pride. The decision to abandon the DM and adopt the euro was thus a controversial decision, but one that was viewed as necessary to gain foreign acceptance of German unification.

Eric Helleiner analyzes one interesting aspect of the debate about the prospects for a North America monetary union (NAMU). This debate has been particularly active in Canada since 1999, and among the strongest proponents have been Quebec nationalists who have stated that they would continue to endorse NAMU even if they were successful in creating an independent sovereign state of Quebec. Since national currencies have historically been an important symbol of national sovereignty, the Quebec nationalist endorsement of NAMU is puzzling. It has also left Quebec nationalists allied with "neoliberal" economists, whose views are normally seen as quite antagonistic to economic nationalism. Helleiner shows, however, that Quebec nationalists endorse NAMU precisely for nationalist motivations. They see it as a way to ease the path to Quebec independence and as an appropriate nationalist response to changing international economic circumstances.

Part 4 analyses how economic globalization is encouraging some newer kinds of economic nationalism. Patricia Goff examines two recent initiatives within the agricultural sector of the European Union that fall within this category: (1) the effort to restrict the circulation of genetically modified organisms (GMOs) with the European market and (2) the attempt to reinforce the rights of authentic producers of food items to use their product names on an exclusive basis. Goff argues that both initiatives are driven in part by the desire to promote national autonomy and preserve national traditions in an era of intensifying international economic integration. They thus represent a new kind of economic nationalism that seeks to protect and even reassert distinct national cultures in a more liberalized economic environment.

Jacqui True examines a different kind of economic nationalism that has emerged in this globalized era. As countries find themselves increasingly locked in global competition for market shares and investment, state policymakers are exploring ways of highlighting their nation's distinctiveness. Here nationalism and national identities influence economic policymaking in a unique way; they are harnessed and reinforced to serve the goals of international competition. True highlights this phenomenon in New Zealand through a study of the creation of a "Brand New Zealand," the international marketing of kiwifruit, and the effort to defend the New Zealand's hold on the America's Cup in yachting.

In the concluding chapter, Eric Helleiner summarizes three principal contributions that this volume makes. The first is to sharpen the meaning of economic nationalism by defining it according to its nationalist content, rather than as a variant of realism or a "protectionist" ideology. As noted above, perhaps the most significant implication of this understanding of economic nationalism is that the term can be associated with a wide variety of policies, including economic liberal ones. Second, the volume challenges the conventional view that economic nationalism is an outdated ideology. The contributors emphasize how nationalism and national identities continue to influence economic policymaking and how economic nationalism and globalization are mutually reinforcing.

Finally, the volume reinforces recent critiques of "rationalist" political economy by calling attention to the significant role that ideational factors play in economic policy. While most ideational analysis in IR and IPE to date has focused on the role of economic ideologies, we examine the economic significance of deeper national identities. This volume contributes to the development of a constructivist approach to the study of IPE that explores the mutual interrelationship between identities and interests, and it highlights the various ways in which identities can be linked causally to policy outcomes.

Part I

Economic Nationalism in the
Post–Soviet Union Context

1

Nationalism and International Political Economy in Eurasia

Rawi Abdelal

Nationalism has four primary effects on governments' foreign economic policies: it endows economic policy with fundamental social purpose, related to protecting and cultivating the nation; it engenders the economic sacrifice necessary to achieve societal goals; it lengthens the time horizons of a national community; and, most significantly, it specifies a direction for policy, away from the group that a nation conceives of as "other" and, often, toward another cultural space. As a result, nationalism powerfully influences the world economy. However, the study of international relations (IR) and international political economy (IPE) lack a theoretical framework to explain how, when, and why this influence occurs. This is a serious deficiency, because it is impossible to make sense of fundamental patterns of interstate economic relations without understanding the influence of nationalism.

Building on a neglected Nationalist tradition in IR theory, as well as on the emerging constructivist research agenda, I specify several necessary analytical components of a framework that links nationalism to the world economy. In doing so, I outline a distinctively Nationalist perspective on IPE—that is, one that explains how nationalism and national identities affect cooperation and discord in the economic relations between particular states. A Nationalist perspective therefore differs fundamentally from the

For their insightful comments on this chapter, I am grateful to Valerie Bunce, Tom Christensen, Matthew Evangelista, Eric Helleiner, Meg Jacobs, Peter Katzenstein, Jonathan Kirshner, Andreas Pickel, Julio Rotemberg, Adam Segal, Debora Spar, and Lou Wells. The research for this chapter was supported by fellowships from the American Council of Learned Societies, for East European Studies, and the Institute for the Study of World Politics, as well as by research grants from the International Political Economy and Peace Studies programs at the Einaudi Center for International Studies, Cornell University, and the Division of Research, Harvard Business School.

two dominant theoretical perspectives in the study of IPE, realism, and liberalism.

Of course, IPE already has something called the "nationalist perspective," presented by Robert Gilpin (1987, chap. 2) in a foundational text of the field. Gilpin's nationalist perspective is, however, a masterly restatement of realist political economy. It is filled with mercantilism and statism; there is no nationalism in it. Nationalism is an expression of a constructed societal identity. Statism is an expression of an autonomous state with interests distinct from society. The equation of the two approaches and concepts, therefore, is an analytical mistake: nationalism is not equivalent to statism; economic nationalism is not equivalent to mercantilism; and thus a nationalist perspective on IPE, if it is to take nationalism seriously as a causal variable, cannot be equivalent to the Realist perspective.

In this chapter I also illustrate the necessity of an approach to IPE based on nationalism by applying the Nationalist perspective to an important puzzle of the post–Cold War world economy. This puzzle is the central question of the political economy of post-Soviet international relations: Why has the Eurasian regional economy both disintegrated, among some states, and reintegrated, among others, during the first post-Soviet decade? In December 1991, after the Union collapsed, all post-Soviet states were economically dependent on Russia. Post-Soviet governments interpreted their dependence in dramatically different ways, however. Some post-Soviet governments, such as Belarus's, decided that dependence was a good reason for economic reintegration with Russia. A second group of post-Soviet governments, typified by Lithuania, interpreted the very same dependence differently; these governments considered economic dependence on Russia a security threat and sought to reorient their economies. Still a third group, typified by Ukraine, failed to choose a coherent economic strategy and remained neither oriented away from nor oriented toward the Russian economy. Thus, post-Soviet governments had contrasting preferences for the political-economic future of the region. Differences in the national identities of post-Soviet societies led to these varying government preferences.[1]

During the 1990s, national identity was the central axis of debate about the regional economy. In each post-Soviet state there were nationalists who advocated economic reorientation away from Russia and toward some other group of states, most commonly the "West" or "Europe." The nationalists argued that the economic costs of reorientation were worth the goal, and that autonomy from Russia would eventually bring its own rewards. They demanded change at the expense of regional cooperation. In opposition, others demanded that the economic ties of the former Soviet Union be

---

1. For a similar argument, which emphasizes the "strength" of national identity and the prior history of statehood, see Tsygankov (2001).

maintained and even strengthened. Invariably, among the groups that insisted on regional economic cooperation and reintegration were the industrialists and other organized business interests. Repudiating the "romanticism" of the nationalists' program, they urged pragmatism and continuity. These incompatible arguments forced post-Soviet societies and politicians to choose between reorientation and reintegration.

The political economy of post-Soviet international relations revolved around one central question: Did post-Soviet societies and politicians agree with their nationalists? Here the former Communists played a decisive role. During the first post-Soviet decade, the defining political difference among the fourteen non-Russian states was the relationship between the formerly Communist elites and the nationalists in each—whether the former Communists marginalized the nationalists, arrested them, co-opted them, bargained with them, or even tried to become like them. These different relationships indicated the degree of societal consensus about nation- and statehood after Soviet rule. Lithuania's former Communists sided with its nationalists, Belarus's former Communists did not, while Ukraine's former Communists and nationalists were deadlocked. These outcomes indicated that Lithuanian national identity was coherent and consensual; Belarusian national identity was contested, fragmented, and ambiguous; and Ukrainian national identity was regionally contested, as west and central Ukrainians largely accepted the arguments of the nationalists, while east and south Ukrainians did not. The Nationalist explanation presented here can be generalized to the overwhelming majority of post-Soviet states.[2]

In this chapter I first specify several core arguments that must be part of an approach to IPE based on nationalism and national identity and show how these arguments differ from the core assumptions and analytical foundations of realism and liberalism. Second, I outline the central empirical puzzle of the economic relations among post-Soviet states and show that a nationalist perspective on IPE is necessary to resolve it. Then I illustrate these politics with three case studies of post-Soviet foreign economic policy-making during the 1990s—Lithuania, Ukraine, and Belarus.

Nationalism and International Political Economy

A rich scholarly literature on nationalism concludes that nations, national identities, and nationalisms are inventions.[3] Nations are not actual groups

2. Here I treat these identity variables as given. The origin of variation in post-Soviet national identities is a separate explanatory task, which I take up in Abdelal (2001, 2002). For an insightful analysis of the material stakes in the Ukrainian and Russian debates about the content of their national identities, see Maya Eichler's chapter in this volume.

3. See especially Brubaker (1996).

of people. Rather, nations are symbols, reifications of a group's collective identity. National identity is a collective identity of a particular kind: it is an identity shared among a population and defined by historical memory and cultural symbols. In addition, many national identities include components of language, ethnicity, and religion. Nationalism is the use of the symbol of the nation for specific political, economic, and cultural purposes; it is the nation connected to a project (Verdery 1996). Nationalists, then, are societal actors who propose the nation's most important goals; they have fundamental goals for the states they seek to create or govern. Moreover, as Valerie Bunce argues (1999, 12–13, 147–51), the projects and goals of different nationalists and, therefore, of different nationalisms vary dramatically across time and political space.

National identities also vary—from society to society, and over time—in two primary ways: in their content and contestation. First, national identity has content: self-understandings and goals that are cultural, political, and economic.[4] The content of a national identity includes definitions of membership in the nation, the fundamental purposes of statehood, and the states that threaten those purposes.[5]

The content of national identity is inherently relational, because nationalist movements arise in interaction with (and frequently in opposition to) other nationalisms and states in the international system. Therefore, the content of a national identity is a direction, a state or ethnicity against which identity is defined. Nations are frequently imagined to have a most significant "other." Nationalism thus leads governments to be averse to close cooperation or integration with specific states in the international system. At the same time, however, the content of a national identity may also include an affinity for another, broader cultural identity. Thus, there is often a two-way (anti and pro) direction in national identity. The content of national identities is both more variable and more consequential than has been acknowledged in IR theory.

Who decides what the content of national identity is? Every society has nationalists, who attempt to link the symbol of the nation to specific goals and, therefore, who seek to define the content of their society's collective identity. Not everyone in society always agrees with how the nationalists seek to construct their identity, however. Sometimes the nationalists cannot even agree among themselves. Nationalists can only offer proposals for the content of societal identity; they cannot dictate the content.

Therefore, national identities also vary in their contestation among all members of society. Specific interpretations of the goals of the nation are

4. On the importance of the content of national identities, see Szporluk (1988, 164, chap. 6) and D'Anieri (1997a).
5. See especially Haas (1997, 45).

sometimes widely shared, sometimes not. Moreover, the further apart the contending interpretations of national identity, the more that identity is fragmented into conflicting and potentially inconsistent understandings of what the goals of the nation should be. Thus, the variable of contestation describes whether the rest of a society agrees (and how it disagrees) with its nationalists. In some societies, and at some moments in history, nationalists' ideas resonate, achieve widespread support, and are converted into policy. In other societies, or at other times, they do not. Mark Beissinger's (1998) metaphor succinctly captures the contestation of national identity: many nationalisms bark, but only some bite. The process of the contestation of the content of national identities is necessarily collective.

Nationalism and the Economy

A shared national identity makes a society more willing to bear the economic costs of pursuing the long-term goals that compose its identity. Nationalism thus engenders sacrifices and lengthens the time horizons of a national community. These were central insights of Friedrich List, the preeminent economic nationalist and theorist of the Nationalist tradition. List, therefore, is not the quintessential statist or neomercantilist.

A shared national identity, in List's framework, creates a national community—a nation. The nation means much more than the collection of individual citizens of a state. The interests of the nation are "infinitely different" from the interests of individuals, if "each individual is to be regarded as existing for himself alone, and not in the character of the national community." Liberal political economy, and its cosmopolitanism—against which List was writing—made the mistake of assuming that individuals were "mere producers and consumers" who "do not concern themselves for the prosperity of future generations." The Liberals, List argued, assumed that individuals were forward looking, but only for themselves, not for the nation. The individuals who populate the theories of Adam Smith are decadent and selfish; "they trouble themselves little about the power, the honor, or the glory of the nation." But, according to List, members of a nation do not think it foolish to make present sacrifices for the benefit of future members. Finally, the state's role in the economy is to change it from a mere "economy of the people" to a "national economy," to give the statewide economy national meaning.[6] The state, for List and other Nationalists, acts on behalf of the nation, not on behalf of itself.

In sum, a distinctively Nationalist perspective on IPE is composed of a few necessary arguments: national identities are socially constructed and vary in their content and contestation; the content of national identities specifies a

6. Quotes from List ([1841] 1966, 172–73, 195, 167, 199).

direction for, and the fundamental social purposes of, economic policy; and shared national identities lengthen the time horizons of a society and create the political will necessary for economic sacrifice. Contested and fragmented national identities do the opposite: limit sacrifice, separate economic activity from national purpose, and shorten time horizons. *Economic nationalism* is a set of policies that results from a shared national identity and therefore bears its characteristics. Thus, economic nationalism is economic policy that follows the national purpose and direction. It is a result of nationalism, not of statism.[7] National purposes vary, moreover, and so must economic nationalisms. This approach is, as Eric Helleiner notes (2002, 326), "best defined by its nationalist ontology instead of its specific policy prescriptions."

Reinterpreting Economic Nationalism and the Nationalist Perspective

Realist scholars have assumed that their tradition subsumes the Nationalist tradition. Such an interpretation assumes that nationalism's effects on economic relations are best understood as reasons of state, rather than reasons of nation. Gilpin, in the most important and influential example of this, suggests that the Nationalist and Realist traditions of IPE are essentially identical. Economic nationalism, Gilpin argues (1987, 31), is conceptually equivalent to "mercantilism, statism, protectionism, the German Historical School, and, recently, New Protectionism." The "central idea" of economic nationalism is "that economic activities are and should be subordinate to the goals of state building and the interests of the state." However, this is a description of the statism that informs Realist theories of IPE. Gilpin concludes, "economic nationalism is based on the Realist doctrine of international relations" (42). Together these arguments composed what Gilpin labels the "Nationalist perspective" on IPE.[8]

Nationalism, however, is not the same as statism. In IPE, nationalism and statism must be distinct concepts: in economic statism, and the Realist tradition of IPE, there is no constituting "other" defined by identity; there is no domestic societal politics, only state building; no social purpose, only state power; and no historical memory—all that is the stuff of nationalism. Therefore, as E. H. Carr suggested (1945, 5–6, 22–23), economic nationalism and mercantilism are different: economic nationalism is social, while mercantilism is statist. Statist self-interest results in policies that are different from those motivated by national purpose. Therefore, I distinguish the Nationalist from the Realist tradition.[9]

7. See especially Crane (1998), Shulman (2000), and Goff (2000).

8. More generally, see Gilpin (1987, 31–34, 41–54).

9. I offer further elaboration of the Nationalist perspective in Abdelal (2001, chap. 2). Realism and liberalism are broad traditions within which diverse theories have developed. Here I focus on their basic assumptions.

There are several important differences between the Realist and Nationalist perspectives on IPE. First, the basic assumptions are different. The central tenet of statism in Realist theories is that the state is a distinct actor with its own interests, which are distinct from the interests of society or various societal actors (Kirshner 1999). Realist political economy is thus fundamentally materialist and rationalist. In contrast, a Nationalist perspective is necessarily constructivist, for the simple reason that national identities are social constructions.[10]

The Nationalist and Realist perspectives understand the internal goals of state authority differently. Realist theories of political economy tend to assume that states are concerned principally with state building and the extraction of revenue from domestic society. In contrast, because nationalisms define membership in the nation, they privilege the economic status of members, thereby politicizing the distribution of income and wealth, patterns of employment, and the ownership of capital (Golay et al. 1969).

Third, Nationalist and Realist political economy predict different patterns of international economic relations. States, according to Realist theories, worry about the relative distribution of power and wealth in the international system. States guard their autonomy jealously and are loath to engage in cooperation that increases their dependence, particularly on strategic goods or strategically important states (Waltz 1979, 104–7; Grieco 1997, 168). Nationalist, like Realist, political economy assumes that governments pursue both relative development and autonomy.[11] But relative development compared to whom; and autonomy from which states? The content of national identity—not the distribution of power—gives these concerns about development, dependence, and autonomy a direction, since nationalisms discriminate between other states, which are understood to be threats to national identity and security, not just because of their power, but also because of how the identities of the two populations have interrelated politically and historically.

Disintegration and Reintegration in the Eurasian Regional Economy

Only a Nationalist perspective on IPE can make sense of the economic relations among post-Soviet states. There was no regionwide economic cooperation among post-Soviet states during the 1990s. These fifteen states composed the most economically interdependent region in the world, and so collaboration seemed an obvious necessity. But their currency union fell

10. See especially Katzenstein (1996a) and Jepperson, Wendt, and Katzenstein (1996).
11. On relative development, see Hayes (1931, chap. 7, esp. 232). Also see Greenfeld (1995, 2001a) and Gerschenkron (1962, esp. 24–25). For an application to East Asian development, see Woo-Cumings's chapter in this volume. On autonomy, see Itagaki (1971).

apart, and monetary relations were disorganized and chaotic. Trade relations were discordant, and by 1996 trade volume among post-Soviet states had declined by more than 50 percent. Part of the collapse of regional trade resulted from economic transition. But leaders, societies, and organized economic actors throughout the former Soviet Union blamed political dissolution more than any other cause and put the region's failed cooperation at the center of foreign economic policy debates.

Most striking about the political economy of post-Soviet international relations was its variety. Some post-Soviet governments sought to redress the failure with regional economic reintegration. Russia, Armenia, Belarus, Kazakhstan, Kyrgyzstan, and Tajikistan all promoted cooperation and the development of regional institutions; they signed bilateral and multilateral agreements to reorganize their currencies and coordinate their trade policies. Another group of post-Soviet governments was much more ambivalent about the desirability and prospects of economic reintegration. Ukraine, Moldova, Turkmenistan, Georgia, Azerbaijan, and Uzbekistan recognized the need to cooperate in money and trade. However, their governments rejected multilateral reintegration, primarily because they feared that the formal institutionalization of cooperation would strengthen Russia's regional hegemony. The three Baltic states, Lithuania, Latvia, and Estonia, composed a third group of post-Soviet governments that unambiguously rejected both economic reintegration and regional cooperation, as well as membership in the Commonwealth of Independent States (CIS). Therefore, the regional economy was characterized by a complex mix of disintegration, reintegration, and the mere persistence of long-standing economic dependences.

During the 1990s, the Lithuanian government consistently interpreted economic dependence on Russia as a threat to state security and, as a result, strategically reoriented its economy toward the West.[12] Lithuania sought to reduce its dependence on Russia by diversifying its trade links, integrating into the EU, and creating an independent currency tied closely to the West.[13] Meanwhile, the Lithuanian constitution expressly prohibits the government from joining any political or economic unions on the territory of the former Soviet Union; CIS membership was simply out of the question. The Lithuanian government negotiated a free-trade agreement with the EU in 1994, but rejected free trade with Russia or the CIS. Economic relations with Russia were severely strained by Lithuania's Western foreign policy priorities. Until 1995 Lithuania was one of only four countries in the world, including the two other Baltic states, not to have received most-favored-nation

12. Ministry of Foreign Affairs of Lithuania, interviews by author, Vilnius, July–August 1998; administration of the president of Lithuania, interview by author, Vilnius, July 1998. See also Nekrasas (1998) and Vilpisaukas (1997).

13. See Lithuania Government (1997) and Lithuania Ministry (1997); also Bank of Lithuania, interview by author, Vilnius, July 1998.

trade status from Russia. In addition, Lithuania was, in October 1992, one of the first republics to leave the region's monetary union after the collapse of Soviet authority. The government pegged its new currency, the litas, to the dollar. The Bank of Lithuania planned to switch to a euro peg in 2001 and ultimately to join European monetary union.[14]

Belarus did essentially the opposite. The Belarusian government interpreted economic dependence on Russia as mutually beneficial exchange, a reason for closer cooperation with Russia and the multilateral reintegration of the post-Soviet economic area.[15] Belarus therefore did not reorient its economy away from Russia and toward the West. Belarus's orientation toward Russia was also strong enough to produce a string of agreements that symbolically united the Belarusian with the Russian state in 1997, 1998, and 1999. Free-trade and customs-union agreements continued to tighten the economic links between the two countries. Belarusian acquiescence paid handsome rewards, since Russia consistently subsidized Belarus's energy imports and forgave its enormous energy debts.

Ukraine's foreign policy orientation was a middle course between Russia and the West. Although the Ukrainian government sought close relationships with NATO and the EU, it did not apply for membership during the 1990s and is not likely to do so in the near future. However, the Ukrainian government did, like Lithuania's, interpret economic dependence on Russia as a security threat, even if it did much less to achieve economic autonomy and reorient its economy Westward.[16] The Ukrainian government decided that close cooperation with Russia was necessary, but, unlike the Belarusian authorities, it ruled out the possibility of multilateral reintegration of the former Soviet economy. The Ukrainian currency is tied to the dollar, though not as tightly as is the Lithuanian currency, and there are no plans for monetary unification with either Europe or with Russia.[17] Ukrainian foreign economic policy during the 1990s was ambivalent.

Competing Explanations

Material variables drawn from domestic and regional politics and economics cannot explain the differences between Lithuanian, Ukrainian, and

---

14. Bank of Lithuania, interview. See also Bank of Lithuania (1997).
15. See Dawisha (1997). For particularly clear expressions of these interpretations and goals, see *Sovetskaia Belorussia* 11 (February 1993) and *Narodnaia gazeta,* June 6, 1995.
16. Ministry of Foreign Affairs of Ukraine, interview by author, Kyiv, June 1998; administration of the president of Ukraine, interview by author, Kyiv, June 1998. See also *Nezavisimaia gazeta,* October 21, 1993; *Pravda Ukrainy,* January 29, 1993. For the best overview, see D'Anieri (1999).
17. National Bank of Ukraine, interview.

Table 1.1. Energy dependence on Russia (as percentage of total consumption)

	Oil	Gas
Lithuania	94	100
Ukraine	89	56
Belarus	91	100

Source: Adapted from Dawisha and Parrot 1994.

Belarusian foreign economic policies. These three states, the western borderlands of the Soviet Union, shared a number of meaningful similarities. In each, the titular ethnic group was the overwhelming majority, representing at least 73 percent of the total population. Each of these states was highly dependent economically on Russia, especially Russian oil and gas imports (see table 1.1). Meanwhile, economic links with the West were minimal—in 1990, 90 percent of Lithuania's total commerce was intraregional, as was 87 percent of Belarus's and 82 percent of Ukraine's (Michalopoulos and Tarr 1992). All three also had very similar economic structures (see table 1.2). They were among the most economically advanced republics of the Soviet Union and, therefore, best prepared to make the economic transition to independent statehood. None of the three faced serious secessionist threats or violent ethnic conflict.

Finally, and most interesting and significant politically, each of these states was ruled by formerly Communist elites for most of the 1990s. In 1992, Lithuania was the first state in the region to return its former Communists to power, and it elected an important Party leader as president. Ukrainian and Belarusian governments and presidents also were drawn from the ranks of former Communists.

Liberal Approaches

Two variants of Liberal IR theory apply to the political economy of post-Soviet international relations; both focus on material incentives. The first,

Table 1.2. Share of economy by sector, 1990

	Agriculture	Industry	Construction	Transport	Other
Lithuania	33.4	34.1	13.4	5.9	13.3
Ukraine	30.3	41.3	9.7	6.0	19.4
Belarus	29.3	44.0	11.8	5.1	9.8

Source: Adapted from World Bank 1992.

neoliberal institutionalism, emphasizes that international institutions make cooperation easier to achieve by reducing transaction costs. The second, more traditional version of Liberal political economy argues that domestic economic actors with different material interests shape foreign economic policies. Both variants of Liberal political economy suggested that, in the short and medium term, material interests would push post-Soviet states toward economic cooperation and even, possibly, reintegration.

Both Liberal theories seem to fit the Belarusian case. However, Liberal theories cannot explain why other post-Soviet states politicized regional cooperation with concerns about autonomy and security from Russia. This politicization led to a failure of CIS reintegration and multilateral economic cooperation in general. For its part, neoliberal theory cannot explain why all of this occurred in one of the most densely institutionalized and interdependent regional systems in the world.

Moreover, economic interests did not pull all the post-Soviet states back to Russia.[18] Contrary to traditional Liberal political economy, nearly *all* organized economic actors, and especially the powerful industrial lobbies, throughout the former Soviet Union preferred regional cooperation and reintegration. And yet in many post-Soviet states their preferences were trumped by the strategic concerns of governments, concerns defined by nationalism.[19] To be sure, there were raw materials and metals suppliers that preferred to sell their goods on world markets for higher prices. But no organized economic actors preferred a rapid and drastic reorientation of trade to the West and the disintegration of the post-Soviet regional economy. Moreover, at the time that Lithuania, Ukraine, and Belarus chose their economic strategies, Russia was still giving them enormous energy and raw materials subsidies, some 60 to 70 percent below world prices. So, as Matthew Evangelista concludes (1996b, 183–84), "it is hard to argue that the policies of the republics in trying to break away from Moscow were driven strictly by pursuit of economic utility. Virtually all of them stood to lose."[20]

---

18. On problems of applying sectoral and coalitional approaches to post-Soviet political economy, see Evangelista (1996a, 1996b).
19. On the preferences for reintegration of the organized economic actors and lobbies in each post-Soviet state, see *Delovoi mir*, January 28, 1994, and the publication of the International Congress of Industrialists and Entrepreneurs, *Vestnik delovoi zhizni*, no. 13, August 1997. On the preferences of these lobbies in Lithuania, Ukraine, and Belarus, see *Baltic News Service*, September 12, 1996; October 9, 1997; *Nezavisimaia gazeta*, November 20, 1993; *Delovaia Ukraina*, October 6, 1992; *Krasnaia zvezda*, January 12, 1993; *Izvestiia*, October 21, 1992; *Kommersant-Daily*, October 21, 1992; *Sovetskaia Belorussia*, March 20 and 30, 1993; *Kuranty*, April 16, 1994; *Nezavisimaia gazeta*, October 9, 1992.
20. See also Evangelista (1996a, 175–85).

Realist Approaches

There are also two possible ways to apply Realist political economy to the former Soviet Union, and like the two Liberal variants, they share a common weakness, although a different one: both are indeterminate. The most general Realist expectation for the post-Soviet regional economy was that some post-Soviet states would, at a minimum, seek economic autonomy from Russia. This pursuit of autonomy would then lead to the following outcomes: cooperation would be difficult; regional reintegration would be impossible; and some post-Soviet states, alone or in concert, would balance against Russian power. On the surface, these Realist expectations seem to have been correct, since autonomy and security have been such prominent features of post-Soviet foreign economic policymaking. Russia is, by far, the strongest state in the region. Furthermore, Russia aggressively, and openly, sought to dominate politics in the former Soviet Union; its intentions to influence all other states in the region were clear.[21] In this Realist account, post-Soviet states should have interpreted economic dependence on Russia as a security threat and have acted accordingly.

However, each post-Soviet government did not interpret economic dependence on Russia as a security threat. Some did, but others did not. This observation leads to the second Realist expectation: instead of balancing against Russian hegemony and seeking autonomy, those post-Soviet states that either lacked available allies or sought to change the status quo might choose to bandwagon with Russia—in other words, to ally with Russia and acquiesce in its regional dominance (Walt 1987). Perhaps, this Realist logic suggests, Belarus allied closely with Russia because it lacked alternatives or was unsatisfied with the post–Cold War settlement in Eurasia. In general, then, Realist theories can accommodate a diverse set of foreign policy patterns, including some of those found in the former Soviet Union.

But the indeterminacy of Realist approaches to post-Soviet political economy is demonstrated by comparing Belarus to Lithuania. Material variables cannot account for the differences between their strategies. Clearly, Lithuania sought economic autonomy from Russia, but Belarus did not. These two small, weak states pursued radically different policies toward Russia, the CIS, and the West. And it is not merely that material variables cannot account for this striking difference; theories that rely on these variables projected completely different patterns of international relations. In late 1991, as both states emerged from the collapsed USSR, Belarus was much larger, richer, and stronger militarily. It even had nuclear weapons.[22] Yet Belarus

21. For an interpretation of Russia's policies toward the region, see Tsygankov's chapter in this volume.
22. In 1992 Lithuania had a population of 3.7 million, GDP per capita of $3,700, and armed forces of 8,900. Belarus had a population of 10.5 million, GDP per capita of $6,800, and

turned out to be much more acquiescent than Lithuania. The Belarusian government never considered autonomy from Russia a legitimate goal.

The availability of allies and trade partners did not determine these governments' foreign policy choices. By the end of the 1990s, the choices that Lithuanian and Belarusian leaders made in 1991 foreclosed options that were once available to them. Belarus alienated the West, Lithuania alienated the East, and the results now appear inevitable. But they were not. The West's reaction to these two new states was a result of Lithuanian and Belarusian policies, not their cause. Indeed, Western support can hardly have caused Lithuania's reorientation, because it was not at all substantial. Lithuania did not become a member of the EU or NATO, and, formally, all it has to show for its efforts to cultivate economic ties with the West is a free-trade agreement with the EU. There are no Western security guarantees that keep Lithuania outside Russia's sphere of influence, only its own efforts.

Realist theories have an even greater problem with Ukraine, because Ukraine is the regional power whose behavior should have conformed most to the expectations of Realist theory. It is, for realism, the crucial case. Ukraine, a large state with significant military capabilities and economic potential, is second only to Russia in material indicators of power in the region. Yet Ukraine did not balance against Russia. This fact means that, in the 1990s, *no* regional balance to Russian power emerged. Ukraine's government, unlike Belarus's, did interpret Russia, and its economic dependence, as a security threat.

Ukraine attempted to achieve autonomy, yet it also maintained close bilateral economic cooperation with Russia. Ukraine's preferences about this cooperation were very specific, however, because the possibility of multilateral economic integration in the CIS was rejected outright. This grudging acceptance of close cooperation with Russia, resulting from a significant reversal of Ukraine's foreign economic policy in 1992–93, was caused by regional divisions in Ukraine's economy and population. Like Lithuania, Ukraine initially pursued a policy of radical economic autonomy from Russia—what Realist theories would have expected. But the Ukrainian government did not sustain its attempt to reorient the economy Westward (D'Anieri 1997b, 21–22). Ukraine's nationalists wanted to continue the autonomy policies, but the rest of Ukraine's society did not. In the Realist logic, states do not have to respond to domestic divisions and societal demands, but the Ukrainian government did. According to the independent variables that inform Realist theory, France-sized Ukraine, not West Virginia–sized

---

armed forces of 92,500. In 1992, Ukraine's population was 52.2 million, its GDP per capita was $5,000, and its armed forces consisted of 517,000 troops (International Institute of Strategic Studies 1994).

Lithuania, should have balanced against Russian power most forcefully; even Belarus was in a better position to do so than was Lithuania.

In sum, both Liberal approaches to post-Soviet political economy expected regional cooperation—organized by regional institutions and sought by domestic economic actors—in the short and medium term. However, neither Liberal approach can explain the variation in post-Soviet economic strategies and the collapse of regional cooperation. Various Realist approaches expected at least some states to seek autonomy from Russia, while others might bandwagon for profit or out of fear. But Realist political economy is indeterminate: it cannot make sense of which governments chose which strategy, or why Ukraine, the only post-Soviet state crucial for Realist theory, chose neither. Lithuania's policy of economic autonomy from Russia seemed to follow some Realist expectations; Belarus's policy of economic reintegration with Russia seemed to follow all Liberal expectations; and Ukraine's incoherent middle course was an anomaly for both theoretical perspectives. An alternate approach must explain why post-Soviet governments interpreted objectively similar economic circumstances and prospects in such different ways.

National Identity as the Explanation

If Lithuanian, Ukrainian, and Belarusian nationalists had their way, their states' foreign economic strategies during the 1990s would have been nearly identical. During the first post-Soviet decade, the mainstream nationalists in these countries had essentially identical ideologies and foreign policy goals.[23] That is, their nationalists strove to define the content of their societies' identities in very similar ways. Lithuanian, Ukrainian, and Belarusian nationalist ideologies had three fundamental ideas in common.

The first was their interpretation of the history and purpose of their statehood. Lithuanian, Ukrainian, and Belarusian nationalists all argued that their statehood, having been lost to Russian influence at various moments in history, had now been restored. Thus, for all three groups of nationalists, Russia is the most significant "other," and the state from which statehood must be defended most of all. And a strong, unified state is necessary to protect and cultivate the nation.[24] Lithuanian, Ukrainian, and Belarusian na-

23. Leaders of the most important Lithuanian, Ukrainian, and Belarusian nationalist parties (respectively, Homeland Union, Rukh, and the Belarusian Popular Front [BPF]) agreed with this observation. Homeland Union, interviews by author, Vilnius, July 1998; Rukh, interview by author, Kyiv, July 1998; Belarusian Popular Front, interviews by author, Minsk, July 1998. Also see Chervonnaia (1993); Lozowy (1994); Rukh ([1989] 1990); Sajudis(1989); TsIMO (1991).
24. Homeland Union, interview by author; Rukh, interview; Belarusian Popular Front, interview.

tionalisms, which began as anti-Soviet, became anti-Russian (Beissinger 1996).

Second, Lithuanian, Ukrainian, and Belarusian nationalists all argued that economic dependence on Russia is a security threat.[25] Indeed, the Belarusian Popular Front calls economic dependence on Russia "the main problem of the security of the Belarusian state."[26] Nationalists in these states do not believe that Russian troops are likely to cross their borders to take over the country. But they do fear that economic dependence will drastically limit their governments' ability to act autonomously, or even to perceive the country's true national interests. Therefore, they rejected close economic cooperation or reintegration with Russia, whatever the costs of autonomy. The nationalists argue that economic sacrifice will not be permanent, since they will reorient their countries' commerce. In the long run they, and future generations of the nation, will be European and rich.

Finally, their states' "return to Europe" is the third fundamental idea that these national ideologies have in common. These three nationalisms are not just anti-Russian; they are also powerfully pro-European and pro-NATO. Their definition of Europe reflects this stance, moreover, since they do not consider Russia to be a part. A Lithuanian member of parliament, for example, when asked to define Europe responded, "Europe is . . . not-Russia!" (Ash 1994). Therefore, Lithuania is "seeking to regain what it thought was its proper place, after being torn away from the Western world and incorporated into the Eastern world" (Nekrasas 1998, 19). Lithuania's anti-Soviet nationalists, Joan Lofgren concludes, "are now among the prime advocates of EU membership" (Lofgren 1997, 47).[27] As Andrew Wilson shows, Ukrainian nationalists' external agenda "is clear and can be neatly summarized as anti-Russian and pro-European." For these nationally conscious Ukrainians, therefore, Europe symbolizes a cultural space that Ukraine shared before Soviet Communism, and, for some parts of Ukraine, before the tsar's authority. And a European state is "democratic," "civilized," and rich, unlike "uncivilized" Russia (Wilson 1997, 113, 179–80; Prizel 1998, 367). For Belarusian nationalists, too, the directions of their proposed policy—anti-Russian, anti-CIS, and pro-European—are equivalent.[28]

In sum, Lithuanian, Ukrainian, and Belarusian nationalists had remarkably similar ideologies. They wanted the purposive content of their societies' identities to be essentially the same. And they wanted similar foreign

25. Ibid.
26. Belarusian Popular Front, interview. See Zaprudnik and Urban (1997, 286–88, 297–98).
27. Also Homeland Union, interview.
28. Belarusian Popular Front, interview. See also Belarusian Popular Front, "Belarus—To Europe! A Strategy of Defense of Independence," in *Documents of the Fifth Congress of the Belarusian Popular Front* (Minsk, June 20–21, 1997); and *Narodnaia gazeta*, October 23–30, 1990.

policies: economic reorientation away from Russia and toward Europe, despite the costs. If Lithuanian, Ukrainian, and Belarusian nationalists had been in charge of their respective governments for the past decade, their states' foreign economic policies would have been virtually identical. However, none of them was in charge, not for the entire decade.

Instead of making policy themselves, Lithuanian, Ukrainian, and Belarusian nationalists had to try to convince the former Communists who were running the government to accept their arguments and goals as their own. Therefore, the central political question was whether the former Communists accepted or contested the goals that the nationalists proposed.

Lithuania: Contestation of National Identity

The arguments of nationalists matter most when the rest of society agrees with them. In Lithuania the rest of society agreed. The vast majority of Lithuanians, and of Lithuanian political parties, accepted the nationalists' arguments for reorientation. There were no influential political parties that contested them. Thus, the content of Lithuanian national identity was widely shared (Senn 1995; Jurgatiene and Waever 1996). In the late 1980s and early 1990s, the coherence of national identity was reflected in the popularity of the nationalists themselves. In the 1990 elections to the Lithuanian Supreme Soviet, nationalist candidates won nearly 80 percent of the seats.

The coherence and consensus of national identity was even more powerfully illustrated when the nationalists lost parliamentary and presidential elections to former Communists. The victorious Lithuanian Democratic Labor Party (LDDP), the successor to the Communist Party, did not dispute the fundamental purposes of Lithuanian statehood or the foreign policy objectives of the nationalists. In fact, the foreign policy goals of the LDDP in 1992 were very similar to those of Sajudis, Lithuania's nationalist movement.[29] Although Algirdas Brazauskas, a former Communist, emphasized the necessity of normalized relations with Russia in his 1993 successful presidential bid, the former Communists and nationalists shared the goal of reorienting Lithuania's politics and trade toward the West and integrating into Western institutions.

Moreover, the LDDP, like the nationalist Homeland Union, connected the symbol of the Lithuanian nation to the goals of reorientation. They, too, proclaimed the goals of the nationalists as their own. The subtle differences

29. See, for example, LDDP, "The Platform of the Lithuanian Democratic Labor Party for the Parliamentary Elections," reprinted in *Tiesa*, October 7, 1992, in FBIS-USR-92-149, 20 November 1992, pp. 96–103.

in their policy programs reflected the LDDP's greater willingness to maintain normal, less hostile relations with Russia, so as not to alienate Russian leaders while Lithuania integrated with multilateral institutions in Europe and rejected them in Eurasia. LDDP leaders insisted that theirs was a wiser policy that achieved the same goal of reorientation. Their goal, the former Communists assert, was identical to Homeland Union's, but the LDDP was, and will be, better at achieving it. As an LDDP leader asserted, "the Communists are more nationalist than the nationalists."[30]

Furthermore, all five of Lithuania's major political parties shared the same foreign policy objectives.[31] That is, all five—Homeland Union, the Lithuanian Christian Democratic Party, the LDDP, the Center Union, and the Lithuanian Social Democratic Party—legitimated these goals of reorientation with the symbol of the nation. These five accounted for over 90 percent of parliamentary seats throughout the decade. When the Lithuanian parliament ratified the Europe Agreement in June 1996, only one member of parliament voted against Lithuania's membership.

In sum, Lithuanians have a clear national identity. They agreed on the fundamental purposes of their statehood, purposes that are derived from their shared historical memory. This clarity caused Lithuania's post-Soviet foreign economic policy to be coherent, purposive, and single-minded. Lithuanian national identity framed the society's political and economic debates. Economic reintegration with the East was an illegitimate option. Lithuanians believed that reorienting their economy toward Europe was the best path to wealth, even if only in the long run. The widely shared content of national identity gave both government and society the political will to endure the economic sacrifice of reorienting toward Europe. The central theme of Lithuania's economic policies was the victory of the long view over the short.[32] And Lithuania's policies clearly were not economic statism: they were motivated by fundamental national purpose, not statist self-interest, and they followed the direction of Lithuanian nationalism, both toward Europe and against Russia. This was economic nationalism, but a national purpose defined as liberal toward the West.

30. LDDP, Vilnius, August 1998.
31. See, for example, their party platforms for the 1996 parliamentary elections: Lithuania's Success (Homeland Union); With Work, Concord, and Morality into the Twenty-First Century (Lithuanian Democratic Labor Party); To Serve for Lithuania (Lithuanian Christian Democratic Party); The New Lithuania (Lithuanian Center Union); Labor, Truth, and Justice (Lithuanian Social Democratic Party).
32. For more on the association of economic hardship with political independence and European reorientation, see Girnius (1997). Also Homeland Union, interviews; LDDP, interview.

Ukraine: Contestation of National Identity

Those same nationalist ideas received a cooler welcome in Ukraine. The ideas and goals of the nationalists were not widely accepted among Ukrainians, even if they were strongly held by the nationalists themselves. It is not the "weakness" of Ukrainian national identity that prevented the country from having a foreign policy of reorientation. Rather, the way that east and south Ukrainians *contested* the content of Ukrainian national identity tempered Ukraine's pursuit of autonomy. Ukrainian national identity was contested regionally, Ilya Prizel argues (1998, 371), "leading to different 'national' agendas advocated by different regions." Although political parties throughout Ukraine and across the political spectrum agreed that Ukraine should have its own state, there was "little agreement as to the purpose of that statehood." The collection of ideas and projects linked to the nation were widely debated. As Paul Kubicek argues (1996a, 39), "different versions of the nation tend[ed] to compete with each other."

Nationalist political parties enjoyed electoral success in the western and central regions of Ukraine, but generally received a minority of Ukraine's parliamentary votes. This was a common pattern in post-Soviet states; in no state were nationalist political parties strong enough to implement their political programs without help from other parties. Few other parties agreed with their program.

The Communist, Socialist, and Peasant Parties, all anti-reform, anti-Western, and pro-CIS, were highly popular in eastern and southern Ukraine, but deeply unpopular in western Ukraine (Prizel 1998, 367–68). The Ukrainian political spectrum therefore was polarized with regard to the foreign policy choices available to the government. Throughout the 1990s approximately 35 percent of members of parliament were in favor of an exclusively Eastern foreign policy orientation, while roughly 20 percent of members of parliament urged an exclusively Western foreign policy orientation.[33]

Rather than a distinctively and exclusively Ukrainian national identity, east and south Ukrainians tended to have multiple and overlapping identities, which included Pan-Slavic, residual Soviet, and regional identities. This caused east and south Ukrainians to question the anti-Russian content of nationalist ideologies formulated in western Ukraine (Kuzio 1998b, chap. 7). Any characterization of east Ukrainians as pro-Russian is therefore misleading. More accurately, most east and south Ukrainians are not anti-Russian. The attempt of nationalists to define Russia as Ukraine's most significant "other" was therefore problematic, because east and south Ukrainians sim-

---

33. Pro-CIS and anti-West parties accounted for 118 of 338 seats (35 percent) in 1994, and 158 of 450 seats (35 percent) in 1998. Anti-CIS and pro-West parties accounted for 40 of 338 seats (12 percent) in 1994, and 95 of 450 seats (21 percent) in 1998.

ply did not interpret Ukrainian and Russian identities to be mutually exclusive. They simply had a different idea of what it means to be Ukrainian (Kuzio 1996, 599).

These contrasting and ambivalent interpretations of the nation had consequences for foreign economic policy.[34] Ukrainians' views on economic union with Russia were indicators of their interpretation of Ukrainian national identity, rather than of their analyses of the state of the economy. East and south Ukrainians were "less likely to worry about what a close integration with Russia would do to their identity, since they already identif[ied] at least as much with Russian culture as with Ukrainian culture" (Arel 1995, 179). Just as in Belarus, pro-Eurasianism was an economic argument, for living better and cooperating more with the East.[35] As Taras Kuzio summarizes (1998b, 85), "In western Ukraine the drop in living standards has been offset by the strength of the national idea." In marked contrast, east Ukrainians preferred wealth to autonomy, and the "drop in living standards [was] blamed largely on the disintegration of the former USSR or the breakdown in economic ties with Russia caused by the former 'nationalist' President Kravchuk."

Ukraine could not choose a singular path. Its national identity was too contested and fragmented regionally for the government to make a decisive break from the CIS and toward Europe, as did the Baltics. At the same time, Ukraine's nationalism was too well developed to be marginalized; the government could not sell political autonomy for economic gain, as did Belarus. Neither a purely pro-Western nor a purely pro-Eastern foreign policy was possible, because either one would have divided the country. The former entailed economic costs that east Ukrainians were unwilling to bear. The latter was unacceptable to west Ukrainians for reasons of identity. Domestic politics undermined Ukraine's economic nationalism.

Unlike in Lithuania, most of Ukraine's former Communists did not become nationalists. However, many of them adopted important elements of the nationalist program both to maintain their power and to mediate Ukraine's regional divides (Kubicek 1996a, 40–41; Bilyi and Bystrytsky 1996). This group of former Communists formulated Ukrainian foreign policy during the 1990s. Thus, Ukrainian nationalists succeeded in framing Ukraine's foreign economic policy debate, convincing some former Communists of the importance of state building, and ruling out the Belarusian option for Ukraine. But they did not fully convince the east and south Ukrainians, nor all the former Communists.

34. See especially Shulman (2000).
35. Subtelny (1995, 194). See also Burant (1995).

Belarus: Contestation of National Identity

Belarusian nationalists failed completely in their attempt to define the content of Belarusian collective identity. Most of Belarusian society rejected their anti-Russian, pro-European program. Belarusian national identity is contested and ambiguous; it is an identity that does not specify clearly the fundamental purposes of the state and foreign policy (Furman and Bukhovets 1996; Marples 1999). Virtually none of Belarus's former Communists turned into nationalists. Indeed, nowhere in the former Soviet Union was there a larger gap between the beliefs of the nationalists and the beliefs of the former Communists about the political meaning of national identity: the nationalists supported reorientation away from Russia, while the former Communists supported ever closer ties. The ideas of Belarusian nationalists were unpopular among most Belarusians, and particularly among Belarusian political elites (Furman and Bukhovets 1996). In the parliamentary elections of 1990, the ones in which Lithuanian nationalist candidates won 80 percent of the seats, the Belarusian Popular Front won less than 8 percent of the seats. The 1995 elections were disastrous for the BPF, which did not win a single seat. Belarusian nationalism barked, but it clearly did not bite (Beissinger 1996, 122–24).

The politics and results of a May 1995 referendum also illustrated the ambiguity of the Belarusian national idea. The debate was clearly cast as between those politicians opposed to integration with Russia and those in favor. Although the nationalists exhorted Belarusians to support national revival and autonomy from Russia, Belarusian voters rejected both. Over 80 percent of Belarusian voters approved of the government's proposal to give the Russian language legal status equivalent to Belarusian *and* the president's attempt to integrate economically with Russia.[36] Throughout the decade the BPF's stock continued to fall. Moreover, Belarusian nationalists are well aware of their unpopularity. Although the BPF insists that the government has manipulated referenda and elections, it admits that "few political parties" share the foreign policy goals of the party, and that their support is no more than 25 percent of the population.[37]

In contrast to the BPF's pro-European and anti-Russian foreign policy stance, no major Belarusian political party opposed close economic integration and political cooperation with Russia (Bobkov, Kuznetsov, and Osmolovsky 1997; Bugrova and Naumova 1996). In the repertoire of Belarusian identities, pan-Slavic and residual Soviet identities were more widely shared than a distinctively Belarusian identity defined in opposition to Russia. Belarus—as an entire country or society—does not "lack" a national

36. *Narodnaia gazeta,* April 19 and May 16, 1995.
37. Belarusian Popular Front, interview. See also *Narodnaiagazeta,* January 14, 1993; *Sel'skaia zhizn',* November 27, 1992.

identity. More accurately, most Belarusians, like east Ukrainians, have mixed identities, combinations of multiethnic and multilingual identities that do not preclude a significant overlap between Belarusian and Russian identities. The meaning and content of Belarusian national identity is therefore ambiguous. Belarusian national identity is fragmented into conflicting interpretations of the nation.

Because Belarusian political elites and most of Belarusian society did not share the nationalists' interpretation of the content of Belarusian national identity, they did not see the point of allowing the post-Soviet regional economy to continue to disintegrate. Not only did pursuing economic reorientation seem irrational, the costs of independent statehood itself seemed excessively high.[38] Belarusians were not willing to bear the costs of economic autonomy from Russia because the goal was not widely shared. Therefore, without a coherent sense of national purpose or direction, the government attempted only to reap short-term economic benefits from the state's relationship with Russia.

Put most simply, Belarus's fragmented national identity allowed economics to influence the foreign policy orientation of the country directly, unmediated by higher national purpose. By the time of the controversial 1994 presidential election, in which Aleksandr Lukashenko was elected, Belarus had already institutionalized its choice to reintegrate with Russia economically under the leadership of Prime Minister Kebich. President Lukashenko therefore continued Kebich's popular pro-Russian policies through the rest of the 1990s (Markus 1996a, 1996b). And at every step of Belarus's primrose path to economic reintegration with Russia, Belarusian nationalists objected, always citing security and autonomy as their reasons.[39]

In this volume Maya Eichler addresses the distributional sources of the contestation of national identities in Ukraine and Russia, suggesting that some leaders in those two countries served their own material interests by instrumentally deploying alternate claims about the purposes of the nation. Here I stress, in contrast, the societal incentives leaders faced to make these claims in the first place. It is not useful for leaders to appeal to ideas of national purpose if those ideas do not resonate in society—if other actors without the same material stake in such definitions do not valorize those claims. The sociological analysis of the context in which leaders were embedded is, therefore, necessary to understand these politics of national identity. Indeed, the fact that the content of a national identity is collectively constituted means that an analysis of the cultural context of decision making can

38. For example, *Sovetskaia Belorussia,* March 27, 1993.
39. For example, *Narodnaia gazeta,* October 29, 1992; *Vecherny Minsk,* December 24, 1993; *Interfax,* October 15, 1993; *Nezavisimaia gazeta,* November 20, 1993; *Segodnia,* February 5, 1994; *Segodnia,* April 15, 1994; and *Izvestiia,* April 20, 1994.

accommodate a variety of behavioral assumptions about leaders. Because those cultural contexts vary, we can attribute variation in policies to variation in contexts, regardless of whether political elites were instrumental or true believers in national purposes defined by society.

The analysis in this chapter also has implications for IR theory and our understanding of the compatibility of economic nationalism and liberal policy. Realist and Liberal theories of IPE produced different expectations for the political economy of post-Soviet international relations. Lithuania followed some Realist expectations, Belarus followed all Liberal expectations, and Ukraine followed none. I argue that one advantage of an approach to IPE based on national identity is its ability to explain this variety.

There are several possible ways to interpret this variety, however. One is to suggest that if Lithuania fulfilled Realist predictions about post-Soviet international relations, but other new states did not, then there must be something internal to all these states that explains whether or not they chose *realpolitik*. The national identities of post-Soviet societies determined whether their governments pursued autonomy from Russia, whether they acquiesced in Russian regional hegemony, or some combination of strategies. Therefore, it is possible that in the former Soviet Union a coherent national identity is the prerequisite for the politics that Realist theories predicted. After all, the issue is the interpretation of threats. Russia's attempts to dominate the region are obvious, and those governments that interpreted the Russian threat are the same governments that balanced, politically and economically, against Russia. This argument, that domestic society and not international anarchy is the source of post-Soviet *realpolitik,* by itself would be a significant challenge to a Realist explanation for the political-economic policies of the Baltic states.

I go further than that. Lithuania's policies were substantially different from what Realist theories of IPE would have predicted. Lithuania's policies were not economic statism, informed by *realpolitik*. Lithuania's policies were economic nationalism, and there is a difference. Two aspects of Lithuania's economic nationalism distinguish it from economic statism.

The first is motivation. Lithuania's economic reorientation has a purpose that is not captured by the concept of statism, in which the state behaves as though it were a self-interested, rational, and unified actor. Rather, Lithuanian nationalism determined the fundamental purposes of Lithuanian statehood. Those purposes, and the Russian threat to them, motivated Lithuania's economic strategy.

An important purpose embedded in Lithuanian national identity was the country's "return to Europe." Thus, the second crucial aspect of Lithuanian economic nationalism is its direction. It is true that Lithuania's national identity led to economic policy that emphasized autonomy from Russia. However, that same national identity led directly to economic policies that

promoted connectedness to the states of western and central Europe. Lithuanian economic nationalism was as strongly pro-European as it was anti-
Russian. The Lithuanian government was not therefore concerned about
economic autonomy from everyone. Although the government clearly in-
terprets economic dependence on Russia as a security threat, a new economic dependence on the EU would not be a threat. In fact, not only would
it not be a threat, it is a strategic goal of the Lithuanian government to become economically dependent on the EU.[40] Thus, it is a foreign economic
policy mix of cooperation and discord whose direction is determined by nationalism—cooperation with the West, but autonomy from the East. Almost
all Lithuanian nationalists sought to pool their newly won sovereignty with
other states in the European Union, but certainly not with Russia or the CIS.
Joining Europe was much more than an escape from Russia; Europe itself
was a fundamental goal, derived from Lithuanian identity. In sum, diverse
aspects of Lithuania's economic nationalism—a specific "other" defined by
national identity, domestic societal politics, social purpose, historical memory, and a powerful impetus toward Europe—distinguish it from economic
statism. This was, therefore, what Helleiner describes as liberal economic nationalism (2002, 319–22).

40. Ministry of Foreign Affairs of Lithuania, interviews.

2

[Europe, Asia, Russia]

The Return to Eurasia

Russia's Identity and Geoeconomic Choices
in the Post-Soviet World

Andrei P. Tsygankov

*F52 F02
P26 P33*

In the post-Soviet era Russia has passed through several distinct stages in geopolitical imagination. The early Russian leaders visualized their country's identity as "Little Russia" and its interest as the pursuit of a direct relationship with the West, even at the cost of severed ties to the former Soviet region. The state soon began to change its perceptions, however, and announced the policy of integrating the former Soviet republics into a coherent union. More recently, Vladimir Putin has introduced a new vision and policies of uniting Eurasia. Instead of pursuing a multilateral and state-driven integration, Putin argues for bilateral and private sector–driven ties in the region.

What accounts for these shifts in the geopolitical/geoeconomic identity and behavior of the Russian state? After the initial readiness to disengage from the region, why did Russia "return" to Eurasia and why does it now perceive Eurasia as of strategic importance? In this chapter I explain Russia's varying images of and relations with its periphery. I draw on recent research in constructivism and critical geography to argue against treating a nation as given, natural, or objective. It is only through viewing national/geographical space as a contested construct that we come close to understanding Russia's behavior in the post-Soviet world.

Russia's geoeconomic nationalism is a complex product of the nation's interaction with the world. Russia's geopolitical images and geoeconomic strategies are reactions to various external and domestic events mediated by the national context and political struggle. The Soviet elites broadly shared the spatial identity of Russia-Eurasia, but the decline and disintegration of the USSR challenged this identity. It set the terms for the contestation of a Russian-Eurasian identity by various elites, each with its own interests and resources. Russia's Westernizers competed against Eurasianists, and it was ultimately new global historical practices that tipped the competition in favor of one policy group at the expense of another. For example, the ideology of Little Russia must be understood within the world context of the post–Cold War euphoria. A coalition of liberal reformers and pro-capitalist elites that promoted the ideology of Little Russia emerged when the late-Soviet elites grew impatient with the lack of practical results from Gorbachev's policies and became attracted to the "Western" model of development.

The turn to Eurasia and Russia's strategy of integrating the former Soviet space has taken place in a different world context. New instabilities and conflicts in the former Soviet Union, Russia's failed neoliberal economic reform, and NATO's decision to expand eastward provided the context for the rise of the new spatial ideology. This context improved the discursive position of Russia's nonliberal forces and paved the way for the new domestic coalition of the former Soviet industrialists, the military, and security services. The state eventually adopted the geopolitical ideology of this security coalition in its regional policies. Finally, Putin's pragmatic vision cannot be fully understood without taking into account new international opportunities made possible by domestic economic stabilization and Russia's cooperation with the West in the aftermath of September 11.

I argue against structurally rationalist accounts of Russia's geoeconomic behavior and insist that we ought to study the *various types* of rationality displayed by distinct Russian elites. After introducing an analytical framework for understanding geoeconomic nationalism under globalization, I explore how Russia's geopolitical ideas and policies evolved through several stages. I provide an overview of Russia's changing perceptions of, and behavior in, the region and then concentrate on two post-Soviet episodes: ideas and strategies during the early Yeltsin years and under Putin.

Globalization and Geoeconomic Nationalism

The end of the Cold War led to the expectation that the economic policies of nations would converge. The neoliberal concept of globalization anticipated that nations would redefine their interests to fit the standards of the newly emerging and Western-defined openness in the world economy.[1] Rooted in the mainstream tradition of modernization theory, the vision of the worldwide ascendancy of liberal capitalism is based on assumptions of the West's moral and institutional superiority.[2] The vision assumes relative

1. For a work emphasizing the global spread of Western political and economic institutions, see especially Friedman (1999). For an earlier work with a similar ideological spin, see Fukuyama (1989).
2. Modernization theory is known for projecting Western views and values across the globe and for offering ethnocentric, context-insensitive policy advice to non-Western societies. For a recent critique of this theory, see Badie (2000).

homogeneity and uniformity of the West relative to the rest of the world. It also implies that countries outside the West can no longer make a creative contribution to world development; at this "posthistorical" point, all that the non-Western world can do is wait patiently to be absorbed by Western-defined globalization.

Many scholars have justifiably criticized the assumptions of global homogeneity and uniformity as vastly unrealistic. Instead of an increasingly Western-defined policy convergence, one observes a rapid emergence of new cleavages and divergences. Globalization led to increased poverty and socioeconomic divisions, created new areas of violence and lawlessness, reactivated arms races, and accelerated cultural change. Instead of relying on the protection and welfare of Western hegemony, nations often seek to reformulate their interests in order to better protect themselves and readjust to their regional environments (Stallings 1995; Mansfield and Milner 1997). In both global and regional organizations, nations redefine their interests in light of their histories and self-images. New regional and global arrangements emerge as ways of accentuating national differences rather than reducing them. In the adjustment to new global challenges, institutional and cultural advantages appear no less important than economic ones.[3]

To make sense of this persisting diversity of national policies, we need to study what "national" means, and we ought to treat "nation" as open to various meanings and interpretations.[4] Furthermore we should view globalization as a phenomenon that is culturally diverse rather than uniform, and open to various interpretations. Here I define geoeconomic nationalism as a geographically specific perception of a nation's regional economic interests and corresponding policies. Following in the tradition of Friedrich List, I propose to view national economic policy as a product of "time, place and degree of development" (quoted in Taylor 1989, 121).

The factors of time and place are emphasized in cultural geography and "critical" geopolitics. In critical geopolitics, geographical space is a product of political and cultural imagination, not a natural or objective phenomenon.[5] By emphasizing the socially constructed nature of geographical space, the new geopolitics draws our attention to the possibilities of a creative reimagining of the political and economic order beyond the traditional boundaries in the world.

The advocates of the new geopolitics advance several key arguments.[6]

3. For earlier institutionalist arguments, see Katzenstein (1985) and Ikenberry (1986).
4. Such an approach has been pursued, among others, by Crane (1999), Shulman (2000), Abdelal (2001), Helleiner (2002), and Pickel (2003).
5. For a sample of works in the tradition of the new geopolitics, see Ó Tuathail (1996), Alker et al. (1998), Dodds (2000), and Rupert (2000).
6. This paragraph draws on Ó Tuathail and Dalby (1998, 1–8).

First, they seek to advance the study of state practices by delineating the cultural mythologies underlying them, such as myths of foundation or national exceptionalism. Second, they concern themselves with boundaries in a broader sense than those of power and domination only. The new geopolitics, to quote Gearóid Ó Tuathail and Simon Dalby (1998, 4), "is concerned as much with maps of meaning as it is with maps of states. The boundary-drawing practices . . . are both conceptual and cartographic, imaginary and actual, social and aesthetic." Finally, scholars working in the tradition of new geopolitics argue for the irredeemable plurality of geographic space and insist on the significance of intellectual and political creativity in shaping spatial constructions. They maintain that concepts such as identity, security, proximity, and responsibility are never entirely neutral and often reflect the biases of self-expression.

If we apply these premises, varying geoeconomic choices make sense as reflecting nations' varying geographic/geopolitical perceptions. In this tradition scholars understand nationalism chiefly as a way to adjust to the world, rather than discriminate against it. James Mayall (1990, 72), for example, has argued that "the political victory of the nation-state at a time of unprecedented economic interdependence . . . has entrenched many mercantilist attitudes and policies and revived others." In the post–World War II order, nationalism reshaped itself not as policies of self-sufficiency, with a potential for xenophobic intolerance, but as "[state] rationality based on the principle of popular sovereignty" (88–89). In linking national historical experience and foreign policy, another scholar has suggested, "national identity is neither constant nor immutable" and usefully identified five distinct categories of national identity; each with its own preferred foreign policies.[7]

None of these national identities is, by definition, antiliberal. Rather, all should be viewed as *aliberal,* pursuing the objective of finding an appropriate niche in the world based on geopolitical imagery. Paradoxical as it may sound, the strengths of national identity may facilitate, not impede, liberal policies of international adjustment. The new states in the former Soviet area, for instance, have demonstrated that those with a stronger sense of national self, such as the Baltic states, pursued considerably more aggressive policies of economic reorientation away from Russia, the former core state.[8] Another example is the Chinese new nationalism, which also is not incompatible with globalization, as several scholars have shown.[9]

7. Nations may imagine themselves as legally political (Anglo-American model), ethno-national (Eastern and Central Europe), state-driven (France), anticolonial (former European colonies in Asia and Africa), and theocratic (Iran and Russia) entities (Prizel 1998, 21–37). For a similar approach to nationalism, see McCrone (1998). For other research linking national identity and foreign policy, see especially Hudson (1996).

8. Tsygankov (2001). For a similar argument emphasizing political contestation of national identities, see Abdelal (2001).

9. See, for example, Hughes (1997), Pettman (1998, 163), and Crane (1999).

What then is the mechanism through which nations develop and connect their geographical self-images to specific policies? The key variable here is the national interpretation of world challenges and its formulation into a dominant foreign policy ideology. Once adopted by a state, such an ideology eventually is integrated into national economic interest and guides policymakers in their practical decisions. Before that happens, however, a society goes through a process of contestation of various foreign policy ideologies and geopolitical images of economic nationhood. Various ideologies compete for hegemony or the ability to shape public discourse. Promoted by various politico-economic groups in both public and private spaces, ideological contestation is intense until one of the available ideologies becomes dominant. Political entrepreneurs, material and ideational resources, institutional arrangements, and historical practices can considerably facilitate this process of persuading the general public and elites. When the persuasion is complete, the state appropriates the dominant national ideology and spatial image as a guide in economic policymaking.[10] Although many other factors and influences may interfere with a decision-making process, one can expect a reasonable degree of policy consistency when it is based on an adopted image of geoeconomic identity.

Understanding Russia's Identity and Geoeconomic Choices

Immediately after the Soviet breakup, Boris Yeltsin pursued policies of disengagement from the ex-republics. The post-Communist leadership emphasized its new commitments to strategic partnership with the West and expressed little interest in preserving close ties in the former Soviet area. The idea was to integrate directly with the West at the expense of relationships with the former republics. To meet this goal, Russia's leaders designed several cultural, economic, and military policies. In the cultural area, the concept of Little Russia served the purpose of maintaining minimal responsibility for the Soviet policies and historical legacies outside Russia. In the economic area, the new leaders meant to stop subsidies to the former USSR, which they viewed as an indicator of the ex-republics' exploitation of Russia. And in the security area, the plan was to gradually withdraw the Russian military and to rely on the assistance of international organizations, such as the Organisation for Security and Cooperation in Europe (OSCE), in solving possible future conflicts in the region.

These policies, however, soon revealed their weaknesses. As early as 1993, Russia's leaders were confronted with challenges in the former Soviet region and began to reconsider their policies of disengagement. By the end of 1994

10. For similar approaches to economic policymaking process in the postcommunist world, see Pickel and True (2002) and Maya Eichler's chapter in this volume.

the newly appointed foreign minister, Yevgeni Primakov, was leading the country's return to the former Soviet region. The idea of Russia's historical responsibility for organizing Eurasia was back to replace the short-lived concept of Little Russia. In the economic area, Primakov formulated the goal of integrating the former Soviet area. Russia's leadership also emphasized the importance of maintaining Russian military presence in at least some of the ex-republics for the sake of stability and peace.

Vladimir Putin's arrival as president signaled another change in policies. The commitment to Russian engagement in the post-Soviet Eurasia has not been challenged; rather, the new leadership is changing the pattern of the country's regional engagement. Instead of pursuing Primakov's multilateral and state-driven integration of the region, Putin has developed a concept of bilateral and private sector–driven ties in the post-Soviet world. The reasoning behind these new policies is that Primakov's Russia overstretched itself. While continuing to honor its regional commitments, Putin's Russia would therefore economize and be more "pragmatic"—a favorite word in the Kremlin's new political vocabulary—in its relations within post-Soviet Eurasia.

The Framework for Understanding

How can we make sense of the observed variation in Russia's economic policies in the former Soviet region? In the rest of this section, I examine the relationship between the world context and patterns of spatial economic behavior in Russia after the Soviet disintegration. In particular, I focus on the Russian elites' ideologies and spatial images and on the specific geoeconomic policies that proceed from these images. My discussion in this section is sketchy, but I will elaborate later on each of the points.

Figure 2.1 explains the general process of formation of Russia's geoeconomic nationalism. Throughout the imperial and especially the Soviet rule, Russia has developed and internalized a spatial self-image of Eurasia as a supranational and supra-ethnic community that combines elements of both European and Asian or non-Western orientations. The Soviet elites broadly shared the spatial identity of Russia-Eurasia, but the decline and disintegration of the USSR challenged this identity and spurred contestation and rethinking. Contestation produced various spatial ideologies, both of Westernist and Eurasianist nature, and eventually from these ideologies the state drew its concepts of national geoeconomic interests and policies.

At various stages, the post-Soviet state was committed to different ideologies and visions of economic interests, and it had divergent policies in the former Soviet region. Andrei Kozyrev, Russia's first foreign minister, was a liberal Westernizer committed to the notion of Little Russia and policies of disengagement from the former Soviet republics. Primakov, the second foreign minister, continued to view Russia as responsible for organizing

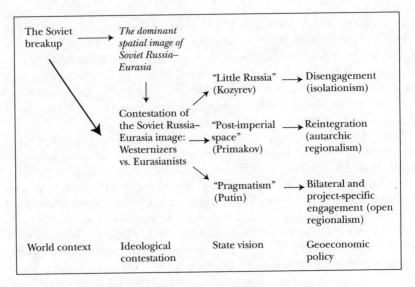

Figure 2.1. Formation of Russian geoeconomic nationalism(s)

Eurasian space and, consistently with this image, designed policies of reintegrating the former Soviet area. Finally, president Putin too demonstrates his commitment to active involvement in Eurasia, but he bases it on a less hegemonic vision of Eurasia.

How do various ideologies and spatial images emerge and eventually get appropriated by the state? Which social forces should be held responsible? Figure 2.2 specifies my reasoning. At stage I, as a result of various historical practices,[11] contacts with the external environment, and intellectual activities, new ideologies emerge and make room for new interpretations of the nation's spatial environment. At stage II, the newly emerged ideologies are intensely debated by elites and promoted through activities of political entrepreneurs, support of prominent politico-economic groups, and conducive institutional arrangements. Finally, at stage III, contestation of various spatial images reaches the point when the state decides to appropriate one of them as its own. The chosen ideology becomes the dominant one and guides state policies. At this point the state chooses to align itself with some prominent politico-economic groups and advance their agenda.[12] The emergence of some new historical practices may, of course, challenge this ideological choice and begin a new cycle of ideological competition.

11. "Historical practices" here refers to the various events and experiences nations go though during their development.
12. For a more extended treatment of relations between economic interests and political power in post-Soviet Russia, see Simonia (2001).

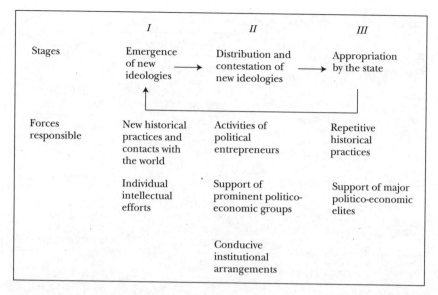

Figure 2.2. Formation of state ideology in Russia

The three dominant Russian geoeconomic ideologies are summarized in table 2.1. Each ideology was adopted in a distinct world context and supported by a distinct coalition of domestic interests. The ideology of Little Russia emerged during the era of the post–Cold War euphoria as a direct challenge to Gorbachev and was promoted by the late-Soviet elites in Russia and other republics. A coalition of liberal reformers and pro-capitalist elites both supported and promoted the ideology of Little Russia.

A challenge to this ideology came from a security coalition that united military industrialists, army, and security services—those who saw no major benefits in adopting the "Western" model and needed an external threat to justify their significance and solidify their influence. The world of the early to mid 1990s provided such a threat. The Primakov-supported ideology of "postimperial space" responded to newly emerged instabilities and conflicts in the former Soviet Union, as well as to NATO's decision to expand eastward. Domestically, this coalition blocked the efforts of liberal reformers, and it benefited politically from the failure of the "shock therapy" reform.

Finally, Putin's ideology of pragmatism is a project of a mixed coalition that includes both commercial and some security interests. Sometimes referred to as the alliance of oligarchs and chekists,[13] the coalition was formed in a new context, one that holds both threats and opportunities for Russia.

13. *Chekist* originates from the Russian *CheKa,* the original name of the Bolsheviks' security service led by People's Commissar Feliks Dzerzhinski. *Oligarchs* are, of course, the superrich captains of Russia's newly privatized economy.

Table 2.1. Dominant Russian geoeconomic ideologies

	Little Russia	Post-imperial space	Pragmatic state
Supportive politicians	Kozyrev, early Yeltsin	Primakov	Putin
Supportive politico-economic elites	A coalition of commerical interests (pro-capitalist elites and liberal reformers)	A coalition of security interests (military industrialists, army, and security services)	A mixed coalition of commercial and selective security interests (oligarchs and chekists)
Geopolitical orientation	Westernism	Eurasianism	Eurasianism
Perceived world context	New opportunities (end of the Cold War)	New threats (conflicts in the former Soviet area, NATO expansion)	Threats and opportunities (terrorism and domestic recovery)

The opportunities come from domestic economic stabilization and possible cooperation with the United States after September 11, and the threats are defined by the new leadership as those of a terrorist nature inside and outside Russia.

The historically established Eurasian identity, therefore, proved to be resilient. During the Soviet era, Eurasianism defeated Russian ethno-nationalism, whose representatives never occupied prominent positions within the ruling elite.[14] After the Soviet collapse, Eurasianism, supported by various domestic interests, successfully resisted the Westernist identity promoted by the Little Russia ideology. As a result of various intellectual and political activities, Eurasianist ideology was reformulated, rather than replaced by Westernism. First, by selectively borrowing from writings of hard-line oppositionists,[15] supporters of new Eurasianism, such as president's advisor Sergei Stankevich, paved their way to the new ideology of "postimperial space" and the political rise of Primakov. Then, the new commercial class with renewed business interests in the former Soviet area reformulated the notion of Eurasia further. Oligarchs, such as Boris Berezovski, advocated a more pragmatic and open regionalism in the former USSR even before Putin's arrival. Their vision of Eurasia—that of multilevel politico-economic arrangement supported by the state but built primarily through private-sector initiatives—was eventually adopted by the Putin government.

14. In the next section, I elaborate on the notion of Russia's Eurasian identity and provide more evidence of its post-Soviet resilience. Outside Russia, Kazakhstan's President Nazarbayev was especially supportive of Eurasianist ideology.
15. This opposition was often concentrated in the newspaper *Zavtra*, edited by Aleksandr Prokhanov.

Table 2.2. Russian geoeconomic policies

	Little Russia	Post-imperial space	Pragmatic state
Concept of regional economic interests	Disengagement	Reintegration	Bilateralization and tri-levelization
Institutional development (CIS)	Loose CIS	Tighter CIS	The end of the CIS
	Low progress in institutional development	More active institutional developments	Subregional institutional developments
Economic policies and initiatives	Unilateral decision to end the ruble zone	Promotion of the Customs Union	Initiation of specific projects, especially in energy and transportation areas
		Political use of subsidies	
	No coordination of price liberalization		
	Protectionism		

Finally, table 2.2 explains in greater detail the spatial economic policies that Kozyrev, Primakov, and Putin pursued, as a consequence of their ideological commitments and their conceptions of Russia's regional economic interests. Kozyrev proceeded from the view that relative disengagement from the former Soviet republics was the best course of action. Accordingly, he advocated a loose conception of the Commonwealth of Independent States (CIS) and was supportive of the view that the organization should facilitate "civilized divorce" and nation building among the ex-republics, rather than encourage their political and economic integration. Consistent with this view, Russia pursued a unilateral design of reformist policy by cutting monetary and commercial ties with the ex-republics and pushing forward with price liberalization. In his turn, Primakov wanted to revive the CIS as a tool for reintegrating the former Soviet space, and he promoted Russia's more aggressive role in developing supraregional economic ties through the Customs Union—for example, by means of economic sanctions such as state subsidies. Finally, Putin acted as if he had no faith in the CIS and instead advanced various specific projects especially in energy and transportation areas.

Alternative Rationalist Perspective

Rationalists might argue that the approach taken in this chapter understates the role of actors' interests and political calculations. For scholars working in this tradition, regional economic strategies are not cultural, and they could not have taken place were it not for leaders' political interests. In reply to what I have said, rationalists might assert that Russia's economic nationalism and turn to Eurasia is political and interest maximizing rather than cultural. These political interests might include the need for elites to present themselves as guardians of Russia's geopolitical interests against the "encroaching" and "hegemonic" West or the "terrorist threat" from the South. The project of Eurasianism may usefully serve as a form of nationalist ideological mobilization. It helps to create the image of an enemy and consolidate public opinion around desired goals. It is appealing politics, if one is motivated purely by an interest in preserving power.

Furthermore, rationalists might argue that this politically calculated nationalism is shortsighted and unhelpful in satisfying Russia's real economic interests, namely, successful global adjustment and integration in the world economy. Any attempts to pursue projects of local or regional significance are a waste of resources, which otherwise could have been invested in economic globalization. For example, some have criticized the view of CIS as Russia's hegemonic project for being too expensive and not in Russia's genuine interests.[16] Others have argued that economic arrangements with countries like Belarus and Kazakhstan are not going to improve Russia's power status. Thus, one rationalist found "particularly puzzling" Russia's "preference to maintain close ties with some of the weaker states" (Spruyt 1997, 325).

The rationalist account is insufficient because it does not spell out the sources of Russia's perception of its economic interests. It is not helpful in clarifying how Russia's elites make their geoeconomic choices and why they choose a regional, rather than a merely global, orientation. The account does not tell us why this perception evolved from the concept of isolationism to integration and then to pragmatism in Russia's economic relations with the ex-republics. It oversimplifies the process of economic interest formation by assuming Russia's institutional and cultural similarity with the Western economies. It also dichotomizes the process of global adjustment by presenting it as an either-or choice between global and regional economic spaces, while in reality this process is a complex dialectic of both. In reality, the Eurasian choice is not necessarily anti-West and anti–global economy. Regionalism may in fact be a bridge to successful globalization. If we are to make progress in understanding the Russia's geoeconomic choices, we need a perspective that is sensitive to how a nation perceives itself. This is what the present study attempts to accomplish.

16. Olcott, Aslund, and Garnett (1999). In Russia, pro-Western liberal politicians and business circles were protective of what they saw as Russian economic interests and objected to Russian subsidies and trade openness to the former republics (for a scholarly critique of the CIS, see Shishkov 1997). I return to this point in the second half of the chapter.

Choice 1: Breaking Away from the Post-Soviet Periphery

Russia's Soviet Eurasianist Identity

Eurasianist identity reflects a cultural belief in the common destiny of Russians and other nationalities living in the geographical space of the former USSR. It is a historical image or myth of the existence of a transnational community in Europe and Asia with Russia as its core, an image that is widely shared by Russian society and elites. The establishment of the image of Eurasia is a product of mutually reinforcing historical practices before and especially during the Soviet era. Russia's imperial policies and developments have often constituted the core of these practices. But Eurasianist identity is anything but static;[17] various ideologies or programs of action have constantly undermined, disputed, and developed the imagined transnational community. Historically, Eurasia has been vigorously contested by ideologies of Russian and Slavic nationalism. More recently, the challenge came from liberal Westernizers, with their ideology of Little Russia and a "civic nation" within the post-Soviet political boundaries.

There are number of ways to demonstrate the vitality of Eurasianist identity in Russia immediately before and after the Soviet disintegration. Statements by politicians of both the left and right indicate the significance of Eurasianism for the political class. Intellectual writings across the spectrum illustrate the endurance of Eurasia as a unifying idea for Russia. And polls of the general public demonstrate that thinking in Eurasianist categories is not alien to Russian society as a whole and has potential for continuous support.

Both conservative and reformist politicians have showed their commitments to Eurasianist identity. Conservative opposition to Gorbachev and Yeltsin articulated the notion of a new Eurasia in newspapers such as *Den'* and *Zavtra* and put forward various projects of reintegrating Russia with the republics.[18] Gorbachev too showed his support for a newly reformulated union of Eurasianist nature.[19] He diverged from his conservative opposition

17. Elsewhere I identify four distinct schools of Russia's Eurasianist thinking (Tsygankov 2003).

18. For various political projects of Zyuganov, Zhirinovski, and others, see Tolz (2001, 257–60).

19. On several occasion, Gorbachev used the term "Eurasia" in his speeches and writings. For example, in October 1988 in his welcoming message to foreign guests attending the Asia-Pacific Region Conference in Vladivostok, he stressed that "the Soviet Union was a Eurasian state . . . to serve as a hopeful bridge bringing together two great continents" (cited in Hauner 1990, 249). And in the 1987 edition of *Perestroika* he upgraded his "common European home" formula by adding the Asian dimension: "The Soviet Union is an Asian, as well as European country" (Hauner 1990, 11). Gorbachev's principal foreign policy advisor Georgi Shakhnazarov (2001, 486) wrote later about his regret that the post-Soviet Commonwealth of Independent States was not named "the Commonwealth of Euro-Asian States," which

about the methods for unifying the Soviet space rather than about the need itself. Among the Westernizers, Andrei Sakharov defended the notion of Eurasia and has even formulated a "Constitution of the Union of the Soviet Republics of Europe and Asia" (1990, 266–76). And leaders of the ethnic autonomous territories were broadly supportive of Eurasianism, which they perceived as capable of guarding against their Russification.[20]

Intellectuals too have demonstrated interest in developing Eurasianist ideologies. The conservative *Den/Zavtra* group led by Aleksandr Prokhanov and Aleksandr Dugin articulated an essentialist vision of Eurasia as a new continental empire and a distinct civilization.[21] Some liberals too have used the notion of Eurasia for characterizing Russia's historical legacy and future development. Before the Soviet disintegration one liberal intellectual, Mikhail Gefter (1991, 460–67), viewed Eurasia as a "country of countries" and group of diverse nations that are nonetheless united by common history. After the disintegration, Vadim Mezhuev and others have argued that Russia should continue to fulfill its mission of preserving a unique supranational community (Tolz 2001, 240).

In addition, the general public has consistently demonstrated relatively strong support for the idea of a transnational community in the former USSR and relatively little support for the idea of Russia's independent cultural existence. Although the support for the existence of a transnational community varied during 1990–2001, it consistently reached 60 to more than 70 percent. Various data on how Russians viewed the Soviet Union and their cultural belonging demonstrate this.

During the referendum of March 17, 1991, which took place in the context of Gorbachev's struggle for a renewed union, and was conducted in all Soviet republics except Armenia, Georgia, Moldavia, and the three Baltics, 147 million people voted and 76.4 percent approved the preservation of the union.[22] Although few Russians wanted the Soviet Union to be restored af-

---

"would have emphasized the unique feature of our country that for centuries has been a bridge between the two great continents and civilizations." Gorbachev's liberal foreign minister Eduard Shevardnadze too referred to the Soviet Union as a "great Eurasian space" and a "world of worlds" (*mir mirov*). Citing the Russian philosopher Georgi Fedotov, Shevardnadze said Russia had to live in a complex political world of both European and Asian nations (see Otunbayeva 1991, 186–87).

20. The Dagestani Ramazan Abdulatipov was actively opposing the new concept of the Russian (*rossiiskaia*) nation as a community of citizens (Tolz 2001, 261–62).

21. Tsygankov (1998). For a history of intellectual debates on Russian place between Europe and Asia, see Hauner (1990) and Neumann (1996).

22. The question was, "Do you support the preservation of the union as a renewed federation of sovereign republics in which the rights of a person of any nationality are fully guaranteed?" The Yeltsin-led Democratic Russia actively campaigned against the referendum (Kotz and Weir 1997, 147).

ter its disintegration, many strongly favored some way of preserving the cultural community in the former Soviet space. In 1994, for example, only 21 percent named the restoration of the USSR as one of the three most important tasks facing Russia, but most Russians would have approved if several of the former Soviet republics were to reunite with Russia.[23] And a survey in January 1997 found that about 84 percent of 1,500 Russians either regretted the disintegration of the Soviet Union "very much" (54 percent) or "to some extent" (30 percent) (Sakwa and Webber 1999, 405).

In addition to regretting the loss of a union, Russians are quite aware of their cultural distinctness from the West. In a December 1994 poll taken by the respected agency VTSIOM, 59 percent of Russians felt that Russia is culturally different from Europe, whereas only 20 percent saw Russia as belonging to European civilization.[24] In another VTSIOM poll taken in 1997, over 70 percent of Russians supported the thesis that "Russia is a special country alien to the West" (Paschenko 2000, 8). And in December 2001, 71 percent agreed with the statement "Russia belongs to the special 'Eurasian' or Orthodox civilization, and therefore cannot follow the Western path of development."[25]

If Eurasianist cultural identity was indeed well established, then the Soviet collapse should not be viewed as evidence of a disintegration of the identity of Eurasia. Rather, it was a disintegration of *one* Eurasianist identity. Gorbachev's failure to reconstruct the Soviet space does not mean that the public support for his efforts was low. However, revolutionary polarization of the political space deprived Russia of a chance to reformulate its Eurasianist identity. What eventually shifted the political balance away from Gorbachev and toward Yeltsin's anti-Eurasianism was the perestroika leader's hesitancy to abandon the old Soviet project, on the one hand, and Yeltsin's radical nationalism, on the other.

The collapse of the USSR has demonstrated then that the Soviet Eurasianist idea has exhausted its vitality and potential for development. It did not demonstrate, however, that some new forms of Eurasianist thinking would not be able to win the minds of Russians. On the contrary: the evidence seems to indicate a future Eurasianist revival.

23. The rate of approval ranged from 84 percent for Ukraine and Belarus, the two Slavic states, to about 50 percent for four Central Asian states, with Kazakhstan falling in between these two poles (U.S. Information Agency, Office of Research and Media Reaction, briefing paper, Washington, D.C., September 1994).
24. *Segodnya*, December 6, 1994.
25. Rossiya: zapadni put' dlia "yevroaziatskoi" tsivilizatsiyi . . . ? *Vserossiyski Tsentr Izucheniya Obschestvennogo Mneniya (VTSIOM)*, no. 32, November 13, 2001, http://www.wciom.ru/vciom/new/press/press12111532.htm.

The Soviet Collapse and the Rise of Pro-European Isolationism

As figure 2.1 illustrates, the Soviet breakup brought about the disintegration of the previously established Russian spatial identity and initiated a process of identity reformulation. Under new conditions, it was the liberal coalition of democratic reformers and the former Communist *nomenklatura* that was able to shape the new political discourse.

United by Boris Yeltsin, the members of the new elite wanted to accomplish different but compatible goals. Reformers wanted fast economic and political change that would bring Russia in line with politico-economic standards of Western countries within a limited time.[26] Members of the former Communist Party *nomenklatura*—those who realized that the return to the Soviet past was no longer possible and had lost faith in the Soviet form of socialism as well as other forms[27]—wanted to obtain control over the state property they had previously managed under the leadership of the Central Committee. This was a fairly broad group. Its two largest parts originated from the Komsomol (the youth branch of the Communist Party) apparatus and the so-called "industrialists" or directors of large state enterprises, both of whom entered private business during 1989–91.[28] The goals of democrats and the former *nomenklatura*, however contradictory, were not entirely incompatible: democrats wanted pro-capitalist reforms, while the Party *nomenklatura* was eager to become a capitalist class.[29]

The new liberal coalition was able to shape the national discourse because it thoroughly undermined the power of Gorbachev. Gorbachev's reforms, especially after the failed coup of August 1991, lost their appeal. This was partly a result of Gorbachev's poor strategic thinking, indecisiveness, and naïve illusions.[30]

It was also due to the influence of the West. The idea of Western modernity powerfully shaped the minds of Gorbachev's liberal opposition. Although politically the Western leaders were supportive of Gorbachev's gradual efforts to dismantle the Soviet system, most of them were critical of

26. Yeltsin and Gaidar typically talked about of one or two years of necessary reforms, after which Russians were to considerably improve their living standards.

27. Some, of course, never gave up on the idea of socialism. Gorbachev was among these, as well as some of his former supporters, such as Nikolai Ryzhkov and Yegor Ligachev.

28. See Kotz and Weir (1997, esp. 109–30) for development and empirical support of the argument about transformation of the party-state elite into the pro-capitalist coalition.

29. See Peregudov (1994, 70) on this convergence of interests. Initially, as Simonia (2001, 272) has argued, two main factions—finance and trade, and raw materials—dominated in the emergence of Russia's new capitalism.

30. One such illusion was Gorbachev's belief that the Soviet Union was not an empire, and therefore the republics should have been grateful to the Soviet rulers for their industrialization and modernization. As a result the existence and the seriousness of the nationality question was fully recognized only in 1990, three years after the first ethnic revolts had taken place in Central Asia and the Caucasus.

his socialist intentions and hoped for the emergence of a Westernized system in place of the USSR. As early as in 1989 the arguments about communism as "the grand failure" won the support of the mainstream discourse in the West (Brzezinski 1989). The leading establishment journal in the United States, *Foreign Affairs,* soon issued the verdict that "the Soviet system collapsed because of what it was, or more exactly, because of what it was not. The West 'won' because of what the democracies were—because they were free, prosperous and successful, because they did justice, or convincingly tried to do so."[31] Russia's liberal coalition too shared the beliefs in the superiority of the Western system.

Having defeated Gorbachev, the new liberal coalition formulated and advanced the ideology of Little Russia. In the postrevolutionary/post-Soviet vacuum of ideas, this ideology quickly became dominant. It called for separating Russia from the former Soviet area economically, politically, and culturally. The argument was that Russia had turned into an "internal colony" of the Soviet Union and, as a result, had suffered from being the core of the Soviet empire, suffered even more than all other republics. For example, as many liberals argued, the USSR had been a constant drain on Russia's resources because the country's oil, natural gas, gold, and other raw materials could have been marketed abroad but instead were sold to other Soviet republics at heavily subsidized prices.[32] Russia suffered politically and culturally too, and it should rebuild its national identity as a nonimperial or "civic" nation-state.[33]

The origins of the ideology were in the Democratic Russia movement, which presented itself as an anti-imperial movement by emphasizing the autonomy of Russia and other republics and openly calling for the dissolution of the Soviet Union.[34] Democratic Russia saw Gorbachev as the last savior of the "empire." Throughout the political campaigns of 1990 and 1991, Yeltsin advanced the "victim Russia" argument, and his advisors eventually wrote a scenario for dissolving the union.[35] Ironically, the argument was borrowed from Russian nationalists, who often complained about Russia's burden of provisioning the rest of the union (although they never supported breaking

31. Pfaff (1991, 48). This vision was finally legitimized on the highest policy level when President George H. W. Bush announced the Cold War "victory" of the United States in his 1992 State of the Union message.

32. For an example of such reasoning, see Kortunov (1995, 144). At about the same time, during the late 1980s, anti-imperial/anti-Russian arguments were advanced in number of the ex-republics as well (see Tsygankov 2001 for details).

33. For elaboration on Russia as a civic nation, see Tolz (2001, 249–65).

34. In early 1991 Democratic Russia called for dissolution of the Soviet Union and even tried (unsuccessfully) to convince Yeltsin to campaign for a No vote in the referendum that year on preserving the Soviet Union (Yitzhak Brudny as quoted in Kotz and Weir 1997, 135 n. 10).

35. Gorbachev (1995) recalls the so-called Burbulis memorandum, in which the idea was articulated by Yeltsin's key aide Gennadi Burbulis.

up the union).[36] Not all democrats agreed with representing the union as the main obstacle to transforming Russia into a market democracy,[37] but the argument won support from the majority of the democratic opposition.

The implications of establishing the Little Russia identity for the country's Eurasian system of values and foreign policy were fundamental. In the words of Andrei Kozyrev, the very system of values was to be changed, which within ten to twelve years would transform Russia into a first-rank country like France, Germany, and the United States. Russia was to accept the priority of the individual and the free market over the society and state in order to develop a "natural partnership" with Western countries.[38] The argument implied that Russia had exhausted the list of alternative development projects; Kozyrev saw no reasons to hide his view that foreign policy was a "tool for advancing Russia's reforms" (1994, 48). Russia's identity turn was, in one scholar's word, an attempt to reverse a four-hundred-year-old political tradition in which the Russian national idea was identical with the Russian imperial idea (Aron 1994, 19).

Geoeconomic Policy

In the former Soviet area, the Little Russia identity implied a considerable degree of Russian isolationism. The leaders of the new Russia saw the country's interests as served by disengaging from the region and developing relationships directly with the Western countries.

In the aftermath of the failed coup of August 1991, Yeltsin first formulated the idea of Russia going it alone. After appointing Yegor T. Gaidar as his main economic advisor, he delivered his famous speech to the Russian Congress of People's Deputies, which was believed to be written by Gaidar. In the speech Yeltsin explicitly committed himself to the strategy of shock therapy—the freeing up of all prices by the end of the year, rapid privatization of both industry and land, large reductions in state spending, and a tough monetary policy—and argued that Russia must go first and provide an example for other republics.[39] Yeltsin shared Gaidar's conviction that economically the republics were nothing but a drain on resources, a "bur-

---

36. Slanislav Kunyayev has argued, for instance, that "of 190 billion rubles of the union's annual profit, Russia leaves to itself a little more than half. The rest of it goes to support the union's bureaucracy and to subsidize the republics, while each Russian family looses around 1,500 rubles a year" (cited in Furman 1992, 13). Similar arguments were made by other leading Russian nationalists, such as Valentin Rasputin and Alexandr Solzhenitsyn.

37. Dmitri Furman (1992), for example, was among those warning about the danger of adopting nationalist strategy by democrats and held democrats directly responsible for the breakup of the Soviet Union.

38. Kozyrev cited in Buszynski (1996, 4 n. 8).

39. *New York Times*, October 29, 1991 (as cited in Kotz 1997, 167).

den on Russian legs," and therefore Russia had a little choice but "break away" (*uiti v otryv*) from the former USSR.[40]

This vision corresponded with Kozyrev's view. In September 1991, for example, he argued that his country's foreign policy should accomplish the key historical task of transforming Russia "from the dangerous sick giant of Eurasia into a participant of the Western co-prosperity zone" (cited in Plyais 1993). Until the spring of 1992, Kozyrev did not even bother to visit the newly emerged post-Soviet states (Donaldson and Nogee 1998, 172).

The liberal foreign policy community was supportive of the new vision of Russia's economic interest. For example, the authors of the prominent report "After the Break-Up of the USSR" warned against Russia's becoming the new center of the Commonwealth of Independent States precisely on economic grounds (Zagorskii et al. 1992, 6–11). They argued that a key interest of Russia was entering the G-7 as a full-fledged participant and moving from the periphery of the world economy to its core. The authors of the report insisted that the ambition of becoming the CIS's center would make it impossible to Westernize and that Russia should therefore be prepared to "give up the CIS orientation in favor of that toward Europe" (Zagorski et al. 1992, 15, 17).

Russian isolationism toward the ex-Soviet republics became apparent in at least three areas: CIS institutional developments, monetary policy, and trade relations. In the CIS area, emphasis was placed on facilitating the ex-Soviet republics' political and economic independence, rather than their cooperation and interdependence. This vision of the CIS as a mechanism for a "civilized divorce" shaped the organization's founding agreements, such as the CIS Charter. Russia was instrumental in developing this perception of the CIS purpose, and its initial policies displayed a "degree of hesitancy, even passivity, in relations with the successor states" (Sakwa and Webber 1999, 402). This attitude began to change in 1993 when Russia initiated the CIS Economic Union agreement and shifted the emphasis to a multilateral economic cooperation in the region.

In the monetary area, the most significant development was Russia's decision in July 1993 to end the "ruble zone." Unilaterally, Russia's government halted money supplies and credits to the ex-Soviet republics and withdrew old Soviet and Russian ruble notes from circulation on its territory. The currency reform, accompanied by price decontrol, created a crisis in the republics that relied on the ruble in their transactions.[41] Although Russia was obligated to consult with the republics in economic policy matters

40. The metaphor of the republics as a "heavy burden" has since obtained a wide currency in Russian liberal circles (see details in Klyachko and Solovei 1995).

41. For example, Ukraine's president Leonid Kravchuk complained that "none of the policies, prices, taxes, or any other, is coordinated" (*Nezavisimaya gazeta,* January 13, 1993, 5).

by the CIS founding principles written into the Minsk agreement of December 1991, Yeltsin chose to proceed unilaterally and disregard his obligations. He believed that Russia would be better positioned for further reforms if it alone occupied the ruble zone (Klyachko and Solovei 1995).

Finally, consistent with its isolationist beliefs, Russia placed commercial restrictions on economic activities with the republics. As soon as the Soviet Union fell apart, Russia began erecting trade barriers and maintained them at relatively high levels even after most-favored-nation and free-trade agreements with the republics had been concluded. In part, these policies reflected Russia's dissatisfaction with the state of payments by several republics. The poor state of payments only reinforced the belief of Russia's leaders that trade with the cash-stripped republics should be sacrificed to advancing economic ties with the countries of the "far abroad" (read: the West).

Despite all efforts, the strategy of economic disengagement from the former Soviet area began to backfire soon after Russia's leaders attempted to implement it. In the two years after 1991, all the successor states experienced negative growth rates of GDP and breakdown of their trade, production, labor, and energy ties (Sakwa and Webber 1999, 386). Inside Russia, a different coalition with economic interests in the former Soviet area took shape, ready to challenge Yeltsin and Kozyrev's early policies. The level of public support for these policies was not very high either, and many Russians continued to favor preservation of a cultural community in the former Soviet space. In addition, Russia's leadership faced opposition from some republics.[42] All these developments limited Yeltsin and Kozyrev's ability to act on their beliefs. In 1993 they both began to depart from their original stances and, at least rhetorically, proclaimed their understanding of the priority of relations with the ex-Soviet republics.

Choice 2: Reengaging the Post-Soviet Periphery

Putin and the New Pragmatism in Eurasia

The new ideology of Russia's national interest in the former Soviet region was advanced by a new coalition that included both commercial and security interests. Putin came to power on the platform of eradicating "extremism" in Chechnya and reestablishing a "strong state" in Russia.[43] Because of

42. Kyrgyzstan's president Askar Akayev referred to the CIS integration as a "dictum of time," while Nazarbayev has argued it reflected "an objective process, a historical necessity" (cited in Webber 1997, 1).

43. The bombs that exploded in Moscow in August 1999 and killed hundreds of residents a few weeks before Putin entered the office of prime minister created the context in which the

his background in security service and the proclaimed beliefs in the strong state, various members of Russia's security class supported him.[44] Many liberals too were strongly behind Putin. Especially important were Russia's oligarchs, the group of superwealthy businesses that emerged as a powerful force in 1996, when they were able to overcome their differences and pool financial resources for reelecting the then unpopular Yeltsin. Oligarchs, particularly those exporting natural resources to the West, were likely to maintain and even increase their influence on Putin.

The alliance of chekists and oligarchs emerged in the new world context. The relative recovery of Russian economy after the August 1998 financial crisis and the higher world oil prices further improved the position of oligarchs. As for chekists, their political standing was strengthened by the intensification of terrorism in the Caucasus and worldwide. Putin did not waste time using the events of September 11 to reshape Russia's relations with the United States and redefine the threats as those of a global terrorist nature.

The new semiliberal coalition adopted and further developed the idea of "new pragmatism" as a key concept for understanding Russia's national interest. "Pragmatism" in foreign policy had two key components. The first one was meant for the noncommercial part of the new coalition and emphasized the need to firmly defend the interests of Russia. It served as a continuation of Primakov's vision, which had argued against cooperation with the West at the expense of Russia's own interests. The second component, however, had a liberal appeal and differed from Primakov's vision.[45] It assumed the significance of geoeconomics over geopolitics,[46] and the need for Russia to defend its national interests by primarily economic means. It also introduced a different regional strategy. Regional integration was to be open and compatible with business interests. It was also to be subjected to the task of gradually integrating Russia into the world economy.

Various media and political forces had long expressed their support of

---

future president shaped his election platform. At that time, Putin's popularity was at the level of 2 percent, but in two months it jumped to 26 percent and, as the war in Chechnya progressed, reached the unprecedented 58 percent in January 2001 (Rose 2001, 221–22).

44. Putin was initially supported by both moderate nationalists close to Primakov (see, for example, Zatulin 2000) and hard-liners like the *Zavtra*-affiliates Prokhanov and Dugin. In about a year, Prokhanov has changed his views and returned to his typical "irreconcilable" opposition to the regime, whereas Dugin has continued to be supportive of Putin.

45. Irina Kobrinskaya has labeled the new emphasis "pragmatic liberalism," as opposed to Primakov's "pragmatic nationalism." She traced the origins of the new concept to the spring of 1997, when Yeltsin signed the Founding Act Russia-NATO and the "Big" Treaty of Russia's relations with Ukraine (Kobrinskaya 1997).

46. Russia's intellectuals organized a series of debates about a Russia's optimal strategy of adjustment to global economic interdependence. See, for example, a discussion of Neklessa's article in *Vostok* (Neklessa 1997; Postsovremenni mir 1998). See also Kochetov (1999), which contains a discussion of Russia's geoeconomic adjustment to the global economy.

such views and dissatisfaction with Primakov's grand foreign policy vision, which included the "integration" of the former Soviet republics. Liberals criticized the vision for underestimating Russia's business interests and for continuing to subsidize some republics in exchange for their political loyalty. Boris Berezovski, a one time CIS executive secretary, delivered a passionate critique of the Primakov-inspired vision of the CIS Economic Integrational Development, adopted in March 1997.[47] Scholars of the influential Institute of the World Economy and International Relations (IMEMO) argued that CIS integration was unfeasible and that the pro-integration efforts and the real economic processes in the former USSR ran in opposite directions.[48] Other liberals criticized the state for being soft on Ukrainian energy debts to Russian companies and faulted the planned Russia-Belarus union as economically asymmetrical.[49]

More nationalist-oriented forces had long argued that Primakov wanted post-Soviet integration at the expense of Russia's resources, and they spoke against what they perceived as Russia's one-sided concessions. For example, Andranik Migranian (1994), once a prominent critic of Kozyrev's isolationism and a promoter of Russia's "Monroe Doctrine" in the former Soviet area, argued that "during the several last years, it became absolutely clear that all the attempts to integrate the post-Soviet space have led to nothing. The CIS is barely able to function."[50]

The new liberal-nationalist consensus was well summarized in the document of the influential Council for Foreign and Defense Policy entitled "Strategy for Russia: Agenda for President—2000." The authors of the document criticized Primakov's concept of a multipolar world as outdated, financially expensive, and potentially confrontational.[51] Instead, the authors offered the concept of "selective engagement," which they compared with Russia's nineteenth-century policy of "self-concentration" after its defeat in the war with Crimea and with Deng Xiaoping's policy in China (Council for Foreign and Defense Policy 2000, theses 5.14, 5.2, 5.5).

With regard to the former Soviet space, the council recommended a "considerable revision" of policy involving abandonment of the "pseudo-integration at Russia's expense" and "tough defense of our national economic interests": "We must begin by changing the very concept of integration. It should be built not from above, but from below—on the basis of support-

47. Berezovski 1998.
48. Shishkov 1997. For similar arguments, see Shmelev 1998. Andrei Zagorskii (1994, 26) concluded as early as in 1994 that Primakov-inspired integrationist efforts would not last long because of the divergence of Russia's economic interests from those of other former republics.
49. See the leader of Yabloko Yavlinski as cited in *Nezavisimaya gazeta*, February 26, 1998.
50. For similar views of another Primakovite, see Pushkov (1998).
51. Both liberals, such as Deputy Foreign Minister Anatoli Adamishin, and nationalists, like the above-mentioned Zatulin, collaborated in writing the final draft of the document.

ing integration of various markets of separate goods and services, creating transnational financial-industrial groups . . . exchanging debts for assets' ownership. The state policy of cooperation and integration should be directed at supporting exactly this kind of activities" (thesis 5.8.1).

It appears that Putin has moved to adopt the ideology of new pragmatism and self-concentration in his foreign policy.[52] Putin selectively borrowed from the ideologies of both Little Russia and postimperial space. Like the supporters of the Little Russia ideology, he is quite critical of the Soviet experience and is aware of the unlimited Soviet foreign policy ambitions. He is also keen to develop relations with Western countries and has demonstrated strong support for U.S. efforts in fighting international terrorism after September 11. In Putin's own words, today's U.S.-Russian relations "are based on a new reading of the national interests of the two countries and a similar view of the nature of world threats."[53] There are also signs that Putin is revising Primakov's concept of multipolarity.[54]

Putin is hardly a Westernizer, however, and he is committed to Russia's traditional values. In his programmatic speech "Russia at the Turn of the Millennium," he emphasized patriotism, a strong state, and social solidarity as key values.[55] Putin also capitalized on his country's ties with Asia and announced, "Russia has always been aware of its Eurasian identity."[56] The new image of Eurasia is that of an open, multilevel politico-economic arrangement planned by the state, but built with the close participation of Russia's private sector.

Geoeconomic Policy

How was the concept of new pragmatism and self-concentration translated into policies toward the former Soviet space? It appears that here the key

---

52. See especially Putin's recent speech to Russian ambassadors from around the world: Vistuplieniye prezidenta Rossiyskoi Federatsiyi V. V. Putina na rasshirennom soveschaniyi s uchastiyem poslov Rossiyskoi Federatsiyi v MID Rossiyi. 2002. Available at http://www .kremlin.ru/text/APPTemplAppearId17449.shtml.

53. *Vistupleniye prezidenta* 2002.

54. Although Putin has signed the 2000 Foreign Policy Concept, in which the term "multipolar world" did exist ("Kontseptsiya vneshnei politiki Rossiyskoi Federatsiyi," *Nezavisimaya gazeta*, July 7, 2000), he subsequently distanced himself from the term. Instead, Putin emphasizes international factors of economic significance and Russia's need to economically survive in the post–Cold War world (see, for example, his state of the nation address in April 2002).

55. Putin (1999). During the presidential campaign in March 2000, he stated that "from the very start, Russia was created as a supercentralized state. This is part of its genetic code, tradition and people's mentality" (CNN, March 26, 2000).

56. Putin (2000). Since 1999, Russia's president has visited key states of the region—the former Soviet area, China, India, Mongolia, North Korea, and Brunei—and he has signed some key agreements, such as the treaty of strategic significance with China.

word for the state policymakers is "bilateralization" of relationships. Consider, for example, this statement by Vice-Premier Viktor Khristenko: "The essence of the current policy of Russia toward the CIS states is an energetic bilateral cooperation based on pragmatism and a reciprocal account of interests. We develop multilateral contacts only in those spheres that have received support from the parties. Following this approach, we move to more advanced forms of cooperation mainly with those partners who express a genuine interest in a tighter integration."[57] The new policy course was first articulated in February 2001 by the secretary of the Security Council, Sergei Ivanov. Ivanov admitted that the new course meant a serious rethinking of Russia's previous policies in the former Soviet area. He argued that previous attempts to integrate the CIS came at a very high price and that Russia must now abandon integration in favor of a "pragmatic" course of bilateral relations.[58]

Igor' Glukhovski, a member of the CIS committee of the Federation Council, further clarified the new thinking of Russian policymakers.[59] His interpretation of foreign policy pragmatism in the region included development of Russia's relations with the CIS states on three separate levels—bilateral, subregional, and regional. According to Glukhovski, in addition to bilateral relations, Russia should participate in subregional arrangements, such as the Collective Security Treaty and the Eurasian Economic Union.[60] Russia should also develop regional forms of participation, particularly when it comes to defending the region from international terrorist threats.[61]

The new concept of bilateral and tri-level CIS relations does not mean a revival of the old style isolationism. On the contrary, the state seems to be seeking various ways to stay engaged in Eurasia. In particular, Putin has stated the need to accelerate development of transportation systems and has initiated a variety of transnational and transregional economic projects in the transportation area (Yakunin 2001). Most of these projects involve transporting oil and gas, of which Russia is one of largest world producers.[62] The Caspian Sea has been one prominent subject of attention. Here Russia has

---

57. As cited in *Nezavisimaya gazeta*, August 2, 2001.

58. By the time of the announcement, the debt of the CIS states to Russia was around $5.5 billion (*Nezavisimaya gazeta*, February 7, 2001). For critical reaction to the new "pragmatic" course, see Kasaiyev 2001.

59. *Nezavisimaya gazeta*, February 13, 2001.

60. The Collective Security Treaty was signed by Russia, Belarus, Armenia, Kazakhstan, Kyrgyzstan, and Tajikistan. Members of the Eurasian Economic Union are Russia, Belarus, Kazakhstan, and Kyrgyzstan.

61. *Nezavisimaya gazeta*, February 13, 2001.

62. Responding to the rising oil prices, Russia has stepped up its production considerably and intends to increase it by more than 2 million barrels a day by the end of the decade, posing a rivalry to Saudi Arabia (Krastev 2002).

been trying to quickly establish a gas supply network to Turkey and Europe in order to nullify the competitive "trans-Caspian pipeline."[63]

In addition to the Caspian Sea, Russia's policymakers have been actively promoting projects of a transregional nature, such as the trans-Siberian railroad, an east-west railway route, and a north-south route. Russia's Transportation Ministry has strongly lobbied for the trans-Siberian project, which involves the completion of the eighty-five-hundred-mile railroad for transporting up to a hundred million tons of cargo a year.[64] An east-west railroad would possibly connect China, Kazakhstan, Russia, and Europe, whereas a north-south one would connect Russia with India, Iran, Kazakhstan, Turkmenistan, and other Persian Gulf states (Blum 2000).

Behind these policy initiatives is a vision of Eurasia as an economically open region, in which Russia occupies a central role and reaps considerable economic and political benefits. The Russian foreign policy community has been debating the benefits of such geoeconomic thinking for quite some time. A favorable outcome would preserve Eurasia as an economically and politically stable region and transform the currently weak CIS into a more cohesive arrangement.[65] Such geoeconomic thinking is increasingly advocated by the Russian state and supported by state-oriented parties, some liberal political movements, and the nationally and regionally oriented private sector.

Many of Putin's efforts remain improvisations rather than products of a well-thought-out strategy. It remains to be seen whether the new Eurasianist policies will be more successful than the previous policies of disengagement (Yeltsin) and state-organized integration (Primakov). The thrust of the current critique of Putin's bilateralism and project-specific engagement is its ad hoc nature and overestimation of the power of the private sector. Critics fear that the new policy may become a new version of Kozyrev's isolationism and will eventually deprive Russia of its strong presence in the region. The previously failed integration should not imply that any integration is a mistake. As one scholar put it, "Despite the current state of the CIS, the idea of integration continues to have a potential for its development. . . . What has

63. Russia also wants to succeed in connecting northern Caspian structures to the Russian oil pipeline system and therefore undermine the Baku-Ceyhan project (Blum 2000).
64. See the elaborate report of the transportation vice-minister Vladimir Yakunin (2001), in which he explains the economic and geopolitical rationales for the "trans"-Siberian project, as well as some other transportation projects. The argument about the trans-Siberian road has been developed in the context of potential competition from TRASEKA, a projected international transportation corridor that would connect Europe, Caucasus, and Asia and was decided in Brussels in May 1993.
65. An example of such thinking is Sergei Rogov's *Eurasian Strategy for Russia* (1998, 26, 50), in which the author proposes that Russia focus on building the "communicational bridge" that would link Eurasia's southern, western, and eastern peripheries through the development of ground, air, and electronic transportation routes across Russia and other ex-Soviet states.

failed so far is not the CIS as such, but the model of economic cooperation that has been dominant during the 1990s" (Godin 2000). Integration continues to be important as a model that bridges the regional interests of the private sector and those of Russia's state. Politics continue to matter, and if Russia makes little effort to rebuild the region by opening up its markets and providing other incentives for the CIS states to cooperate, other states may quickly fill the geoeconomic vacuum.

In returning to Eurasia, Russia went through three distinct stages: it moved from its early isolationism to the strategy of "reintegrating" the former Soviet states republics and then to "pragmatic" bilateral cooperation in the region. I have argued that Russia's geoeconomic choices resulted from its interaction with the world's historical practices, which empowered some national elites and disempowered others.

Russia's early isolationism resulted from the post–Cold War euphoria, which had empowered liberal reformers and politically isolated Gorbachev. Primakov's "reintegration," on the other hand, could not have been possible without alarming new developments such as military conflicts in the former Soviet republics and NATO's decision to expand toward Russia's borders. Accompanied by the failure of shock therapy, these developments increased the influence of the security coalition and its role in policymaking. Finally, Putin's revision of Russia's identity has responded to the country's new global environment and is currently supported by a mixed coalition of economic and security interests.

Each of these three visions of Russia's economic interests in Eurasia can be viewed as a rational response to new global developments. Yet, each was rational in its distinct way, and this helps us better understand Russia's complex geoeconomic trajectories. Without problematizing "nation" and viewing its interests and identity as contested, one cannot fully appreciate the observed geoeconomic choices in the post-Soviet world. Nations certainly compete and debate *with other* nations, but—no less significantly—they debate *within* themselves by constantly redefining their visions in the world. When neither a nation nor the world is assumed to obey a single rationality standard, researchers have the benefit of observing a greater variety in state behavior than realists and liberals commonly assume.

3

Explaining Postcommunist Transformations

Economic Nationalism in Ukraine and Russia

Maya Eichler

Postcommunist transformations are fundamentally about conflicts over restructuring political and economic power in society. The transformation path adopted is not simply a question of common sense (of "market and democracy"); it is inherently political, and hotly contested by economic and political actors. Struggles over the form property should take, the control of economic resources, and government policy take place not only at the economic and political level but in the ideological realm. The main issue for those groups seeking power *and* stability therefore becomes: how to legitimate a particular path of transformation and make it appear incontestable?

I approach this question by focusing on the role *economic nationalism* has played in postcommunist transformations. By economic nationalism I do not refer to the Realist doctrine associated with protectionist, statist, or mercantilist policies (see Abdelal's critique in this volume). I use the term more generically to explore the relationship between political economy and national identity in the postcommunist transformation. I understand economic nationalism as the attempt by state and societal actors to link economic prescriptions to a particular understanding or "variant" of national identity in order to create greater legitimacy for their economic policies. Economic nationalism thus can be endowed with different contents, depending on the interests of the actors involved and their relative strengths.

In this chapter, such an understanding of economic nationalism is applied to the study of postcommunist transformation in Russia and Ukraine. I do

I thank the participants of the Trent IPE Centre Workshop "Rethinking Economic Nationalism: National Identities and Political Economy," August 24–25, 2002 for their comments on a previous draft of this chapter. I also thank Andrea Harrington for sharing her unpublished papers, and Daniela Mussnig and Govind Rao for helpful comments on earlier drafts.

not undertake a direct comparison of the two cases, but rather wish to high-light the different ways in which economic nationalism can effect postcom-munist transformation. I argue that in both countries the struggle over economic transformation has become linked to competing notions of na-tional identity. More specifically, the new ruling elites have used national identity to legitimize—as their critics have used national identity to con-test—a particular course of economic policy. Russia's early form of eco-nomic nationalism linked radical domestic reforms to a pro-Western definition of Russian identity. In Ukraine, the perceived Russian threat to Ukrainian independence helped justify calls for economic autonomy from Russia and slower economic reforms. As the two cases illustrate, economic nationalism can engender very different transformation paths.

Theorizing Postcommunist Transformations

Neoliberal economists, who have long dominated policy and scholarly de-bates on postcommunist transformations, initially assumed a linear transi-tion from communist political and economic systems to democracy and capitalism. Path-dependency scholars, on the other hand, pointed to the negative effects that socialist legacies were having on the progress of transi-tion. Michael Burawoy and Katherine Verdery (1999, 14), however, are right to argue that it is misleading to "conceive of the transition as either rooted in the past or tied to an imagined future. Transition is a process suspended between the two." In examining postcommunist transformations I therefore emphasize *contemporary* societal struggles over the favored path of transfor-mation. These struggles endow the transformation process with elements of both change and continuity. Transformation is by its very nature dynamic and contested, its outcome uncertain (cf. Burawoy and Verdery 1999).

The crisis and collapse of the old regime set the stage for the contestation of power and the redistribution of economic and political resources. Post-communist transformations entail the restructuring of power relations in society along existing social cleavages such as class, gender, region, or na-tionality. Rather than theorize the transformation as a process that works it-self out upon society, it should instead be seen as the *object* of struggle among different actors in various arenas. While the state is the central agent in de-termining the transformation process, and thus a certain state-centricity is unavoidable in our analysis, even within the state, ministries, agencies, and levels of government often disagree on the course of reform. Similarly, within society, various social actors such as former state enterprise managers, workers, nationalists, opposition groups, or NGOs work to influence or con-test the government's reform policies.

Postcommunist transformations touch all aspects of life and are best seen as a multiplicity of connected economic, political, ideological, and cultural processes. Commentators tend to disagree as to whether material or ideational factors should be emphasized as the driving force of transformation.[1] In another context, Mark Neufeld and Sandra Whitworth argue for the "active and non-reductive role played by ideas/ideologies," while emphasizing that "dominant ideas and ideologies are not neutral, but regularly serve the interest of power and privilege" (1997, 198).[2] Ideas and ideologies play a central role, but they need to be understood in their interplay with changing material conditions and particular social actors (ibid.). For example, the neoliberal ideas that informed Russia's early reform program need to be linked to the domestic pro-capitalist actors in Russia (although they were not yet dominant), to the interests of Western capitalist states, and to the inflow of Western experts financed by the U.S. Agency for International Development, the World Bank, the European Bank for Reconstruction and Development, and the European Community (Blasi, Kroumova, and Kruse 1997, 36). Thus, we need to be attentive to the connections between the various aspects of transformation, especially to the linkages between material factors and ideas/ideologies.

In addition, postcommunist transformations are constrained by the structures of the global political economy. The crisis and eventual collapse of the Soviet bloc coincided with the rise of globalization and concurrent neoliberal restructuring, which limited the "set of transition choices" available to postcommunist countries (Pickel and True 1999, 3). The geopolitical context of Cold War rivalry demanded that the "defeat" of communism be made irrevocable and strengthened the imperative for a fundamental restructuring of Russia's economy along neoliberal lines. The linkages between transnational actors such as the International Monetary Fund (IMF) and domestic pro-capitalist actors played a central role in bringing capitalism to Russia. In the case of Ukraine, its peripheral position within the world economy and power politics partly explains why there was less international pressure for a radical restructuring of its economy. It is therefore inappropriate to focus on either international or domestic factors, as the disciplinary divide between international relations and comparative politics encourages, because postcommunist transformations have evolved in the interplay between global and national contexts.

1. For example, Appel (2000) argues that materialist analyses have overlooked the crucial impact of ideology on the design of privatization programs.

2. Neufeld and Whitworth here draw on the ideas of the Canadian political economist Harold Innis.

Economic Nationalism: Linking National Identity and Political Economy

The dissolution of the Soviet Union confronted post-Soviet leaders with two fundamental challenges: redefining the country's identity and restructuring its political economy. Ukraine's newly independent status and Russia's loss of "empire" prompted a reformulation of identities. In Ukraine, the early post-Soviet elite emphasized Ukraine's distinct history and prolonged struggle for national independence in an effort to strengthen the legitimacy of the new state. Boris Yeltsin's reform team defined Russia's identity as post-imperial, and Russia as part of the West. Transforming their command economies into market economies was seen as the other preeminent task for postcommunist governments. Russia and Ukraine chose different economic strategies in the early post-Soviet period: while the Russian government rushed to introduce radical market reforms, Ukraine took a more gradual approach and instead focused on establishing political and economic sovereignty.

In the literature on postcommunist transformations the study of national identity has largely remained separate from the study of economic restructuring. Students of national identity focus on historical and cultural aspects, paying only scant attention to questions of political economy. Similarly, scholars of political economy, whether liberals, institutionalists, or Marxists, have mostly assumed questions of national identity to be marginal to our understanding of changing economic structures. This neglect of the relationship between national identity and political economy is unfortunate, as it leaves central features of the postcommunist transformation unexamined. To see how these seemingly separate aspects of transformation interrelate, we must integrate the study of national identity and nationalism with the study of political economy.

Recent attempts to bring together questions of national identity and economic policy have begun by critically examining the meaning of economic nationalism. Scholars such as Rawi Abdelal or George Crane (1998) point out that the conventional realist conception of economic nationalism fails to account for nationalism, national identity, and their influence on the economy. As Abdelal argues in this volume, economic nationalism "is a concept that describes (or should describe) the effect of nationalism on the economic relations between particular states." Andrei Tsygankov, on the other hand, highlights the process by which a nation's geopolitical self-image gets translated into economic policy via domestic structures and political struggles. In contrast to these constructivist approaches, I suggest that we conceptualize the relationship between national identity and political economy from the perspective of *critical political economy*.

The basic assumption, which separates this chapter from many of the other contributions, is that national identity should not be seen as basis of explanation but rather as that which itself requires explanation. I build on Verdery, who emphasizes the ideological significance of the nation and proposes the following questions: What is the context in which one or another definition or symbolization of nation operates? What is it accomplishing? Is it doing work for arguments aimed elsewhere rather than at national questions per se? Verdery argues that we should "treat nation as a symbol and any given nationalism as having multiple meanings, offered as alternatives and competed over by different groups manoeuvring to capture the symbol's definition and its legitimating effects." Furthermore, she concludes, the nation is "a construct, whose meaning is never stable but shifts with the changing balance of social forces" (Verdery 1996, 228, 230). This does not, of course, inevitably lead us to the position that ideas with regard to national identity can be arbitrarily constructed: lived experience and history still frame the boundaries of possible definitions. Nonetheless, history is not so much a legacy as it is "a terrain of struggle, manipulated by forces contending in the present" (Burawoy 2001, 1115). With this understanding of nationalism in mind, economic nationalism can be reconsidered in the following three steps.[3]

First, economic nationalism can be understood generically in terms of the relationship between national identity and political economy. Economic nationalism can take on a variety of ideological contents (e.g., economic liberalism), and thus its meaning cannot be known in advance. It rather depends on the historically specific balance of social forces in which it is situated. Any given meaning of economic nationalism needs to be specified by its historical and social context. Also, in contrast to some authors in this collection (e.g., Abdelal, Helleiner), I am not concerned specifically with the economic ideas of nationalists, but rather with the conceptions of national identity put forward or supported by state and economic actors. Such an approach focuses on how the nation and understandings of national identity are rooted in a country's political economy.

Second, I assert that we should examine economic nationalism as a form of domestic political struggle. Economic nationalism can be defined as the attempt to link a particular understanding of national identity to certain economic prescriptions, and thus take advantage of the legitimating effects that the concept "nation" brings with it. In such cases, the politics of national identity can be seen as a terrain of struggle between and among state and societal actors over the course of economic policy. Thus, national identity becomes a political tool in the struggle over economic transformation. A similar dynamic becomes evident, for example, in Hilary Appel and John

---

3. This three-step rethinking of economic nationalism draws inspiration from work done by Pickel (2003).

Gould's (2000) analysis of the Czechoslovak transition. The authors demonstrate how identity politics came to represent an important resource in the struggle over economic reform within and between the Czech and Slovak republics during the early 1990s. They argue that the Czech government's anticommunist, pro-European rhetoric effectively delegitimized industrial managers and their critique of radical reforms, while appeals to national identity were used by Slovak managers (and eventually by Prime Minister Vladimír Meciar himself) to criticize the economic reforms of the federal government. Appel and Gould describe a close relationship between identity politics and the politics of economic reform: The divisive debate over "the appropriate form of relations with the Czech lands . . . generally served as the sub-text for most other debates—including an ongoing conflict over the appropriate path of economic reform. Conversely, frustrations with economic programmes imposed by an 'external' federal government served to fuel the debate over identity" (Appel and Gould 2000, 124). As the quote illustrates, debates over national identity are shaped by, and in turn shape, the struggle among economic and political actors over the course of economic transformation.

Third, I argue that economic nationalism can help explain postcommunist transformation. Economic nationalism, as I understand it here, addresses the central problematic of legitimacy in postcommunist states at the intersections of national identity and political economy. It highlights the fact that postcommunist transformations are not linear processes with given outcomes, but rather the result of social and political struggles. The concept of economic nationalism encourages us to make the link between the political, economic, and ideological moments of the transition. It highlights how conceptions of national identity are defined by the balance of social forces and are used as a political tool in the struggle over economic reform. Official constructions of national identity play a crucial role, not only in furthering the legitimacy of postcommunist states, but also in legitimizing a particular course of economic transformation. And finally, the concept of economic nationalism makes visible the fact that national transformations are embedded within regional and global contexts. Definitions of national identity as well as economic policies are affected by developments in the global political economy, while policies that aim at integration (with the West, Europe, or Eurasia) are linked to particular domestic projects of change and continuity.

Russia: Capitalist Transformation and Eurasian Identity

Historically, questions with regard to Russia's development path have been closely tied to issues of national identity, in particular Russia's relationship to the West. Nineteenth-century intellectuals disagreed on whether Russia was a natural part of the West, and should thus emulate the Western model of development, or had a distinct identity and must therefore find its own development path.[4] During the Cold War, opposing economic systems formed the basis for antagonistically defined Soviet-U.S. identities. In the post-Soviet period too, strategies of economic transformation have become associated with particular notions of national identity. This section discusses the forms that economic nationalism has taken in Russia in the recent past and their effects on the transformation process.

During the late *perestroika* period economic nationalism became a central player in the struggle between Mikhail Gorbachev and the president of the Russian Republic, Boris Yeltsin. Their political struggle was defined by disagreement over the extent of economic reforms to be implemented, with Yeltsin pushing a more radical agenda. Yeltsin eventually linked his endorsement of radical economic reforms to a nationalist struggle for Russian sovereignty.[5] He used nationalist themes to gain popularity, strengthen his own position vis-à-vis the Union state, and legitimize an alternative economic program (cf. Steele 1994, 235–48). In June 1990 the Russian Congress of People's Deputies declared Russia's sovereignty. This declaration should be seen in the context of attempts to take a more radical reform path, and only minimally as an expression of Russian nationalist feelings.[6] As David Kotz and Fred Weir argue (Kotz 1997, 147), "It was Yeltsin and the pro-capitalist coalition's plans for *socioeconomic change,* which were blocked by Gorbachev and the Union state, which motivated the key act, from which followed a process that ultimately tore the Union apart" (emphasis added). While the claim to sovereignty was based on the idea of a Russian nation, it cannot be explained by nationalism as such. Rather, Yeltsin's use of nationalism helped justify as well as create the necessary conditions for a radical restructuring of Russia's economy.

With the breakup of the Soviet Union in sight, the Russian leadership embarked on the complex task of transforming Russia into a market economy. Yeltsin's reform team adopted the neoliberal agenda of "shock therapy," which entailed sweeping price liberalization, macroeconomic stabilization,

---

4. For a discussion of the Westernizer/Slavophile debate see Petro (1995).

5. Compared to the situation in the other republics, the democratic movement in Russia took up the national question relatively late (only in 1989).

6. The significance of sovereignty became clear, when soon after its declaration the Russian government adopted the proposal of radical reformers, the so-called "500-day program" put forward by Grigorii Yavlinsky. While initially supported by Gorbachev too, the Soviet government in the end presented its own program calling for "continued reform of the existing system and the formation of a market regulated economy without extensive privatisation" (Cox 1996, 124). The "war of programmes" was paralleled by a "war of laws," with the Russian government adopting its own laws on property and enterprises, and utilizing the reform of property relations to assert its economic sovereignty (125).

and privatization.[7] At the same time, Yeltsin and the radical reformers defined Russia as part of the Western world, arguing that good relations with the United States were central to Russia's development. Their "Atlanticist" agenda linked Russia's self-definition as Western with a pro-Western foreign policy and radical economic reforms at home. The ultimate goal was for Russia to join the ranks of the leading capitalist states and thus regain its status as a great power (Zagorskii 1993, 44). In early 1992, speaking before the Supreme Soviet, Yeltsin argued that the two crucial tasks in relations with the West were "to strengthen Russia's entering into the civilized world; [and] to secure the maximum support for our efforts in transforming Russia" (45).

On the flip side, Russia's early reformers perceived closer ties with the other post-Soviet states (the so-called near abroad) as incompatible with the undertaking of radical economic reforms. As Ilya Prizel explains (1998, 244), "writings by the liberal school often perceive the near abroad as a burden that prevents Russia from modernizing and achieving its full potential as a great power." Indeed, coordinating economic policies with the other Soviet successor states (even if they had been willing) would have constrained the Russian leadership's agenda of shock therapy. In this way, radical economic reforms called for a postimperial identity that viewed the Russian/Soviet "empire" as a burden rather than an essential part of Russia.

The economic nationalism espoused by Russia's early reform government was thus underpinned by neoliberalism and the conceptualization of Russia as postimperial and Western. How did this form of economic nationalism come about? Initially, it had some popular appeal because of disillusionment with the old system. For ordinary Russians who had suffered from the late Soviet regime's increasing inability to provide improving standards of living and the failure of Gorbachev's economic reforms, the promises of the market and integration into the West touched hopes of a better future. But more importantly, this form of economic nationalism was supported by a coalition of domestic and international actors interested in the establishment of liberal capitalism in Russia.

Domestically, the coalition consisted of an alliance between elements of the state apparatus (especially Yeltsin's reform team, the Ministry of Finance, and the Ministry of Foreign Affairs)[8] with Russia's capitalist class and liberal intellectuals. The nascent capitalist class consisted of members of the former *nomenklatura,* such as directors of state enterprises who had gained control over their enterprises during perestroika through so-called spontaneous privatization, or state and Party/Komsomol functionaries whose "cap-

7. Yeltsin's reform team included Gennadii Burbulis, Yegor Gaidar, Aleksandr Shokhin as deputy prime ministers and Anatolii Chubais as minister of privatization and chairman of the State Committee for Management of State Property.
8. The Foreign Ministry was led by Andrei Kozyrev, one of the strongest advocates of Russia's pro-Western orientation in the early post-Soviet period.

ital of social connections" had enabled access to profitable business activities (Silverman and Yanowitch 1997, 114). It also included people operating in the former shadow economy who were able to legalize their activities, thanks to new laws passed during perestroika, and people entering business for the first time, mostly from the technical and scientific intelligentsia (114–15). Among liberal intellectuals, economists such as Yegor Gaidar (who joined Yeltsin's reform team) who were influenced by Western neo-liberalism in the manner of Hayek and Friedman, played a crucial role in the ideological legitimation and implementation of shock therapy (cf. Flaherty 1991). Early on, the pro-capitalist (or "anticommunist") coalition still had some support from the working class. The part of the working class that most clearly allied itself with Yeltsin in the final phase of perestroika was the miners, whose strikes in 1989 and 1991 significantly weakened the Soviet leadership. Their union leaders had seen the transition to a market economy as a means of gaining greater independence from the Union state and its institutions (Kotz 1997, 141).

Internationally, support for Russia's pro-capitalist coalition came from leading capitalist states (the G-7) and international financial institutions in the form of advisors, political support, and (albeit limited) financial loans (Lane 1999, 9; cf. Roche 1996). Western advisers helped draft Russia's economic reform program, which was designed to gain support from the IMF (Blasi, Kroumova, and Kruse 1997, 31). Close relations with the West and its institutions were instrumental in pushing through reforms, as the domestic coalition was too weak to have succeeded on its own.

Indeed, resistance began to form quickly in reaction to shock therapy. Within weeks Yeltsin's reform team was confronted with opposition in parliament over the effects of price liberalization. In April 1992 the G-7 countries stepped in with political support and the promise of financial aid ($24 billion) to bolster Yeltsin's position vis-à-vis parliament. While this helped the government continue its reform program, it was still forced to make concessions, for instance, by continuing to supply industry with soft credits and budget subsidies (Rutland 1994, 1111). Industrial directors appeared as a key force in opposition to shock therapy, which represented a split in the pro-capitalist coalition that had supported Yeltsin (Kotz 1997, 202). They did not oppose capitalism as such, but their concern over the decline of industrial production and their own status made them favor more state intervention and a slower transition. These industrial directors were organized in the Civic Union, an organization founded by Arkadii Volsky in an attempt to defend the interests of industry.[9] The Civic Union was able to ally itself with trade unions in opposition to further liberal reforms (McFaul 1999,

9. Volsky is a former CPSU Central Committee member and adviser to Yuri Andropov and Gorbachev, with strong ties to industrial directors (McFaul 1999, 215; Kubicek 1996b, 39).

215). The go-slow agenda of the industrial directors was also supported by parts of the state, especially by the Ministries of Industry, Agriculture, and Defense (Lane 1999, 9).

In their domestic struggle for influence, these anti–shock therapy forces drew on an alternative understanding of Russia's identity. They criticized Yeltsin's pro-Western policies, which had failed to establish Russia as a great power or even to end the free fall of the Russian economy. Instead they argued that Russia should draw on its dominant role over the territory of the former Soviet Union and assert itself as a Eurasian great power. These groups, as James Richter writes (1996, 80), "shared a preference for greater state intervention in the domestic economy to shore up industrial production and to preserve Russia's status as a Eurasian great power distinct and independent from the West." Such a redefinition of Russia's identity was in the interest of key industrial sectors, such as the military-industrial complex or the energy sector, who called for a reorientation of policy toward the other post-Soviet states and former Soviet allies. They perceived closer integration within the Commonwealth of Independent States (CIS) as vital to their economic interests (Malcolm and Pravda 1996, 18; Pravda and Malcolm 1996, 297; Zagorskii 1993, 50).[10]

In addition to the resistance among industrial actors, other developments further undermined Russia's early economic nationalism before it could take root. First, the effects of shock therapy,[11] combined with the lack of substantial financial assistance from the West,[12] eroded the legitimacy of Yeltsin's liberal reforms and pro-Western policies. The erosion manifested itself most clearly in the 1993 elections, in which Yeltsin's communist and nationalist opponents were able to win substantial support.[13] In addition, the planned eastward extension of NATO to the exclusion of Russia made it ever more difficult to portray the West as a "friend" interested in helping Russia. These events increased popular support for a redefinition of Russia's national identity as Eurasian rather than Western.

Government policy was amended to acknowledge the dwindling support

10. The CIS was founded on December 8, 1991, by the leaders of Russia, Ukraine, and Belarus as a mechanism to dissolve the Soviet Union. They were soon joined by the other successor states, with the exception of Georgia and the three Baltic states.

11. One indicator of the economic crisis is the fact that GDP contracted by almost 20 percent in 1992 and by still another 12 percent in 1993 (Tikhomirov 2000, 231, 234). Further, life expectancy among men dropped from 63.8 in 1991 to 57.6 in 1995, and among women from 74.3 in 1991 to 71.2 in 1995 (168).

12. For example, the $24 billion aid package mentioned above, only partly materialized. Russia received a $1 billion credit in August 1992 and another $600 million in 1993. Only the $11 billion which were trade credits for commercial deliveries—and which, as Götz (2001, 1291) points out, cannot be understood as aid—were fully realized.

13. The Communist and Agrarian parties together received about 20 percent of the votes and Vladimir Zhirinovsky's far-right nationalist party won almost 23 percent (the largest number of any single party) (Urban and Gel'man 1997, 193).

for shock therapy and a pro-Western definition of Russian identity. One the one hand, Yeltsin brought a number of former industrial managers (who had the support of the Civic Union) into his government from mid-1992 on, such as Viktor Chernomyrdin and Vladimir Shumeiko. This led to a more gradual pace of reform, although it clearly did not entail the abandoning of capitalist reforms. Chernomyrdin, who replaced Gaidar as prime minister in December 1992, argued that Western economic methods could not simply be transferred to Russia (Kotz 1997, 203). On the other hand, the siege of the White House (Russia's parliament building) in October 1993 and the adoption of a new constitution helped undermine parliament and thus moderate its ability to interfere with the executive's reform agenda. These limits on democracy were an important precondition for the continuation of capitalist reforms in Russia. Finally, Yeltsin attempted to restore legitimacy to his position by taking a more nationalist, anti-Western stance. He adopted rhetoric to the effect that Russia was a Eurasian state with its own unique identity. The countries of the former Soviet Union became defined as Russia's sphere of vital interests,[14] and economic and political integration within the CIS was declared a foreign policy priority. This shift entailed a more assertive and skeptical stance toward the West.[15]

Russia's second variant of economic nationalism was mostly a defensive strategy, aimed at diffusing resistance to shock therapy. It allowed the government to claim to be defending the interests of the Russian nation while continuing Russia's capitalist transformation. A decisive step in this transformation was the cash privatization of major state industries starting in 1995 (especially the "loans-for-shares" program), which led to the creation of powerful Russian financial-industrial groups.[16] The close ties between the state and the presidents of the biggest financial-industrial groups, the so-

14. This reflected the earlier recommendation for a Russian Monroe Doctrine in the post-Soviet space by the chairman of the parliamentary Committee on International Affairs and Foreign Economic Relations, Yevgenii Ambartsumov (Eggert 1992, 6).

15. The replacement of Russia's pro-Western foreign minister Kozyrev with Yevgenii Primakov in early 1996 was indicative of this shift. Kozyrev, though, had been forced to take a more balanced stance even earlier. For example, in October 1992 he had announced before the Supreme Soviet that "Russia must not narrow its framework of cooperation by choosing between East and West" (cited in Plyais 1995, 71).

16. The beneficiaries of the loans-for-shares privatization, the bank-led financial-industrial groups and their presidents, often referred to as Russia's "oligarchs," comprise a handful of business people who—thanks to their wealth—have gained influence in politics too. This group includes B. Berezovsky (LogoVAZ), V. Potanin (ONEKSIMbank), V. Gusinsky (Most-Group, MediaMost), M. Khodorkovsky (MENATEP, YuKOS-Rosprom), A. Smolensky (SBS-Agro), M. Fridman and P. Aven (Al'fa-Group), and V. Malkin (Rossiiskii Kredit). Other important members of the economic elite are R. Viakhirev (director of Gazprom, formerly headed by V. Chernomyrdin), A. Chubais (head of EES Rossii, one of the biggest energy producers), V. Alekperov (LUKoil), and V. Bogdanov (Surgutneftegaz). These people represent the top echelon of Russian business and were invited to participate in meetings with President Yeltsin and other government officials during 1997–98 (Schröder 1999, 968–71).

called oligarchs, became visible during the presidential election in 1996, when the oligarchs funded Yeltsin's campaign heavily. Once reelected, Yeltsin made an effort to reinitiate economic reforms and brought prominent oligarchs into his political team (e.g., Vladimir Potanin). This development reflects the decreasing power of the industrialists and the rise of the internationally oriented wing of Russia's capitalist class: the financial and export-oriented sectors (Aron 1998, 44–45). In the meantime, Russia's attempts to reintegrate the post-Soviet countries had failed, and Yevgenii Primakov, the foreign minister, was beginning to define Russia's external relations more in economic terms.[17] These developments brought about a new official understanding of Russia's economic nationalism, which has become even more clearly articulated under Vladimir Putin.

This latest form of economic nationalism aims to disassociate Russian nationalism from an antireform, anti-Western agenda. It links the notion of a unique, non-Western identity with the goal of Russia's increasing integration into the global capitalist economy. Putin stresses traditional nationalist themes: he has emphasized the need for a stronger state (centralization) and for a strong sense of nationhood (Nicholson 2001, 869). His promotion of patriotism and Russia's distinct identity has not, however, entailed a turning away from the West. Rather, he sees a strong national foundation as key to solving Russia's economic problems and as a means for Russia's fuller participation in the global economy. He has also argued that Russia's relations to the CIS as well as the West should be guided foremost by economic interests (Melville 2002, 15–17). Key goals have been defined as "state support for Russian business abroad," "state measures against Russia's discrimination in the world markets," and "Russia's participation in international trade organizations" (17). Russia's new economic nationalism thus openly equates the parochial interests of Russian business with the interests of the Russian nation, which indicates a maturing of oligarchic capitalism in Russia.

The redefinition of Russia as a Eurasian great power has not halted Russia's capitalist transformation. Rather, the government's rearticulation of national identity has become a central ideological component of its ability to promote further liberalization and integration into the global economy. While this shift in Russia's economic nationalism is primarily the outcome of domestic struggles over the path of economic reform and the ability of various groups to capture the meaning of national identity, external factors have also played a role (e.g., the lack of Western financial support and the failure of CIS integration). In the final analysis, to define Russia's leading

17. At the CIS Summit in March 1997, Yeltsin admitted that the prospects for CIS integration had become bleak (Alexandrova and Timmermann 1997, 1031). In March 1998, Primakov, the foreign minister, suggested giving economic issues a higher priority in foreign relations, for example, by supporting Russian business abroad (Baur 1999, 247).

business activities as "in the nation's interest" creates greater legitimacy for a domestic political economy that is skewed toward the interests of Russia's oligarchs rather than the nation as a whole.

Ukraine: Economic Stagnation on the Road to Europe?

In post-Soviet Ukraine, questions of national identity and political economy have been framed in relation to the former center. This has informed Ukraine's main postindependence dilemma: how to renegotiate economic dependence on Russia while protecting a national identity that is threatened by Russian influence (D'Anieri 1999, 4). Close historic ties and the presence of a large ethnic Russian and Russian-speaking population in eastern Ukraine delayed Russia's acceptance of Ukrainian independence.[18] In addition, close economic ties and heavy reliance on Russian oil and gas supplies have been perceived as an obstacle to real autonomy (15).[19] In this section I show that Ukraine's transformation has been shaped by attempts to resolve this dilemma. These attempts, which entail the legitimation of particular economic strategies through national identity, represent various forms of economic nationalism.

In a referendum held in December 1991, three-quarters of all Ukrainians (90.3 percent of those who voted) endorsed national independence. The nationalist argument that Ukraine's economy was being exploited by Russia,[20] as well as the positive assessment of Ukraine's development potential by international experts,[21] led to the widespread conviction that Ukraine's economy would take off "naturally" once separated from the rest of the former Soviet Union (van Zon 1998, 608). Ukraine's early economic nationalism combined an understanding of national identity, which defined Ukraine as part of Europe and in opposition to Russia, with the call for economic autonomy from Russia. It did *not*, however, entail arguments for domestic economic liberalization.

The central idea guiding state-building efforts in the early post-Soviet period was a perceived Russian threat to Ukrainian independence and sover-

---

18. The Russian minority in Ukraine makes up more than 20 percent of the population. In western Ukraine 5 percent of the population are ethnically Russian and 90 percent choose to speak Ukrainian. In eastern Ukraine 36 percent are ethnically Russian and 80 percent prefer to speak Russian (Pleines 1998, 365).

19. In the early 1990s, Ukraine was confronted with a 90 percent dependence on Russian crude oil and a 65 percent dependence on Russian natural gas supplies (Pankov 1996, 542).

20. This argument was originally made by the Ukrainian economist Mykhailo Volobuiev during the 1920s. Volobuiev claimed that Ukraine was an "internal colony" of the Soviet Union/Russia (Wilson 2000, 253).

21. In particular, a report by Deutsche Bank in 1990 gave Ukraine the best economic chances of all Soviet successor states (van Zon 1998, 608).

eignty. Ukraine's first president, Leonid Kravchuk, once put it dramatically, "What concerns Russia, it is the problem of all problems for Ukraine" (cited in Alexandrova 1994, 68).[22] In the economic realm, Ukraine's postindependence government aimed to protect the national economy from Moscow's influence. Kravchuk's March 1992 program called Fundamentals of National Economic Policy included plans to create a national currency, reduce trade with Russia, reorient exports to other countries of the former Soviet Union and to the West, and set up customs controls (D'Anieri 1999, 111; van Zon 1998, 609).

Although this form of economic nationalism was portrayed as beneficial to the nation as a whole, it corresponded to the interests of Ukraine's political and economic elite. National independence and a turning away from Russia allowed the local elite to consolidate its power. It offered the "national Communists" or "sovereignty Communists" a new basis of legitimacy. Most prominently, Kravchuk, the former chief of ideology of the Ukrainian Communist Party, adopted the nationalist program of Ukraine's independence movement (Rukh) and thus gained the support of the national democrats. Ukraine's early economic nationalism also served the class of top managers, whose autonomy was limited during Soviet times when, it is estimated, as much as 85 percent of the country's industrial stock was organized under the All-Union ministries (Prizel 1997, 345). As Prizel argues, "After the managers had pushed through the nationalization of Soviet property in 1990, political independence assured the undisputed control of the country's wealth." In the early phase, the political and economic elite also had the support of the miners' movement (from the eastern region of Donbas) in their coalition for independence. The miners supported the national state in the hope that it would bring improved working conditions and more subsidies and investment directly from Kiev (Crowley 1995, 58; Wittkowsky 1998, 579).[23]

Ukraine's early variant of economic nationalism constrained the opportunity for a radical restructuring of Ukraine's command economy. This is not surprising when we consider that the government was supported by those state and social actors opposed to radical liberalization.[24] Neither in-

22. This idea was translated into various policy areas, including foreign affairs and national defense. Anatolii Zlenko, Ukraine's first foreign minister, defined the basic principle governing foreign relations as "the guarantee of state independence and sovereignty" (Zlenko 1993, 6). In the military sphere, a policy of nonalignment and neutrality and the creation of national armed forces were aimed at strengthening national identity and independence (Strekal 1996, 50).

23. The situation in Donbas deteriorated after Moscow changed its investment priorities in favor of Siberian coal mines in the 1960s. With independence, new subsidies were expected to come directly from Kiev (Wittkowsky 1998, 579).

24. In addition, Ukraine's marginal position within the international political economy meant that international pressure for economic reforms was limited. In the early transition

dustrial managers nor Ukrainian miners favored such a strategy. Kravchuk and his team adopted only minor economic reforms, in fear that more radical ones would threaten social and political stability.[25] This concern was reflected in calls for a "Ukrainian way" or a "Ukrainian third way," an alternative to shock therapy that would avoid social disruption (Kubicek 1996b, 36). In addition, the speed of reforms undertaken in Russia was framed by policymakers as a threat to Ukraine's autonomy in deciding its own pace of reform.[26]

Against expectations, national independence and greater economic autonomy did not bring economic prosperity. Instead of economic takeoff Ukraine experienced severe economic decline.[27] The collapse of the Soviet economic zone, within which Ukraine had been overwhelmingly integrated, and Ukraine's isolationist economic strategy resulted in the disruption of trade and industrial production (van Zon 1998, 608–9).[28] Kravchuk lost support among workers and industrial managers in eastern and southern Ukraine. They criticized Ukraine's turning away from Russia and the weakening of its ties to other CIS members, on whom they relied for supplies and markets. Coal miners in Donbas staged a new wave of strikes, forcing early elections for 1994 (D'Anieri, Kravchuk, and Kuzio 1999, 192). In the meantime, Kravchuk reconsidered his strategy of economic autonomy from Russia and began taking steps toward reestablishing economic ties. By 1993, Ukraine seemed willing to participate in a free-trade zone with other members of the CIS, although Kravchuk finally opted for "associate status" only. These developments signaled the failure of Ukraine's early form of economic nationalism.

The presidential elections in 1994 were dominated by the question of Ukraine's relationship to Russia, in terms of both national identity and economic policy. Kravchuk portrayed himself as a defender of independence and Ukrainian national identity, while Leonid Kuchma argued that Ukraine's security was threatened more by the country's dismal economic situation than by Russia. He stressed the need to tackle the economic crisis, mostly by improving economic ties with Russia and the rest of the CIS, but

---

period, the attention of international actors like the IMF or G-7 was instead focused on Russia's reform process.

25. Some prices were liberalized in July 1992 and small-scale privatization was initiated, but the old structures generally stayed in place. In particular, the government maintained high subsidies for industry and agriculture, thus contributing to hyperinflation.

26. As D'Anieri (1999, 107) writes, "The dispute over implementation of reform went a long way in convincing the Kravchuk administration of the need to cut off ties with Russia."

27. GDP declined by 16.8 percent in 1992, 14.2 percent in 1993, and another 23 percent in 1994 (Wittkowsky 2001, 250).

28. Ukraine's economy was overwhelmingly integrated with the Soviet Union—90 percent of Ukrainian exports went there, and 75 percent of imports came from other parts of the Soviet Union in 1987 (van Zon 1998, 608).

also by adopting market reforms. Kravchuk was supported by the national democrats, the western part of Ukraine, and those sectors of the economy that exported mainly to the West or that feared Russian competition. For example, the metallurgical sector (whose export markets lie outside the CIS) and the nuclear power industry (which competes with Russian oil and gas imports) favored Kravchuk's policies of turning away from Russia. Kuchma's support was concentrated in eastern Ukraine and among sectors that depended on closer ties to the CIS, in particular the coal industry and the military-industrial complex (Kuzio 1997, 61–62).[29] He also had the backing of key economic associations such as the Inter-Regional Association of Enterprises and the Union of Industrialists and Entrepreneurs (Kuzio 1998a, 36).

In his election campaign against Kravchuk, Kuchma had adopted an alternative understanding of Ukraine's national identity in relation to Russia. In his inaugural speech as president, Kuchma explicitly redefined Ukraine's official conception of national identity: "Historically, Ukraine is part of the Euro-Asian cultural and economic space. Ukraine's vitally important national interests are now concentrated on this territory of the former Soviet Union" (cited in Burant 1995, 1138). Unlike Kravchuk, who had portrayed Russia as a threat (while acknowledging Russia as Ukraine's dominant partner), Kuchma argued that Russia was a *necessary* partner (Kuchma 1995, A489). He linked a Eurasian notion of Ukraine's national identity with the need for closer economic ties to Russia and the other Soviet successor states. He also attempted to incorporate market reforms as an element of this new form of economic nationalism.

Kuchma began his presidency not by moving closer to Russia, but by attempting to advance the country's domestic liberalization. A program of neoliberal reforms was worked out in cooperation with the IMF and in view of gaining its financial support. These efforts led to a substantial liberalization of prices and to monetary stabilization, which allowed for the introduction of the new currency, the hryvna, in 1996. As early as 1995, however, the reform process started to slow and its path was modified, due to pressure from the antireform wing of the Ukrainian Union of Industrialists and Entrepreneurs (Kubicek 1999, 75). Reforms were constrained, in the absence of a broad coalition favoring radical restructuring along capitalist lines. Andreas Wittkowsky (2001, 251–52) argues that the state's pursuit of reform instead reflected short-term economic interests: Kuchma's team "wanted to stop the free fall of the economy in order to open up new prospects for the heavily affected arms industry and gain access to international credit." Thus, even the state's stop-and-go reform efforts were not so much informed by a genuine development strategy as by the elites' short-

29. Kuzio points out that the workers often follow the recommendations of their manager in terms of what kinds of policies they support and for whom they cast their ballot.

sighted interest in gaining access to economic resources (cf. Wittkowsky 1996, 377; van Zon 2000, 40).

Under both Kravchuk and Kuchma, opposition to radical restructuring has been articulated in terms of an alternative "Ukrainian way," which is evoked to legitimize a gradual approach. In September 1995, Kuchma argued against blindly emulating foreign models and instead insisted that economic policy should be "based on the historical traditions, genetic roots, national identity and culture" of Ukraine (cited in Wilson 2000, 259). In practice, this "Ukrainian way," which Kuchma continued to pursue over the following years, has entailed an interventionist state and the continuation of subsidies to industry.[30] As a result, Ukraine's economy finds itself partially reformed. Keeping it that way could in fact reflect the interests of those in power, as Hans van Zon has argued (2000, 46): "It seems that in Ukraine the ruling elite has an interest in keeping the economy in limbo between a centrally planned and a market economy in order to continue its rent-seeking behaviour." This is reflected in the state's lack of a development strategy and has given rise to a "bureaucratic corporatism" in which economic and political elites cooperate in plundering state assets and gaining control over property (Bojcun 2001, 7).

While Kuchma's critics interpreted his calls for economic integration with Russia as a threat to Ukrainian independence, Kuchma's actual policies have pursued a dual strategy of normalizing relations with Russia while seeking closer ties to Europe. This strategy has been informed by "a desire to move closer to the affluent West, while keeping such a 'strategic partner' as Russia at arm's length" (Molchanov 2000, 280). In this vein, Ukraine has signed a Treaty on Friendship and Cooperation (1997) and a ten-year program on economic cooperation (1998) with Russia, and has sought closer ties with NATO (1997 NATO-Ukraine Charter on a Distinctive Partnership) and the European Union (1998 Strategy of Integration into the EU). While pursuing this balanced policy, the government has replaced Kuchma's previous understanding of Ukraine's Eurasian identity with an emphasis on Ukraine's Europeanness, but defined it in socioeconomic rather than cultural terms. As Kataryna Wolczuk points out (2001, 668), "The ruling elite has attempted to reformulate the 'national idea' as an imperative for socioeconomic and technological modernization, which is exemplified by Europe, rather than for cultural and linguistic revival."[31] One would assume such a

---

30. Wittkowsky (2001, 247) identifies this struggle over soft budget constraints as the main problem in the Ukrainian economy. These subsidies made up 20 percent of GDP in 1997 (Wilson 2000, 260).

31. With respect to Ukraine's European orientation, Rontoyanni argues that "apart from being a more promising welfare provider, the West has prevailed over Russia as the Ukrainian governing elite's integration partner of choice also because its influence has been perceived as more diffuse and less antagonistic of politically powerful economic interests within Ukraine" (2001, 8).

definition of national identity to be linked to a program of economic reform. But this developmental definition of national identity stands in stark
contrast to the government's lack of a reform program and the slim chances
of Ukraine joining the EU in the near future.

In contrast to the Central and Eastern European countries, there is hardly
any correlation between the official narrative of European identity and comprehensive economic reforms in Ukraine.[32] In fact, Ukraine's pro-Western
orientation in foreign relations and its domestic appeals to a "Ukrainian
third way" are not two different visions of economic nationalism, but rather
two components of the Ukrainian variant of economic nationalism that took
shape in the second half of the 1990s. It represents a delicate balance between the state's interest in maintaining bureaucratic corporatist structures,
on the one hand, and its promise of economic progress along European
lines, on the other. Because a strong domestic coalition of state and social
actors supporting capitalist reforms is absent, the developmental definition
of Ukraine's European identity is ambiguous. It is not a vehicle of national
economic recovery, but rather helps legitimize the status quo, and thus cor-
responds to the state's desire to maintain social peace amid widespread economic crisis.

In this chapter I have argued that we cannot separate the politics of national identity from the struggle over economic transformation in postcommunist states. Rather, we must examine how notions of national identity
have become associated with particular strategies of economic transformation, to the benefit of some state and social actors over others. Thus, national
identity is an important legitimizing tool in the struggle over the direction
of change. I have argued that economic nationalism is a useful concept in
understanding this relationship between the ideological/cultural and economic aspects of postcommunist transformations. I have followed a three-
step retheorization of economic nationalism: as a generic ideology, as a form
of domestic political struggle, and as an explanatory heuristic for the study
of postcommunist transformation.

We have seen that in the case of Russia, neoliberal reforms were supported by a coalition of state and social actors who defined Russia as part of
the West. Those actors who advocated a more gradual transition to capitalism, and who cultivated ties with the other Soviet successor states, linked
their agenda to an alternative understanding of Russia as a Eurasian great
power. In reaction to this pressure, the Yeltsin government moved toward a
more skeptical stance vis-à-vis the West and instead emphasized Russia's dis-

32. In contrast, Pickel and True have argued that in the Central and Eastern European countries "there is a very high correlation between the desire to be western, to join the European
union and the likelihood that comprehensive political and economic reforms are adopted"
(1999, 9).

tinct Eurasian identity, while continuing to pursue Russia's capitalist restructuring. More recently, Putin has linked such an understanding of the Russian identity to the promotion of Russian business interests abroad and Russia's further integration into the global economy. This move of Putin's challenges any assumption that capitalist development and integration into the world economy necessarily require a definition of Russia as part of the West. In contrast, Ukraine's early definition of national identity in opposition to Russia helped justify a strategy of economic autonomy. This form of economic nationalism allowed the political and economic elite to consolidate its control over the national economy and its resources while avoiding radical economic reforms that would have threatened their power base. In the election campaign, Kuchma stressed Ukraine's special location between Russia and Europe, arguing for closer economic ties with Russia in addition to economic reforms. However, Kuchma's government has claimed that Ukraine will eventually develop into a European nation, and it has pursued a strategy of integration into European structures. This promise of economic prosperity seems unlikely to be kept, considering that neither the state nor other important social actors have an interest in comprehensive economic reforms.

This analysis has shown, first, that economic nationalism can prescribe divergent economic policies: shock therapy or gradual reforms, economic integration or economic autonomy. What is needed, therefore, is a closer examination of domestic actors, their interests, and linkages to external actors. Second, it has highlighted the centrality of national identity in the struggle over economic policy. Resistance to shock therapy in Russia and to a strategy of economic autonomy in Ukraine were aided by appeals to alternative understandings of Russia's and Ukraine's identity. And finally, this examination of economic nationalism makes clear that we cannot assume that a pro-European definition of national identity promotes the economic reforms necessary for European integration (as seen in Ukraine's case). Likewise, we cannot assume that a notion of national identity that has developed in reaction to the West and capitalist reforms will necessarily inhibit integration into capitalist Western structures (see Russia). The two cases show that economic nationalism can push postcommunist countries toward radical change just as much as it can legitimate the status quo.

Part II

Developmental States and Economic Nationalism in East Asia

4

Back to Basics

Ideology, Nationalism, and Asian Values in East Asia

Meredith Woo-Cumings

In this chapter I want to refocus on the essential elements of development in Northeast Asia: I want to go back to basics, and those basics are the economic nationalism and the logic of national security that animated Japan, Korea, and Taiwan—two fundamental elements that made these three places so different from the countries of Southeast Asia. A focus on these two essential factors will enable me to clear the air of all the ubiquitous verbiage about "crony capitalism," "neoliberalism," "transparency," "accountability," "globalization"—terms that emerged with the Asian crisis, as both its cause and cure, and that raised the possibility of an end to the peculiar developmental trajectory of East Asia. Then I readjust my focus to the longer term, where the binding elements of nationalism and international security have been, and remain today, critical to future East Asian development.

The 1997 crisis threatened to destroy a generation of economic growth in Northeast Asia, but in its aftermath the powers that be offered no new diagnosis of the essential problem: if "crony capitalism" was the problem, it had *been* a problem for many decades in Japan, Korea, and Taiwan; there was nothing new about it. No "cronies" are more reliable than one's immediate family, and the Japanese *zaibatsu* and the Korean *chaebôl* organized successive eras of rapid industrial growth that looked suspiciously like capitalism in a handful of families. If "neoliberalism" was the remedy, it would appear that you need a liberalism that can be "neo-ed" in the first place, but no rooted liberalism existed in the region. Crony capitalism was a presentist fantasy masquerading as the instantly discovered malady of these economies, just as "market-conforming" measures were the chimeras occupying the minds of Western economists trying to explain the past successes of Northeast Asian growth.

To write the remedy for the 1997 crisis requires first of all that you give the patient a proper diagnosis. Two diagnostics, nationalism and security, offer the most powerful explanations of success (and failure); they illustrate both the enormous difference between the northeastern and southeastern patterns of Asian development and the vast space between the imaginings of Western economists and the realities of East Asia. I will examine the ideological bases and institutions of the Northeast Asian pattern in the spirit of Albert Hirschman's dictum that ideas are the binding agents of economic development, and in the magical words of Alexander Gerschenkron's famous metaphorical invocation of visions that generate and sustain excitement about development. For both thinkers, originality and creativity in development came not from copying, followership, or one-size-fits-all dictums based on the Western experience, but from inventive and iconoclastic deviations—sudden industrial spurts and leaps forward, skipping over Rostovian "stages," carving out new sequences, and reinventing the role of states and markets (Hirschman 1986, 15; Gerschenkron 1962).

I examine these binding agents in several parts: first, I revisit the core of my own scholarship, which argues for an overarching nationalism in East Asian industrial development, an experience that might appear to have mimicked Western experience but in fact did not—because nationalism was a flexible vehicle for deviation and innovation. This work will be familiar to some readers, but I need to establish a basis for criticizing alternative conceptions—if only to argue that ultimately they made little difference—especially that overarching ideology that many analysts thought lay behind this developmental experience, namely, "Asian values." As the reader will see, I find no basis for sustaining a relationship between these putative Asian values and economic development. Much more important were *security* concerns, particularly those of the Cold War period, which provided a flexible vehicle for economic mobilization, often under the philosophically vacuous but catchall rubric of "anticommunism."

But that was then and this is now: the Cold War ended in Europe more than a decade ago, and it has not yet ended completely in East Asia. But we still have nationalism: I will conclude that the uses of economic nationalism in the service of mobilizing the populace for vast projects of national security or economic development have not yet run their course in Japan, Korea, and Taiwan, and that they offer far more promise for organizing China's development. Older forms of nationalism no longer have the appeal or clout that they once did, mostly because the two great endeavors that nationalism served—postcolonial emergence and Cold War struggle—have little relevance today. Security against communism is also far less important in a twenty-first-century context where average citizens in China, North Korea, and Vietnam are probably more "anticommunist" than the populations of their capitalist counterparts. But new forms of nationalism for this new century will emerge in a region that still has few multilateral institutions and little or no movement toward any overarching regional unity—a nearly complete contrast to the European Union.

Nationalism as a Vacant but Efficacious Binding Agent

In Northeast Asia, I have argued, those looking for Hirschman's "binding agent" found it in nationalism. Economic nationalism there may have seemed a simple elaboration of the Western experience, but in fact it wasn't—it was highly innovative and idiosyncratic. Yet we still have very little work that explores the relationship between nationalism and economic development. In many ways what we call "nationalism" was a cover for change and innovation. In *Imagined Communities* Ben Anderson (1983, 5) contrasts "the 'political power' of nationalism" with the "philosophical poverty and even incoherence" of nationalist doctrines: "In other words, unlike other isms, nationalism never produced its own grand thinkers: no Hobbes, Tocqueville, Marx, or Weber, just a series of local and highly eclectic responses. This 'emptiness' at the core of nationalism easily gives rise, among cosmopolitan and globe-trotting intellectuals, to a palpable condescension. Like Gertrude Stein witnessing Oakland, one quickly concludes that there is 'no there there.'"

There *was* a there there, but in recent decades economists never could understand nationalism, just as in the nineteenth century the majority of economists could not understand the mercantilist ideas that were associated with nationalism. As Joseph Schumpeter (1954, 336) wrote, "[The liberal economists] could see nothing but error in them . . . and developed a practice according to which it was all but sufficient for putting a work out of court to attach to it the slightest tinge of mercantilism." Schumpeter's bêtes-noires were the Anglo-Saxon economists, Adam Smith above all, who famously found much to criticize in mercantilist analysis. But mercantilism was a pragmatic adaptation: not a theory with no praxis like the hypothetical free market, but a theory *of* economic practice. Not a theory of how economies *might* operate, all other things being equal, but a plan of action to *make* them operate, in search of something else becoming "equal"—the late-developing nation-state. As Perry Anderson (1974, 36) put it, "Mercantilism was precisely a theory of the coherent intervention of the political state into the workings of the economy, in the joint interests of the prosperity of the one and the power of the other." These practices constituted, at the end of the day, adequate means to obtain rationally defensible ends, such as state building, national autonomy, and the augmentation of national power. But this was also the purest economic heresy: anyone refusing to believe in free trade (the "absolute and eternal wisdom for all times and places") must be "a fool or a crook or both" (Schumpeter 1954, 397).

Like the earlier mercantilist arguments, the thesis about the Northeast Asian "developmental states" derives from observations about actual economic practice—first in Japan and later in South Korea and Taiwan. The idea that coherent state intervention into the workings of the market might have something to do with Japanese growth has a long scholarly pedigree. The works of E. H. Norman (1975) on the role of the Japanese state and William Lockwood (1968) on Japanese economic history are perhaps the best examples of this tradition in the English language. But rudimentary notions of the developmental state were also at the heart of the writings of early development economists, such as Gunnar Myrdal, Paul Baran, and Simon Kuznets.

Perhaps the most representative account in English of pragmatic Japanese development is Chalmers Johnson's *MITI and the Japanese Miracle.* This work became influential not because of its original theoretical or analytical power but because it spoke the truth about a Japanese predicament that was instantly recognizable to anyone who has lived it, or who can imagine it. He shows how the Japanese, faced with the harsh reality of a world dominated by the Western powers, devised a system of political economy that was simultaneously successful, admirable, and dangerous. Johnson's contribution was to make the Japanese experience explicable. He conveyed the truth that the Japanese state was, like the Korean or the Chinese states later on, a hard-bitten one that chose economic development as the means to combat Western imperialism and ensure national survival: for most of the twentieth century, economic development was a recipe for overcoming the depression, war preparation and war fighting, postwar reconstruction, and finally independence from U.S. aid (Johnson 1982, 308).

Still, the East Asian state's economic interventions and the developmental determination shown by its population present a vexing phenomenon, a true problem of comparative understanding. To Albert Hirschman (1958, 8) this was the most important puzzle to reckon with. In *The Strategy of Economic Development,* he wrote:

> If we were to think in terms of a "binding agent" for development, *are we simply not saying that development depends on the ability and determination of a nation and its citizens to organize themselves for development?* [emphasis added] Perhaps this is not as tautological and vague as it sounds. By focusing on determination, for instance, we are taking hold of one of the specific characteristics of the development process in today's underdeveloped countries, namely the fact that they are latecomers. This condition is bound to make their development into a less spontaneous and more deliberate process than was the case in the countries where the process first occurred.

What the East Asian developmental states had in common with the late-developing European nations of the past, and with contemporary developing societies in Latin America and elsewhere, is not the application of a uniform model that could be adapted everywhere, but different adaptations to varying arrangements of state and society in different international and security environments. All of twentieth-century East Asian development occurred in the midst of war, Great Power rivalry, and continuous concerns about security, whereas two world wars and the Cold War barely touched Latin America (with the exceptions of outlying nations like Cuba and Chile). Hirschman (1968) argued that these different security contexts explained why Latin America could not evolve along the continental European model and adopted instead the "late late development" pattern, relying on import substitution and overvalued exchange rates.

Asian nationalism was not an abstract ideal but a reality born of struggle with the enemy: Japanese nationalism grew in the context of Anglo-American dominance in the Pacific, just as an acute sense of national sovereignty was Korea and China's response to more than a century of imperialism. Japan was a case of "an economy mobilized for war but never demobilized during peacetime," which led Johnson (1995, 10) to think that "the Japanese capitalist developmental state seemed to have squared the socialist circle; it involved very high levels of social goal setting without the known consequences of communism."

Johnson's *MITI and the Japanese Miracle* is a country-specific study without much reference to the external world, but it became more than an account of idiosyncratic practices analyzed in isolated splendor. It was an implicitly comparative account, containing within it a truth about East Asian developmental regimes and their outlook. This is why a whole generation of scholars in comparative politics can deploy any number of country cases (the larger the N the better) and still not grasp the basic truth about the political economy of any single country, and why a single case study by an astute analyst of politics can generate insights that are instantly recognizable as true for many different societies. In fact, the pull of nationalism—catching up and getting even—is such an important motivating force behind state action that Johnson wondered if economic development might not have been a mere side effect of the pursuit of economic nationalism. But in the cases of Korea and Taiwan, we could say it was also the side effect of the pursuit of national security.

Nationalism and Warfare

> The concept of the state presupposes the concept of the political. . . .
> In contrast to the various relatively independent endeavors of human
> thought and action, particularly the moral, aesthetic, and economic, the
> political has its own criteria which express themselves in a characteristic

way. . . . The specific political distinction to which political actions and motives can be reduced is that *between friend and enemy.*

—Carl Schmitt, *The Concept of the Political*

Looking back at the days of the Cold War, we find that the question of national security was much simpler and easier then. Among the nations within the free world, a broad relationship of credibility and fraternity existed. In times of emergency, friends could be counted upon. Not so any more.

—Park Chung Hee, *Korea Reborn*

Another insight that has long eluded American social science work on South Korea and Taiwan is a crushingly simple one: these states were born of civil wars that have not yet ended, and the subsequent Cold War against their respective communist enemies defined the parameters of state action in these countries, subsuming developments of social and economic institutions to exigencies of national survival. The Cold War in East Asia, and the vicissitudes of American strategic calculation with regard to the region, had a determining influence over the choice of industrial programs in South Korea and Taiwan. This, in a nutshell, is my argument: security counts. It made a huge difference, if not the *whole* difference, and added to the prevailing economic nationalism of East Asia, a life-and-death proposition: either grow industrially or die. Meanwhile, with the exception of the two Vietnams that merged into one in 1975, no Southeast Asian state has ever faced a comparable threat of simple extinction. An extreme security dilemma concentrates every mind, but this is not something that happens in Southeast Asia.

Carl Schmitt (1976, 34), a leading thinker in Weimar Germany, once theorized that political actions and motives could be reduced to merely this: those between friend and enemy.

War is neither the aim nor the purpose nor even the very content of politics. But as an ever present possibility it is the leading presupposition which determines in a characteristic way human action and thinking and thereby creates a specifically political behavior. . . . The political does not reside in the battle itself, which possesses its own technical, psychological, and military laws, but in the mode of behavior which is determined by this possibility, by clearly evaluating the concrete situation and thereby being able to distinguish correctly the real friend and the real enemy.

Taiwan and South Korea both had enemies who sought their extinction and nearly succeeded in 1950; thereafter, an ever-present possibility of war has continued to define the relationship of state to society in both countries:

Korea was governed by military dictators for thirty years, while Taiwan had a martial law regime for four decades (1947–87). If for Japan economic nationalism was an attempt to correct status inconsistency with the United States and the European countries, for Korea and Taiwan it meant catching up to Japan—or to a comparable level of industrial development—as a means to hold off the communist enemy.

Warfare and security long helped to shape the rise of developmental states in East Asia. If Johnson (1999, 55) thought that the critical experience defining the world view of the men who dominated MITI was that they were "men born in the middle to late Meiji era who virtually all survived the war and continued to work for the government as if they were uniformed military officers," I have argued the same for South Korea's economic policymakers who came into their adulthood toward the end of the war, either in the Japanese military or in its colonial bureaucracy. For Korea, it was Japanese imperialism that bequeathed what Hirschman might call a "growth perspective," comprising not only the developmental determination but also the perception of the essential possibility of a path leading toward that goal.

War and colonialism as the deep background for the Korean developmental state was an idea first advanced by Bruce Cumings in *The Origins of the Korean War*. In that book he argued that the Japanese created a kind of developmentalism in Korea that was profoundly predatory but that also achieved rapid industrial growth; in other words, the early 1960s were not the first time for such growth in South Korea. He also argued that massive social mobilization and dislocation caused by the Pacific War and war-related industrialization led to popular rebellion and civil war after 1945. In my book *Race to the Swift* I also argued for the critical importance to colonial Korea of the wartime period. Korea, as an entrepot between Manchuria and Japan, and as a natural supplier of an abundant variety of mineral resources, cheap labor, and hydroelectricity, was a logical location for a forced industrialization program of the most brutal kind. The political ruling coalition was based on an alliance of the repressive state and "the new *zaibatsu*" (as the prototype *chaebôl*, the Korean transliteration of *zaibatsu*), using the same system of credit-based industrial financing that came to characterize postwar Korea.

In South Korea and Taiwan during four decades of Cold War, a nationalism that so incessantly demanded economic sacrifices and compliance by the populace was based on the military standoff with communist counterparts, backed by big-power guarantors. The Cold War against their respective enemies long defined the parameters of state action in these countries, subsuming the development of social and economic institutions to exigencies of national survival. The extraordinary embeddedness of Korea and Taiwan in the Cold War international system concentrated the minds of state leaders and led to cultivation of the art of deflecting international pressures, an incessant search for autonomy vis-à-vis the outside world, and a shrewd exploitation of their nested invulnerabilities as wards of a hegemonic power so economically munificent as the United States, which could not easily exchange Seoul and Taipei for more compliant clients.

All this made the security situation of late development in East Asia fundamentally and qualitatively different from that experienced in Latin America. The "determination of a nation" in East Asia did not reside primarily in the economic but in the political, with economic growth often viewed as the indispensable means toward obtaining military security. This should not be so surprising because South Korea and Taiwan still remain locked in to their respective civil wars, still perched on the twentieth century's last geopolitical fault line, still armed to the teeth. Security concerns have therefore defined the states of South Korea and Taiwan for most of this century, both in the colonial period and afterward; in the aftermath of their civil wars, the overwhelming raison d'être of these states has been the survival of their sovereign entities, achievable in the end through the annihilation of the communist enemy—or short of that, through wealth and power.

The political economy of South Korea and Taiwan is thus inexplicable without grasping the logic emanating from the perpetual mobilization for war, lasting for half of the twentieth century if not longer. But it is precisely at this point that we face a conundrum: we do not have a theory to explain this phenomenon. It is a reality that remains uncaptured by theorizing about Latin American "bureaucratic-authoritarianism" or about totalitarianism in its communist or fascist variants. Perhaps the term Harold Lasswell (1997) gave to the national security apparatus, the "garrison state," comes close, but the institutional structure of the American garrison state is a far cry from the reality we wish to explain here. If American history were bereft of precedents and theories that could have anticipated East Asian developmental trajectories, where might one turn for comparative insights? Once again, theories of economic development that grew out of the security experience of continental Europe provide useful reference points. To understand the logic and essential tension in anticommunist security states, and to grasp the notion of the political to which the economic and cultural spheres are subsumed, we can turn to Carl Schmitt.

The normative concern behind *The Concept of the Political,* the only work by Schmitt in English translation, rested with maintaining the viability of Germany in the aftermath of its defeat in World War I. For Schmitt, the Weberian understanding of the state—an entity with a monopoly of violence within a given territory—was a meaningless description that eviscerated the essential political and emotional tension that defined *raison d'état* and the power that flows from it. In seeking the simplest and the most concrete criterion of the political, Schmitt thought that a binary distinction between friend and enemy ultimately undergirded the power of the state. By enemy he meant a collective hostile entity that invokes concrete antagonism, expressed in everyday language culture, defining the collective "we" against the alien "other." The political enemy need not be morally evil or aesthetically ugly; he need not appear as an economic competitor, and it may even be advantageous to engage with him in business transactions. But he is, nevertheless, the stranger, the Other; and it is sufficient for his nature that, in a specially intense way, he is existentially something different and alien, so that in the extreme case he can be killed (Schmitt 1976, 27).

The latent potential conflict with the enemy explained for Schmitt the position of the state as the highest and most decisive entity, with ultimate authority to shape the economy and society in order to preserve the integrity of the collectivity against the existentially opposed enemy. War, Schmitt argued, was neither the aim nor the purpose nor even the very content of politics. But as an ever-present possibility it was the leading presupposition that created a specifically political behavior. Only real combat revealed the most extreme consequence of the political grouping of friends and enemies, and from this most extreme possibility human life derived its political tension: "The political does not reside in the battle itself, which possesses its own technical, psychological, and military laws, but in the mode of behavior which is determined by this possibility, by clearly evaluating the concrete situation and thereby being able to distinguish correctly the real friend and the real enemy" (Schmitt 1976, 37).

Pluralism assumes that an individual is a member of many human associations of equal weight—including the state itself. The essential fact of political life for Schmitt, as a Catholic and organic thinker, was that pluralism, left unchecked, would destroy the political integrity of Weimar Germany, and it would succumb to enemies from within and without, sooner or later. This dangerous argument could have justified the pathological extremes of the Third Reich (although later Schmitt was roundly criticized by the Nazis, perhaps for his Church-oriented and anticapitalist views). But the point I wish to underscore is that Schmitt's point does capture the orientation of states engaged in perpetual civil war, and it explains not only the logic and the manner of state intervention in the economy, but why for so long the policies of the state, even when they were so grotesquely ill conceived and executed, were suffered and tolerated by the citizens.

Schmitt's notion of the "political" anticipates the mobilizational and state-oriented aspects of East Asian economic development by explicating the siege mentality—the binary "we" versus "they" in internationalized civil conflicts—that undergirded the culture of political compliance and acquiescence in Taiwan and South Korea. This is to say that societal compliance has more to do with immediate existential angst and authoritarian controls than with residual cultural habits, whether thought to emanate from the political economy of hydraulic power (Wittfogel's 1957 *Oriental Despotism*) or the eternal fount of Confucianism's presumed authoritarian dictums. The intellectual link between fin-de-siècle continental Europe and postwar East Asia is this: the essence of the modern European state, which Schmitt sought to distill down to its uncompromising tension of hostility, came to its full atavistic bloom in East Asia—and first in Meiji Japan.

The Meiji oligarchs, including Ito Hirubumi (later the first resident-general of Korea), were assiduous students of the apparatus of the Prussian military state. Ito had traveled extensively in Europe and came away fascinated by Prussian military and bureaucracy, which he saw as a route to Western rationality and modernity but also as an alternative to Anglo-Saxon liberalism. He was largely responsible for making the Prussian-style bureaucracy the absolute, unassailable base and center of political power in the state system (Woo-Cumings 1995, 439). What Otto Hintze (1975, 201) said about Prussia could easily apply to the state structure that emerged in East Asia in the first half of the twentieth century.

> The absolutist military state [in sixteenth- and seventeenth-century Europe] developed into the tutelary police state, which understood the *salus publica* inscribed on its banner, not in the sense of the individual felicity of its subjects but in the sense of the preservation and strengthening of the state as a whole. At the same time the institutions of the army insinuated themselves in an important way into the realm of civil administration. This was particularly evident in Prussia, generally the classic example of the militarist state.

Japanese interest in Taiwan and Korea after the 1880s also sprang from regional security concerns, broadly conceived. In the words of Marius Jensen, the compass of Japan's strategy concern radiated in concentric circles outward from the homelands to the "cordon of sovereignty," encompassing territory vital to the nation's survival and under formal occupation, and the "cordon of advantages," an outer limit of informal Japanese domination, seen as necessary to protect and guarantee the inner line. The territorial contiguity of Japanese imperialism and this security concern, combined with Japan's status as a developing country, meant that Japanese policy in its colonies would be significantly different from that of, say, Britain. Japanese control of its colonies was much more extensive, thorough, and systematic; the economic structure of the colonies had to undergo radical and brutal transformation tied to the needs of a rapidly growing homeland.

The militarization of civil administration was even more evident in colonial Korea than in Japan proper. The Korean governor-general always came from the army, and in the aftermath of the 1931 Manchurian Incident, Korean society was mobilized for war to a greater degree than was Japan. In the industrial sphere Korea was one of the logical locations for a crash industrialization program: hence the slogans describing Korea as "Chosen as a base of war supplies" and "Chosen as a base of penetration" (Woo 1991, 31).

The colonial state was not accountable to its domestic constituents, nor was it subject to the supervisional scrutiny of the Japanese cabinet or the parliament (it reported to the Ministry of Colonies in Tokyo, which tended to ratify what the colonial governments proposed). This resulting separation both from colonized societies and from superordinate Japanese influence was reinforced by the highly articulate, well-organized, and militarized state machinery, replete with a "thought police" and a "spy system," to buttress the civil and police bureaucracy that was probably better developed in Korea than anywhere in the world.

Taiwan had a colonial legacy similar to Korea's, with the same kind of coercive apparatuses but with perhaps less necessity to use them among the comparatively quiescent Taiwanese. But post-1949 Taiwan had another coercive experience to draw on: the civil war on the mainland and the excessive militarization of the Kuomintang apparatus, both of which had major implications for economic policy in Taiwan. The militarization of the Kuomintang party-state structure has a long pedigree, going back to the late 1920s when Chiang Kai-shek came to dominate the party, primarily through his military struggle to establish control over China. The institutional development of the KMT was a residual effect of military penetration, and one that was profoundly influenced by the German military (and later by Soviet advice, characterized by an independent military council that controlled military operations as well as political and industrial programs). Not only were the weapons German made, but many military officers were German trained, and the whole military organization and industrial development was German inspired. The KMT adopted the German tradition of maintaining the military independent of legislative interference, and military command separate from administrative functions (Lewis 1993, 83). The founder's sons, Chiang Ching-kuo and Chiang Wei-guo, were also trained by the German military (with Ching-kuo having the added experience of training in Soviet Russia). The military character of the KMT increased with the war against Japan, as elites shifted from party operatives to military officers, a changeover that reached its zenith in a full-blown civil war with the communists (81). To the extent that Taiwan's post-1949 economic program was predicated on security needs, it conformed to a historical pattern of civil conflict on the mainland going back to the early 1920s.

The second point worth considering about the Japanese colonial legacy is the relationship between the colonial state and business, especially the prewar *zaibatsu* that came to invest in its colonies. The colonial state offered big business two fundamental preconditions for business engagement and practice: political stability and a guarantee of state investment in industrial infrastructure—political and social overhead, so to speak. The *zaibatsu*, in their turn, were to serve the military and its security goals of the Tokyo leadership, which, in the crisis conditions after the Sino-Japanese War began in 1937, turned them into tightly woven accomplices of Japanese militarism. (Indeed, this security linkage was the prime one driving American occupiers to dismantle the *zaibatsu* after 1945.)

If colonialism left a multitude of bad memories, it also left an edifying memory for latter-day industrialists. The colonial industrialization pattern, deeply imbricated with militarism, *worked:* Japan and its colonies constituted one of the most rapidly growing economic regions in the world in the late 1930s. The colonial state's role in the comprehensive and coercive channeling of capital to target industries set a precedent for a similar mobilization in the 1970s in both Taiwan and South Korea, especially the "big push" of the mid to late 1930s that brought new industries to Korea (steel, chemicals) and Taiwan (aluminum), along with very high growth rates. If it is true that a "growth perspective" is garnered only through an experience of growth, then the war-induced colonial political economy was important in providing such a perspective in postwar years.

True, the Japanese pattern also had a devastating effect on the development of that class which has carried all before it in the modern world: the entrepreneurial element. Certainly there were Koreans and Taiwanese who, after doing quite well under the Japanese, parlayed their capital and entrepreneurial skill into a fortune in the postcolonial era. But the Japanese presence in the colonies was too overbearing for one to argue the case of entrepreneurial continuity. It was the bureaucrats who "continued" into the postwar period, armed now with a new concept of state-guided development. The smothering of local entrepreneurial talent, combined with revolutionary upheavals that bedeviled both countries (further wiping out what little entrepreneurial continuity there might have been), in the end cut both ways in terms of the development of postcolonial Korea and Taiwan: bereft of powerful and entrenched local business interests, the new states were also less hamstrung, especially by entrenched interests closely tied to the metropole.

The defeat of the Kuomintang in China did not have the effect of transplanting a retreating cluster of businessmen in Taiwan. Few leading mainland capitalists followed Chiang Kai-shek to his island redoubt; most preferred instead to go to the United States or Hong Kong. The few that went to Taiwan thought it was a temporary sojourn, and eschewed significant commitments of capital until a bilateral treaty between Washington and Taipei guaranteed the island's security. This also tended to reinforce the state's role in postwar Taiwan.

The third point is the relationship between the state, militarism, and the rural sector. Unlike the European colonialists in Latin America—or for that matter, elsewhere in Southeast Asia—the Japanese colonial government did not drive the peasants off their land to establish plantations (although it did not care to enact reforms to redistribute land, either). Instead it preferred to use police and administrative methods to root the landlords firmly in the countryside, to secure a reliable extraction of agricultural outputs and taxes, and to keep the lid on peasant unrest. This was the key reason why Barrington Moore (1967) linked landed elites to Prussian and Japanese militarism in his classic book, *Social Origins of Dictatorship and Democracy*. Korea and Taiwan had differences from Japan, of course; Korea's landed class was of centuries' duration whereas Taiwan, as a nether region of China, never had deeply developed landlordism. Instead it had a significant group of "rich peasants," furnishing another reason why Japan could extract resources in Taiwan through incentives, instead of often having to use coercion as in Korea. By 1945 both countries did have wealthy landlords by virtue of strong growth in the agrarian sector. But the landlords in postcolonial Taiwan and Korea did not have long to enjoy their privileges, unlike the latifundia owners in Latin America.

As the historian Bruce Cumings argued, the defeat of imperial Japan burst asunder the "pressure cooker" that was colonial Korea, leading eventually to war and instability; in the midst of this chaos, even the conservative South Korean state had to quickly enact a thorough and extensive land reform, at the prodding of the United States, lest the revolution in the north spill over. In Taiwan land reform in 1950 was likewise swift and decisive, enacted by the Kuomintang (with a lot of help from American advisors), who were nervously looking over their shoulders toward the revolutionary mainland and hoping to nip peasant upheaval in the bud.

How then do we sum up the colonial legacy for the latter-day industrialists in Korea and Taiwan? We can do so by noting the relative absence of entrenched interests, both industrial and agricultural—either because local entrepreneurial talents were not nurtured in the smothering intensity of Japanese imperialism, or because they were shattered to smithereens when the colonial pressure cooker blew up, as in the case of the agrarian interests. This discontinuity had a powerful leveling effect, equalizing incomes more than in most developing countries and providing a fertile ground for instituting effective interventionist states, which were given a relatively free hand to forge a developmental coalition as they saw fit. And it worked because the resources for this coalition did not depend on internal sources but on the external succor of a big power: the United States. But this gets us ahead of our story. The main point here is to remember how deeply both Korea and Taiwan were affected by the twin experiences of war and development—long before anyone imagined a Cold War.

So the state structure was there, and the lessons—in the form of a demonstration effect, the know-how of engineering industrial policy—were there.

The disruption caused by colonialism and war, the wiping out of the entrepreneurial and landowning class, meant that state-led industrialization was
overdetermined, and that the historical task of the Korean and Taiwanese
states was to construct, in the vacuum left by colonialism and war, a social
class that could carry the burden of industrialization. Korea and Taiwan
went about doing this in different ways, however, and here we see a sharp divergence in how both countries dealt with colonial legacies.

Korea essentially replicated the Japanese pattern of nurturing large conglomerates, at least under Park Chung Hee and Chun Doo Hwan (1961–
88), whereas Taiwan nurtured only a couple of big firms while emphasizing
small business. What accounts for the difference? The reasons are primarily
historical. Because of Korea's mainland connection to Manchuria and
North China, Japanese colonizers and *zaibatsu* corporations developed
heavy industries and spent huge amounts on social overhead in Northeast
Asia, especially in northern Korea but also in the south, thus stitching together a large marketing, communications, and transportation infrastructure tied to the mother country. Taiwan did have heavy industries like
aluminum and electric generating by the end of the colonial period, but the
country was much more oriented toward light industry and agriculture, and
much of its product was exported (sugar in great amounts to Japan, for example). This history bequeathed bigness to Korea, small-scale practices to
Taiwan.

As Thomas Gold (1986) and others have shown, Nationalist rule on Taiwan also brought with it Nationalist methods in the economy—a state-
centered rather than firm-centered pattern, often called "bureaucratic capitalism" in the literature. Personal connections in the ruling Kuomintang
party were often the avenue to upward economic mobility. An additional
Chinese pattern, drawn from the interstitial economic practice of the Chinese diaspora in what Ralph Clough (1978) aptly called "island China,"
yielded the family as the prime economic unit, specializing in small business
(the stereotypical Chinese laundries or Chinese restaurants throughout the
United States are examples of a far wider pattern of family business in Southeast Asia). This tended to promote greater emphasis on small business in
Taiwan. Taiwan also sought niches in the world economy, quite like Singapore—but quite unlike Korea, whose leaders always wanted a fully developed industrial structure. For Taiwan, securing a foothold in the world
economy was to be accomplished when the mainland was retaken, but not
on an island.

All these factors led to a divergence in Korean and Taiwan economic practice by the 1980s. But there was still an essential similarity up to that point,
and the greatest resemblance was in something economists pay no attention
to: security. Here there was also a vast difference from the Latin American
cases. The relation of these two "NICs" (newly industrialized countries) to

the world was also the relation of two highly developed security states to the world, especially in regard to their relations to the United States in the context of the Cold War.

The Political Economy of Security in Postwar East Asia

The most obvious—if often overlooked—way in which security made a critical difference in postwar Northeast Asia is the enormous amounts of aid that were pumped into the region. Washington has a great deal of difficulty in appropriating taxpayers' money for many programs, but not for security: in the 1950s under a Republican administration, even the interstate highway system could be justified as a security measure against the USSR. What better way to support security abroad than to shower money on two frontline states? After the Korean War, both Taiwan and South Korea catapulted forward in the American global calculation as bulwarks of anticommunism, whose retrieval from the abyss in 1950 and subsequent survival necessitated a massive infusion of capital. In Taiwan during the 1950s economic aid equaled about 6 percent of GNP and nearly 40 percent of gross investment, and military aid was even bigger (Wade 1990, 82). From 1946 to 1976 the United States provided $12.6 billion in economic and military aid to South Korea and $5.6 billion to Taiwan. Combined with additional contributions from Japan and international financial institutions, the total per capita assistance to South Korea in the midpoint year of 1960 was $600 for three decades, and $425 for Taiwan (Woo 1991, 44). This munificent aid helped to stabilize the economy, society, and regime of the recipient countries; it boosted investor confidence and financed extensive land reforms and other social measures. It also gave a big push to domestic capitalists through noncompetitive import quotas and licenses, access to bank loans, aid funds and material assistance, and the noncompetitive award of government and U.S. military contracts for reconstruction activities.

In the end, though, the true significance of the American role in the choice of economic programs had less to do with the programs themselves than with U.S. ability to manipulate the parameters of economic action in East Asia. The three major policy choices in postwar South Korea and Taiwan—import-substitution industrialization in the 1950s, export orientation in the late 1950s in Taiwan and early 1960s in South Korea, and the defense-related industrialization, deepening in both countries in the late 1960s and early 1970s—were predictable responses to America's changing geopolitical calculations and its perennial indulgence of these two anticommunist clients.

The early phase of ISI (import substitution industrialization) in South Korea in the 1950s was not an ill-conceived outcome of home-grown economists (or even a well-thought-out policy in a decade where ISI was a developmental norm and not an aberration) but a catch-as-catch-can political solution to sink foreign-aid dollars into infrastructural and industrial development and keep the foreign-aid spigot open. In South Korea, open trade or export orientation as a way to earn foreign currency was fiercely resisted, especially because it involved an American effort to create a viable regional market to revive the Japanese economy. Syngman Rhee was well aware of the American plan to solve two intractable problems at once—the revival of the Japanese economy and the maintenance of viability in the two Cold War wards—by linking them into a regional market, which meant recycling U.S. aid dollars in Taiwan and South Korea to purchase goods from Japan: the specter of another Co-Prosperity Sphere. Rhee called the scheme of regional integration "the American policy to secure two dollars of benefit— one for Japan and one for Korea—from every dollar expended" (Woo 1991, 56). What this mercantilist wanted instead was dollars to benefit Korea alone, to nurture Korean industries with U.S. aid in a zero-sum game. Rhee thought expansion of Korean industry should have its counterpart in suppression of Japan's. In other words, he would refuse to have a part in the long-run global solution for the "dollar gap," which, to rectify the massive structural disequilibrium in world trade, required rebuilding the economies of Europe and Japan. This resistance worked, as did the resulting program of ISI (at least for some years).

The situation was somewhat different for Chiang Kai-shek. In the aftermath of the Korean war, the United States was unequivocally committed to staying in Korea, which only increased the political clout—and recalcitrance—of Syngman Rhee. This was not a luxury that Chiang enjoyed. (In 1960 the largest MAAG operation in the world was in Taiwan. Still, this was nothing like having massive American ground troops present as in South Korea, a tripwire to ensure an instant American involvement in the event of war.) Of the three states to enjoy strong support by the American right— Taiwan, South Korea, and South Vietnam—Taiwan under Chiang was to suffer the deepest penetration by American aid agencies and to implement therefore the most far-reaching economic and social reforms.

In 1950, the relatively weak hand of Chiang—compared to Rhee—led to a quick capitulation on the issue of restoring trade ties with Japan, which in turn led to a Japan-Taiwan trade agreement engineered by American aid officials and the SCAP (Supreme Commander of the Allied Powers). By 1953 Japan absorbed half of Taiwan's exports of rice, salt, and sugar and exported to Taiwan almost as much in textiles, fertilizers, and machinery (Lewis 1993, 207). Periodically Chiang would enjoy upsurges of American military and economic aid, as he did during offshore island crises in 1954–55 and 1958. But in general Taiwan was more subject than South Korea to reduction in foreign-aid commitments, as suggested in the Prochnow Committee report, implemented soon after the second offshore island crisis.

We can say, then, that to the extent that the ISI program characterized Taiwan's policy in the 1950s, it did not stem from Chiang's refusal to earn foreign exchange from Japan. Rather, it had to do with the need for expanding state revenues, through tariffs and other duties associated with the program of ISI, in order to support the huge military. By the late 1950s the ROC possessed the seventh largest land army in the world and fifth largest among the noncommunist countries. Over 6 percent of the population actively served in the armed services, not including the enormous reserves, making it the most militarized of the noncommunist countries.

Another reason for ISI in Taiwan had to with the dispersal of colonial industrial and infrastructural enterprises in Taiwan. Unlike in South Korea, where vested enterprises were sold to the private sector, in Taiwan such companies were passed on to the public sector as financial rewards to mainlanders who became the mainstay of the KMT. The state enterprises were often in infrastructural and heavy industries, and the program of ISI became a way to channel resources to those industrial enterprises controlled by the KMT.

In the end, however, both the South Korean policy of making Korea "another Japan" while keeping the real Japan at bay (and being succored by an indulgent America), and the Taiwanese policy of concentrating national resources to beef up the KMT-controlled public sector while increasing defense expenditure (which rose 656 percent between 1951 and 1961), could not stand. The Decade of Mutual Security came to an end, and with it a precipitous reduction in aid to South Korea and Taiwan. Taiwan was forced to turn outward by the end of 1950s, and South Korea by the beginning of the 1960s (the South Korean delay had to with the uncertainty caused by the coup d'état in 1961).

The export-led program in the 1960s, then, was less the result of the American technical advice than a function of declining U.S. aid. This is a point entirely missed in the American political science literature on the East Asian NICs, which prefers to interpret the export-oriented reforms either as emanating from USAID to insulate the native technocracy from political pressures of the Nationalist leadership in Taiwan, or as the result of the institution of a reform-oriented coalition in South Korea (Haggard 1990). But then, as if these two nations were fated in the twentieth century to be rescued by war, along came Vietnam.

When the Cold War turned into a regional conflagration in Indochina, U.S. aid to South Korea and Taiwan reversed its brief early-1960s decline. Washington pumped yet more resources into these countries. Much as Japan fueled its postwar takeoff with the economic windfalls from the Korean

War, so did Taiwan and South Korea with the Vietnam War. Taiwan was seen as a strategic asset maintaining pressure on China, as well as a critical source of logistical support for U.S. forces operating in Southeast Asia. As a part of the island chain that surrounds China, Taiwan was an important link in U.S. containment policy, and Taiwan in turn benefited from American purchases of agricultural and industrial commodities, use of military facilities and depots for repair of equipment, designation of Taiwan as a site for R and R, and contract work for and in Vietnam.

South Korean involvement in Vietnam was more direct. It sent more than three hundred thousand troops by the time the war was over; this was more men per capita than any nation in the world, including the United States. The total cost to the United States of equipping and paying for these was "peanuts compared to what it would be for a comparable number of Americans," but those "peanuts" went a long way to finance Korea's takeoff. The total economic and military aid that Korea received as a direct payment for partaking in the Vietnam War came to more than one billion dollars (Woo 1991).

If the first phase of ISI in the 1950s was politically motivated, the second phase of deepened substitution in heavy industry in the 1970s was no less so, as it coincided with another shift in hegemonic policy having apparent adverse effects on the security of South Korea and Taiwan. We can call this shift the Nixon difference. The fulcrum of the new economic program, the need for military self-sufficiency and thus defense-related heavy industrialization, was occasioned by a rapid procession of events: the declining American fortunes in Vietnam, increasing North Korean guerrilla infiltration of South Korea, the Pueblo incident, the downing of the American EC-121 by the North Koreans, and, to top it all, the Nixon Doctrine.

The first place (besides Indochina) where the axe of the Nixon Doctrine fell was South Korea. During the Johnson presidency the National Security Council had recommended reducing the U.S. troop commitment to South Korea in five or more years depending on the Korean pace of military modernization, but the Nixon administration accelerated the withdrawal out of budgetary pressure: some twenty thousand American soldiers were removed from South Korea by the middle of 1971, with the rest to be phased out in the next five years. Seoul had little to say in the decision, having lost its trump card once the United States had determined upon Vietnam disengagement (Woo 1991, 123). This was followed by the opening to China in 1971 and 1972.

In what was perceived to be a security crisis caused by the waning days of Pax Americana, the first goal in South Korea was to purge all uncertainties from the body politic by tightening the grip of authoritarian politics and, once the steering mechanism was thus made predictable, to veer toward the Big Push: massive investments in steel, shipbuilding, machine building, chemicals, and metals. The development of heavy industries also held the promise of a vibrant defense industry and thus and end to dependence on American largess in weaponry and the attendant political interference. This conception of national security meant a clear departure from the export-oriented, non-sectoral-biased strategy adopted throughout the 1960s.

Taiwan's response to Nixon's policies was as determined and swift as South Korea's. As early as 1967, Nixon intimated in *Foreign Affairs* that China should be included in the family of nations, and by 1970 Taiwan was aware of U.S. overtures to the mainland. As in South Korea, Taiwan intensified the crackdown on domestic dissent, raised military preparedness, and tightened the state's control over the economy. But the new regime of political economy that emerged in Taiwan was not subject to the kind of international scrutiny that South Korea received. This was in part because Park Chung Hee had to create a strong authoritarian politics through the KCIA (Korean Central Intelligence Agency), founded in 1961; the 1972 constitution, which ushered in a ruthlessly authoritarian regime; and periodic declarations of martial law. The KMT always had a well-structured Leninist organization and had ruled Taiwan through martial law ever since 1947. In other words the intensification of martial law in Taiwan was a much better orchestrated affair, and faced less concerted opposition than in South Korea.

In the late 1960s Chiang Ching-kuo proceeded to strengthen his hold over the armed forces, the secret police, the China youth corps, the retired servicemen's association, and vital sections of the bureaucracy (Lewis 1993, 272). He also concentrated the decision-making power in the newly formed National Security Council, made up of the KMT regime's military and political elites and empowered to coordinate the nation's military strategy and security-related affairs. Chiang Ching-kuo began focusing on a comprehensive program of economic development with the strategic objective of increasing national self-sufficiency by reorganizing the military and becoming the world's major arms importer and manufacturer; he also strengthened Taiwan's defense capabilities, emphasizing air and naval power rather than ground troops and a shift from the offensive posture to defensive.

The kind of programmatic shift that Taiwan underwent required careful planning, so as to forge links among the industrial, research, and defense sectors. The capacity to form these links was facilitated by state control of Taiwan's financial sector, educational system, and large-scale manufacturing operations. It is important to note that many state enterprises served dual (commercial and military) functions. Examples include Taiwan Machinery Manufacturing, China Shipbuilding, Taiwan Aluminum, China Petroleum, Taiwan Metal Mining, BES Engineering, China Petrochemical Development, China Steel, Chung-Tai Chemical Engineering, and the Aero-Industry Development Center (Lewis 1993, 309). In 1971 Chiang Ching-kuo called for a gigantic investment program centering on the development of heavy industry and chemicals, especially plastics and resins, machinery, ship-building, electrical equipment, and steel—exactly the foundations of defense industry.

If in Taiwan the agents of heavy industrialization were state-owned enterprises, in South Korea they were private enterprises—the huge conglomerates known as the *chaebôl*, nurtured by the state through "financial repression," which is the policy of provisioning big business with capital at rates much lower than what the market would have dictated. This policy of "financial repression" had a profound impact on re-configuring the class structure in South Korea, giving a huge boost to a constellation of domestic enterprises, marking their birth as world-class conglomerates. It also altered the nature of the state's relationship to big business, eliminating any arm's-length relationship that might have existed before.

The state's financial strategy of allocating credit through preferential low interest rates meant that banks offered loans (in the context of the virtually absent equity market) to subsidize the chosen—namely, entrepreneurs who had proven their mettle through good export records, risk takers who entered into heavy and chemical industries, and the faithful who plunged into the untried sea of international competition with new products—and relied on the state's good offices to rescue them, should they fail. It was really these entrepreneurs who made the defense-oriented program possible, and thus the drive for industrial maturation.

To join the chosen few, enterprises had to be big: size was an effective deterrent against default, forcing the government into the role of lender of last resort. The importance of size in this sense cannot be overemphasized, since highly leveraged firms, exposed to the vagaries of the international market, live with a constant specter of default. It was for this reason that the expression "octopus-like spread of the chaebôl" came into wide circulation in South Korea. But the chaebôl tentacles gripped not only the economy but the state as well: big state and big business would have to sink or swim together. A credit-based financial system, mediated by an interventionist authoritarian state, became the basis of Korea Inc.

The flipside of the state–big business symbiosis was an effective suppression of popular protests and a thorough evisceration of labor as a political force—almost always done in the name of anticommunism and the specter of North Korea just across the border. This is a stunning contrast to the situation in Western Europe, where the development of governmental institutions of representation was powerfully shaped by an effort to cope with such popular sectors. It is also fundamentally dissimilar to the experience of Latin America, where the evolution of corporatist structures was an institutional solution to the demands of labor, and where economic policies, such as ISI, obtained political legitimacy through populist attempts to redress gaping economic inequality. True, oppressive political conditions for labor in Taiwan and South Korea were somewhat mitigated by firm-level paternalism; but labor remained weak and systematically excluded in both countries, shackled by continuing considerations of national security and international economic competitiveness.

What the foregoing discussion points to is that the contours of state and society in South Korea and Taiwan are powerfully shaped by international conflicts, from the agony caused by late-bloomed Japanese imperial ambition to civil wars, revolutions, and the Cold War. With the easing of Cold War tensions, combined with greater prosperity in Taiwan and South Korea, both the political terror and developmental frenzy subsided. The greatest task of the recent reform program begun in 1997 became one of redressing the excesses of the past. This meant, in Korea, reassessing the relationship between the state and business, and, in both countries, finding ways to institutionalize the popular sectors that shouldered much of the burden of such rapid development. While Taiwan today confronts a tense security situation in the Taiwan Strait, Korea suggests optimism about a final end to the Cold War—primarily because President Kim Dae Jung dramatically changed South Korea's orientation to the North when he came into office in 1998.

Asian Values

So far we have discussed the historically and regionally shaped values of Northeast Asian industrial development and national security. These values were justified by doctrines of nationalism and anticommunism that succeeded as ideologies precisely because of the intellectual emptiness of the doctrines at their core: they were known more by what they proposed or opposed than by a coherent and intellectually satisfying set of ideas. Park Chung Hee or a Chiang Kai-shek argued this before their people: my authority derives from my not being a Communist, and my legitimacy will come from economic development. Everything else was opaque. In a sense this was the opposite of twentieth-century communism: at its core Marxism-Leninism was full of coherent ideas—how the world got to be the way it is, and how it could be changed through revolution—while being bereft of practical ideas of development. Except for Stalinism, that is, which found a way to push industrialization forward in the context of a horrendous security threat in the 1930s, and with increasing recourse to old forms of Russian nationalism.

The American discourse on the political economy of South Korea and Taiwan tends to go through periodic and predictable permutations, depending on the state of American bilateral relationships with the two countries. Thus in the late 1960s the unanticipated economic success of South Korea and Taiwan, coupled with their steadfast support of the American effort in

Vietnam, led the American academic community to portray the economic systems in South Korea and Taiwan as liberal and open, as miracles of market-led development, and often as vindications of economic reforms enacted under American supervision. However, when pressed to explain why economic development was clearly not following the Western model, and in particular why that development was leading not to democracy but rather to deepened authoritarianism, they typically had recourse to a catchall category—"culture," specifically Asian culture: Confucian values, a strong family system, patriarchal leadership, and the presumed tendency of all three to promote authoritarian politics.

In the 1980s that interpretation changed, amid deep anxiety about Japan's skyrocketing trade surplus and a perception of American decline and the loss of U.S. competitiveness. As more American scholars and trade negotiators uncovered Japanese practices of industrial policy, similar practices in South Korea and Taiwan also came under scrutiny: Suddenly these two countries were seen as microcosms not of liberal America but of illiberal Japan. And their authoritarian politics was thought to proceed directly from the state's overbearing role in the economy. (Japan was clearly a democracy, but in an influential 1989 book, *The Enigma of Japanese Power*, Karl Van Wolferen argued that behind this facade was an opaque "system" that made all the important decisions.) In a much-publicized assessment of economic growth in East Asia, the World Bank proffered their own view that the governments of South Korea and Taiwan were interventionist in a "market friendly" way, thus splitting the difference between the two earlier views.

Such periodic reversals of opinion in this country would seem to highlight the absence of a basic intellectual framework within which East Asia's modern experience might be apprehended. Of all the discourses seeking to explain (or to warn about) Asian success, however, "Asian values" still strikes an expert on the region as the most inexplicable. Where did it come from, this very pale reflection of the nationalist and security ideologies that mobilized the populace of Northeast Asia in the past century? Another curiosity, bordering on intellectual if not mental imbalance, is that the most prominent "Asian values" arguments (by leaders like Lee Kuan Yew and analysts like Lucian Pye) refer to the multiethnic, multicultural countries of *Southeast* Asia, countries having tangential relation to Sinic or Confucian influences and with relatively short periods of independence following lengthy experience with European colonialism. Meanwhile Japan, Korea, and Taiwan came roaring into the modern world in the late nineteenth century with cultures, values, and philosophies steeped in centuries of Chinese learning, civil service, and statecraft, not to mention written, official languages; furthermore they were homogeneous ethnically and subject to no Western colonial influences. From a *Northeast* Asian perspective, it often seems that no one would ever have mentioned "Asian values" if Lee Kuan

Yew hadn't picked this idea up while picking up his Chinese (as a child he spoke only English), or if Prime Minister Mahathir (now there's a Confucian name) hadn't imbedded his form of nationalism in an anti-Western discourse—an often forgotten *Islamic* discourse to boot.

To make this long story short, I would argue that these Southeast Asian leaders see so much virtue in "Asian values" because they have so little of it. Their "Asian" values are precarious and weak precisely to the degree of their saturation in Western thinking, absorbed through colonially influenced educational systems and languages, and *that* is why Southeast Asian leaders prattle about Asian values. They are trying to leave Europe and join Asia, the reverse of Japan's famed *Datsu-A* (or "leave Asia") orientation. In other words, the idea of Asian values is a measure of what is absent in Southeast Asia, not what exists; it is about what one thinks needs to be invented, often as a means of sustaining authoritarian rule in the one historical environment in East and Southeast Asia where liberalism and the rule of law has made some serious inroads, if only under British imperial tutelage. In short, no deep structure of values has shaped these leaders' development. Much of Mahathir's rhetoric in Malaysia about how Asia is not inferior to the West, for instance, can be understood only in the context of colonial history and its needs: the need to find a national identity in a multiethnic society and to keep the people bound to it; the need to respond somehow to the problem of disorder amid the effects of rapid modernization and accompanying social ills; and as always, the need to find a "concept of the political" to justify autocracy.

Lee Kuan Yew famously pioneered a model for a "soft" form of authoritarianism, described by Ralf Darendorf as follows: "law-abiding citizens who assiduously attend to their own affairs and otherwise live inoffensive private lives need not fear the wrath of their leaders. . . . But those who criticize government for its unaccountable power, those who use their freedom of speech to expose nepotism, those who dare put up alternative candidates in election—these people are in trouble" (Bell 1997, 7). But Lee Kuan Yew was perhaps just a bit too close to the "soft power" of the colonizer. After all, simultaneously with its empire upon which the sun never set, the leading thinkers of the United Kingdom pioneered most if not all of the great ideas of modern liberalism—something that Edward Said has memorably analyzed in *Culture and Imperialism*. According to his own autobiography (1998, 183), Lee (né Harry Lee Kuan Yew) did not speak or write Chinese until over the age thirty, when he organized the People's Action Party (PAP) and was accused by opponents of being unworthy to run the country because he did not speak or write Mandarin or Hakka or Hokkien—whereupon he hired himself tutors in those languages.

Even the contemporary exponents of Confucian values are not sure where these ideas came from. In *Asian Values and Human Rights*, William

Theodore de Bary writes that when he was first asked about Asian values, "fifty years of studying, teaching, and writing about Asian civilizations and Asian humanities did not help much in answering the question. 'Asian values' is a new concept in current political parlance, and one could not help wondering what this new usage was all about" (de Bary 1998, 1). In other words the most prominent scholar of Confucianism in the United States had never heard of Asian values until Lee Kuan Yew began talking about them; meanwhile Singapore has as strong a British or Anglo-Saxon background as it does a Chinese one, and indeed has been a central, prosperous, and typically promiscuous trade entrepot for Southeast Asia for at least two hundred years.

For his part Mahathir (in a speech called "The Asian Values Debate," May 21, 1996) sounded like a hybrid Southeast Asian in search of Confucianism:

> I believe in community-building. . . . For centuries, so many of us in Asia believed that our Asian values and ways were second-rate. If today, Asians have discovered that Asian ways and values are not inferior simply because they are Asian, and often are superior despite the fact that they are Asian, perhaps we may be forgiven. . . . I would like emphasize here that the difference between people, is not their physiognomy, ethnicity or skin color. What distinguishes them is their culture, that is the system of values which they believe in.

He also sounded like Samuel Huntington (*Political Order in Changing Societies*) in his concern for mere political stability. In the same speech Mahathir said, "The survey found that the six societal values most valued by the East Asians were: first, having an orderly society; second, societal harmony; third, ensuring the accountability of public officials; fourth, being open to new ideas; fifty, freedom of expression; and sixth, respect for authority." He also says that for the West, the leading values are freedom of expression, personal freedom, the rights of the individuals, open debate, thinking for oneself, and the accountability of public officials. He notes that accountability comes sixth here in the West, whereas it is third in the East.

This chapter started with the observation that social science theories are often more revelatory of the social scientists than the subjects of their inquiry. If the biography of the author is so important, then perhaps it is incumbent on me to explain my particular personal and historical grounds for insisting on the importance of the "political" (as Schmitt understood the term) in undergirding the economic mobilization of East Asian security states. The historical experience I draw on is the knowledge bred in the bones of anyone growing up in postwar South Korea or post-1949 Taiwan, namely, the intensive emotional loathing of communism that was so successfully drilled into every schoolchild, the constant admonition that national survival was contingent on economic development, and the drumbeat of military preparedness that demanded endless personal sacrifice. This is the kind of lived experience that is deeply internalized, even if it has long dwelt in the shadows of much Western imagination about the golden-era of the Pacific Rim and its supposed unfettered capitalism. It explains how the most ruthless societal mobilization for economic growth worked and for so long.

If we briefly look at these same Northeast Asian states during and since the 1997 financial crisis, we find the following: Taiwan was virtually unscathed and continued apace its remarkable developmental pattern amid a continuing security threat—made manifest in March 1996, when Washington mobilized two carrier task forces into Taiwan waters, after China conducted missile tests off the island's coast. And then its apparent great comparative advantage—its masterful silicon chip and computer manufacturing industries—set the economy up for an unprecedented fall with the implosion of the dot-com economy in the United States in 2000. For Japan 1997 was another year of drift, punctuated by a serious banking crisis in November and December. Because it is the world's largest creditor country it easily survived the financial panic, but its inability fundamentally to reform its economy and restore a strong growth pattern bespeaks the domestic strength of the political-economic coalition that governed that growth in the first place. Japan Inc is the author of its own problems, the victim of its own past success, and today is the initiator not of any brilliant long-term growth strategies but of a seemingly perpetual economic malaise. At the end of 1997 South Korea's political economy appeared to have been demolished by a freight train called the Asian financial crisis, but in 1999 it had the strongest growth rate in Asia, over 10 percent; growth slowed a bit with the 2000 global recession, but 2001 and 2002 were again strong growth years. Korea succeeded by reinvigorating the state's interventionist role in the economy, this time to achieve transparency and accountability at the nexus between government and corporate power, and to bring Korea's huge state-favored banks under the control of market forces, something greatly aided by allowing foreign interests to buy large chunks of these same banks. Kim Dae Jung thus used the strong state to accomplish a miracle of reinvention. If a strong nationalism still drives Korean growth, though, the security situation is much less tense and determining than before, which is a key reason for the growth of Korea's democratic politics in the past decade. We can conclude this brief review by noting that none of the following terms made an appearance: crony capitalism, Asian values, free markets, or neoliberalism. In other words Northeast Asia continues to move along its own distinctive path of political economy.

Does this make the developmental experience of South Korea and Taiwan idiosyncratic, bereft of lessons for other developing countries? The answer, I think, is a mixed one. In a comparative discussion of developmental states in Northern Europe and East Asia, one scholar has argued that Austria, Finland, South Korea, and Taiwan (the four countries he examines) shared four attributes of successful state intervention. First, old bureaucratic traditions existed that were capable of providing competent administration; this is unquestionably true of all four. Second, again in all four, the outcome of the wars they suffered shook up the prewar power blocs and rearranged the previous distribution of power among domestic elites, paving the way toward a more developmental "embeddedness." Thus the history of South Korea and Taiwan may not be as unique as one might be led to believe. Third, the external position of each of the four countries in the international system was precarious, posing security threats possibly leading to their annihilation—which very nearly happened to South Korea and Taiwan in 1950. Lastly, in spite of their positioning between two major international power blocs, all four maintained a basic commitment to the bourgeois legal order (if only in form sometimes) and respected private property. In the end all four adopted major policy tools that were remarkably similar: investment subsidies, price controls, credit rationing, and maintenance of interest rates at artificially low levels (Vartiainen 1999).

What, then, are the lessons for development, in light of the foregoing discussion of power and plenty in the context of security states? The genius of the states in South Korea and Taiwan was in transforming very real fears of war and instability into a remarkable developmental energy, which in turn became an abiding and binding agent for growth. The pursuit of power and plenty, in the context either of the security state or of catching up with the rest of the world (usually both), is vastly more effective in generating developmental energy than a general appeal to increased welfare, à la Latin American "populism." We are back to the vacant center, a unique, regionally specific species of nationalism and security.

But isn't there still quite a bit of space for development driven by nationalist and security concerns, particularly in East Asia? The new century has not dissolved into the globalized, multilateral, interdependent world that seemed to be materializing in the late 1990s. Instead the American economy experienced a period of Japanese-style stagnation of (at this writing) indeterminate length, a stunning inversion of "crony capitalism" in the collapse of Enron and its (presumably transparent and accountable) accountant, Arthur Anderson (the fifth largest of the American accounting firms that dominate the global market), and a frightening new security threat after September 11, 2001, that, in its ubiquitous, anonymous, and globe-roaming terror, made many security analysts long for the predictable routines of the Soviet-American Cold War conflict. If September 11 gave to East Asian–American relations a temporary "pass," in contrast to the rivalry many expected would develop between the United States and China, it is just a temporary lull in a region still given to strong nationalisms and security rivalries. Japan remains distrusted above all by those closest to its shores, in Korea and

China. Korea and China remain divided, and in response to September 11 the United States proposes to deepen its military position in the region, while all the old reasons for it have mostly disappeared (containing communism, etc.). Meanwhile economic nationalism remains a powerful ideology in the region, with its headquarters now centered in Beijing.

A big question one can pose, without really being able to answer it as of this writing, is whether the age of *developmentalism* on the East Asian pattern is over. Clearly it isn't over for China, but it is hard to imagine how China's rapid growth can proceed into the foreseeable future without straining economic growth in its neighbors, and in the world generally. But a glance at "Communist" China's contemporary rhetoric and propaganda shows that whatever the world economy's tolerance for rapid developmentalism, China goads its own people with limitless recourse to nationalism, and invokes the very real oppressions suffered at the hands of the imperialist West. They also reveal remarkably exaggerated displays of piqued national sovereignty whenever a mishap occurs in its relations with the United States (for example, the American spy plane that crash-landed on Hainan Island on April Fool's Day, 2001).

For a quarter century Deng Xiaoping and Jiang Zemin have parlayed a menu of nationalism and past Western and Japanese insults into economic development, and into a political justification for the paradox of a Chinese Communist Party sitting astride all this development. When the Chinese invoke "nation," the West understands it as jingoism. But if we look at China's experience at the hands of imperialists, or understand one of the main dilemmas of Chinese development to be the center-periphery conflict (or the paradox of the central government and the provinces, which Mao Zedong talked about all the time), the question of asserting nationhood and territorial sovereignty gathers paramount importance. But Chinese nationalism will find its pièce de résistance, its greatest legitimation, in rapid economic growth. And in that sense it will merely be recapitulating the developmental trajectories of Japan, Korea, and Taiwan.

5

Japanese Spirit, Western Economics

The Continuing Salience of Economic Nationalism in Japan

Derek Hall   F52

Japan is arguably the single most important country in the international political economy (IPE) literature on economic nationalism. The spectacular success that the Japanese state has enjoyed in promoting economic development, both during the Meiji period in the late nineteenth century and during the high-growth decades of the Cold War, has made the country the most effective advertisement for economic nationalism since interest in the concept began to reemerge in the early 1970s. The precise mix of policies that Japan has employed in spurring economic growth is, of course, the subject of scholarly debate. There is widespread agreement, however, that mechanisms such as industrial targeting, directed lending, protection and subsidies for infant industries, efforts to procure and indigenize technology, and state control over finance have been central to Japan's success. While Alice Amsden coined the phrase "getting the prices wrong" to describe South Korea's industrial policy (1989, chap. 6), the willingness of the Japanese state to change price incentives in the economy has been a key part of the country's economic nationalism. During the 1980s, Japan was touted as a model not only for the rest of Asia, where various states made efforts to emulate Japanese policies (Wade 1996b), but even for the United States itself. At a more theoretical level, much of the discussion about economic nationalism in IPE took Japanese policies as paradigmatic.

Given that Japan's economic success has had so much to do with both the study and the advocacy of economic nationalism, it is not surprising that the country's prolonged doldrums during the 1990s have encouraged critics of

For their comments and suggestions, I thank Andrea Harrington, Eric Helleiner, Kato Kozo, Peter Katzenstein, Dave Leheny, Elayne Oliphant, Andreas Pickel, Steve Power, Matt Rudolph, Lisa Sansoucy, two anonymous reviewers for *New Political Economy,* and the participants in the workshop "Rethinking Economic Nationalism: National Identities and Political Economy," Trent University, Peterborough, Ontario, August 23–24, 2002.

nationalist economics. Japan's "lost decade," and the 1997 Asian financial crisis which laid low many other states ostensibly following the Japanese model, have widely been seen as decisive refutations of economic nationalist policies. Indeed, with the Asian crisis following on the heels of the collapse of the Soviet Union, liberal economists (particularly in the United States) were quick to argue that both communist and nationalist economics had been discredited and that liberalism was now the only game in town. Whatever usefulness Japan's nationalist economic policies may have had in earlier decades, they were hopelessly obsolete in an age of economic globalization, and served only to hobble both Japanese economic growth and the world economy as a whole. Thus, while vested interests and "reactive nationalism"[1] will likely continue to prop up Japan's calcified political economy, efforts being made in Japan toward liberalization, internationalization, and globalization represent the best, if not the only, hope for the country's future. Frank Gibney has stated the argument succinctly (1998, 11): "Given the lightning moves of world trade, finance, and investment, however, in the new computer-networked society, the once marveled 'bureaucratic development state' has become a badly worn piece of furniture. So are the premises of economic nationalism that once sustained it."

Defenses of economic nationalism and of the "developmental state" have certainly not vanished. Some scholars have presented alternative views of the Asian crisis, arguing that the worst-hit countries had either dismantled key parts of their developmental states or had never had such states to begin with (Henderson 1999; Weiss 1999). Others have argued that while Japan certainly needs to undertake reform, the postwar system contains valuable elements that should not simply be jettisoned en route to the introduction of "Anglo-Saxon," laissez-faire capitalism (Sakakibara 1998; Dore 2000). In this chapter, however, I take a somewhat different perspective on the future of economic nationalism in Japan. Building on recent reformulations of the concept in IPE,[2] I will argue that economic nationalism has itself been an important force in shaping the drive for economic liberalization in Japan and the specific forms that liberalization has taken.

I make this claim, and use the concept of economic nationalism, in two different ways. In the first section of the chapter, I follow the arguments of authors who contend that IPE should define economic nationalism not in terms of a specific set of *policies* (such as protectionism and infant industry promotion) but rather in terms of its *goals*. When economic nationalism is understood in terms of goals or motivations, the seeming contradiction that "liberal" policy is often promoted—in Japan and elsewhere—for "economic

---

1. Susan Pharr (2000, 178) has used the term to refer to Japanese resistance to the demands of its trade partners for market access.

2. In addition to the contributions to this volume, see Crane (1999), Goff (2000), Shulman (2000), Abdelal (2001), Helleiner (2002), and Pickel (2003).

nationalist" reasons is resolved. Thus, even if we keep to the goals that are associated with economic nationalism or "neomercantilism" in IPE, economic nationalism remains alive and well in calls for liberalization in Japan. In the second section of the chapter, I treat economic nationalism quite differently by using the insights of recent scholarship that relates it primarily to national identity rather than to state purpose. I demonstrate that the perceptions of the Japanese "national character" held by promoters of liberalization (both in Japan and abroad) have affected the kinds of reforms that Japan has been called on to undertake. Liberalizers have been profoundly concerned that the national identity of the Japanese people will itself present a barrier to liberalization and internationalization, and they have advocated a wide range of measures aimed at reeducating the Japanese to be more "liberal" or "international." I argue further that the current crisis over the nature of the links between the economy and the national character is a central part of Japan's prolonged malaise.

In terms of the distinction between statist and identity-based understandings of economic nationalism that Eric Helleiner highlights in the conclusion to this volume, the first section of this chapter keeps more closely to the statist conception prevalent in IPE but argues that the goals associated with this conception can motivate liberalization. The second section fits more closely with the other contributions to this volume by arguing that liberalization is shaped by perceptions of national identity.

Before proceeding, I will make two points of clarification. First, Japan's "reform" debate is obviously complex. While advocates of reform frame and combine their arguments in a variety of ways, the key proposals include trade liberalization, the deregulation of domestic economic activity, the reorientation of the economy away from the interests of producers and toward the sovereignty of consumers qua rational individuals, and the dissolution of the various forms of "relational contracting" that characterize Japan's political economy.[3] While I am conscious of the dangers of lumping these various proposals together (particularly because, as Steven Vogel points out [1996], liberalization can often entail more rather than less regulation), I will, for the sake of brevity, refer to this reform agenda as "liberalization" except in cases where the specifics of reform proposals are particularly important.

Second, my objective in this chapter is not to argue that these alternative understandings of economic nationalism can provide a full explanation of liberalization and deregulation in Japan. Diverse factors shape actual policy outcomes, including the organizational structures of industry and the bureaucracy, the electoral system, pressure from outside the country (*gaiatsu*), and sectoral characteristics.[4] What I hope to analyze is rather the *reasons* that

3. Ronald Dore (1999) gives an excellent overview of this debate.
4. Important sources on deregulation and liberalization in Japan include Vogel (1999a),

promoters of liberalization think Japan should follow their proposals. My aim is thus the relatively modest one of suggesting that even in an age of globalization, the two variants of the concept of economic nationalism highlighted above will retain significant importance in any explanation of Japan's liberalization.

Why Liberalize? Liberal and Nationalist Motivations

> Japan is a country without resources so it must create a free trade world. . . . In a sense, Japan must promote free trade and technological development in order to survive.
>
> —Imai Takashi, chairman of the Japan Federation
> of Economic Organizations, January 7, 2002

It is not at all difficult to understand why globalization and economic liberalization are taken to be inimical to Japanese economic nationalism. Japan has emerged as a key country in the literature on economic nationalism because of the argument that the country's rapid industrialization has been promoted by development-oriented state intervention. The willingness of the state to involve itself in guiding the economy away from the outcomes that would prevail under free-market conditions and toward prioritized sectors is at the heart, for instance, of Chalmers Johnson's conception of the "developmental state." For Johnson (1982, 17–23), the developmental state worked according to a "plan-rational" logic which differentiated it from "market-rational" countries like the United States and "plan-ideological" states like the USSR. Liberalization and deregulation both represent mortal challenges to such a political economy: the former because arranging outcomes in an open economy with significant foreign participation is much more difficult than trying to shape an economy that is protected and primarily "national," and the latter because the opportunity for administrative discretion and the imposition of regulatory solutions are crucial to the model.

More recently, Richard Samuels and Eric Heginbotham (1998) have made a coherent statement of Japanese economic nationalism (without using the term) in the foreign policy sphere, arguing that Japan follows a

---

Schoppa (1997), Kusano (1999), and Gibney (1998). Vogel (1999a, 15) writes that "Japan's distinctive approach to liberalization has been characterized by slow and incremental change; elaborate political bargains, typically involving compensation for the potential losers from reform; considerable efforts to prepare industry for competition; and continued bureaucratic monitoring and manipulation of the terms of competition."

"mercantile-realist" strategy organized around advancing the country's technoeconomic position in the international system. Japan, they argue, has balanced against the United States economically while bandwagoning with it militarily, and has used industrial and trade policy in order to promote critical high-technology industries. Here again, the Japanese state is playing a key role in determining the trajectory of the economy, a role that would be threatened by liberalization and deregulation. The desire to smash this "plan-rational" or "mercantile-realist" state has been clearly stated by reformers both inside and outside the country. Ichiro Ozawa's (now defunct) Liberal Party, for instance, put strong emphasis on the need to shift from a state-led to an individual-led economy, and the need to reorient Japan's political economy away from its prioritization of producers and toward consumers.

The fact that liberalization and deregulation pose a serious threat to Japan's postwar political economy does not necessarily mean, however, that they are inimical to economic nationalism. Recent scholarship in IPE has argued that economic nationalism should be identified, not in terms of its policy content, but rather in terms of its nationalist motivation or connection with national identity. This perspective opens up the possibility that even liberalizing or deregulatory policies can be seen as instances of economic nationalism if they are promoted for nationalist reasons. Eric Helleiner (2002, 320), for instance, has recently identified a group of nineteenth-century "liberal economic nationalists" who advocated liberal policies in the belief "that these policies would strengthen national identities, the prosperity of the nation and/or the power of their nation-states." Similarly, Glenn Drover and K. K. Leung (2001) have argued that nationalists in Quebec have used the liberalization of trade as a means of promoting nationalist goals. The identity that most of the IPE literature perceives between economic nationalism and statist, protectionist economic policy is thus coming to be seen as a false one.

Precisely what this means for the analysis of economic policy formation, however, is not clear. A shift in focus of the term "economic nationalism" from policies to motivations and identities—from what people do to why they do it—obviously implies that analysis of the reasons for policy implementation must be foregrounded. At present, however, the literature does not contain a set of distinctions that would allow contrasts to be drawn between nationalist and nonnationalist motivations for liberalization that is equivalent to Abdelal's (2001) distinction between statism and economic nationalism. Given the extraordinary pervasiveness of nationalism in modern thought, this situation runs the risk of allowing almost any behavior to be defined as nationalist. This lack of attention to the motivations for liberalization—or rather, the assumption that such motivations are obvious—has also characterized much of the writing urging Japan to change its ways. It is telling, for instance, that the chapter titled "Arguments for Change" in Edward J. Lincoln's *Arthritic Japan* is devoted almost entirely to detailing the inefficiencies of the Japanese political economy. Precisely why inefficiency is a problem, and on whose behalf it needs to be overcome, are questions that the chapter does not address. Suggestively, however, Lincoln later argues that only liberalization that is driven by a ground swell of support from below (as opposed to being pushed primarily by bureaucrats) counts as "true" liberalization (Lincoln 2001, 154–57).

I would like to put forward three "liberal reasons for liberalization," which can be counterpoised to the nationalistic reasons that will be detailed below. The first two are derived from liberal political philosophy, while the third relates more to liberal political economy. First, liberalization can be inspired by an ideological commitment to utilitarianism, that is, the idea that economic policy should aim at the greatest total welfare for the greatest number of people. The argument that economic protectionism and regulation lead to inefficiency and (static and dynamic) welfare losses has been central to the push for liberalization and deregulation around the world, and to the extent that the problems with these welfare losses are conceptualized in terms of their divergence from utilitarian ideals (rather than, say, in terms of the problems they cause for state power), it seems reasonable to view this motivation for liberalization as a liberal one.[5]

A commitment to economic freedom as a basic human right independent of its welfare implications—that is, a rights-based, rather than utility-based, view of liberalization and deregulation—constitutes a second "liberal reason for liberalization." The argument for liberalization here is that states are illegitimately infringing on the rights of their citizens when they prevent them from engaging in commerce across national borders or impose regulations upon their behavior beyond the minimum degree of regulation justified by the theory of the "night-watchman" state. Associated with thinkers such as Friedrich Hayek, this view has greatly increased in prominence in "Anglo-Saxon" countries in particular since the early 1970s.

Third, liberalization may also be seen as having had liberal origins if it is brought about by political pressure mobilized by groups and individuals who are concerned primarily with promoting their own individual economic self-interest. This force for liberalization is well articulated in an influential article by Jeffrey Frieden and Ronald Rogowski (1996), who argue that increasing internationalization creates incentives for competitive sectors in the domestic economy to push for liberalization.

While these "liberal motivations for liberalization" are all reasonably straightforward, it is more difficult to determine how economic nationalism

---

5. This view, obviously, implies acceptance not only of utilitarianism as an ethical principle but also of the basic correctness of neoclassical economics.

might motivate liberalization. As a number of authors have recently pointed out, "economic nationalism" refers most often in popular (and even academic) discourse to a loose set of interventionist policies associated with trade protectionism, infant industry promotion, and economic discrimination against foreigners. The term, for the most part, simply refers to policies of which liberal economists disapprove. This formulation of economic nationalism is undermined, however, by two facts: the policies it refers to can be promoted for nonnationalist reasons (trade protectionism, for instance, can be motivated by socialist economic goals), and nationalism can be a motivation for liberal policy. Economic nationalism is thus better understood in terms not of its content but of its goals. Identifying just what these goals are is complicated by the fact that "economic nationalism" tends, in the IPE literature, to be used synonymously with various other terms, such as "neomercantilism." I would argue, however, that "economic nationalism" in IPE fundamentally refers to the goal of promoting the survival, strength, and prestige of the state and/or nation in a competitive international system. Robert Gilpin (1987, 31), for instance, writes that the "central idea" of the economic nationalist perspective on IPE "is that economic activities are and should be subordinate to the goal of state building and the interests of the state."[6] Meredith Woo-Cumings (1999, 6), meanwhile, has built on the work of Johnson and Liah Greenfeld in arguing that for Japan "economic nationalism is an attempt to correct status inconsistency with the United States and the European countries." While the literature has tended to assume in practice that this goal will be promoted by interventionist or "developmental" policies, there is no reason why liberalization cannot be promoted for reasons of national power and prestige. Indeed, even the promotion of second-order economic nationalist goals such as state independence, sectoral/national competitiveness, and industrialization can, as I will show, lead to liberalization.

Liberal and economic nationalist motivations for liberalization need not be contradictory and can overlap. In the Japanese context, Ronald Dore has argued that the self-interest of particular social groups favoring liberalization can be framed in "patriotic" terms, and he has shown how "neoclassical" and "patriotic" arguments coexist happily in government documents (Dore 1999, 88, 75). I argue, however, that to the extent that liberalizing policies are driven not by appeals to the prosperity and rights of individuals or by self-interested pressure groups à la Frieden and Rogowski, but rather are justified in terms of their contribution to national strength and prestige, economic nationalism (in the standard IPE sense) motivates liberalization.

To what extent, then, is liberalization in Japan framed in terms of an ap-

6. It should be noted that, for Gilpin (1987, 34), economic nationalism does not rule out the pursuit of liberal economic policies.

peal to liberal, rather than economic nationalist, principles? Note first that pressures for liberalization—whether motivated by liberal thinking or not— have been fairly weak in Japan. The Japanese state has been deeply split on this issue, and what proposals for liberalization have been put forward tend to be rather vague (Yamaguchi 2001, 15–19; Nagano 2002, 20–25). Japanese business associations have been halfhearted in their calls for liberalization, and consumer groups have generally either not supported liberalization or else have actively opposed it. Steven Vogel's (1999a, 1999b) observations regarding the general resistance of Japanese consumers not only to liberalization but even to the very idea that they should define themselves as "consumers" are particularly striking, given that standard economic theory would expect that Japanese consumers have a great deal to gain from deregulation of Japan's producer-oriented political economy. Vogel (1999a, 9) argues further that the recognition by Japanese political parties of widespread industry and consumer opposition to liberalization helps to explain why "no Japanese political party has ever stood unequivocally in favor of economic liberalization, and no party is likely to do so in the foreseeable future." Lincoln (2001), similarly (though more despondently), calls attention to the absence of any real ground swell of support for economic liberalization in Japan (see also Nakatani 1997). That said, it remains the case that the amount of public commentary recommending liberalization and deregulation on what are basically liberal grounds has dramatically increased since the collapse of the bubble economy in the early 1990s. It is now very common to hear economists, journalists, business leaders, and politicians calling for consumers to be set free and for the construction of a society that is based upon the desires and freedom of the individual.[7]

On the other hand, the rhetoric of liberalization and deregulation in Japan suggests that these policies are perhaps being pursued for economic nationalist reasons. The quotation at the head of this section alludes to a first possible nationalist motivation for liberalization and deregulation in Japan: these policies are often seen as being vital for the nation's survival in a globalizing world. Economic globalization is frequently presented by both sides of the reform debate as posing a threat to Japan. An often-used metaphor is the "return of the *kurofune*," the American "black ships" commanded by Commodore Perry that forced the opening of Japan to trade in the 1850s and brought to an end the *sakoku* (closed country) period, on which more below. This is an extraordinarily versatile metaphor in Japan, in that it can be used to describe virtually any external force that is likely to change the country in some way; the 2002 World Cup, for instance, has been described

---

7. Dore (1999) traces the history of these calls. For a selection of proposals that basically fit within this framework, see, for instance, Itō (1992), Keidanren (1992), and Yashiro (1999, 2000).

in terms of the *kurofune,* as has Tokyo Disneyland (Kawabata 2002; Raz 1999). Similarly, Iwabuchi Koichi writes that the Japanese media often compares the impact of transnational satellite broadcasting to the black ships, with the implication "that Japan can no longer enjoy a self-contained domestic market, but rather is now under threat of being forced to open its doors to the world" (Iwabuchi 2002, 4). In the economic realm, then, the metaphor implies, economic globalization requires that Japan open its borders and deregulate its economy in order to survive. It is important to note here that not all liberalizers invoke the *kurofune* metaphor: some, indeed, reject the idea that economic globalization represents a threat to Japan, preferring to see it instead in more liberal terms as an opportunity. The prevalence of the metaphor, however, suggests that this view of liberalization as a response to threat rather than as potentially beneficial is fairly widespread.

Undertaking liberalizing policies for the economic nationalist purpose of responding to external threats is far from novel in Japan. Richard Samuels argues (2003, 85), for instance, that the privatizations accompanying the Matsukata reforms in the early 1880s "had nothing to do with liberal principles," but rather represented an effort to get government finances under control in order to avoid raising foreign capital and allowing foreign control over Japanese industry. In this case, then, the *kurofune* of foreign capital were kept at bay precisely by liberalizing moves at home. Some of the complex contemporary policy consequences of this view of globalization-as-threat are well illustrated in William Grimes's work on Japanese finance (2000, 2003). Grimes makes the case that the renewed interest in the internationalization of the yen since the late 1990s is partly a defensive response to globalization. Greater international use of the yen, particularly in Asia, is being promoted as a way of shielding Japan and the region from the destabilizing effects of the global financial system. Among the various ironies of this situation that Grimes identifies, we may note that various liberalizing policy moves in the financial sphere have been undertaken in order to promote yen internationalization for the purpose of *insulating* Japan from globalization. It is also notable that Grimes has described internationalization as promoted by a coalition of "economic nationalists" and those who see liberalization as desirable for its own sake.

A second, and related, motivation for Japan's liberalization and deregulation that can be understood in traditional economic nationalist terms is policy change brought about in response to foreign political pressure, or *gaiatsu.* The United States has been exerting almost constant pressure on Japan to liberalize and deregulate its economy since the 1960s, and has gradually expanded the range of reforms it wishes to see implemented. The amount of weight accorded to *gaiatsu* in the academic literature on Japan's liberalization has lessened in recent years, with more consideration being given to the way that external pressure interacts with forces for change within Japan (Schoppa 1997; Kusano 1999). It is interesting to note here, however, the often-made argument that pro-liberalization forces in Japan use external pressure to argue that the country has no choice but to accede to American demands. In such appeals, again, actors within Japan tend to avoid making a direct appeal to liberal principles in support of their projects and instead frame liberalization in terms of Japan's relations with a powerful external actor and of Japan's position in the international system as a whole. While arguments that change is inevitable because of foreign pressure can obviously be made simultaneously with liberal calls for liberalization, such calls do tend to reinforce a common theme in the history of Japan's economic nationalism: that sweeping changes must be made in the country's organization because of pressure from the international system.

Third, liberalization is often promoted in Japan for the purpose of enhancing the economic competitiveness of key sectors or of the economy as a whole (identified above as a second-order goal of economic nationalism). This argument for liberalization stresses not so much the utilitarian greatest good for the greatest number as it does national or sectoral competitiveness in the international system, although the two can overlap. Leon Hollerman has stated this argument clearly, writing that from the 1960s "big business was able to make its case for liberalization in the name of the national interest. It was clear that business had to be unshackled in order to stand its ground in competition with the West" (Hollerman 1998, 265). Lincoln has argued that deregulation in Japan will be "clearly producer oriented" as fears of declining national competitiveness prompt the bureaucracy to ease some regulations (Lincoln 1998, 67). Ronald Dore has also called attention to a "Schumpeterian" strand in "patriotism/economic necessity arguments" for deregulation that stresses the way Japan is losing out in the race for innovation as a result of its excessive regulations (Dore 1999, 75–76).

The financial sector again provides a useful example of such thinking. It is often argued that the difficulties Japan's financial institutions have faced in international competition derive not simply from the excesses of the bubble years but also from the lack of exposure of these institutions to international "best practice" in the domestic market. Liberalization and the exposure of Japanese firms to foreign competition here become aspects of the promotion of a key national sector. As Sakakibara Eisuke, then director-general of the International Finance Bureau, put it at the time (paraphrasing Edmund Burke), "sometimes in order to conserve what is good for the country you have to implement very radical reforms."[8]

---

8. For examples of this kind of thinking with respect to Japan's "Big Bang" financial sector reforms, see Hartcher (1998, 250–55). The quotation from Sakakibara is on p. 252.

Particularly interesting in this context is the attitude of the Ministry of International Trade and Industry, the famous MITI,[9] which, Chalmers Johnson argued, was responsible for coordinating Japan's industrial policy after World War II. In the early 1990s, MITI made a much-heralded turn toward promoting economic deregulation and liberalization, a stance that has increasingly brought it into conflict with more conservative ministries. In this turn to deregulation, however, we see strong echoes of the major goals of Japan's postwar industrial policy. In a 1994 magazine article titled "MITI Transforms Itself into the Ministry of Deregulation," for instance, the overwhelming concern of the bureaucrats interviewed is the transformation of Japan's industrial structure and the improvement of industrial productivity, goals that have always been key objectives for MITI. What seems to be changing here, then, are MITI's methods rather than its goals. Kumano Hideaki, then MITI's vice-minister (the highest bureaucratic post in the ministry), expressed this point of view very clearly when he argued that "deregulation itself is a central pillar of industrial policy."[10] MITI's thinking here meshes well with the widely voiced idea that Japan's economic system, while successful during the catch-up period, is no longer appropriate in an age of globalization and needs to be liberalized in order to secure national and sectoral competitiveness. The key issue, of course, is whether national competitiveness is seen as a goal as such, and it seems that it still is.

When Japanese economic nationalism is understood in terms of a set of specific policy preferences—industrial policy, for instance, or trade protectionism—liberalization and deregulation constitute obvious threats. However, each of the three motivations for liberalization and deregulation that I have noted above—ensuring the nation's survival in a globalizing world, responding to foreign pressure, and promoting the international competitiveness of key sectors or of the economy as a whole—resonate strongly with the goals of Japanese economic nationalism as traditionally understood in IPE. None of these reasons for liberalization is inconsistent with the advocacy of what I have termed more "liberal" arguments for change in Japan's political economy. But to the extent that these motivations prevail over more liberal ones in government rhetoric, in the thinking of businesses, and in the minds of the Japanese public, liberalization is consistent with Japan's economic nationalism from Meiji on (indeed, we might remember here that the introduction of capitalist economics was a key part of the Meiji project).

Determining the relative weight of these positions in debates over Japanese economic policy is an empirical project that goes beyond the scope of

9. Called METI since the 2001 reorganization of the ministerial structure.
10. "Kisei Kanwa Suishinshōni Henshin," *Nikkei Business,* October 24, 1994. The quotation is on p. 16.

this paper. However, the rhetoric that has accompanied Prime Minister Koizumi Jun'ichiro's calls for economic reform provides an intriguing window onto the possibility that liberalization is a nationalist project. There is certainly nothing unusual about the idea that economic reform is likely to be painful for some, and it is not strange that politicians promoting liberalization might spend a good deal of time asking people to steel themselves against this pain. Given that the primary economic justification of deregulation and liberalization is that these policies increase efficiency and leave the nation as a whole better off, however, it seems natural that politicians would be more likely to accentuate the positive rather than the negative aspects of deregulation. It is thus not surprising that Koizumi's repeated calls during 2001 for the Japanese people (*kokumin*) to bear the pain (*itami*) of reform provoked a certain amount of comment.

Whether Koizumi intended it or not, the primary image his speeches conveyed was not the positive vision of a new Japan but rather the image of pain that would have to be shouldered in order to get there. The vagueness of Koizumi's calls for "structural reform," discussed below, may have contributed to this outcome. Indeed, to some observers, Koizumi's constant reiteration of the reformist slogan "no pain, no gain" emerged as the most critical issue of the July 29, 2001, House of Councilors election.[11] Notable here is the fact that while reformers did indicate that the worst of this pain would be borne by workers in inefficient, protected sectors,[12] Koizumi's exhortations were directed to the citizenry as a whole rather than primarily to these workers. The overall impression one is left with is a call to the Japanese people to shoulder burdens for the sake of a great national project. Hayano Toru, in an article for the *Asahi Shinbun,* has summed up the message as follows: "This is a challenge not for Koizumi alone, but for everyone in the country. Give a hand to help Koizumi face this challenge." Hayano's article is particularly apt because it compares Koizumi's calls with a previous attempt to mobilize the populace to endure for the sake of a liberal project: Prime Minister Hamaguchi Osachi's 1929 efforts to return Japan to the gold standard. Hamaguchi's campaign included a leaflet written under his name titled "I appeal to all of you—the people of Japan," which included the line "You have to have the courage to bear the small complaints in your daily lives for the good of the future." The project was also promoted by a popular tune called the "Austerity Song."[13]

11. Hayano Toru, "Farewell to 'Tora-San's World,'" *Asahi Shinbun,* July 30, 2001.
12. For instance, Sakaiya Taichi, former director-general of the Economic Planning Agency and a reformer, stated in an interview that "the people who will suffer the most pain are workers of small businesses and self-employed people" (ibid.).
13. Hayano Toru, "Voter Manipulation, Past and Present," *Asahi Shinbun,* June 29, 2001.

Liberalization, Deregulation, and the Japanese "National Character"

When Koizumi describes the pain that must be endured in order for economic reform to take place and for the Japanese economy to recover, the pain he refers to is economic: in particular the loss of jobs that will accompany the mass bankruptcy of inefficient firms. The rhetoric of those who wish to reform Japan suggests, however, that the country's citizens are likely to face painful adjustments in ways that go far beyond the economic. Both in Japan and abroad, many reformers claim that liberalization will not truly take hold in Japan until there have been wide-ranging changes in the psychology of the Japanese people—that is, in what we might call the Japanese national character. While the specific changes that are called for vary, there is a strong sense that there is something about "Japaneseness" that both holds back the move toward deregulation and greater participation in the international economy and would continue to inhibit such participation even if regulations were fully rolled back. Rather than seeing the Japanese as rational consumers who will naturally prefer cheaper goods and deregulated markets, reformers often argue that the nation needs to be reeducated before liberalism can properly take hold in Japan.

These claims resonate powerfully with the new focus on identity in the IPE literature on economic nationalism that is highlighted in this volume. Various scholars have recently argued that the major problem with the traditional IPE conception of economic nationalism is precisely that there is no nationalism in it; rather, it is a theory of statism. These authors have refocused the study of economic nationalism on the ways that the nation is perceived or "imagined" by its constituents and the important implications these imaginings can have for economic policy (Crane 1998; Helleiner 2002). Abdelal (2001), for instance, has argued that the economic policy trajectories of post-Soviet states, and in particular their efforts to integrate with or draw away from the Russian economy, have been profoundly influenced by variations in national identity. In this section I take up this new approach to the study of economic nationalism in two different ways. First, I identify two common themes regarding the nature of Japan's national character in the works of reformers: the country's "insular" mentality and the putative fondness of its citizens for regulation. These themes, I show, can be found in writings by Japanese and by foreigners, and by academics and popular writers. Without committing myself to either theme (I disagree strongly with some of the works I cite), I suggest that the reformers' perceptions shape the kinds of reforms they advocate and have resulted in real policy consequences. I then make a more general claim that during the 1990s Japan entered a period of "identity crisis" regarding the relationship between national identity and the economic system, and that this crisis is an important factor in slowing political economic change.

Sakoku Mentality and the Need to Be Regulated

In his book *Importing Diversity* the anthropologist David McConnell explores Japan's insularity and identifies several points that are common to work on the topic. First, he notes that most observers see Japan's insular mentality as creating problems for the country, most notably in its foreign policy, but also in its ability to adapt to change. Second, he shows that the sense that Japan is an insular country is shared both by the Japanese and by foreigners. With respect to foreign criticism of Japan's insularity, McConnell writes (2000, 16), "Now Japan is being asked to go beyond appropriating skills and knowledge to transforming its entire value system. What foreign criticism amounts to is a demand that the Japanese reconstitute themselves and their society so as to make them more compatible with international norms and institutions." On the Japanese side, similarly, his study shows that the question of how Japan can be "internationalized" is being taken up with great seriousness by the Japanese government. As early as March 1980, for instance, MITI issued a report blaming Japan's economic system for its failure to produce "internationalist" workers who would be able to maintain the country's economic competitiveness. Finally, McConnell argues that it will be extremely difficult for Japan to change this situation, stating that while Japan does have a long history of adaptation to other cultures, the "social, cultural, and historical barriers to a broader formulation of Japan's national purpose are truly formidable" (17–18, 30).

McConnell's discussion of Japan's insular national psyche appears tame when compared with some other formulations. In *Cartels of the Mind,* for instance, Ivan P. Hall, an American who has spent thirty years working and teaching in Japan, launched a blistering attack on the country's exclusionary practices in such fields as law, journalism, and education, arguing that in these areas it is virtually impossible for foreigners to find permanent employment. To Hall (1998, 7), the "intellectual closed shop" that the country maintains in these fields is again a function of insularity: "That Japanese intellectuals maintain these barriers with enthusiastic conviction, and with no visible desire to reciprocate the open access they themselves enjoy in other countries, simply confirms the depth of Japan's insular mentality." In a formal academic treatment of Japan's efforts toward "internationalization" (*kokusaika*), the political scientist Mayumi Itoh draws a distinction between Japan's "outward" internationalization, which has been mostly related to the expansion of economic influence and has been "nationalistic and superficial," and "inward" internationalization, which is "genuine and qualitative" and "refers to the assimilation of the Japanese mind to foreign values and the transformation of Japan's domestic systems to meet internationally accepted norms and standards" (Itoh 2000, 5). We may note here that to Itoh, the inward project is clearly nonnationalist: as she writes, "It may be argued that the necessity for an inward *kokusaika* grew out of the very success of the nationalistic and superficial outward *kokusaika*."

Itoh argues that this inward, and more important, form of internationalization in Japan has been stymied by the *sakoku* mentality. *Sakoku,* or "closed country," refers to the policies of cutting most contact with the world beyond Japan that were pursued during the Tokugawa era, and continues to be used to refer to isolationism and insularity. (The Japanese-language edition of Hall's *Cartels of the Mind* is titled *Chi no sakoku,* literally "closed country of the intellect.") To Itoh, the *sakoku* mentality is a vital construct for understanding Japan's foreign policy, and a serious barrier to the country's liberalization. She argues that "Japanese exclusionism, protectionism, racial prejudice, and xenophobia, all derived from the *sakoku* mentality, constitute the attitudinal prism of Japanese foreign policy decision makers (as well as of the public), which has retarded Japan's liberalization and internationalization even today" (Itoh 2000, 15). Itoh, like McConnell, also argues that the views of *sakoku* Japan that are held by foreign policy makers outside of Japan (that is, foreigners' sense of the Japanese character) have been important in forming the demands that they make of Japan and the kind of behavior they expect from the country (7).

The need for Japanese to "internationalize" their closed minds and redefine their national character has reached beyond policy proposals and academic reporting. The Japanese government has taken concrete, and expensive, steps toward promoting internationalization. One of the most striking is the Japan English Teaching Program (JET), initiated in the mid-1980s, that McConnell analyzes in *Importing Diversity.* This program, which brings thousands of native English speakers to Japan each year to teach in the country's public schools at an annual cost of $500 million (McConnell 2000, ix), was created for a number of reasons, and one of the strengths of McConnell's book is the way he weaves together the different bureaucratic and political motivations that gave birth to JET. It is quite clear, however, that a key force behind creating the program was the desire to internationalize Japanese children by exposing them to *gaijin* (foreigners) at an early age. Indeed, this goal may be more important in the running of JET than the project of teaching English itself, a fact that causes some disgruntlement among the foreign teachers. The JET Program, as "the centerpiece of a top-down effort to create 'mass internationalization'" (McConnell 2000, ix), represents a concrete outcome of a widely held sense that economic liberalization in Japan will not yield the expected results, or indeed may not even occur, until Japan has become a more "normal" country and conformed to global standards of mental openness.

David Leheny (2003) has demonstrated that similar dynamics are at work in Japanese leisure and tourism policy. Leheny argues that ever since the late nineteenth century, the sense of national identity held by Japanese bureaucrats has led the government to actively encourage Japanese participation in more "normal" leisure practices—that is, practices that more closely mirror those in the "advanced industrial nations"—while retaining a Japanese flavor. During the 1980s, various ministries became concerned that the failure of Japanese lifestyles to "catch up" with those of the West was beginning to create problems in Japan's foreign relations. These concerns led to the attempt, by the Ministry of Transport through its Ten Million Program, to persuade more Japanese not only to travel overseas (in order to facilitate the recycling of Japan's trade surplus) but also to become less "insular" as tourists, more "individualistic," and less likely to go on package tours. Leheny argues that for the MOT, the value of the program "to the nation would be not only in terms of its improvement of Japan's international relations but its doing so through making Japanese enjoy themselves in a manner befitting an advanced industrial nation" (2003, 151). MITI was also involved in these efforts to make Japanese leisure more "normal." The ministry "continued to promote the development of a 'society that gives me space to do my own thing' as one of its major objectives of the 1990s. Even as its reports stressed the importance of this better lifestyle for Japanese, they also pointed to the relevance of this better lifestyle in Japan's foreign relations" (114).

If the discussion of Japan's need to overcome the *sakoku* mentality is mostly concerned with relations between Japanese and the outside world, analysis of another putative aspect of Japan's national character that is understood to inhibit liberalization—the tendency of Japanese to accept, and even expect, a high degree of regulation in their personal lives—has more to do with social relations within the country. As with the *sakoku* mentality, attention has been drawn to an ostensible Japanese desire to be regulated both within and outside Japan. Several of the articles written by American liberals in the 1998 Brookings Institution–edited volume *Opening the Bureaucrat's Kingdom* claim that this desire will be an impediment to the adoption of deregulation in Japan. Frank Gibney (1998, 14), for instance, argues that "sweeping deregulation" in Japan is "not so much a matter of policy as it is a matter of mind-set." Edward Lincoln writes that in Japan, "the public is taught to acquiesce in detailed regulation of their lives from an early age" (1998, 61–62). Similarly, Steven Vogel (1999b) has written of the tendency of consumer organizations in Japan to lobby against liberalization and in favor of regulation. One of the most spirited condemnations of the Japanese tendency to welcome and expect regulation was written by Miyamoto Masao (1995), a psychoanalyst who worked as a bureaucrat in Japan's Ministry of Health and Welfare before turning to writing popular books condemning Japan's bureaucratic culture. Miyamoto views the process of socialization in Japan, and the school system in particular, as designed to produce a "castrated" citizenry. This state of castration is a central impediment to deregulation and individual initiative in Japan that will need to be confronted before any real change can be achieved: "Once castrated, humans become less aware of what is going on around them and stop questioning what they see. . . . Naturally, it becomes hard to generate the will to bring about change. So the status quo continues in a virtual bureaucrats' paradise" (Miyamoto 1998, 76).

Referring back to the "liberal reasons for liberalization" introduced earlier, we can argue that these reformers are berating the Japanese precisely for not being liberals. According to these observers, then, liberalization and deregulation in Japan are not simply a matter of changing rules, opening borders, and freeing up the economy in order to give free rein to consumer choice; rather, they involve the Japanese reconstructing themselves as "consumers." Precisely what will bring this change about is not always made clear by those who advocate it. Miyamoto, in a call that may reflect his training as a psychoanalyst, suggests that the change must come from within each individual. He writes that "it is important to liberate one's self from the regulations that have become a part of the inner self" (Miyamoto 1998, 77). Other prominent liberalizers have seen the deep-seated resistance to deregulation and liberalization stemming from the Japanese national character as necessitating a radical and total systemic reform.[14] Reform cannot simply be limited to the economy, or even to the political system, but must extend to social organization and ways of thought. Amaya Naohiro (1994, 208–11), for instance, argued that while Japan's first "opening" to the outside world (in the 1850s) took place at the level of the skin, and the second (after World War II) at the level of the flesh, the third, contemporary opening must penetrate to the bones or even to the soul (*tamashii*). We might note with reference to JET and the Ten Million Program, however, that it is often argued that Japan's state itself has a key role to play in defining and guiding this process. This argument underpins a recent comment by Tanigaki Sadakazu, Japan's minister of finance, who quoted the former finance minister Miyazawa Ki'ichi to the effect that now that Japan has caught up with the West, there is no longer an image of what the people's lifestyle (*kokumin seikatsu*) should be like, and that as a result there is at present no desire to invest. According to Miyazawa (and Tanigaki), it is up to politicians to create such an image.[15]

I should stress here again that my aim in rehearsing these arguments is not to commit myself to any particular image of the Japanese national character. Determining whether the Japanese are in fact insular xenophobes with a pathological dependence on regulation is not the point. The point,

14. See, for instance, Ohmae Ken'ichi, cited in Sakakibara (1998).
15. Tanigaki, interviewed in Yamaguchi (2001); the quotation is from p. 128. Amaya (1994, 235) makes a similar argument.

rather, is to show that for many people committed to the liberalization and deregulation of Japan, both inside and outside the country, Japan's national character is perceived to be profoundly illiberal. The idea that there is something about Japanese society and psychology that generates resistance to laissez-faire economics is not limited to defenders of Japan's existing political economy or to proponents of *Nihonjinron* theories of cultural uniqueness. It is shared, rather, by liberalizers themselves. Ironically, the perceived need for cultural transformation in order to bring about liberalism may be greater with reference to capitalist Japan than it was in postcommunist Eastern Europe. The concept of economic nationalism—referring, in this section, to the ways in which ideas about national identity influence economic policy—thus seems to be highly relevant for an understanding of the way that liberalization is being promoted in Japan. Indeed, Japanese "liberalization," requiring the reeducation of the Japanese populace under (in some formulations) the guidance of the state, is a rather strange example of the breed.

Toward a New Model?

In making the above argument, I attempted to steer clear of any positive claims regarding Japan's "national character," preferring to focus instead on the claims that are made about it by reformers. Now I will make a bolder claim about the relationship between Japan's political economy and Japanese national identity. It is widely assumed that the postwar success of the Japanese economy constituted a source of great pride (which in the late 1980s turned into hubris) for the Japanese people.[16] This pride, moreover, emerged not simply from the sense that the Japanese had created one of the world's foremost economies, but from the feeling that economic success was directly derived from the Japanese national character. Japan's labor relations, for instance, and the *keiretsu* style of economic organization, were taken to be expressions of fundamental characteristics of Japanese social relations, group loyalty, and capacities to create lasting interpersonal bonds.[17] The prolonged economic stagnation of the 1990s has, of course, shaken both pride in the economy and the Japanese sense of how the country's "unique" social relations were able to create a superior economy. George Crane has outlined the problem nicely (1999, 217): "In the boom years of the 1980s Japanese success was interpreted in some quarters as a manifestation of a unique national character, which has made the recession of the

16. Itoh (2000, 14), for instance, contends that the economic system had "become the principal symbol of national pride" in Japan.
17. It is not particularly significant here that many of the relevant aspects of Japanese culture are in fact of quite recent provenance; see Johnson (1982) and, on invented traditions in Japan more generally, Vlastos (1997).

1990s something akin to an identity crisis: how can we decline when we are destined to succeed?" Indeed, much of the criticism of Japanese *sakoku* mentality and preference for regulation may be seen as a backlash against the assumption that Japan's economic success proceeded directly from Japan's cultural characteristics. While most Japanese would not accept the more dramatic of these claims, it is certainly the case that Japan's economic crisis has been interwoven with a crisis in the understanding of what Japan's national culture is and what it entails for the economy.

While the mainstream IPE literature on economic nationalism has, as noted above, tended to focus primarily on statist and protectionist economic policies, it is difficult not to see the tight connections drawn in Japan between national character and the organization and success of the economy as another form of economic nationalism, albeit one that preoccupies sociologists and anthropologists more than political economists. It is thus possible to see the 1990s as having dealt a blow to Japanese economic nationalism, not only in the statist, IPE sense, but also in the more sociological and identity-oriented sense. The Japanese are now profoundly uncertain about the connections between their culture and their economy. I would prefer, however, to examine this crisis of identity not so much in terms of what it says about the collapse of Japan's postwar political economy as in terms of what it implies for efforts to carry out reform and build a new economic system. In Japan at present there is a widespread sense that some kind of profound reform is required in order to pull the economy out of its slump: hence Koizumi's incredible popularity during 2001. There is an equally strong sense, however, that this reform cannot simply involve importing Anglo-Saxon socioeconomic institutions, and that Japan's political economy must remain in some important sense "Japanese": hence the vagueness of Koizumi's proposals, which most analysts agree was key to his popularity.[18]

There is virtually no agreement on what a reformed but still "Japanese" political economy would look like. Indeed, I would argue that the failure to reconcile these three issues—the sense that reform is necessary, the desire that it be "Japanese" reform, and the difficulty of imagining precisely what such reform would entail—contributed profoundly to the reform deadlock of the 1990s. In this sense, then, it is not so much the Japanese understanding of the connections between national identity and political economy that is relevant for the reform debate, but rather the *lack* of such an understanding. In the absence of more inspiring efforts by intellectuals and political parties to create such a vision, it is difficult to imagine reform moving forward quickly.

18. For two examples of the desire for specifically "Japanese" reform, see Tett (2003, 194–95, 275–76).

Japan's "miraculous" economic development in the century following the Meiji Restoration is widely considered to be the most successful example of economic nationalism in world history. The slow-motion crisis of the Japanese economy during the 1990s has thus led many commentators to argue that economic nationalism has no place in a global economy and that Japan will return to prosperity only by embracing liberalization and deregulation. Whatever successes Japan's policies may have brought about in the past, the age of economic nationalism is now over. This argument does not necessarily imply that Japan will in fact adopt liberal policies and "converge" on the ideal-typical Anglo-Saxon political economy; it does mean, however, that to the extent that Japan becomes liberal, it will abandon economic nationalism, and to the extent that it remains committed to nationalist economic policies, it will continue to be illiberal. Economic nationalism and liberalization/deregulation are thus seen to be in a zero-sum relationship. In this chapter, I have suggested that recent developments in the theorization of economic nationalism indicate that this may not be the case. Just as Vogel (1996) has shown that the relationship between liberalization and economic regulation is not zero-sum, and that "freer markets" can in fact require "more rules," so I have argued that economic nationalism can in fact support liberalization. It is thus possible that "freer markets" can accompany "more economic nationalism"—or, at any rate, that they can be consistent with economic nationalist goals.

In this chapter I have used recent work in IPE to make two claims for the continued relevance of economic nationalism in Japan's political economy. In the first section, I stuck fairly closely to the traditional sense of economic nationalism in IPE but emphasized not the specific policies that have been associated with the concept but rather the goals that it prioritizes—for instance, the survival of the nation in a competitive international system and the promotion of key industrial sectors. Focusing on these motivations, and contrasting them with what I characterized as "liberal reasons for liberalization," I argued that much economic liberalization and deregulation in Japan is in fact consistent with, rather than inimical to, the goals of economic nationalism. I also suggested that much pro-liberalization rhetoric in Japan is framed as a plea for citizens to make sacrifices on behalf of the nation, rather than in terms of the benefits of liberalization. While I do not want to imply that Japan's government is currently pursuing a coherent economic nationalist strategy in world politics—it is too fragmented to be able to do so—I do argue that much of the motivation behind liberalization, for instance in pro-liberalization ministries like METI, is compatible with traditional understandings of nationalist goals.

We might note here that such nationalist motivations for liberalization are not restricted to Japan. In an article on the relationship between foreign direct investment, economic liberalization, and democratization in China,

Mary Gallagher has argued that the massive flows of FDI that China has received have contributed to reformulating ideological debates in a way that supports further economic liberalization. Gallagher argues that most post-communist transitions run into ideological difficulties because moves to privatize the economy are framed in terms of a debate between public and private ownership that threatens core principles of the regime's legitimacy. Thus "the debate over privatization leads to mortal divisions both within the party-state and between the state and society" (Gallagher 2002, 359). The competitive pressure that foreign firms in China exert on Chinese firms, however, means that in China it has been possible to reformulate the debate in a way that stresses not the public-private dichotomy but rather the competition between Chinese national industry and foreign industry. In this debate, which does not explicitly call the core principles of the socialist state into question, privatization is seen to be necessary "so that Chinese 'national industry' . . . can be revitalized and strengthened to meet its global competition" (361). While Gallagher does not explicitly discuss the concept of economic nationalism, her case that privatization in China is being promoted for nationalist reasons resonates with the claims made in the first part of this chapter.

In the second section, I moved further away from the traditional IPE understanding of economic nationalism to explore connections between political economy and national identity in Japan. I focused on the extent to which reformers, in Japan and abroad, identify elements of the Japanese "national character" that are likely to stand in the way of liberalization and deregulation. The ideas that Japanese are insular and that they tend to accede to, and even expect, high levels of regulation in their lives are common in reform discourse, and these ideas have shaped the kinds of proposals that reformers have made (biasing them toward calls for sweeping reform of Japan's entire social system and of Japanese psychology) and have led the government to implement specific pro-internationalization policies like the JET Program and the Ten Million Program. I also argued in this section that an identity crisis regarding the connections between national identity and a failing economy, in combination with a strong desire to maintain some elements of "Japaneseness" in the economy, have slowed movement toward a new economic system. Whatever one thinks of the necessity of economic liberalization in Japan, then, economic nationalism—both as a set of state goals and as an understanding of the connections between the economy and national identity—will continue to be highly salient in Japan.

Part III

Monetary Policy, Liberalism,
and Economic Nationalism

6

(Germany)

Nationalist Undercurrents in German Economic Liberalism

Klaus Müller

FS2

A reconsideration of economic nationalism derives its significance from two sets of claims. The first set comprises globalist claims, according to which in a world of free-flowing capital, ideas, and people, nationalism is an outdated ideology. The second set comprises (neo)realist conceptions of international relations and trade that analyze national economic policy in terms of theories of endogenous growth or strategic trade. Both sets of claims are problematic. The globalist claim that national affiliations have been replaced by transnational spaces, practices, flows, and identities is surely exaggerated. A home bias can be observed even in the most globalized financial markets: U.S. investors hold only a small part of their equity wealth in foreign stock markets, much less than would be required by rational risk management (Lewis 1999). Border effects, that is, preferences for domestic goods over imported ones, work in the border regions of Canada and the United States as well as inside the European Union (OECD 2000, 179–82). Thus, some nationalism seems to be present even in supposedly rational decision making by investors and consumers. As for the second set of claims, economic nationalism cannot be reduced to its neomercantilist rationalizations in terms of national competitiveness. While there may be some theoretical models to justify export promotion, industrial policy, or protecting sensitive industries, most of these policies are in practice of no "strategic" advantage at all (Krugman 1996). French films, Japanese rice, or German coal will never be competitive. Thus if there is something "national" in economic nationalism, there must be an additional dimension associated with it according to which "national sensitivity" makes more sense in those sectors than for tariffs on steel, meat, or shoes. This dimension is usually related to sentiments of identity, autonomy, unity, pride, prestige, and distinctiveness, if not superiority or uniqueness, and may be part of the cultural code of a society.

If we accept this understanding, there nevertheless remains an open question: how exactly can we relate national identities and symbolic systems to economic liberalism? Conceptually this is no easy problem. Classical liberal economic theory had no place for nations or even nationalism, while nationalists seldom had a sense for economic affairs. Modern economic theory conceptualizes the economy as a subsystem of society governed by rationality, efficiency, and growth. This conception leaves no room for the role of national identity, which is not necessarily instrumental but whose meanings and symbols receive their motivating power from the sphere of ultimate values (Hayes 1928).

Postwar West Germany is an instructive case to examine how economic liberalism and nationalism work together. It also illustrates that nationalism is not necessarily expressed in an overt manner, like "a flag which is being consciously waved with fervent passion," but may be "banalized" into everyday routines, like "the flag hanging unnoticed on the public building" (Billig 1995, 8). I will argue that in the Federal Republic of Germany, economic liberalism has been the main "nationalizing mechanism" (Pickel 2003) for half a century, even though historical and political contexts during that period changed rather drastically. I proceed in three steps, which correspond to these changing contexts. I start with the surprising liberalist turn that West Germany took in the late 1940s. A radical currency reform and a set of liberalizing policies set the stage for an unexpected recovery. Interestingly, Germany's so-called social market economy after World War II was a forerunner of economic liberalism at a time when Britain and the United States were relying on macroeconomic management. More important than the limited economic content of this concept was its association with a form of socioeconomic organization that became the prime object of national pride and identity. In the next section, I consider the second dimension of German economic nationalism, which emerged after the country's "economic miracle." Monetary competition in the post–Bretton Woods era promoted the deutsche mark (DM) to a world currency, which the German public cherished as a common good of paramount significance. The Bundesbank's leadership in European monetary affairs nurtured a German monetary nationalism, whereas the rest of Europe had to bear the deflationary consequences of the German "stability culture" far into the 1990s. Why then was Germany prepared to give up its monetary supremacy and become part of a currency union in which it has no more say than Luxembourg? The final section contrasts two interpretations of this event, which pose a serious challenge for realist models of "national capabilities" in terms of a rational state utility function. On the one hand, Germany may have fallen back into traditional political nationalism: its currency was the international price to be paid for national unity, even though the burden of unification made it the "sick man of Europe" in terms of employment and growth. On the other hand, the advent of the Euro may signal an important step beyond the monetary sovereignty of nation states. Whether this marks the beginning of a postnational European identity or that of a European economic nationalism remains to be seen.

"Economic Miracle" and "Social Market Economy"— Foundations of German Economic Nationalism

The emergence of a German brand of economic liberalism was the most significant and most surprising turn in German politics after 1945. Until then, German nationalism was associated with the collectivist methods of a *Staatswirtschaft:* strongly opposed to British individualism, characterized by an understanding of international economic competition as war by other means, cartelized industries and a work force disciplined in a quasi-militaristic manner (Greenfeld 2001a, 218–23). On the one hand, the highly organized structure of the German economy and its authoritarian features were held responsible for the rise of Nazism in the late Weimar Republic (Parsons 1942); On the other, Lenin took Germany's planned organization of industry as the latest stage in capitalist management practice and as a role model for a socialist economy.

Against this background, it seemed rather unlikely that economic liberalism would become the strategic formula for a reconstructed Germany. That this nevertheless happened against strong opposition from both sides of the political spectrum is understandable in the historical context of the postwar era, which also explains why a political nationalism was not an available option. The situation in which Germany found itself after 1945 was depressed in every sense of the term: the country was destroyed and divided, most of its political culture was devalued, and its leading intellectuals had either died or emigrated. Conservatives spoke of a national catastrophe, social democrats and socialists of the catastrophe of nationalism.

The latter interpretation became dominant, at least in the long run. Even today most Germans do not feel that they constitute a normal society. "National identity" in political or even cultural terms is anathema. If asked to define Germany's national interest, most politicians of any party would probably answer: the interest and the future of Germany is Europe. This political skepticism in defining a national identity is reflected in German social science theory. Jürgen Habermas, who a quarter of a century ago posed the question of whether complex societies could develop an identity at all, offered an answer that became part of Germany's public philosophy: the only possible way to organize politics in a globalized world takes the form of a postnational democracy. Old-fashioned nationalism, then, is replaced by a "constitutional patriotism"—the pride to be part of a democratic society

(Habermas 1998, chap. 4). From this point of view the German catastrophe refuted the possibility of a German nation-state, and of the nation-state as an object of collective identification. In a survey reported in the *Economist* of November 8, 2003, only 19 percent of those asked in 2001 if they were proud to be German answered in the affirmative, compared to 80 percent in an American sample.

Nevertheless, most Europeans do not seem to be prepared to take this German "negative nationalism" very seriously. As A. J. McAdams notes (1997, 282), "In a world in which many states would prefer to justify their entitlement to special treatment by underscoring their exceptionality, the Germans' obsession with wanting to be perceived as 'just like everybody else' may look anomalous." When Helmut Kohl assured Margaret Thatcher that he was a European first, she is said to have remarked how terribly German he was. Why, in fact, should the extreme experience of Germany be relevant for other countries at all?

If national self-denial is typically German, it should be understood as a symptom: national identity is not articulated in a straightforward way, it is built into the political economy. The grand ideological formula that helped the Germans regain self-confidence in the immediate postwar era was the "economic miracle" and the associated doctrine of "social market economy."

The historical reality of the "economic miracle" can be summed up in a few words. In the short span of four years after policies of economic liberalism were launched in 1948, the West German economy reached a positive trade balance, which it has maintained ever since. Also, the current account was positive for most of the years since 1951, the year in which prewar levels of GDP and industrial productivity were reestablished. Most spectacular, of course, were the extraordinary growth rates averaging 5.6 percent a year between 1950 and 1965, which were considerably above the OECD level. From 1950 to 1973 West Germany realized the highest growth among all Western economies (Maddison 2001, 186). In addition, this development was accompanied by the lowest inflation rates in the world. No one had expected this in 1945. Standard explanations of German "supergrowth" usually refer to the currency reform in 1948 and the accompanying set of internal deregulations, helped by the Marshall Plan aid, catch-up processes to U.S. productivity levels, technology transfer, and the reconstruction of international trade (Carlin 1996). Other studies demonstrate, however, that German industries were not as devastated as widely believed (Abelshauser 1983).

More significant than the economic data and explanations in the present context is that the economic miracle became the founding myth of the West German identity—a myth that lived on even after the economy lost its momentum in the late 1960s and after Ludwig Erhard, architect of economic liberalism, was removed as head of government. And this is where economic nationalism came in. Three factors in what constituted a new West German national identity were more important than growth per se.

First, the currency reform which introduced the deutsche mark (DM) was perceived as a radically new start (*Stunde Null*). The drastic depreciation of the Reichsmark was conceived as a clear break with an inglorious past. The new currency, which preceded the constitution of the Federal Republic by nearly a year, had a deep and lasting impact on the future course of Germany. Economically the black, gray, and barter markets dried up immediately thanks to stabilized monetary expectations; literally overnight shop windows were filled with goods. Politically, the establishment of the DM deepened the rift between West Germany and Soviet-occupied East Germany by signaling that the West would prefer freedom to unity. Designed in the United States and managed by an independent central bank, the DM was incompatible with a planned economy. A separate currency reform in the East, and thus competing monetary regimes, provoked the first Cold War clash in Germany: the Soviet blockade of Berlin in 1948. Socially, the initial endowment of all West Germans with an equal amount of deutsche marks symbolized a common starting point into a new life and laid the ground for the social mythology of a society beyond classes and social strata (*nivellierte Mittelstandsgesellschaft*) (Schelsky 1954, 393).

Second, the growth rates of the 1950s not only introduced an unknown consumerism into German society but were interpreted as an act of salvation. Intellectuals diagnosed an "inability to mourn" about the victims of the recent past and observed that economic restoration came together with a "characteristic new self-esteem." For lack of either a positive political identity or an acceptance of the Nazist catastrophe as a specific challenge to the national society, "libidinous energies were concentrated in the economic sphere" (Mitscherlich and Mitscherlich 1967, 24–45). In fact, public sentiment was preoccupied by the country's wondrous rise from the ruins to its partnership in the newly founded European Council and the Montan Union in 1951. A meteoric rise of this kind, then, encouraged a certain exceptionalism: "I think it can and should not be regarded as arrogance if I say that hardly any other country ever had to deal with such a gigantic task from the position of complete chaos as it was incumbent upon us in Germany" (Erhard 1953, 132). Thus, a movie like Kurt Hoffmann's *Wir Wunderkinder* (1958) was not entirely a parody. In a sense, the religious connotations of an "economic miracle" were taken seriously. They constituted a modern equivalent to the Protestant ethic, which takes economic success as a sign of salvation. A people achieving such extraordinarily high growth rates cannot be totally damned. Spelled out in the profane everyday language of that time: "We are somebody, again!"

Third, the most enduring aspect of the first phase of German economic nationalism was subsumed under the label "social market economy." The principles of the social market economy had been formulated since the early 1930s by the so-called *Ordo* liberal school, whose proponents tried to reconcile spontaneous market processes with rules that would allow for a socially equitable order.[1] The political message was rather elementary: the state has to provide for an adequate price system, a stable currency, and free competition in open markets. To achieve this aim, the rule of law was to be guaranteed, especially with respect to private property and the freedom of contract. Economic and legal policies are required to keep the markets free from organized interests and power groups. If the regulatory framework proposed by the *Ordo* liberals left room for wide interpretation, it was clear that economic policies should strictly conform with the rules of the market. So the "social" in the social market economy was not to be attained by political means but would emerge spontaneously from a properly functioning competitive order. On the other hand, markets were not conceived as "self-organized." A strong state was indispensable to reign in a destructive pluralism of interest groups and to provide public goods within the limits of "subsidiarity" (Eucken 1952, 348), the principle according to which lower units of society or individuals should retain as much responsibility as possible.

The interdependence of the economic system with the orders of state, law, and society was the core of the *Ordo* doctrine. The holistic promise of an order beyond demand and supply, which would transcend collectivism, class conflicts, and political cleavages made it suitable as an integral ideology flexible enough to cover a broad political spectrum. According to common understanding, this formula meant that market failures had to be corrected by state intervention, the tax system, and social welfare. But this was plausible only by projecting the 1970s back to the 1950s. For not until the 1970s, then under a Social Democratic government, were social reform policies tackled seriously. In the early 1950s French proposals that market integration should be complemented by a progressive harmonization of social security legislation were rejected in Bonn as the attempt to "burden German industry with the French social security system" (cited in Mahant 2003, 16).

In the 1950s the "social market economy" was designed for ideological purposes, especially the containment of widespread anticapitalist sentiments, not only among trade unions and the Social Democrats but also

---

1. The insistence on a strong state above society is the main difference between German "neoliberalism" and classical liberalism of the nineteenth century or Hayek's individualist approach. In fact, although Hayek promoted many members of the *Ordo* circle abroad and an article by him opened the first volume of *ORDO*, the circle's yearbook, in 1948 he remained highly suspicious of the "social" in the "social market economy" as a backdoor for socialism. It is not necessary here to discuss the wider context of this doctrine; for this see Zweig (1980), Starbatty (1997), the—mostly apologetic—contributions to Peacock and Willgerodt (1989a, 1989b), and, from a critical point of view, Haselbach (1991).

among many Christian Democrats. If market forces and social values could be reconciled, there would be no need for a socialism of any kind. More specifically, the vision of a "social market" proved quite helpful in preventing certain key industries from being nationalized—as envisaged by some Länder constitutions. Thus, the West German government after 1948 chose an economic "*Sonderweg*" beyond the German "Keynesianism before Keynes," which had emerged after the Great Depression and also in contrast to international postwar Keynesianism (Abelshauser 1991, 12). Germany, as Andrew Shonfield observed, was "not in the mainstream of modern capitalism" (Shonfield 1965, 273). Above all, the social market economy was set against East Germany's planned economy. National unity was to be achieved by economic rather than political means. This meant that if you could grow faster than the newly established planned economy in the East, you would not have to roll back communism by military means. The government in Bonn clearly preferred what it called the "magnet theory": sooner or later prosperity would attract the East Germans to the West, thereby delegitimizing communism.

On the other hand, *Ordo* liberalism was hardly a theory in the strict sense of the term. As even admirers concede, the writings of its proponents "may sound vague and strange to Anglo-American mathematical model builders" (Zweig 1980, 24). Probably the authors of the doctrine would agree: according to their self-perception, the social market doctrine was "admired all over the world" not only for its singular success but even more so for "supraeconomic, state-sociological and spiritual reasons" (Rüstow 1957, 75). Combining the medieval concept of *ordo*—i.e., justice counterposed to the *perversio, corruptio,* and *malum* of the world— with the nineteenth-century concern about the "social question" and the Austro-liberal's aversion to collectivism made for an unusual syncretism: "tricky in its argumentation, dogmatic in its inspiration, very German" (Hentschel 1996, 73).

Had it not captured the ideological predispositions of postwar West Germany, the social market doctrine would have probably remained a curiosity. Under the peculiar circumstances of the time, in particular the simultaneous rejection of Nazism and communism, the doctrine became the new social consensus of the 1950s: in 1959 the Social Democrats shelved their Marxist tradition and made friends with markets and private property. The most effective boost, however, came from the real achievements of economic reconstruction. While British and American economists feared a sharp decline into unemployment and deflation—a scenario that gave support to Keynesian options in both countries (Hutchison 1979, 432)—the German government ascribed the surprising revival of the country's economy to its liberalization policy, which it had pursued against the advice and will of the allied administration. The social market doctrine appeared post factum not only as an attractive political slogan but as the proper explanation for postwar success.

The surprisingly successful postwar reconstruction boosted its ideologues' excessive self-importance. The German model was recommended not only to other countries but to whole continents if not the whole world. "We are the only state in the free world," Rüstow wrote, "whose government has a sound economic programme, while all other governments have to struggle with the changing compromises of a pluralism, known to us only now too well from the Weimar Republic" (Rüstow 1957, 75). Wilhelm Röpke made the nexus between economic conception and national dignity evident by presenting the social market doctrine as a "noble way" to compensate the international community for the damage done by the Nazi war economy; and he could not help but feel deep satisfaction in history's judgment. After having overcome their mistrust and hostility, the victors of World War II were emulating the superior model of the former enemy. Britain, for example, if it followed Germany's counterapproach to the "inflationary-collectivist mixed systems," could get off the road to Moscow along which Labour's "welfare-statist policies of nationalization" were taking it. In the late 1950s, Röpke observed (1961, 5–6), members of the American cabinet came to Bonn to ask for support for the dollar "with an impetuousness like capital-hungry developing countries." And if the economic integration of Europe should proceed, then the most natural approach to overcome the "backwardness" of countries like France and Italy would be to adopt the most advanced German program (Rüstow 1957, 75–76).[2]

All these statements clearly expressed the most deeply rooted sentiments attached to one's nation—the sense of being superior to others—now, for obvious reasons, not articulated in historical, cultural, or political terms but referring to the nation's economic organization. The primacy of an economic identity of the nation was also reflected in public opinion. In 1959, 33 percent of West Germans (compared to 7 percent of Americans) took pride in their economy, while only 7 percent (compared to 85 percent in the United States) cherished their political system (Greiffenhagen 1997, 71).

---

2. These are only some examples of the pompous self-confidence of the doctrine's proponents, arrogant enough to teach the U.S. Treasury about the "heavy sins" of their economic policy (Röpke 1961, 7). Anticipating the "Washington Consensus" by three decades, Röpke denied the special claims of development economics; the same "neoliberalism" that made possible the German success story should lift the dead hand of the state in Latin America and India (ibid.). In fact, Ludwig Erhard in his later years toured in South America to advise the governments in Brazil, Argentine, and elsewhere how to install inflation-free market economies (Hentschel 1996, 904). With some success: Sanchez de Losada, who enforced the first so-called shock therapy to end high inflation in Bolivia in 1985 named Erhard as his mentor (Skidelsky 1995, 140). Maes (2002) explains the long history of the German-French EMU controversy starting since the late 1950s not only by different views on economic policymaking, but also against the background of different "metacultures", i.e., national traditions, regarding the role of the state, elite formation and ideas about a future Europe.

German Monetary Nationalism: Deutsche Mark and Bundesbank

While the primary identification of West Germans with their economy was based on actual economic performance, the second act of German economic nationalism was played out in the monetary sphere. As exceptional growth rates faded with the end of the "economic miracle," class conflicts, political protest, and rising unemployment clouded the postwar consensus of a wealth-generating "export nation." Clearly, all countries had to adapt their policies during the turbulence of the 1970s, chiefly the end of the Bretton Woods system and the energy crises. Germany, however, managed to redefine its economic nationalism even under radically changing historical conditions by switching to a "DM nationalism." Germany's monetary regime rested on two pillars: the Bundesbank, which was one of the most remarkable institutions of the Federal Republic, and a sophisticated, if implicit, sociopolitical mechanism for coordinating monetary policies with collective bargaining and government budgets.

The Bundesbank's enormous authority was usually explained with reference to its formal autonomy from political interference and its mandate to keep inflation low. The Bundesbank Act of 1957 made it the most independent central bank in the world, which took "safeguarding the currency" as its prime objective. After the breakdown of the Bretton Woods system, the bank led the international trend toward monetary targeting as a new strategy. Monetary stability was declared the prime goal of economic policy, now pursued by a Social Democratic government at considerable cost in terms of employment and growth. But no government—until the 1990s—dared to try macroeconomic populism in order to win elections. The enormous power of the Bundesbank was demonstrated by the fact that three German chancellors lost their majority in parliament after disputes over monetary policies (Marsh 1992, chap. 7).

The extraordinary authority of the Bundesbank, which, unlike the U.S. Federal Reserve, was responsible to neither the electorate nor elected politicians, could hardly be explained by its legal standing alone. Notwithstanding the conventional view, the Bundesbank Act had no constitutional status; in addition, the Bundesbank was required by law to support the government's general economic policy. Generally, a central bank's independence is unsustainable if it is not politically supported, whatever its legal status (Posen 1993). One might think that a consensus on monetary stability was established easily, since the advantages of a strong currency seem so obvious. In fact, steadily improving terms of trade delivered cheap imported goods and cheap holidays in foreign countries. On the other hand, competitive exports could be secured only by dampening labor costs and through strong productivity growth, which in many cases simply meant lost jobs. Ever since the Bundesbank switched to monetary targeting in December 1974, Germany has seen nothing like the growth rates and employment levels of the economic miracle days. There is no conclusive macroeconomic evidence for the claim that autonomous central banks whose primary mandate is price stability deliver real growth (Stiglitz 1998; Bruno and Easterly 1998). Why then should trade unions be receptive to the policies of a central bank that never compromised on employment and growth? And why have politicians shied away from altering the Bundesbank Act even though this would have required only a simple parliamentary majority?

Here the second layer of German monetary nationalism came into play: a general societal and political consensus on a strong currency and low inflation, even if this implied sacrifices and fiscal restrictions. The trade unions and the Social Democrats shared the concern for the stability of the national economy and its position on international capital markets. Competitiveness vis-à-vis the world's other leading economies became a collective good in the self-declared "export nation" and has remained a political dogma to the present day—even among those who have had to bear the major burden of repeatedly enforced deflations. Though concern about the general wage level in the economy is not the primary task of trade unions in Germany's highly centralized system of collective bargaining, they accepted the responsibility to keep labor costs down. As a "social partner" in the nation's "productivity pact" they traded moderate wage increases for a rather egalitarian wage structure, thereby fostering profitability and monetary stability as well as reaffirming the social market ideology. In this way the corporatist traditions of Germany were of benefit for a credible and stable monetary policy.[3]

"Stability culture," as even its proponents admit, is a diffuse concept. Though easily identified empirically by the inflation rate as its "most important indicator," it is meant to refer to types of cultural patterns, predis-

---

3. Herr (1991, 237–39). More generally the institutional design and stability of central bank autonomy is path dependent on a nation's capital-labor relations, especially the wage-bargaining system (Hall and Franzese 1998), legislative-government relations (Bernhard 1998) and specific historical events. The individualism-collectivism axis in Greenfeld's typology of nationalisms (Greenfeld 2001b, 261) is reflected in different ways (decentralized/centralized) to coordinate wage bargaining via trade-union and/or employer organizations, which in turn are favorable for certain monetary arrangements. The often-cited historical reasons that made the German public especially inflation-averse, namely, the devaluation of their savings between 1920 and 1923 and after 1945, are spurious, since this happened in other countries too. "Typically German" was to turn the underlying causes of these inflations, namely the costs of two world wars, into a question of central bank autonomy—a clear displacement in the psychoanalytical sense. In reality, the Reichsbank, though independent since 1922, fueled the hyperinflation of 1923 by following erroneous theories. The selective memory of the German central bank mythology ignores that the darkest episode of German history was prepared in part by a fatal monetary policy the consequences of which are trenchantly summed up by Wilhelm Hankel (1972: 242): "With the inflation from 1920 to 1924 Germany caused damage only to itself, whereas the deflation from 1930 to 1932, on the other hand, did damage to the whole world."

positions, and institutions that allow for cooperation and mutual trust across class lines (Bofinger et al. 1998, 16). The German desire to lend metaphysical depth to strategic questions of monetary politics is well known. Well aware that this may sound to some people as "currency religion" (as to Andre Glucksmann, *Rheinischer Merkur,* September 3, 1993), Issing seems to argue that mere technical knowledge even in strictly rule-bound systems is not sufficient: "Ethical categories and moral aspects are expressed, first, at the level of the central bank constitution and, second, at the level of individual and collective behaviour within the prescribed institutional framework" (Issing 1995, 13). Cultural distinctiveness, accordingly, made the difference between Germany and its strike-plagued neighbors. Country-specific attitudes toward monetary stability were held responsible for diverging macroeconomic developments—which confirms Schumpeter's dictum (1970, 1) that "the often passionate and always great interest in practical questions of the monetary system and monetary value can be accounted for only by the fact that a people's monetary system reflects everything this people strives for, does, suffers, and *is.*" What this meant in terms of national exceptionalism was made explicit by a manifesto signed by a group of prominent German professors articulating their concerns about thoughtlessly giving away the DM for the sake of Europe: "A consensus to give priority to the stability of prices, as traditionally displayed in Germany, has so far not existed anywhere in Europe" (Bofinger et al. 1993).

In fact, the Bundesbank claimed the most prestigious role in the institutional framework of German "stability culture." While the trade unions were usually held responsible for unemployment and inflation, the DM and the Bundesbank's management always remained the public's central object of identification. According to survey data, the institutional trust in the Bundesbank (2.1) ranked above law courts (1.4), the parliament (0.9) and the government (0.6) (Balkhausen 1992, 87). This was confirmed by a later survey on "stability culture" that covered political actors, the business elite, the banking sector, interest groups, the trade unions, and the economic profession (Bofinger et al. 1998, 128–46). Not surprisingly, most people erroneously believed in the constitutional status of the Bundesbank's autonomy. Use of the term "monetary constitution" to refer to the economy was not just the technical jargon of economists; it also reflected the common people's attachment to their currency.[4] Monetary nationalism thus balanced the advantages and disadvantages of a strong German mark. Feelings of pride in the domestic currency were enhanced by feelings of superiority—

4. The unique attachment to the national currency is observed by foreigners with some perplexity: "It is safe to say that no other country in the world enjoys quite the same sacred status in its country's iconography. . . . Only in Germany is the coin of the realm the country's veritable national symbol, more exalted than either the national flag or the splayed black German eagle" (Bonfante 1998).

not al least vis-à-vis East Germany. It was easy to compare the relative strength
of West Germany and East Germany by the exchange rate of their currencies. During the 1970s the DM had about four times the value of the East
German mark. No wonder then that the former became the parallel currency in the East and a symbol that wealth could be brought about by choosing the right money.[5]

More impressive for the outside world than public opinion data was the
manner in which the DM paved the way for Germany's return to international politics. In fact, wage restraint for the sake of monetary stability and
public affection for the faceless bureaucracy of a central bank is only one indicator of a nation's identification with a strong currency. This identification was supported by the structural power exercised by German monetary
policy in relation to other nations. The external power of the Bundesbank
unfolded with the transition to flexible exchange rates: "The breakdown of
Bretton Woods was in part due to the extreme relative credibility of the Bundesbank's commitment to price stability, and the concomitant appreciation
of the Deutsche Mark" (Posen 1997, 11). Now even the United States was
confronted with an uncompromising Bundesbank that was not prepared to
cooperate in stabilizing the weakened dollar. Monetary targeting as the pre-
dominant central bank strategy explicitly introduced in late 1974 implied a
nationally focused view on the domestic labor markets and public house-
holds. The last attempt to coordinate international monetary policy brought
forward by the U.S. administration in 1978 was blocked by an intransigent
central bank. In the complacent account of Otmar Emminger (1986, 384),
then its director: "The Bundesbank asserted itself at that time and no agreements on target zones for exchange rates were made."[6] When Paul Volcker,
head of the Federal Reserve Board, arrived in Hamburg in 1979 he "was lec-
tured on the need for stern adjustment measures first by Helmut Schmidt"
(Helleiner 1994, 133).

While there was no intention to compete with the dollar as world currency, DM hegemony characterized European monetary relations. The
mark was the only currency that was not depreciated, was the second most
frequently used international money, and became the anchor currency of
the Exchange Rate Mechanism (ERM). When David Marsh characterized
the Bundesbank as "the bank that rules Europe" (Marsh 1992), this was
surely exaggerated. To make his story even more forceful he mobilized a
widespread British perception of German nationalism when he wrote that

5. To be sure, DM colonization was initiated in the East with East Berlin's decision to sell
high-quality goods on its own territory to its own citizens, but only for West German currency.
6. And, like Röpke in 1961, he celebrated the Bundesbank's victory, the latest in a long tradition: "The result was definitely perceived as failure on the American side. . . . In fact, the
German 'singular course of stability' had already started in 1952/53" (Emminger 1986, 396,
35).

"the Bundesbank has replaced the *Wehrmacht* as Germany's best-known and best feared institution, . . . (holding) sway across a larger area of Europe than any German *Reich* in history" (10). Nevertheless, this overstretched rhetoric contained a true core. Given its strong currency and positive current account, Germany could exert considerable power over those European countries that had to cover their trade deficits through German loans. As a critical observer from Italy put it: "Germany has reasons to accumulate financial power for subsidiary objectives of commercial and economic policy: great financial power enables Germany to extend its imperialistic influence by consolidating its sphere of commercial and political hegemony. It is enough to recall the experience of German loans to southern Europe: Italy, Portugal, and now even Turkey." Regarding his own country he could cite Chancellor Helmut Schmidt with the following words: "We have given Italy enough to keep its head above water. . . . It is necessary that a precise division of labour be brought about in Europe" (Parboni 1981, 135). Whatever this meant concretely, Germany was not prepared to squander its external surpluses through expansionary domestic policies. Instead it dictated its own philosophy of monetary stability all over Western Europe, thereby dampening employment and demand.

By this general mechanism, the policy domain of the Bundesbank was extended beyond the borders of the Federal Republic. Since the mid-1980s monetary policy for France, Denmark, Austria, and the Benelux countries was made in Frankfurt. In the 1990s not only the Bundesbank's policy style but also its institutional design was transferred to the European level. The independence of the Bundesbank, widely regarded as the world's most successful central bank of postwar times, was enshrined into the statute of the European Central Bank. In the German public mind this was not at all monetary imperialism but a cultural mission, namely to export the German "stability culture" especially to the South.

How can assertive monetary nationalism be reconciled with the German commitment to European integration? As far as German economic liberalism is concerned, it has always been at odds with European political integration, from the early days of Ludwig Erhard to the final days of the DM. Since the early 1950s Erhard had strongly opposed any institutional form of economic cooperation and preferred currency competition. He suspected that the European Payments Union, which was of great help for Germany around 1950, worked in favor of French statism. While still only minister of commerce and industry he challenged Chancellor Adenauer's foreign policy toward Europe. Clearly, his favorite conception of Europe followed Britain's intergovernmental realism, which he backed against France's supranational inclinations. Against Jean Monet's plans for an economic and political deepening of Europe, Erhard drew up a counterproposal in which he contrasted the "romanticism" of institutional integration with the "functional integration" in restricted economic matters as exemplified by the GATT, IMF, and OECD (see Hentschel 1996, 297–318). No doubt, he would have applauded NAFTA, a pure trade agreement without further political obligations.

In Erhard's days, European integration was in any event a rather limited affair, confined to economic cooperation in a few areas—agriculture, energy, and tariffs. The more integration affected sensitive areas of national sovereignty, the more alternative views on the future of Europe came to the fore. And why, one might ask, did it take thirty years to establish a common currency when it had been planned in some detail as early as 1969? Sensibly enough, Germany countered French ambitions to shape a common monetary policy in a politically nonconfrontational manner. Rather, it simply insisted on a special theory of how monetary union was to be achieved. For a long time Paris had favored the so-called cornerstone theory: a commonly defined monetary policy as the starting point for far-reaching political integration. The Germans, on the other hand, insisted on what they called the crowning theory: only after far-reaching policy coordination and after economic convergence had been achieved would a common currency become viable. Both sides were not very specific on the final shape of a unified Europe. The reason for this strategic ambiguity was continuing economic nationalism on both sides.

German Unification and the Advent of the Euro

How then was it that the euro nevertheless finally did arrive? Had the German tradition of postwar supranationalism, which had always loomed in the background, somehow won a late victory? Is the transnational European Central Bank a definite break with national economic policy? The advent of the euro was rather complicated and followed a dialectical twist. Ironically, the surrender of the deutsche mark was the price the German government was finally willing to pay for the third stage of German economic nationalism: unification.

"Unity" in the most comprehensive and, at the same time, unqualified sense plays a key role in any discourse on national identity as well as economic nationalism (Shulman 2000). One would expect that after decades of partial sovereignty and division Germany would reconstitute, and in this sense "normalize," itself as a nation-state next to others in the redrawn political landscape of post–Cold War Europe. Normalization, in fact, became a highly contested theme: "It is hard to think of a group of contemporary politicians more obsessed with debating their state's normalcy than the Germans. With the opening of the Berlin Wall in November 1989 and the unification of the two German states one year later in October 1990, the theme of normalcy has been an undercurrent to just about every significant policy debate in the Federal Republic of Germany" (McAdams 1997, 282).

Nevertheless, German unification was approached in the typical way: not as a political act, which would have required the convocation of a common constitutional assembly. Germany remained an economically constituted society—though it now became a victim of its own national economic mythology. The drama of unification unfolded in three acts. The first was the belief that the successful currency reform of 1948 could be repeated. Even before the political union was arranged, the Kohl government extended the currency area of the deutsche mark eastward—a move which, no doubt, corresponded to eastern sentiments, since DM nationalism was deeply rooted on both sides of the border. So it was understandable at that time that East Germans confounded the adoption of a strong currency with personal wealth. The West German government, on the other hand, simply believed in the economic myths of the past. As the minutes of government consultations show, the currency union of 1990 was thought to induce a "second economic miracle" in the East.[7] The cost of adjustment to the market was to be financed by the proceeds from the privatization of state-owned enterprises and additional growth. The decision for unity had been made by Helmut Kohl alone, inspired by his transfigured memories of the 1950s and the irresistible idea that he could use national sentiments for his (then doubtful) reelection.

To be sure, economic nationalism was the prevalent mode of self-identification on both sides of the wall and was to become a driving force as well as a burden for "reunification." Like the West, the GDR was primarily integrated economically and not, as Poland or Hungary, by a strong political nationalism (Offe 1996, 138–43). In its foundational phase the regime cleared itself of the blame of Nazism by claiming to represent the "better Germany," which had abolished the classes of industrialists and Prussian aristocrats responsible for the rise of Hitler. But in the late 1950s, encouraged by respectable growth rates over the whole decade, ritualized antifascism was supplemented by Walter Ulbricht's famous promise to catch up with and surpass West Germany. After some trial and error with economic de- and re-centralization, the leadership invented the "identity of economic and social policy," a program that took up the old Bismarckian welfare tradition and mimicked the West's social reforms (Beyme 1977, 24–25). To set incentives for productivity growth and to appease a dissatisfied population that always compared its standard of living to the western neighbor, welfare

---

7. Marsh (1992, chap. 8); for the conditions of the currency reform of 1948 compared to those of the monetary union in 1990, see Smith (1994, 25–34) and Hoffmann (1993, chap. 1).

assistance, housing construction, and pension entitlements were upgraded considerably, and the supply of consumer durables was improved. All this nurtured the impression of a belated East German *Wirtschaftswunder* in the "Golden Seventies," whereas the West fell into stagflation after the first oil crisis (Ritschl 1996, 519).

As György Dalos observed (1993), the elites of the Warsaw Pact states did everything to develop a kind of national pride, mostly at the expense of their neighbors. With the second largest industry and the highest living standard in the socialist world, the GDR cultivated a special feeling of superiority. Always trying hard to present itself as the closest ally of the Soviet Union, East Berlin condemned the economic reforms in Hungary, supported the invasion of Czechoslovakia, and denounced Poland's crisis in the early 1980s as the result of strikes in a politically unreliable socialist country. This "arrogance of the bulwark" (Dalos 1993) came to an absurd conclusion when the East Berlin leadership turned itself against Gorbachev's last reform efforts—with the presumptuous comment that "there was no need for new wallpapers just because a neighbor was redecorating his flat" (cf. Schroeder 1998, 292).

More momentous, since it survived the GDR, was the myth of ranking tenth in the league of the world's industrial states. In 1976, and only in that year, the World Bank made some statistical errors when calculating national income figures for the countries of the world. With some heroic estimates about output and purchasing power, the GDR was placed ahead of Britain (Morgan 1992). East Germany not only used these figures to boost its international reputation but also capitalized on them in international credit markets. Despite declining returns on investment and a growing divergence between productivity and wages, the illusion of economic strength was upheld for some years thanks to external sources: cheap oil from the Soviet Union, credits from the West, and access to the European markets via West Germany. Rather late it became obvious that this path was unsustainable. Severe balance-of-payments crises and a rising debt burden in the 1980 made the GDR more and more externally dependent. Only in the last days of the regime was this reality conceded by a secret report to the politburo of the Socialist Unity Party of Germany (SED). The unacceptable alternative now was to lower the general consumption level by 30 percent or to declare external default and become a client of the IMF (Schürer et al. 1989).

Whether by chance or necessity, reunification came as the recovery of the East's dignity and as fulfillment of Chancellor Kohl nostalgic remembrance of the 1950s. In the "hour of national sentiment" (Habermas 1989) sweeping over Germany in late 1989 everything seemed possible: unity, full national sovereignty, and a "second economic miracle," which would save East Germany from the collapse of the COMECON. Economic calculations like those made in a special report by the Council of Economic Advisers (SVR

1990) seemed pedantic. According to Kohl's famous saying, unity could be purchased using the petty cash for postal expenses. Misguided by false historical analogies, the West German government chose the fatal strategy of "Economic, Monetary, and Social Union"—a formula that might have been issued by the East German politburo. In this way, western and eastern identities, constructed primarily in economic terms on both sides, were short-circuited. By suggesting continuity with the "identity of social and economic policy", on the one hand, and with the "social market economy" under the umbrella of a common currency on the other, the West assumed liability for East Germany's heavily indebted industry and overstretched social security system, which were to become one of the largest burdens of unification (Ritschl 1996, 520).

Introducing the deutsche mark as the new currency was the first step toward unity, predating political unification by several months. This, no doubt, appealed to West German memories of the *Stunde Null* in 1948 and at the same time matched the East Germans long-practiced identification with the DM. At this point, however, West German economic nationalism also lost touch with economic reality and became dysfunctional. Most of the damaging effects of unification can be explained only by a *sacrificium intellectus* in the name of national unity. Nobody would ascribe the same value to the British and the Egyptian currency units just because both are denominated in pounds. This is precisely what happened in Germany in the summer of 1990: the exchange rate was elevated into a national symbol itself, so that large quantities of East German marks were converted into DM at a rate of 1:1. The inflated expectations associated with this operation were aptly described as "Christmas in July" (Heilemann and Jochimson 1993).

In the real world of adjustment, however, a heavy price had to be paid on both sides. East Germany's industry broke down under the weight of its old debts, which now had to be serviced in hard currency. In the first three years of unification, the East German GDP shrank by one third while industrial production declined by 60 percent. Nevertheless, without considering the productivity gap, East German workers—now organized by West German trade unions—insisted on equal pay: converging wages were considered a condition of becoming a "full German." Unfortunately, this economic nationalism from below priced East German work out of the market. Productivity grew only in the early years and is now stagnating at around 59 percent of the western level (Czarnitzki 2003). Despite a slew of counteracting labor market policies, registered unemployment has remained at 20 percent until the present. Economic activity in the West was adversely affected as well. The cost of unification had the effect of a general tax increase as well as rising labor costs. In recent years Germany's growth rate has been one of the lowest in Europe. Even the current account was negative for some years. Today, market wages, unemployment, and growth rates in the West and the East are diverging once again (Burda and Hunt 2001). The sectoral structure of the eastern economy is still distorted, now due not to a planning bureaucracy but to industrial policies, which privileged fixed capital formation while neglecting investment in human capital and service-intensive production (Klodt 2000, 300). Not only compared to the West but also compared to postcommunist Eastern Europe, economic reconstruction remained disappointing despite all subsidies. Take the following comment from the World Bank (2002, 38–39): "Now East Germany seems to suffer from exactly the same phenomenon as the least successful transition economies in the Commonwealth of Independent States—anaemic growth of new enterprises that have been the main drivers of growth elsewhere in transition. . . . The East German case demonstrates how poor policy choices at the start of the transition can undermine even the most favourable environment."

How to explain these poor results in the frame of a once very successful socioeconomic formation? And why have the early mistakes, which could be observed already in the early 1990s, not been rectified in the following years? Why is the German polity across all parties prepared to continue a strategy with disastrous results until the year 2019? Taking the political trends of the 1990s seriously, the political economy of Germany has changed in a way that most Germans were not prepared to face. It needed observers from the outside to remark that a "conspiracy of silence had wrought its fearful work."[8]

In a nearly unnoticed process that altered the rules of the game, two central elements of Germany's socioeconomic system were discarded in favor of national unification (see Müller 1995, 19–33). First, the economic rationale of the social market: in East Germany the "productivity pact" that linked earnings to labor productivity was supplanted by a politically driven program of wage equalization. In 1991 the target date for equal wages in both parts of the country was set for 1996. Characteristically, it was not the strongest industrial trade union, the IG-Metall, that set the pace in wage bargaining in the East but the overstaffed public sector. Since this meant rising labor costs and higher unemployment, the whole system of collective wage bargaining was called into question. Because pensions and unemployment benefits were linked to wages, social expenditures exploded: in 1992 they amounted to 67 percent of East Germany's GDP, and in 1997 were still high at 54 percent. For a while the illusion of a second economic miracle was stabilized by western transfer payments, which amounted to 5 percent of GDP

8. Morgan 1992. The *Times* (London) of October 29, 1992, felt obliged to point out the international repercussions of Germany's self-oriented behavior: "For the past two years, the whole of Europe has paid dearly for the failure of Germany, its pivotal economic power, to put unification on a sound financial footing"; and it prophesied: "the costs of cowardice will be high." For another view from the outside see also the *New York Times*, April 17, 1997: "Bonn's Blank Check Buys Hollow Economy in the East."

annually. From 1990 to 2000 transfers amounted to 770 billion euro; in the same period public debts rose from 40.4 to 60.2 percent of GDP (Sachver-ständigenrat 2003, table 38). Transfers of this volume could be mobilized only if they were defined as a national project. In fact, no party ever risked questioning the primacy of rebuilding East Germany. In the tradition of West German corporatism, policies were put into place, this time not for pro-ductivity growth but for nationalist reasons: a "solidarity pact" for public transfers, a "solidarity surcharge" on income tax, an "employment pact," and recently a "national stability pact" to keep public deficits in the range of the Maastricht criteria. In a sense, welfare socialism was kept alive by transfers from the West—a surely unique constellation, but also unsustainable: "Such a primacy of social thinking and such a strong tension between social pro-tection and economy has never existed in the Western world before, not even in Italy's Mezzogiorno" (Schmidt 1999, 304).

The Kohl government managed these tensions by creative accounting. The public debts resulting from the legacy of the GDR, the currency union, and the running transfer payments to the East were "fanned out," as the Bundesbank complained, into a multitude of shadow budgets (Deutsche Bundesbank 1997, 20). Early on, the Bundesbank gave warning of a debt trap that put other countries participating in the European Monetary Union (EMU) at risk. Not until 2003 was this warning taken seriously. Since then, ironically, a government led by Social Democrats is trying to bring the pub-lic deficits under control—not by spreading the cost of unification more equally via the tax system but by cutting back the welfare state. While taxes in relation to GDP fell to a historical low point in 1997, the unemployment insurance and pension system had to transfer considerable surpluses from the West to the East, which from 1991 to 1997 added up to 95 billion euro—a heavy blow to the foundations of the social market economy: "By shifting parts of the financial consequences of unification into the area of social in-surance the system of security by solidarity was overburdened and, thereby, discredited. In no type of insurance is it possible to join after the damage has occurred. Precisely this, nevertheless, was expected of the public social insurance, which consequently ran into a financial crisis, calling into ques-tion the system of social security" (DIW 1997, 729). This course has also been maintained by Social Democratic governments after Kohl. If the *Agenda 2010*, the cornerstone of the present government's economic pol-icy, will come into effect by 2005, then welfare as the Germans knew it will end by gradually privatizing old-age security and health insurance and by in-troducing elements of "workfare" into the labor market.

Second, for the first time in its history the Bundesbank was forced to back down in a confrontation with the government. Otto Poehl, then its presi-dent, resigned in protest over the monetary union. As was to be expected, the Bundesbank tried to keep monetary expansion at bay by sharply raising interest rates in the early 1990s, thus putting the European currency system under unbearable pressure. The *Economist* was right, after all, in asserting that German unity was the biggest single shock for European unity. And as Helmut Schlesinger (1991) of the Bundesbank had accurately predicted, the experience of unification made European currency union much more difficult. This might have been viewed as a blessing in disguise since the Bundesbank had always been skeptical about the feasibility of EMU in the foreseeable future. The old "coronation theory" had declared a common currency as the final seal of an integrated economic policy, without exactly saying when this stage would arrive. Only by threatening to alter its status could Chancellor Helmut Schmidt bring the Bundesbank to accept the European Monetary System in the 1970s (Smith 1994, 193–94); later Schmidt (1997) sensed that the Bundesbank's strong preconditions for EMU were a hidden agenda for preventing it.

In fact, resistance against EMU was widespread in Germany. Public opinion strongly opposed "sacrificing" the DM on the altar of European unity. In 1992 more than 70 percent of Germans rejected the idea of a common currency; in 1998 two-thirds of the respondents to a survey declared that they would vote against EMU in a referendum (Güllner 1998, 134). East Germans especially saw their newly won monetary self-esteem already endangered: "Most East Germans felt enormously uplifted by possessing the D-Mark. . . . If access to a currency is a gain in quality of life, then loss of that currency is a loss in quality of life."[9] The public's skepticism was backed by some unusual steps, made by prominent members of the economic profession. In 1992 sixty German economists signed a manifesto warning that the Maastricht criteria were too weak to filter out those countries that could not live up to the German stability culture (German economists 1994). In 1998 a group of professors, including a former member of the Bundesbank council, felt obliged to sue the government at the constitutional court: EMU would end Germany's more than 120-year-old tradition of social responsibility and "plunder savers and pensioners." The old rivalry with France was reactivated: "The French understanding of the relations between the central bank and politics is different" (Hankel et al. 1998, 129, 61). Others either feared more generally that EMU would favor the "southern countries of the EU" or simply wanted to keep the Bundesbank's seignorage at home (Sinn 1996).

But at that time the Bundesbank had already lost its secret battle against EMU. True, it had raised discount rates in late 1991 to their highest level in postwar times to fight off the inflationary consequences of unification. Its distinctive role was underlined by the privileged part it played in the EMU

9. So writes Friedrich Schorlemer (1998, 234), a prominent member of the civil rights movement in eastern Germany. On the other hand, Jürgen Trittin, minister in the Red-Green government, used the negative nationalism of the West German left to explain his pro-euro attitudes: as a long-term obligation resulting from the holocaust (Trittin 1998, 355).

negotiations, in which it was continuously involved (in contrast to the Banque de France). But all the political prerequisites it established for a common European currency, which in fact were intended to delay it as long as possible, were overtaken by political events of a different order (Marsh 1992, chap. 9.4; Overturf 1997, chap. 6).

Paradoxically, German unity opened the door for the most decisive step toward a united Europe. The euro finally was introduced, not as a result of economic reasoning but as a political compromise. France, as one of the four Allied powers still having sovereign rights over Germany, was prepared to endorse unification only in exchange for a common currency no longer under German control. In informal communications, kept in the strictest secrecy in order to minimize public attention, François Mitterrand persuaded Helmut Kohl to make the final stage of EMU "irreversible"; only under this pressure did the German negotiators "shelve their fundamentalist 'coronation' theory" (Dyson 1999, 38). So Germany agreed, but its surrender was conditional.

The last act of the Bundesbank was to transfer its monetary exceptionalism into the construction of EMU. The euro was to be "at least as stable" as the deutsche mark, and it would be safeguarded by a so-called Stability and Growth Pact, which would limit inflation rates, restrict budget deficits to 3 percent, and reduce public debts to less than 60 percent of GDP. Supranational policy coordination, according to the old principle of subsidiarity advocated by the German government, was limited to only a few areas. While the supranational European Central Bank (ECB) had (and still has) the sole and narrow mandate to keep annual inflation below 2 percent, the institutional framework of the Stability Pact is confined to the Broad Economic Policy Guidelines, which require an annual review of all national stability programs whose goal is to achieve a balanced budget or even a surplus. In the case of "excessive deficits" the European Commission is authorized to initiate a gradual process of enforcing policy revisions in the member states or even recommend to the Council of EU finance ministers (ECOFIN) the imposition of fines on nonconforming countries (OECD 1999, chap. 2).

Germany's Dilemmas—European Solutions?

Ironically, a decade after Germany forced its conditions on EMU, it finds itself entangled in the restrictions of the common monetary policy for the Euro area. Overconfident that a second economic miracle would pay for reunification, it tried to manage three things simultaneously, which became more and more contradictory over time: transferring the social market economy to the East, pursuing a sound fiscal policy, and playing a constructive role in Europe.

After billions had flown into the East to restructure obsolete industries, rebuild decrepit infrastructures, and modernize the public administration, the effects on the labor markets were nevertheless modest. Since the burden of unemployment and early retirement schemes had been passed on to social security contributions, labor costs also soared in the West, dampening growth and employment. Germany's average annual growth rate from 1990 to 2001 was merely 1.5 percent. Between 2001 and 2003, growth rates fell back to less than 0.4 per cent. Shrinking tax revenues, sharpened by risky tax policies, widened the public deficits at all state levels (Deutsche Bundesbank 2003a). While the government blamed rigid labor markets and generous social expenditures, the dismantling of the welfare state will not solve the real problem. Throughout the 1990s and until 2003, health, unemployment, and pension insurance systems in the West provided considerable surpluses, which were transferred to the East German *Neue Länder.* The government had the choice between breaking the consensus on which the social market economy had rested for five decades or confronting East German voters by fading out transfers and further reducing a still oversized public sector. As indicated above, the Social Democratic–led government also played the national card and extended the "Solidarity Pact II," the code name for continued transfers to the East, until the end of 2019—without knowing how to pay for it.

This decision runs into a second dilemma, a severe conflict with the institutional structures of EMU. On the one hand, having transplanted its uncompromising stability culture into the ECB, Germany cannot—as hoped for at the G-8 meeting in Evian in June 2003—expect consideration for its special problems with growth. Instead, the ECB responded to "deflation *angst*" in Germany (OECD 2000, 14; cf. IMF 2003, 24–72; Posen 2003, 17–19) with the same monetary arrogance that the rest of the world was used to expect from the Bundesbank. The ECB asserted that the concept of deflation makes no sense inside a currency union (ECB 2003, 85–86). So German growth may be the first victim of the deflationary policies by which the ECB tries to enhance its reputation (*Economist,* June 14, 2003, 84). On the other hand, the Stability and Growth Pact, originally designed by the Kohl government to keep Italy out of EMU for reasons of protecting the "stability culture," now has come to haunt Germany. The fact that Berlin received warnings from Brussels not to overstretch its budget is simply an unforeseen consequence of its economic nationalism in the context of unity. That the European Commissioners even tried to impose budgetary conditions on Germany demonstrates that they were no longer prepared to accept unification, nearly fifteen years after it happened, as a "special circumstance" justifying "excessive deficits."

And this is the dilemma of German economic nationalism today: how to pursue its project of unity without further damaging European institutions.

A solution may take the road of renegotiating the Stability Pact to allow for more public spending, as has been under discussion for some time. But an agreement will not be reached without serious conflict. In his clash with the European Commission in November 2003, the German minister of finance made a remarkable revision of the German point of view: the Stability Pact should no longer be interpreted as an automatism, but as a political arrangement with room for compromise. This corresponded to the French understanding and received support by Italy and Britain but was opposed by Spain and some smaller countries. Surely, there are good economic reasons to revise the ill-conceived Stability Pact, especially its sanctioning mechanism. Ironically, and also symptomatically, this mechanism was made "as hard as possible" on German initiative: to prevent categorically that the EU would become a transfer union like the unified Germany. Since internal problems could not be solved at home, they were displaced to the European level. Unfortunately, the excessive rigidity of the Stability Pact was relaxed not by agreement but by the combined power play of France and Germany, a gambit that could, in the worst case, lead to a return to an overt policy of national interests in the supposedly postnational EU.

On the other hand, even the supranational ECB may, in the long term, modify its understanding of stability, as its implicit change in monetary strategy suggests. May 8, 2003, marked a profound defeat for the Bundesbank: on this day the ECB revalued its "two pillar" strategy and shifted the emphasis from "monetary analysis" to "economic analysis," so that real economy indicators would play a more prominent role (ECB 2003, 86). Even worse, according to the proposals for a European Constitution, the ECB would become an institution of the EU like others; in contrast to the Maastricht Treaty, price stability would no longer be an explicitly constitutional goal. Hardliners from the Bundesbank, like its present director, already fear that the ECB could loose its "special status as an institution *sui generis*" (Welteke 2003, 3). The Bundesbank therefore perceives a breach of trust. The continuity of the "monetary constitution" was a precondition for the German public "to bring the DM into the European work of unification . . . ; this has to be borne in mind now" (Deutsche Bundesbank 2003b, 67, 73).

In any event, in its recent confrontation with the European Commission, Germany has already lost some of its supranational standing. And more generally it is true that German politics in the 1990s made it "less a model and magnet for other European countries" (Anderson 1999, 206). In a sense, this may at long last bring a certain kind of normalcy to Germany, now acknowledging that it is saddled with regional disparities much like France or Italy.

7 /Canada/

Why Would Nationalists Not Want a National Currency?

The Case of Quebec

Eric Helleiner

Quebec nationalists have emerged as one of the strongest supporters of proposals to create a North American monetary union (NAMU). If Quebec was to become a sovereign state after the creation of such a union, these nationalists have indicated that they would favor the preservation of NAMU instead of the creation of a new Quebec currency. This position is surprising, since the issuing of a national currency has traditionally been strongly associated with nationalist identities and has been seen as a key symbol of the sovereignty of a nation-state. It is also unusual because most other supporters of NAMU are "neoliberal" thinkers who see monetary union as a way to accelerate international economic integration and domestic deregulation as well as to provide external discipline on the ability of politicians to pursue discretionary monetary policies and fiscal spending. These neoliberal goals are also hardly those we traditionally associate with economic nationalism.

How can we explain this conundrum? This chapter begins by examining the historical roots of the Quebec nationalists' position in the NAMU debate. Since the origins of the modern Quebec nationalist movement in the 1960s, its leadership has always argued that Quebec sovereignty would not be associated with the creation of a national currency. Until their recent decision to endorse NAMU, they promised that an independent Quebec would continue to use the Canadian dollar. Interestingly, this promise was strongly criticized at key moments by many of their own followers who argued that sovereignty without a national currency would be a hollow shell. Federalist

I am grateful for research help I received from Fred Deveaux, Asha Gervan, Samuel Knafo, and Vince Sica, as well as for financial support from the Social Sciences and Humanities Research Council of Canada. I am also grateful to the following people for their helpful comments: Rawi Abdelal, Feyzi Baban, Jim Driscoll, Patti Goff, Derek Hall, Andreas Pickel, Andrei Tsygankov, and Meredith Woo-Cumings.

politicians also criticized—even taunted—Quebec nationalists on the monetary question, arguing that a "true" nationalist movement should be advocating the creation of a national currency. Despite this heavy criticism—which has continued with their recent decision to endorse NAMU—Quebec nationalist leaders have stood their ground.

Their position, I argue, is in fact much more consistent with nationalist goals than their critics suggest. It partly reflects some short-term political considerations relating to the need to reassure Quebec voters that the path to sovereignty will not be accompanied by monetary instability. The importance of this objective stems from the fact that nationalist leaders in Quebec have long recognized that political support for their project of building a sovereign state is far from universal in the province, a point that has been reinforced by their loss of two referendums on the question in 1980 and 1995. In this context, the impact of nationalism on economic policy has been quite different than in many of the other cases examined in this book. As Rawi Abdelal notes in his chapter, nationalism often promotes economic sacrifice to achieve societal goals. In the Quebec case, however, nationalist policymakers have been forced to acknowledge that a large segment of the population of Quebec is unwilling to undergo such a sacrifice. Indeed, a central political task for these policymakers has been to convince undecided voters that very little sacrifice would be involved in creating a sovereign state. For this reason, they have viewed the creation of a national currency in a very different way than, say, the Lithuanian leadership that Abdelal analyzes. Because domestic support for their nationalist project was very high, the latter could ignore the economic risks associated with the creation of a new national currency, and they played up the symbolic significance of this monetary reform. Quebec nationalist leaders did not have this luxury. They have been forced to view this monetary question through a strategic lens that examines its impact on undecided voters. To persuade these voters that sovereignty would not be associated with monetary upheaval, they have deliberately downplayed the symbolic role of a national currency in the nationalist cause, describing it as an issue of mere "plumbing" that did not interest them.

Their stance on monetary issues has also been influenced by changing external circumstances. When downplaying the significance of a national currency, nationalist policymakers in Quebec have frequently identified some important ways in which the relationship between nationalist goals and currency structures have been changing across the world in recent years. They argue that in an age of increasingly powerful global financial markets, national monetary sovereignty is a thing of the past. A national currency can even be a liability from a nationalist standpoint, they suggest, because it can become a target of speculation in these global markets. The creation of the euro is also said to demonstrate how the traditional relationship between sovereignty and currency structures is changing. The Quebec nationalists' decision to back NAMU has also partly reflected Quebec's deepening economic integration in North America as well as arguments about the negative effects of Canada's monetary policy and its depreciating dollar on the Quebec economy.

Although they find themselves allied with neoliberals, Quebec nationalists thus have very different reasons—nationalist ones—for backing NAMU. The endorsement of NAMU by Quebec nationalists, then, is not a repudiation of the ideology of economic nationalism. It is instead an embodiment of it. The Quebec case, thus, provides important support for the argument in this book that we must move beyond traditional understandings of the term "economic nationalism." It also reinforces the book's thesis that the policy content of economic nationalism will be heavily influenced by the distinct domestic and external contexts in which nationalists find themselves.

The Deep Roots of Quebec's National Currency Question

The question of whether an independent Quebec would create its own national currency emerged as central in Quebec sovereignty debates from the very origins of the emergence of the modern Quebec nationalist movement in the 1960s. René Lévesque's dramatic departure from the Liberal Party in 1967 is widely seen as the central moment in the rise of this movement as a significant political force. From the very outset, Lévesque made clear his belief that a sovereign Quebec should not have its own currency. Instead, he proposed a five-year experiment in which an independent Quebec would share a currency union with the rest of Canada. The joint currency would, he suggested, be managed by a central bank with a joint board of directors (which would include the deputy ministers of finance of both countries as nonvoting members). The top positions of the bank would be distributed proportionately between the two countries, and the positions of governor and deputy governor would alternate between officials from the two countries (Lévesque 1968, 45).

Lévesque's vision of a Canada-Quebec monetary union immediately invited criticism. Initially, the sharpest criticism came from federalists, most notably Robert Bourassa. Lévesque had hoped that Bourassa would join him in leaving the Liberal Party, but Bourassa had refused and the reason he gave publicly was his disapproval of Lévesque's monetary ideas (Lisée 1994, 145; Fraser 1984, 41). If Quebec nationalists wanted true political independence, Bourassa argued, they should create an independent currency. A monetary union with Canada would, in his view, ultimately require some form of political union, both because common fiscal policies would be necessary and because the two countries would each need a voice over monetary policy.

Would Bourassa have supported Lévesque if Lévesque had called for an independent currency? The answer was still no. In Bourassa's view, the creation of a new Quebec currency would produce the risk of massive capital flight and monetary instability. Since these risks could be avoided only by continuing to use the Canadian dollar, and since the continued use of the Canadian dollar required political union, then Bourassa would remain a federalist. His decision to back the federalist cause was thus justified on this very pragmatic ground that the monetary costs of true sovereignty would be too high. Bourassa repeated these arguments in his political battles against "sovereigntists" throughout the 1970s, often with considerable success.

Criticism also came from the backers of Quebec sovereignty. Conflict broke out within Lévesque's newly created Parti Québécois (PQ) on the issue in 1972, with economists such as Jacques Parizeau pushing for the idea of an independent currency (Parti Québécois 1972, 135; Pentland 1977, 225; McRoberts 1988, 259). Even when Parizeau became finance minister in the PQ government after its election in 1976, he and others initially continued to express skepticism about the idea of monetary union (e.g., *Globe and Mail* 1978; Gibbens 1978; McRoberts 1988, 304; Daignault 1978; Hadekel 1978). They argued as Bourassa had: a monetary union with Canada would force Quebec to coordinate fiscal and other economic policies with Canada in ways that would severely undermine the significance of sovereignty. In Parizeau's 1977 words, it "would put huge constraints on them and on us" (*Vancouver Sun* 1977; see also McRoberts 1988, 308; Gibbens 1978; Leslie 1979, 23). Kenneth McRoberts (1988, 308) also notes that many nationalists argued in favor of an independent currency on the grounds that "currency can constitute a tangible symbol of national status, to which citizens are daily exposed." In addition, it was noted that an independent currency would provide useful seigniorage revenue to the Quebec government (Lemco 1994: 137).

Despite these arguments, the PQ continued to endorse the idea of monetary union. Its proposals in this area in fact became more elaborate. During the 1980 referendum on sovereignty, the party proposed that Quebec continue to use the Canadian dollar and create a Bank of Quebec, which would control the banking system and act as the government's fiscal agent. The PQ suggested that the Bank of Canada and the Bank of Quebec be combined into a new monetary authority that would make key decisions about exchange-rate and monetary policy. The party's 1979 white paper titled *Quebec-Canada: A New Deal* proposed that the leadership of this authority would be "chaired alternately by a governor named by each government; the number of seats allocated to each party on the board of directors will be proportional to the relative size of each economy" (quoted in *Globe and Mail* 1979). In the event of disagreement between the representatives of the two countries within the monetary authority, a newly created "community council"—involving cabinet ministers from both countries—would have the power to give guidelines to the authority. Only if negotiations with Canada over the creation of this monetary union failed, or reached an impasse, would Quebec create its own currency (Leslie 1979, 17).

Parizeau ultimately agreed to support these proposals, but other nationalists did not. At the PQ's 1979 convention when the idea of economic association with Canada was endorsed, the resolution on monetary proposals provoked enormous debate. In Leslie's words (1979, 17–18), it was the only resolution "which appeared to be in any real danger of rejection. . . . [T]he debate on this omnibus proposal focused almost entirely on one issue: monetary union. There were some powerful speeches against it, and they were well received. Two attempts to break up the 12-part resolution to allow a separate vote on the currency issue [were] narrowly defeated—one by a vote of only 642 to 611."

The PQ's monetary proposals in the 1980 referendum campaign also exposed them to severe criticism from federalists at the time. Bourassa spoke frequently during the campaign on his common theme that monetary union would ultimately result in a form of continued political union: "a common money means you must have a common fiscal policy, and that in turn means you must have a common elected Parliament to direct it. The concepts form a triangle whose points cannot be separated" (quoted in Phillips 1980; see also Fraser 1980; Bourassa 1980). Other observers also ridiculed the PQ for not proposing an independent currency. Writing in *Montreal Gazette,* Graham Fraser's comments were typical of many: "the idea of political sovereignty without a currency is a virtual contradiction in terms. . . . When the PQ gives up the idea of a currency for a sovereign Québec, it is seriously compromising the nature of the sovereignty is seeking" (Fraser 1980).

Although their defeat in the 1980 referendum set back the PQ politically, the collapse of several efforts to renew Canadian federalism revived the sovereigntist cause by the early 1990s, and a second referendum was held in 1995. In the lead-up to this referendum, nationalist leaders once again stuck to the position that a sovereign Quebec would use the Canadian dollar. A surprising twist was also added to this long-standing proposal: many nationalists now argued that Quebec would be prepared to adopt the Canadian dollar unilaterally in the event that Canada refused to negotiate the terms of a monetary union. This idea was first mentioned by the 1991 Bélanger-Campeau Commission (1991, 58), which had been set up with representatives of all parties in Quebec and various interest groups to analyze Quebec's future. Interestingly, one of the people who then picked up the idea with great enthusiasm was Jacques Parizeau—now head of the PQ and Quebec premier—who had been more supportive of an independent currency in the 1970s. Parizeau and other nationalists seemed to delight in making the argument that Quebec could continue to use the dollar whether Canada liked it or not (Freeman and Grady 1995, 124–26; MacDonald 1991; Parti Québécois [1993] 1994, 57). Bourassa's case that a monetary union would require a political union because of the need for fiscal coordination was also now questioned more strongly. Parizeau, for example, pointed to the example of the Ontario provincial government at the time, having a distinctive fiscal policy within the Canadian monetary union (Lemco 1994, 139).

In some ways, the enthusiasm with which this idea was embraced by some nationalists was puzzling. Unilateral adoption of the Canadian dollar would, after all, prevent Quebec from having any say over the management of the currency; Quebec's monetary conditions would be set by the Bank of Canada. It would also prevent Quebec from demanding a share of the seigniorage stemming from currency circulating in Quebec.[1] For these reasons, many nationalists refused to endorse the idea. This was true of both the Bloc Québécois (which had been created in 1990 by Lucien Bouchard as a sovereigntist party in federal politics) and the Action Démocratique du Québec (a more moderate nationalist party in Quebec politics). They each supported that idea that Quebec would form a partnership with Canada in which decisions over monetary policy would be shared in an arrangement very similar to that proposed in the 1980 referendum (Cornellier 1995, 129–30).[2] These ideas also found support among many PQ members (e.g., Scott 1991; Parti Québécois [1993] 1994, 60).

Interestingly, the general idea of sharing Canada's currency—whether unilaterally or through a negotiated monetary union—met much less opposition within sovereigntist circles than it had in the 1970s. The new consensus was reflected in the fact that the "O" of the "Oui" signs in the referendum campaign contained a picture of Canada's one-dollar coin (showing the side with the loon rather than the Queen). But the idea continued to be ridiculed by federalists. They were particularly scathing about the proposal to adopt Canada's currency unilaterally. Daniel Johnson, the Quebec Liberal leader, asked "how can you tell Quebeckers that a separate

1. It could, however, compensate by demanding to pay a smaller share of federal debt, as the Bélanger-Campeau Commission suggested (Laidler and Robson 1991, 25–26; Robson 1995, 12–13).
2. The Bloc, for example, discussed a common monetary authority whose board of directors would be made up a members appointed by Quebec (4) and Canada (8), as well as (in a non-voting capacity) the deputy finance ministers of the two countries and the heads of the Bank of Canada and Bank of Quebec. Decisions would be made when nine votes were cast in favor, and the governor and deputy governor would be appointed by a committee involving ministers from both countries, which would also have ultimate authority over the board in the event of a conflict.

Quebec will give another country, a foreign country, Canada, the right to determine those elements of fiscal and monetary and economic policy?" (quoted in Mackie 1995). Similarly, Paul Martin, then Canada's finance minister, argued: "To go from a full say in the monetary policy of the country to no say is just simply nuts." He continued: "I don't understand why anybody who talks about sovereignty would essentially shackle themselves the way that he [Parizeau] would the Quebec economy. It just doesn't make any sense to me" (quoted in Graham 1994).

In the 1995 referendum, the federalist cause won, but only very narrowly. As a result, the cause of sovereignty remains alive politically within the province. The monetary proposals of Quebec nationalists have, however, shifted in an interesting direction. While still rejecting the idea of a Quebec currency, they began in 1998 to endorse the idea of North American monetary union. In December of that year, the leader of the Bloc Québécois, Giles Duceppe, first suggested that Mexico and Canada should consider adopting the U.S. dollar (*Globe and Mail* 1998). Quebec's finance minister, Bernard Landry, then took up the idea, calling for a task force to examine the idea of a Canada-U.S. currency union. In March 1999, the Bloc moved that a special committee of the House of Commons be established to consider the idea of a monetary union embracing all of the Americas (a motion that was defeated by the government). Jacques Parizeau also began to support the proposal for Canada to adopt the U.S. dollar in this period. The Quebec premier Lucien Bouchard also indicated interest in the idea during a trip to partially dollarized Argentina in May 2000.

The Quebec nationalists' interest in a North American or even a Pan-American monetary union reflected a broader interest in this idea across Canada and the rest of the Americas (for reasons I have analyzed elsewhere; see Helleiner 2003a, 2003b). But it also drew strength from the fact that many Quebec nationalists had endorsed the idea of adopting the Canadian dollar unilaterally in the lead-up to the 1995 referendum. If Canada were to adopt the U.S. dollar, Quebec nationalists are very aware that they—like all Canadians—would have little say, if any, in U.S. monetary decision making. In the 1970s, this situation would have caused more concern. But in the 1990s, many Quebec nationalists had already embraced the idea of adopting the Canadian dollar unilaterally, and it was not a very big next step to advocate adopting the U.S. dollar.

This did not stop politicians in the rest of Canada from continuing to criticize their position. Nelson Riis, MP, for example, questioned why nationalists would support dollarization when the adoption of the U.S. dollar would turn Quebec "into a banana republic" (quoted in *Montreal Gazette* 1999b). Questions have also been asked about the political allies that nationalists find themselves making in the NAMU debate. Elsewhere in Canada, support for NAMU has come primarily from neoliberals who see the project as advancing their free-market goals internationally and domestically. These neo-liberals hope that NAMU will accelerate North-South economic linkages on the continent and impose greater market discipline on firms and unions domestically (because greater wage and price flexibility will be required to compensate for the loss of the exchange-rate tool of adjustment to external shocks. They also hope that NAMU will discipline governments by constraining fiscal spending (as monetary union has in Europe) and by preventing future Canadian governments from engaging in activist discretionary monetary management. As critics have pointed out, none of these neoliberal goals are very compatible with traditional "economic nationalism," not to mention the social-democratic values that have historically been associated with the Quebec nationalist movement (Nystrom 1999, 309).

Explaining Quebec Nationalist Views

Quebec nationalists, thus, present us with a puzzle. Throughout the nineteenth and twentieth centuries most nationalist movements have expressed a desire to create a national currency when their state achieved political independence (Helleiner 2003c). For over thirty years, however, Quebec nationalist leaders have bent over backward to say that they don't want one. They have stuck to this position even in the face of strong criticism from their supporters and opponents, both of whom have argued that this position is not compatible with nationalist values. In the current context of the NAMU debate, their position has also landed them in a strange alliance with prominent neoliberals in the rest of Canada whose economic views they would not normally share. What explains this pattern of behavior?

Although this position appears incompatible with nationalist goals, it is not. As many of contributors to this volume observe, nationalist economic policy does not have a fixed content. It varies according to the circumstances in which nationalists find themselves as well as according to the specific content of the relevant national identities in each context (see also Abdelal 2001; Crane 1998; Goff 2000; Helleiner 2002; Pickel 2003). For a variety of reasons, Quebec nationalist leaders have found that the rejection of a national currency served their nationalist goals over the past thirty years. Their views, thus, are best understood as a form of economic nationalism rather than as a rejection of it.

Short-Term Strategic Concerns

The first reason that Quebec nationalists have endorsed the idea of monetary union is a short-term strategic one: they believed it would help them win more support for political independence. They have long recognized that much of the Quebec population is fearful of the monetary instability that might result from the creation of an independent currency after political independence. Their opponents have certainly been quite successful in exploiting these fears with their predictions of large-scale capital flight and the rapid depreciation of a newly created currency. As early as the 1970 provincial election campaign, the provincial Liberals produced a sample Quebec dollar bill and predicted the collapse of its value in an independent Quebec.[3] During the 1973 provincial election, Bourassa was also very effective in playing on popular fears that an independent Quebec's currency would depreciate in value vis-à-vis the Canadian dollar (McRoberts 1988, 309). The political saliency of these predictions has also been reinforced by the capital flight generated by the election of the PQ in 1976, Parizeau's speculations about the creation of a Quebec currency in 1978 (Anderson 1978), and the lead-up to the 1980 and 1995 referenda.[4]

Nationalists have seen their endorsement of monetary union as a way to allay these fears. In 1979 Lévesque explained the need for a common currency to an interviewer: "As you know this subject [of a national currency] belongs to an area about which, as a whole, public opinion very easily becomes nervous" (1979, 85; see also Lévesque 1968, 40). Similarly, in 1991, Parizeau acknowledged: "The creation of a Quebec currency invariably sparks widespread panic among people. It has never stopped me from sleeping but you have to live in the world you're in" (*Calgary Herald* 1991). In 1994, the PQ also highlighted this point in explaining the need to maintain the use of the Canadian dollar after independence: "maintaining a common currency would represent a significant guarantee of stability" (Parti Québécois [1993] 1994, 85). Indeed, it was revealed after the 1995 referendum that the PQ was prepared to devote considerable resources to defend the stability of the Canadian dollar in the event of a yes vote, in order to calm the population's fears about independence. In an interview taped just before the referendum but not shown until afterward, Parizeau stated: "We are the co-defenders of the Canadian dollar. I find the Canadian dollar admirable. . . .I will support the Canadian dollar, with the support of the Bank of Canada, with the Caisse de dépôt, with the federal finance ministry, with the Quebec finance ministry. Everyone supports this glorious Canadian dollar. We will never let it fall" (quoted in McKenna and Freeman 1995).[5]

This motivation also helps to explain why federalists have been so critical

3. For a picture of this bill, see *Globe and Mail,* November 2, 1979, 12.

4. Nationalists also anticipated the danger of large-scale capital flight. In advance of the 1995 referendum, the PQ suggested that they had made $37 billion of liquid funds available that could be used in the event of a yes vote for activities such as defending the Canadian dollar or purchasing all Quebec and Hydro-Quebec bonds in circulation in case of a panic. See "PQ Stashed Away $37-Billion as Panic Fund," *Globe and Mail,* May 18, 1996; McKenna and Freeman 1995.

5. See preceding note.

of the idea that Quebec would continue to use the Canadian dollar. If they could convince the Quebec population that Quebec sovereignty would produce a new Quebec currency, they would win political support. As we have seen, one way to do this was by questioning the sincerity of the Quebec nationalist commitment to the idea of a monetary union by arguing that it was not compatible with "normal" nationalist objectives. Another line of argument, especially prominent in the 1995 referendum debate, was that even if nationalists were sincere in their interest in a common currency, events would quickly force them to change their minds and introduce a national currency. This argument drew on the predictions of those who, like William Robson (1995), highlighted how capital flight might generate domestic financial instability in Quebec that the government could most effectively handle by creating a national currency.

If the promise to use the Canadian dollar was designed to calm Quebec fears of monetary instability, the more recent idea of endorsing a North American monetary union was potentially even more effective.[6] An independent Quebec that adopted the U.S. dollar would be better insulated from potential currency instability because of the U.S. dollar's wide use. This is not to suggest that the monetary change would be simple; complicated issues would arise such as Quebec's sudden need to access U.S. dollar payments systems and lender-of-last-resort facilities as well as its need for adequate U.S. dollars to facilitate the currency changeover. For this reason, the ideal scenario would be one in which Canada adopted the U.S. dollar before a Quebec referendum debate, thereby allowing these issues to be resolved in advance of Quebec independence.[7]

More generally, under either scenario, an independent Quebec would also be less vulnerable to Canadian pressure if it no longer relied on the use of the Canadian dollar (Parizeau 1999, 8). Indeed, if NAMU was not yet in place, Parizeau has noted, the threat to adopt the U.S. dollar might provide Quebec with considerable bargaining power in negotiations with Canada

6. This raises the question of why the idea of an independent Quebec adopting the U.S. dollar unilaterally had not been raised earlier. It was in fact raised in the 1990s by some people. Landry mentioned the idea in 1991 but rejected it then since it "would give the Americans a bigger influence over the Quebec economy, which would not be desirable" (quoted in Scott 1991). When running for the PQ in 1994, Richard Le Hir (former head of the Quebec Manufacturers Association) had also raised the idea, but Parizeau apparently told him to drop it (Gibbens 1994; Ditchburn 1998). Parizeau himself had briefly mentioned it in 1995 (Picard 1995).

7. One more negative effect, however, would be that Quebec might bear more of the financial cost of political uncertainty in the province. Without NAMU in place, Quebec's separation would undoubtedly produce downward pressure on the Canadian dollar, thereby effectively ensuring that all Canadians would bear some of the cost of this political uncertainty. If NAMU was in place, however, financial markets would likely simply charge higher interest rates on Quebec government borrowing. The rest of the country would thus be more insulated from the financial effects of separation (Courchene and Laberge 2000, 315).

(Bueckert 2000). It is certainly true that if Quebec were to leave the Canadian monetary union, the disintegrative pressures facing the rest of the country would be considerable. Ontario would have a strong incentive to use the same currency as Quebec, and it might not want to be stuck with a currency whose value was now more influenced by the other commodity-exporting provinces. At the same time, those other provinces might worry about Ontario's more dominant economic presence in the smaller monetary union (Beine and Coulombe 2003; Atkinson 1991, 55; Weatherbe 1997; Courchene and Laberge 2000, 294).

The endorsement of monetary union has been designed by nationalists to reassure not just Quebec citizens but also business interests outside the province. If political independence could be achieved in an environment of monetary stability, the confidence of foreign business interests in the new state would be enhanced and disruption to international economic relationships could be minimized. In justifying the need for a Canadian monetary union as far back as 1968, Lévesque, for example, drew attention to the importance of ensuring continuity in Ontario-Quebec relations: "There is no good reason for precipitately severing the extremely intricate relationship between the two great financial markets of Montreal and Toronto. . . . [U]nless we should be forced to do so, why destroy this financial mechanism by a monetary break-away, when the normal evolution of a common market inevitably would lead us toward setting up again sooner or later?" (Lévesque 1968, 42). Similarly, Claude Morin, a PQ minister, argued in 1980: "Think of the hundreds of millions of dollars that have been invested in Quebec in the past and now from people based elsewhere in Canada. They are very happy that it should be the same money. They told me so in Toronto. It would be very awkward for them to have to deal with another currency side by side; it would be awkward for us too" (quoted in Saunders 1980).

Questioning the Need for a National Currency

Short-term strategy was not the Quebec nationalists' only justification for rejecting a national currency. Quebec nationalists have also argued that changing international conditions are diminishing the benefits, and increasing the costs, of having a national currency from a Quebec nationalist standpoint. To begin with, they argue that the quest for monetary sovereignty is increasingly futile for smaller countries when faced with today's powerful global financial markets. Small countries find themselves increasingly vulnerable to speculative financial attacks from these markets, which can severely undermine a government's ability to pursue an autonomous domestic monetary policy. Volatility in foreign exchange markets also ensures that the national exchange rate is often the *source* of external shocks to the domestic economy, rather than a means of adjusting to such shocks as nationalists have traditionally argued. In these new conditions, a national currency is increasingly seen as a liability from a nationalist standpoint. Joining a monetary union looks increasingly attractive, since it can insulate smaller countries from the effects of speculative currency attacks and exchange-rate volatility.

These arguments about the limitations of national currencies today are hotly debated in economists' circles. But they certainly find enough support to give them value in the political arena. Lévesque used them as far back as the late 1960s to justify his call for a monetary union with Canada: "Let us again recall—and it is not wrong to insist, given the strength of the illusions held by some on the subject—what a narrow margin for manoeuver is retained in monetary matters by nations subject to the interdependence that is the rule in advanced economic systems" (Lévesque 1968, 43; see also Pentland 1977, 225; Lévesque 1979, 86; Dostaler 1988, 85). In a key paper prepared for the PQ in advance of the 1980 referendum, Bernard Fortin (1978) made a similar case, arguing that a monetary union with Canada would in fact provide the best way for Quebec to preserve a degree of monetary sovereignty because Quebec would be better protected against the power of international speculative capital movements.

These arguments have become more persuasive in the last decade as financial globalization has accelerated. In advance of the 1995 referendum, Parizeau—in contradiction to his 1991 statement—sometimes justified his disfavoring an independent Quebec currency on the grounds that this currency would be too vulnerable to speculative traders whose power had grown so much since the 1970s (Picard 1995).

The more recent decision to back NAMU has also frequently been justified in this way. In 1999, Richard Marceau, a Bloc Québécois MP, argued that NAMU would insulate Quebec from the kind of speculative financial flows that were evident a year earlier in the Asian financial crisis. The U.S. dollar, in his words, was "a strong currency right close to home that provides a shelter when the world economy nose-dives" (Marceau 1999; see also Bloc Québécois 2002). Similarly, another Bloc member, Yvan Loubier, argued that a common currency is needed to counteract "unscrupulous speculators who destroy national currencies, thus threatening the countries' economic future and job creation efforts" (House of Commons 1999). Loubier's comment also highlights how some nationalists are also able to associate NAMU with social-democratic values (e.g., a commitment to full employment).

They make this association in another interesting way. Some neoliberals in the rest of Canada see NAMU as a way to prevent the Canadian government from pursuing activist Keynesian-style monetary policy in the future. But nationalists are more worried about preventing a repeat of the late 1980s and early 1990s when the Bank of Canada pursued an aggressive zero-inflation strategy that resulted in a severe recession in Canada. In Quebec—

as in many other parts of the country—this neoliberal policy was very unpopular, especially since it was seen as primarily designed to counter inflationary pressures in Southern Ontario (Lemco 1994, 140–42).[8] Quebec
nationalists have argued that NAMU might result in a monetary environment more conducive to their social-democratic goals of employment
growth because American monetary authorities have taken a less rigid neoliberal monetary stance in recent years. In Marceau's words (1999), "if the
past is any indication of the future, the American pro-employment monetary policy might be more advantageous for our economy than an anti-in-
flationary Canadian monetary policy designed to reflect the prerogatives of
Ontario."

In response to arguments that Quebec would have little say over U.S.
monetary policymaking, Quebec nationalists have made two arguments.
Parizeau has sometimes argued that the worldwide trend toward the creation of independent central banks indicates that this issue is less significant
today than in the past. He and others have also suggested that the Quebec
government has never had a formal say in the operations of the Bank of
Canada anyway. This latter argument was also used in the lead-up to the
1995 referendum to explain why Quebec's unilateral use of the Canadian
dollar would not result in any further loss of "sovereignty" (Parti Québécois
[1993] 1994, 57–58; *Vancouver Sun* 1995). As Parizeau put it in 1992, "a lot
of people argue we wouldn't have any control over the monetary policy of
the currency we employ. And that's perfectly correct. But, as far as I'm concerned, Quebec doesn't have any control over the policies of the Bank of
Canada right now. So what have we got to lose?" (*Globe and Mail* 1992). Even
the Quebec Liberal Party's 1991 Allaire report, commissioned by Bourassa
after the collapse of the Meech Lake accord, recognized the power of this
argument; it argued that if the Canadian federation was to be renewed, the
Bank of Canada should be reformed to guarantee regional representation
(Lemco 1994, 35).[9]

The issue of distinct regional monetary preferences within Canada is important in another way for the Quebec nationalist argument for NAMU.
Since the introduction of the Canada-U.S. Free Trade Agreement in 1989,
Quebec's economic links with the United States have grown dramatically,
and Quebec now trades more with the United States than it does with other
provinces. This position has strengthened the case for creating a monetary
union with the United States, since currency-related transaction costs would
be eliminated for U.S.-Quebec trade (Marceau 1999). In fact, Quebec na-

8. Recent internal memos from the Bank of Canada note that the bank's reputation in Quebec is still hurting from this policy episode (Toulin and Bellavance 2001).
9. The bank's board of directors is supposed to have regional input, but the board exerts very
little power in practice. Other groups outside Quebec were also calling for a stronger regional
voice in the Bank of Canada at this time (e.g., Corcoran 1991).

tionalists have long been very prominent supporters of free trade with the United States because they see closer commercial ties with their southern neighbor as a way to reduce their dependence on the rest of Canada (Shulman 2000). As in the NAMU debate, they found themselves allied with neoliberals in the rest of Canada during the Free Trade Agreement debate of the late 1980s for this reason.

At the same time that Quebec's economic ties with the United States have intensified, Beine and Coulombe note (2003), the business cycles of Quebec and Ontario are becoming increasingly similar to those of the United States. In this circumstance, Canada's floating exchange rate is of less value to these provinces, and may even be detrimental if it produces currency movements that respond primarily to the needs of the commodity-exporting provinces in the rest of the country. Reinforcing this argument is the analysis of Courchene and Laberge (2000, 296), which suggests that when the value of the Canadian dollar responds to commodity price shocks, these changes do in fact tend to be disruptively pro-cyclical in the Quebec context. These developments provide a further reason for Quebec to favor NAMU.

Some nationalists—including Landry (Smith 2001; Toulin and Bellavance 2001) and Marceau (1999) (see also Bloc Québécois 2002)—also argue that Canada's fluctuating exchange rate has undermined the competitiveness of Quebec businesses (as well as those in the rest of Canada). They argue that the gradual depreciation of the Canadian dollar since the 1970s has discouraged firms from investing in productivity improvements. In Marceau's words (1999), "It could be argued that if the crutch supplied by a Canadian currency that has been quietly devaluing for the last thirty years were eliminated, Quebec businesses would have a much greater incentive to invest in improving productivity." In making this "lazy manufacturing" argument, nationalists find themselves allied with some neoliberal economists. Again, however, their nationalist motivations for endorsing this argument are distinct from those of neoliberals.

If these arguments explain the economic drawbacks of a national currency from a nationalist standpoint, we are still left with the fact that a national currency has long been seen as a potent symbol of sovereignty. Why have Quebec nationalists not seen it in this way? In the late 1960s, Lévesque argued that the issue was not a significant one for the Quebec population because it did not have a historical tradition of associating currency with national identities. Whereas European countries associated their currencies with "a whole slice of national culture," Quebec was different: "We, who at the moment have neither agencies nor specialists nor any cultural patrimony depending on an indigenous 'piastre,' have nothing to gain by insisting on an attribute of independence which evolution is in the process of turning into a liability" (Lévesque 1968, 44). According to Fraser (1984,

41–42), Lévesque also dismissed this issue as insignificant in his discussions with Bourassa: "Monetary system, economic system, all this is plumbing. One doesn't worry about plumbing when one fights for the destiny of the people." He made a similar argument in 1979 in discussing the prospect for monetary union between Canada and Quebec: "Looking at the European experiment, it would seem to be a difficult thing to realize. It is not simple. But unlike the old countries, we do not have that tradition of monetary sovereignty which is almost related to the national image, which makes the franc, the franc, and the lire, the lire" (Lévesque 1979, 85–86). In fact, he went further to suggest that the desire for a national currency on symbolic grounds would represent a kind of immature chauvinism (Fraser 1980).

Lévesque's argument that Quebec nationalists have historically attached little symbolic value to the creation of a national currency was overstated. We have seen how some supporters of Quebec sovereignty did want the creation of a national currency for this reason in the 1970s. Before this, I have also found at least two other episodes when Quebec nationalists associated national identities with currency issues. The first was in 1842 just after the Act of Union had joined Quebec and Ontario (then Lower and Upper Canada) into the new Province of Canada. At this decisive moment in Quebec's history, the new province ended the legal tender of old-regime (pre-1972) French coins as part of its effort to create a more standardized currency. These coins had been very commonly used in Quebec; indeed, accounts were even kept in livres and sols at the time (Shortt 1986, 216–25). According to Adam Shortt (1986, 220), the move was deeply unpopular in Quebec in part because many French Canadians saw the old coins "as part of that cherished nationality which marked [their] independence of British institutions." Many French Canadians were also skeptical of bank notes because they were issued by English banks, and tokens issued by the English-dominated Bank of Montreal in the late 1830s were often refused "on patriotic grounds" (Shortt 1986, 387). A century later, nationalist concerns were again raised in a debate about whether the new Bank of Canada's notes should be bilingual or not. When the Bank had been created in 1934, a provision mandated that its notes be printed in either French or English. Quebec politicians pushed successfully that they be made bilingual instead, seeing this as a symbol of the equality of French and English (Dominion of Canada 1934, 4237–47; 1936, 3623–32).

Although Lévesque overstated his case, his arguments were interesting in that they deliberately tried to downplay the symbolic role of money from a nationalist standpoint. He may have done this partly to reassure undecided voters that the PQ had no intention of introducing a national currency. The strategy also helped him to deflect criticism from Quebec nationalists who did favor a national currency. Lévesque's approach has continued in more recent nationalist discourse. Indeed, developments in Europe have made it easier for nationalists to question the significance of national currencies. As European countries have succeeded in creating a monetary union, Quebec nationalists have increasingly cited that experience to highlight how the link between national identities and national currencies is no longer a necessary one. For example, in 1991 when defending the idea of a currency union with Canada, Landry argued that the European situation showed how monetary issues were mere technicalities of nation building that would increasingly be managed by international bodies. In his view, "sovereignty refers more to the style of life—language, education, health and environment, these types of things" (quoted in Scott 1991). Similarly, Marceau (1999) argued that the creation of the euro "demonstrates how closely the sovereigntist plan proposed in 1995 [a currency union with Canada] reflects the modern world!"

At first sight, the monetary proposals of the Quebec nationalist leaders over the past thirty years appear to represent an odd rejection of economic nationalism. Historically, nationalists in most parts of the world have been strongly attached to the idea that their country needs its own national currency for both economic and symbolic reasons. Quebec nationalist leaders have consistently rejected this position, even in the face of severe criticism from their supporters and opponents. In the recent debate on NAMU, Quebec nationalists have even allied themselves with neoliberal thinkers whose views are normally seen as quite antagonistic to economic nationalism. Indeed, Quebec nationalists have at times seemed to delight in their rejection of traditional nationalist values. For example, when prominent Canadian politicians have rejected the idea of NAMU, Bernard Landry has criticized them for acting out of "narrow-minded nationalism" (*Montreal Gazette* 1999a).

I have argued in this chapter that the monetary proposals of Quebec nationalist leaders are less strange than they first appear. They are in fact driven by nationalist goals and thus should be seen to represent a distinct form of economic nationalism. The distinctiveness stems partly from particular domestic political circumstances. In a context where many voters are wary of Quebec sovereignty, Quebec nationalist leaders have felt it necessary to calm fears about the prospects for monetary instability after political independence in order to build support for their cause. Not surprisingly, this strategy has at times alienated nationalist supporters, who have questioned what kind of sovereignty an independent Quebec would in fact acquire without a national currency. Interestingly, however, these questions have diminished in recent years. As I have shown, a key reason is that external circumstances have changed. As global financial markets have become increasingly powerful, Quebec nationalists have associated the creation of a national currency with fewer economic benefits and more economic costs. The creation of the common currency in Europe has also strengthened the long-standing argument of nationalist leaders that the economic and symbolic value of national currencies for sovereign states is overstated. More recently, the arguments for NAMU have also been reinforced by Quebec's changing economic position in North America and the pattern of Canadian monetary and exchange-rate policymaking.

This study of the distinctive economic nationalism of Quebec nationalist leaders thus reinforces a key analytical point made by other contributors to this volume: the specific content of economic nationalism is a product of the singular domestic and external environment that nationalists find themselves in. Interestingly, the arguments of Quebec nationalist leaders against the creation of national currencies are not unique. Nationalists in many smaller European countries have seen the creation of the euro as desirable for many of the economic reasons that Quebec nationalists have put forward. Prominent economists, such as A. Alesina and R. Barro (2001), have also noted that the cost of separation for regions *within* European countries has diminished with the creation of the euro. The Quebec nationalist movement is then not entirely distinct in the contemporary world. Indeed, in developing these arguments against national currencies more than thirty years ago, it pioneered this form of economic nationalism.

Part IV

New Forms of Economic Nationalism
in a Globalizing World

8

It's Got to Be Sheep's Milk or Nothing!

Geography, Identity, and Economic Nationalism

Patricia M. Goff

What counts as economic nationalism in a global economy? Typically, the term "economic nationalism" evokes a specific set of practices, ranging from the erection of tariff walls to the promotion of autarky. In the contemporary global economy, however, such practices are increasingly undesirable and difficult to implement. Does this mean that economic nationalism is obsolete? My research suggests that the answer is no. Following George Crane (1998, 74), who contends that "economic nationalism is expressed in many different forms beyond trade protectionism and industrial policy," I argue that governments still use economic policy to serve national goals. Indeed, globalization and the dictates of the global trading regime arguably demand such policies. However, the prevailing understanding of what counts as economic nationalism often obscures recognition of its contemporary incarnations, as well as its motivations and purposes. Many contemporary examples of economic nationalism are not traditional examples of protectionism at all. Rather, they are policies that seek to preserve or promote a set of shared understandings, cultural values, or social practices bound up with evolving notions of national security and held dear by a significant portion of a national citizenry.

I have written elsewhere about how these policies manifest themselves in the culture industry sector—film, radio and television broadcasting, video and sound recording, and periodical and book publishing (Goff 2000, 2002). But for the purposes of the current chapter, I turn my attention to the realm of agriculture. I examine European Union policies that restrict the circulation of genetically modified organisms (GMOs) in the European

I thank the contributors to this volume, especially Eric Helleiner and Andreas Pickel, for helpful comments on this chapter. I also thank Peter Katzenstein, Bob Wolfe, and an anonymous reviewer.

market. In addition, I consider a class of policies—generally known as geo-graphical indications—that are expanding and being reinforced and de-fended by such free-trade luminaries as the European Union commissioner for trade Pascal Lamy. These are policies that give producers of certain food-stuffs—mostly artisanal in nature—exclusive rights to product names. Those not recognized as authentic producers of these goods must market their products under another name. These agricultural initiatives represent important contemporary examples of economic policies that promote na-tional autonomy and preserve national traditions.

Both of these policies are, on some level, responses to globalization. As Robert Gilpin suggests (2001, 81), "fear that economic globalization and the integration of national markets are destroying or could destroy the po-litical, economic, and cultural autonomy of national societies has become widespread." Measures that resist GMOs and strengthen geographical indi-cations are motivated by a concern that specific national practices and tra-ditions may be threatened by economic liberalization. Governments and citizens want their societies to remain distinct cultural entities, even as they integrate with others economically. The desire to reassert collective identity and modes of national identification may be even more urgent in this era of globalization.

Economic Nationalism in a Global Economy

In the current period, any mention of economic nationalism in many of the advanced industrialized states elicits reactions ranging from skepticism to outright denunciation. Many officials and analysts automatically assume that economic nationalism is synonymous with protectionist measures, including tariffs, quotas, and subsidies. Economic nationalism ostensibly implies re-striction on foreign investment and on foreign ownership of domestic assets and may lead to distortions in the "natural" patterns of trade. Economic na-tionalism supposedly involves the promotion of autarky and is often por-trayed as the economic dimension of the state-centric theory of political realism. At bottom, economic nationalism is, by all accounts, in opposition to economic liberalism. Consider Robert Gilpin's definition of economic nationalism: "Economic nationalism, like economic liberalism, has under-gone several metamorphoses over the past several centuries. Its labels have also changed: mercantilism, statism, protectionism, the German Historical School, and, recently, New Protectionism. Throughout all these manifesta-tions, however, runs a set of themes. . . . Its central idea is that economic ac-tivities are and should be subordinate to the goal of state building and the interests of the state" (Gilpin 1987, 31).

A quick perusal of representative political economy texts confirms the narrow understanding of—as well as the negative regard for—economic nationalism. For example, David Balaam and Michael Veseth identify economic nationalism as "the ideology of mercantilism" (2001, 459). Joan Spero and Jeffrey Hart define economic nationalism as follows: "The set of practices that dominated international economic interactions during the interwar years and eventually brought about the collapse of the international monetary system in the 1930s. Foremost among these practices are instituting competitive exchange rate devaluations, formation of competing monetary blocs, adoption of beggar-thy-neighbour trade policies, and aversion to the norms of international cooperation" (Spero and Hart 1997, 374).

The sorts of policies depicted in these descriptions of economic nationalism seem distantly removed from the reality of the contemporary global economy. Indeed, many discussions of economic nationalism imply that it is generally associated with the past. In the post–World War II period, the governments of the advanced industrialized economies have taken the lead in liberalizing the international economy and removing barriers to trade. Eight rounds of GATT talks have successfully dismantled tariff barriers and eased the global movement of goods and services. Talks at the multilateral level continue with the launch of the ninth round of trade talks, marked by a shift of focus to nontariff barriers and to an ever-widening list of goods, services, and intellectual property previously not under the purview of the trading regime. Of course, the recent establishment of the World Trade Organization created a robust dispute-settlement mechanism to ensure greater compliance with the principles of liberal trade. Because the principles of liberal trade are now institutionalized in the global economy, it is increasingly difficult to contravene these principles if states are so inclined.

All this leads many to assume that economic nationalism is dead, or should be. Protectionism is synonymous with economic nationalism. Protectionism is in direct opposition to economic liberalism. If economic liberalism has triumphed, then there is no longer a place for economic nationalism. Such a conclusion, however, would be appropriate only if we accept the narrow definition of economic nationalism as protectionism. Like other contributors to this volume, however, I side with Eric Helleiner when he writes that "the ideology of economic nationalism should be defined by its nationalist content rather than by its endorsement of specific economic policies or as an economic strand of realism" (2002, 325).

Defining economic nationalism in terms of its nationalist content shifts our focus away from specific strategies that economic nationalists have used in the past to the *goals* of those strategies. Rather than conflating economic nationalism with protectionism, we find economic nationalism in economic policies that promote national security, sovereignty, and/or identity. Such a conceptualization, moreover, approximates what initiators of the debate over economic nationalism understood it to be. Adam Smith, for example, notes in *The Wealth of Nations* that "the first duty of the sovereign" was "that of protecting the society from the violence and invasion of other independent societies" (quoted in Harlen 1999, 737). As Christine Harlen argues (1999, 741), one of the points on which Smith and economic nationalists like Alexander Hamilton and Friedrich List converge is that protectionist policies were but one means of serving "the real end" of national security. At the risk of making an obvious point, neither List nor Hamilton advocated protectionism for protectionism's sake. For each, developing a manufacturing base and becoming independent economically was crucial to national security in the face of British economic supremacy. Protectionist policies were a way to do that, but as Harlen and others demonstrate, both List and Hamilton placed specific constraints and conditions on when such protectionist policies should be used. Indeed, List felt that free trade was a worthy goal, but he worried that it was unattainable as long as power inequalities existed among the major economic powers. His main concern was national security, which he understood quite broadly: "A nation is a sovereign political body. Its destiny is to safeguard and to maintain its independence by its own efforts. Its duty is to preserve and to develop its prosperity, culture, nationality, language, and freedom—in short, its entire social and political position in the world" (List [1837] 1983, 31).

When our understanding of economic nationalism prioritizes goals over strategies, we can identify examples of economic nationalism even in a time of concerted liberalization. Indeed, it is precisely the continued march toward liberalization that can trigger policies of economic nationalism. As William Dymond and Michael Hart contend (2000, 2), we have seen a "major paradigm shift" in recent years in the trade regime:

> The WTO not only requires governments to live up to their GATT commitments, but also to adopt and implement specific policies, practices, and procedures. These additional rules reach well behind national borders and engage public policy issues that transcend the relationship between national economies and the global economy. . . . The object and purpose of trade policy has been transfigured from trade liberalization through trade barrier reductions to positive rule-making aimed at ensuring the capacity of producers around the globe to fully contest the markets of member states.

As liberalization increasingly challenges domestic regulatory practices—practices often bound up with sociocultural goals—questions of national sovereignty, autonomy, identity, and security frequently arise. Liberalization, as Dymond and Hart define it, threatens the very things that economic nationalists seek to promote and preserve. The nature of the contemporary threat is, however, different. The threat is not increased competition from outside national borders. Rather, it is that membership in a powerful, rules-based multilateral entity will result in national practices and policies being aligned with those of other governments.

Accompanying this new threat is the recognition that security has taken on new meaning in an era of regionalization and globalization. How we define security is largely contingent on the nature of prevailing threats. Security in the mercantilist era, from which contemporary economic nationalism ostensibly springs, meant ensuring a constant state of readiness for war. The threat was invasion and usurpation of territory. As a result, national security required the accumulation of wealth to purchase or manufacture costly weaponry, as well as self-sufficiency so as not to depend on external sources for key resources. In the immediate post–World War I period, especially in Europe, providing for state security meant focusing on economic goals, such as rebuilding a decimated manufacturing sector and fostering competitive industries.

While these conceptions of security are still relevant, other dimensions of national security have surged to the fore in recent years, dimensions that are intimately tied to the features of the global economy. Not just goods, services, and money, but people, ideas, and images cross borders at an alarming rate. As Crane puts it (1998, 230), "autarky is simply out of the question." Even old enemies like France and Germany now use the same currency and find their economies and polities inextricably intertwined. Interdependence is the norm. The strongest economies are not immune to the effects of financial crises or stock market shifts occurring thousands of miles away.

Many have noted that war is unlikely among the advanced, industrialized democracies. No longer worried about advancing armies or the fragility of burgeoning industry, the advanced industrial states conceptualize security in other ways. Territorial sovereignty is not threatened. Economic sovereignty is voluntarily breached. Such goals as "cultural sovereignty," however, and "food sovereignty" become the catchwords of security in the new millennium. Germany no longer fears an advancing British navy, but it does fear the disease that might enter its territory in British cattle. France has no fear of American armies and welcomes American investors. Yet it recoils against the "Hollywoodization" of its film and television industries, the increasing use of anglicisms by native French speakers, and the effects of fast food on traditional culinary habits. These examples constitute threats to security because they threaten the survival of the nation as citizens have come to know it. Indeed, one could argue that it is precisely because globalization is occurring that new threats are surfacing. As threats to national security and autonomy take on different forms, economic nationalists fashion appropriate responses. As Helleiner puts it in his study of several economic nationalists (2002, 323), "each economic nationalist placed emphasis on different nationalist values such as the promotion of national prosperity, the quest for national power, or the promotion of national identities and culture. The differences could also be rooted in the different contexts in which economic nationalists found themselves."

The current context is a regionalized and globalizing one. Integration of markets and the expansion of transnational economic interaction may bring many benefits. It may also be increasingly difficult to maintain distinctive national practices and to reproduce national social bonds. In other words, the very survival of the "national system of political economy," as Gilpin calls it (2001), and the nation more generally, is endangered, representing a threat to national security arguably unique to this period of globalization.

Ole Waever (1995) has done pioneering work on how the integration project in Europe has led to a reconceptualization of European security. He contends that when officials in Europe express fears about fragmentation of the European Community or about an unraveling of the integration project, they are making a security-driven argument. The integration project is part alliance/balance of power and part security community, but it can fulfill this function only if it stays in motion. Waever goes on to argue that identity has become a security problem in the European Union: "Some people in Western Europe question the integration project and show increasing concern for their national identities. Notably, this concern operates in a security mode: It is argued as a matter of survival, as an issue that should take precedence over any other" (1995, 403). Waever fuses identity with security using the notion of societal security. "Societal security is about those ideas and practices that identify individuals as members of a social group" (405). As our understanding of security expands to include such concerns, so will the repertoire of strategies that states employ to protect it.

Crane maintains that "we should expect specific policy prescriptions of economic nationalists to vary with representations of the economic nation" (1998, 74). In Europe, the "economic nation" includes membership in a regional project and participation in a single market that transcends national borders. Given the novelty of this "imagined economy," it should not be surprising to see novel manifestations of economic nationalism. I argue here that policies concerning genetically modified organisms and geographical indications are just that.

Genetically Modified Organisms

In the early 1990s, the European Union introduced a range of policies designed to ensure full disclosure on the part of operators dealing in products containing genetically modified organisms. These measures require special product labels, as well as monitoring or "tracing" of products once they have found their way onto the market. Later in the decade, the EU stalled its approval process for a time—in the wake of the mad cow disease scare, among other things—to update and complete its GMO labeling laws. From the perspective of the largest producer of GMOs, the United States, these policies meant a ban on GMOs in the European market and, therefore, closure of the European market to imports of genetically modified American goods. In 2003 this led the United States, Canada, and Argentina to activate the World Trade Organization's (WTO) dispute settlement mechanism by requesting consultations with the European Union over its GMO regulatory framework. After short consultations, the United States apparently concluded that the EU and the complainants would not themselves find a satisfactory solution and requested that the WTO establish a panel to consider the dispute. At the time of this writing, the panel has not yet rendered a decision.

American producers and political officials seem convinced that a desire to shield the European agricultural and biotech industries from foreign competition inspired the laws. Such a standard interpretation of this debate—in narrow terms of free trade versus protectionism—suggests that the economic interests of a specific sector are motivating the policies. This view obscures the ways in which European GMO regulations are bound up with general concerns about food safety, "food sovereignty," identity, and evolving notions of national security. As Ian Cook, Philip Crang, and Mark Thorpe put it (1999, 223), "everyday practices of commodified food provision and consumption involve the production and consumption not only of foods but of social imaginaries." It is in fact difficult to identify a specific commercial group in Europe that has sought—and derives—economic benefit from GMO regulations. Instead, the policies appear to be motivated by broader citizen concerns over food security and national self-determination.

The European Union defines GMOs (and genetically modified microorganisms [GMMs]) as "organisms (and micro-organisms) in which the genetic material (DNA) has been altered in a way that does not occur naturally by mating or natural recombination. . . . It allows selected individual genes to be transferred from one organism into another, also between non-related species" (Commission of the EU 2002a, 1). European consumers have loudly and vehemently opposed the introduction of GMOs into the European market. Polls suggest that between 70 and 80 percent of Europeans oppose GMOs in their food (Ford 2001). Whereas consumers in other parts of the world are only now questioning the costs and benefits of GMOs, Europeans from very early on resisted their unregulated use. They do so for a variety of reasons. They oppose the use of biotechnology for food on moral and ethical grounds. The European experience with mad cow and hoof-in-mouth disease has brought consumer safety issues to the fore. From a cultural standpoint, citizens do not want culinary traditions and customs compromised. As Olivier Cadot, Akiko Suwa-Eisenmann, and Daniel Traça argue with regard to Europe (2001, 16), "Nowhere have the ideas of free trade and economic efficiency less legitimacy than in the agri-food sector, as food is considered in countries like France as part of culture and something that ought to escape industrial logic, at least to some extent." Additionally, sovereignty is a key motivation. Europeans maintain that they do not want culinary habits imposed from without and they want to ensure their right to establish a higher domestic standard for GMOs than required in international agreements, such as the Biosafety Protocol of the Convention on Biological Diversity, Codex Alimentarius, or the WTO Agreement on Sanitary and Phytosanitary Measures. Strong environmentalist traditions also play an important role here.

One report, investigating why French protesters chopped down an experimental crop of genetically modified corn, quotes a protester as saying that "at the heart of the protest . . . was a simple desire to maintain the traditional quality that small-scale farmers using conventional methods say they alone can ensure." The protester continues, "In this country we still have a system of small farmers doing sustainable agriculture and it works. We want to keep it" (Ford 2001). Similarly, Roger Cohen notes that "Alain Duhamel, a French political analyst, believes that a widespread rejection of cultural and culinary dispossession is at the root of the protests" against GMOs (Cohen 1999).

One of the better-known European voices speaking out against GMOs is José Bové. Bové entered the public consciousness in August 1999 when he participated in the partial dismantling of the McDonald's franchise in Millau, in the Aveyron region of France. The European Union had recently renewed its ban on the entry of hormone-treated beef into the European market. The United States retaliated by slapping tariffs on a range of European products, including Roquefort cheese, one of the main exports from the Aveyron region. Bové and fellow farmers, enraged both by the harm done to Roquefort producers in their hometown and by the effort to redefine European resistance to hormone-treated beef as a trade issue, rather than an issue of quality, health, choice, and cultural identity, proceeded to dismantle the McDonald's as the global symbol of industrialized foodstuffs. Describing McDonald's fare, Bové remarks, "The food is completely uniform; the hamburgers have the same shape and content all over the world. In fact, it's 'food from nowhere'" (Bové and Dufour 2001, 55). He goes on to explain what motivated the farmer's protest that August day in Millau: "The word 'hormone' worries people—so do the initials 'GMO,' because they raise questions about the integrity of food. . . . So on one side of the Atlantic a wholesome product like Roquefort was being surcharged, while on this side we were being forced to eat hormone-treated beef!" (13).

Bové's fellow leader in the Confédération Paysanne, François Dufour, asserts that "people understood that agriculture is not a separate sector, that it can't be reduced to just another aspect of production. Eating habits, quality, gastronomy, cultural identity and social relations all depend on farming, and define what we refer to as agriculture" (Bové and Dufour 2001, 26). In the course of Bové's activities in response to U.S. tariffs, he popularized the term *malbouffe* to capture one of his primary concerns. The term has no good translation into English. It is typically translated as "junk food" or "foul food," but Bové explains that such renderings are insufficient: "The first time I used the word was on 12 August, in front of the McDonald's in Millau. . . . 'Malbouffe' implies eating any old thing, prepared in any old way. . . . For me, the term means both the standardization of food like McDonald's—the same taste from one end of the world to another—and the choice of food associated with the use of hormones and GMOs, as well as the residues of pesticides and other things that can endanger health. So there's a cultural and a health aspect" (Bové and Dufour 2001, 53–54). François Dufour adds, "Today the word has been adopted to condemn those forms of agriculture whose development has been at the expense of taste, health, and the cultural and geographical identity of food" (54).

Turning to the unenthusiastic participation in elections for the European Parliament, Dufour links citizen resistance to GMOs to the new global context, characterized by regionalization and globalization and the security threats they imply.

> People are not against the building of Europe *per se,* they simply want to protect the traditions and rhythms of farming life. Many abstentions and votes cast for the candidates on the "Hunting, Fishing, Nature, and Tradition" (CPNT) slate result from the loss of identity. It wasn't just the hunters who voted for the CPNT; there were many who felt a loss of cultural identity. Agricultural identity is part of this; you don't have to be a farmer or live in the country to feel rooted to the land. Such roots connect all parts of the country in a unifying whole, and this can't be undermined by Europe or globalization. The McDonald's issue came just at the right time to stir up such feelings. Even the most liberal economic milieux had to admit that the downgrading of agriculture and its appropriation by factories was destroying those roots. People don't want to be uprooted. This is essentially what public opinion boiled down to—much more than to a sense of solidarity with the economic hardship being suffered by the producers of Roquefort and other affected products. (Bové and Dufour 2001, 27)

Farm workers and consumers are not the only ones to have expressed such misgivings. European Union trade commissioner Pascal Lamy has been quoted as defending "specific traits of European civilization—the insistence on high-quality foodstuffs, cultural identity in a world without barriers and a reluctance to see some activities reduced to a commercial footing" (Hornblower and Beech 1999, x).

As a result, EU legislators have established strict regulations that, for a time, amounted to a ban on newly approved GMOs entering the EU market. Franz Fischler, European commissioner for agriculture, rural development, and fisheries, noted the shift in EU policy in an April 2002 speech at the European Food Summit.

> Until some years ago, quality was only an asset, but not really a policy objective. The main goal of agricultural policies was the increase of productivity. Consequently, if you read the founding treaty of the European Community, you will not even find the mention of quality under the chapter [on] agriculture. . . . [Today,] however, things are quite different. In the latest reform of the CAP [Common Agricultural Policy], the Agenda 2000, the European Union has set out new goals for our policy, with competitiveness, food safety, and food quality as the first objectives. (Fischler 2002, 2)

EU legislation on GMOs has three main requirements: approval and registration, labeling, and "traceability." Directive 90/220/EEC, the original legislation governing GMOs in the EU, established a multistep approval process through which any GMO or product containing GMOs must successfully pass before entering the European market. A new directive, 2001/18/EC, which came into force in October 2002 and repealed 90/220/EEC, updates and strengthens the approval process.

The Regulation on Novel Foods and Novel Food Ingredients (Regulation (EC) 258/97), as well as a handful of other provisions, complement Directive 2001/18/EC. They provide for mandatory labeling of foods and food ingredients that contain, or consist of, GMOs. They also mandate that GMOs be traceable through all stages of production and distribution "from the farm to the fork." Producers and dealers in GMO products must have procedures in place to identify from whom the products were obtained and to whom they are made available. More recently, new legislation passed by the European Parliament in the summer of 2003 extends current labeling and traceability laws and streamlines the authorization process. Among the provisions enacted by this legislation are labeling requirements for feed to complement those for food, as well as more specific traceability obligations for business operators.

Between 1991 and 1998, eighteen GMOs were authorized for release onto the European market (Bates 1999, 8). No further authorizations were granted after 1998, although approximately a dozen applications were pending. Individual member states have taken further action against GMOs that extends beyond the provisions of EU legislation. For example,

Both Austria and Luxembourg have flat-out refused GM trials in their countries, and France is currently being challenged by the EU Commission over its decision to withhold pro forma approval of two strains of GM rapeseed—strains that were approved by the Commission in 1997. On the issue of ethics and GMOs, Sweden has taken the lead by demanding that ethical considerations be taken into account in issuing licenses for the marketing of GMOs. Denmark, Spain, and Greece have supported Sweden's stand on ethics and, further, have vowed never to approve products that may cause resistance to medicinal antibiotics. (Sandblom 2000, 11)

In response to concerns by citizens and member governments, the EU essentially froze its GMO approval process in 1999 pending reform of GMO regulations, a move designed to increase the confidence of the European consumer and to ensure the existence of an environment in which Europeans could make independent and informed choices about food purchases. The 2003 legislation arguably signals the end of this process, thus clearing the way for a removal of the ban on GMOs in Europe. The United States, Canada, and Argentina have yet to cancel their claim before the World Trade Organization.

The fact that the United States, Canada, and Argentina are using the WTO dispute settlement mechanism to protest the European GMO regulatory framework effectively redefines the debate as a trade issue. The regulatory framework comes to be understood primarily—even solely—as a barrier to trade (with all the attendant negative connotations) rather than as a broader effort to promote a set of sociocultural goals revolving around food security, sovereignty, and culinary identity.

We must await the ruling from the WTO panel. Nonetheless, it is apparent that the European GMO laws do not conform to a traditional understanding of protectionism. This understanding is summarized well by Melvyn Krauss (1978, 6): "The conflict between the economic interests of specific groups within the community and the economic interests of the community as a whole is the essence of the free trade versus protectionism controversy. Free traders argue from the standpoint of the overall economy; protectionists argue from the standpoint of particular interest groups." The particular interest groups that benefit from protection are usually producers; economists demonstrate that consumers generally benefit from free trade.

Yet these oppositions are not in play in the GMO controversy. Rather than pitting the economic interests of a specific domestic group against those of their foreign counterparts, or against the aggregate economic interests of the community, GMO legislation in Europe sets up unfamiliar oppositions. The American biotech industry claims that it loses as a result of European GMO laws. The ban on approvals did restrict the access of non-European producers to the European market. However, it is important to recognize that during the period of stalled approvals, European producers of GMOs ran up against the same sorts of restrictions that Americans and others did. It is not that no new *American* GMOs were approved during that period; no new GMOs were approved at all. Meanwhile, some foreign producers bene-fited from the regulations. Brazilian farmers, for example, who produce non-GM soy crops, were able to increase their exports to Europe under the moratorium.

The policy framework does not protect those who produce organic or non-GMO foods either. It is apparent that these producers do not need pro-tection since GMO products do not tempt European consumers. Who ben-efits, then, in Europe? If we use the language of trade, it would appear that these measures protect consumers who wish to be informed about the con-tent of their food purchases. It may, however, be more accurate to take our cues from Friedrich List. As Helleiner cites him in the concluding chapter of this volume, List counsels us against categorizing people merely as pro-ducers or consumers, rather than citizens. From this perspective, GMO reg-ulations exist to preserve a way of life, a range of choices, and an identity.

That certain domestic constituencies might actually incur an economic cost as a result of these policies might compel some analysts to conclude that these policies are therefore not examples of economic nationalism. Such a conclusion makes sense, however, only if we understand economic nation-alist policy in terms of security. When economic growth and industrial de-velopment were equated with national security, no economic nationalist would allow added economic costs. But when promotion of national iden-tity and autonomy are associated with security, economic cost may be ac-ceptable. It is worth remembering that List's core goals were "prosperity, civilization, and power," not just prosperity. (See Helleiner 2002 for a fuller discussion of this). It may be in the general interest to remove barriers to the movement of GMOs if we measure the general interest in terms of max-imizing wealth. But if we also measure the general welfare in terms of cul-ture and identity, it may make sense to retain these barriers.

Geographical Indications

In the realm of intellectual property rights, the European Union lists "im-prove[d] protection for geographical indications" as one of its four "key ob-jectives" for the ongoing discussions of intellectual property, as well as for the Doha round of WTO talks. "Protected geographical indication" (PGI) is perhaps the term most commonly associated with this class of protections, but it is not the only one. "Protected designation of origin" (PDO) is also common, and periodically we run across "certificates of special character"

(CSC), "certification registration mark" (CRM), and "traditional specialty guarantees" (TSG). Both the European Union and the WTO, under the auspices of the Agreement on Trade-Related Aspects of Intellectual Property Rights (TRIPS agreement), provide for geographical indication protections, although the definitions differ slightly, as do the categories of products enjoying protection. The United States, Canada, and other countries offer similar protections, although they often fall under trademark law.

For the EU, "PDO covers the term used to describe foodstuffs which are produced, processed and prepared in a given geographical area using recognised know-how." For a PGI, "the geographical link must occur in at least one of the stages of production, processing or preparation. Furthermore, the product can benefit from a good reputation." "A TSG does not refer to the origin but highlights traditional character, either in the composition or means of production."[1]

The EU initiated this program in 1992 under regulations 2081/92 and 2082/92. Article 2, section 2, of 2081/92 reads as follows:

2. For the purposes of this Regulation:
   (a) designation of origin: means the name of a region, a specific place or, in exceptional cases, a country, used to describe an agricultural product or a foodstuff:
   —originating in that region, specific place or country, and
   —the quality or characteristics of which are essentially or exclusively due to a particular geographical environment with its inherent natural and human factors, and the production, processing and preparation of which take place in the defined geographical area;
   (b) geographical indication: means the name of a region, a specific place or, in exceptional cases, a country, used to describe an agricultural product or a foodstuff:
   —originating in that region, specific place or country, and
   —which possesses a specific quality, reputation or other characteristics attributable to that geographical origin and the production and/or processing and/or preparation of which take place in the defined geographical area.[2]

Article 3 of 2081/92 distinguishes between those products that merit protection and those whose names have become generic. "For the purposes of this Regulation, a 'name that has become generic' means the name of an agricultural product or a foodstuff which, although it relates to the place or the region where this product or foodstuff was originally produced or

1. See www.europa.eu.int/comm/agriculture/foodqual/quali1_en.htm.
2. Ibid.

marketed, has become the common name of an agricultural product or a foodstuff." A product whose name has become generic cannot be registered.

Article 4(1) of Council Regulation 2082/92 specifies that "in order to appear in the register referred to in Article 3, an agricultural product or foodstuff must either be produced using traditional raw materials or be characterized by a traditional composition or a mode of production and/or processing reflecting a traditional type of production and/or processing."

PDO status carries a variety of other requirements: the region or soil must contribute to the character or quality of the product and proof of this must be offered as part of the registration process; specific raw materials required in the production of the product must be available in the specific region only, a region that is clearly delimited; the product must be produced according to a special manufacturing technique; and the production of the product must be based on the knowledge of manufacturers, built up over generations. Protection is given only to groups. Individuals cannot apply for PDO status. Rather, producers of a good seeking protected designation of origin must form a representative association.

Over five hundred products are registered with the EU. Certain products are covered by both regulations 2081/92 and 2082/92. These include fresh meat, cheeses, other products of animal origin (eggs, honey, milk products excluding butter, etc.), oils and fats (butter, margarine, oils, etc.), fruits, vegetables, cereals, fish, beer, bread, pastry, cakes, confectionery, biscuits, and other bakers' wares. Other products are covered only by regulation 2081/92. They include natural mineral waters and spring waters, natural gums and resins, essential oils, hay, and cork. Specific examples of products that have garnered protected designation of origin status are Kalamata extra virgin olive oil, Proscuitto di Parma, Roquefort cheese, Irish Timoleague Brown Pudding, Cornish Clotted Cream, Tyrolean Grey cheese, French Foin de Crau hay, Scotch whisky, and Feta cheese.

The latter is a particularly interesting example because it is among the PDOs and PGIs that have generated court cases before the European Court of Justice. For several years, feta producers, in consultation with the Greek government, have fought a battle to ensure that feta has PDO status. The EU Commission first accepted the proposal that feta receive protection in 1996. Three other member states (and "feta" producers)—France, Germany, and Denmark—immediately protested this decision, asking that the decision be annulled. Their request was based primarily on the assertion that feta is actually a generic term. In other words, they argued that feta does not denote a particular cheese that hails from a particular location. Rather, it denotes a particular product, a white cheese that can be produced anywhere using a variety of ingredients and methods of production. According to this argument, Danish feta, for example, which resembles in color and texture "authentic" feta cheese, could be sold under the name "feta" because consumers do not expect that their feta necessarily comes from Greece. Nor would they necessarily expect it to be made according to traditional manufacturing practices, with the milk of ewes that have grazed on distinctive local flora in the Greek countryside, as the Greeks maintain.

Acting on the assertions of the French, Danes, and Germans, the European Court of Justice rescinded feta's PDO status and launched a series of investigations that included Eurobarometer polling, as well as consultations with various experts in cheese making. The EU Commission concluded in June 2002 that consumers do actually associate feta cheese with Greece. Furthermore, the Commission established that Greek feta has production requirements that differentiate it from its non-Greek counterparts: "The interplay between . . . natural factors and . . . specific human factors, in particular the traditional production method . . . has thus given 'Feta' cheese its remarkable reputation" (Commission of the EU 2002b, 11). Feta had not, therefore, become a generic term and the Commission reinstated feta's PDO status.

At the WTO, geographical indications are part of the TRIPS agreement. Part 2, section 3 of TRIPS contains specific provisions governing products that "have a specific quality, reputation, or other characteristic that derives from the particular location where the product originates."[3] Article 22(1) of TRIPS says that "geographical indications are, for the purposes of this Agreement, indications which identify a good as originating in the territory of a Member, or a region or locality in that territory, where a given quality, reputation or other characteristic of the good is essentially attributable to its geographical origin." Article 22 continues in the following manner:

2. In respect of geographical indications, Members shall provide the legal means for interested parties to prevent:
   (a) the use of any means in the designation or presentation of a good that indicates or suggests that the good in question originates in a geographical area other than the true place of origin in a manner which misleads the public as to the geographical origin of the good;
   (b) any use which constitutes an act of unfair competition within the meaning of Article 10bis of the Paris Convention (1967).
3. A Member shall, ex officio if its legislation so permits or at the request of an interested party, refuse or invalidate the registration of a trademark which contains or consists of a geographical indication with respect to goods not originating in the territory indicated, if use of the indication in the trademark for such goods in that Member is of such a nature as to mislead the public as to the true place of origin.

---

3. This quote and the legal quotes that follow are from www.wto.org/english/docs_e/legal_e/27–trips_04b_e.htm.

4. The protection under paragraphs 1, 2 and 3 shall be applicable against a geographical indication which, although literally true as to the territory, region or locality in which the goods originate, falsely represents to the public that the goods originate in another territory.

Article 23(1) of TRIPS provides even stronger protections for wines and spirits, requiring each member state to

provide the legal means for interested parties to prevent use of a geographical indication identifying wines for wines not originating in the place indicated by the geographical indication in question or identifying spirits for spirits not originating in the place indicated by the geographical indication in question, even where the true origin of the goods is indicated or the geographical indication is used in translation or accompanied by expressions such as "kind," "type," "style," "imitation" or the like.

The provisions included in the EU regulation and in the TRIPS agreement are not the first to recognize designations of origin. Individual countries have had such laws on their books for decades. For example, as far back as 1955, the Italian government granted protected designation of origin to the recognized producers of Grana Podano cheese. In 1966, the British government granted a certification trademark to the Stilton Cheese Makers Association, specifying that only cheeses produced by seven dairies in Derbyshire, Leicestershire, and Nottinghamshire could sell cheese under the Stilton name. In addition, France has long maintained a body of *appellation d'origine controlée* laws concerning the authenticity of wines and spirits associated with specific regions. Designations of origin protections have also been previously enshrined in international agreements, including the Paris Convention for the Protection of Industrial Property and the Lisbon Agreement for the Protection of Appellation of Origin and Their International Registration.

Although geographical indications are not new, their current reinforcement is noteworthy. In a period characterized by sustained efforts to remove barriers to trade, the EU and the WTO (under the auspices of the TRIPS), seem to be flouting their liberalizing mission by embracing and expanding PDO and PGI protection. Indeed, many who oppose these provisions and seek their removal categorize them as straightforward protectionism. For example, the American National Food Processors Association (NFPA) recently responded to a call from the Office of Trade and Economic Analysis of the U.S. Department of Commerce with comments designed to assist in the preparation of the Annual National Trade Estimate Report on Foreign Trade Barriers. In the section on the European Union, the NFPA says the following:

Throughout Europe, a political "consumers' need to know" agenda is driving a multitude of burdensome and complex labeling regimes. . . . The labeling extremes are well documented in a recently released FAS GAIN report #FR1062 describing French and the EU Product Origin and Quality Labeling standards and the various related logos. These include for France: (1) appellation of origin; (2) Label Rouge; (3) organic agriculture denomination; (4) certification of conformity—a quality mark. The EU has other protective logos: (1) Protected designation of origin; (2) Protected geographical indication; (3) Traditional specialty guaranteed. . . . *NFPA maintains that these so-called "marks of quality" are designed to protect the EU domestic producers and specific rural production areas from imported competition.* (NFPA 2001, 5; emphasis added)

Likewise, Jenny Mosca (2000) argues that geographical indications serve as a barrier to the free movement of goods and the fact that products receive protection as PGIs or PDOs represents an exception to the free movement of goods. The American government makes a similar argument in its dispute against the European Union. In 1999 the United States—later joined by Australia—asked the EU to enter into consultations regarding regulation 2081/92. The United States revived this issue in 2003, in the run-up to the Cancun ministerial meetings, asking for additional consultations. In August 2003 the American government requested that a panel be struck in the wake of failed efforts to resolve the issue in the consultation phase. At the time of this writing, the panel has yet to offer a decision. The U.S. request identifies the core problem as one of national treatment: "Regulation 2081/92 does not provide the same treatment to other nationals and products originating outside the EC that it provides to the EC's own nationals and products, does not accord immediately and unconditionally to the nationals and products of each WTO member any advantage, favour, privilege or immunity granted to the nationals and products of other WTO Members" (U.S. Mission to WTO 2003, 1). The European Union registers non-European products only when the non-European country provides reciprocal protection to EU products. The United States and Australia do so in limited cases.

It is not entirely inaccurate to suggest that geographical indications have protectionist effects. Nonetheless, as is true for GMO regulations, geographical indications are not the straightforward example of protectionism that some portray them to be. For example, it is worth noting that while PDO and PGI protection shields domestic producers from unfair competition, it can also discriminate against domestic producers who do not belong to the recognized consortium of product manufacturers to whom PDO or PGI protection has been accorded. Similarly, within the European context, the feta case clearly demonstrates that EU members challenge *each other* on lists of registered foodstuffs. Therefore, geographical indications are not simply pitting domestic producers against foreign ones or European producers against non-European ones. If indeed these policies are merely protections for local producers, it is puzzling that they are not being dismantled with other barriers. Even the U.S. complaint against the EU faults the Europeans less for the existence of the geographical indications framework than for its apparent incompatibility with its TRIPS counterpart. Europeans actually share U.S. goals to some degree. Both the EU and the United States arguably want to see a fragmented system of national trademarks and geographical indications harmonized. Where they part company is on the extent to which this might be permitted and the range of products they would like to see registered. Ironically, though, both the United States and the European Union claim, for different reasons, that the regulations governing geographical indications are insufficient.

Who loses, then, in Europe as a result of the PGI and PDO regulations? The losers are both foreign and domestic entities who hope to sell inauthentic products under registered names. Who wins? The producers of recognized authentic products do, as do consumers who assume that foodstuff names are indicators of quality, origin, and authenticity. Again, List's reminder—remember the citizen—seems relevant here, since geographical indications are concerned with local knowledge and traditional know-how. They are bound up with concerns about national security, autonomy, and collective identity in ways that the language of protectionism and outdated understandings of economic nationalism do not capture.

That there might be an explanation for geographical indications grounded in identity and security considerations seems convincing since acceptance of PDO or PGI status obliges producers to contravene some basic commercial principles. For example, in order to gain PDO protection, producers vow that the manufacturing techniques used are, and will remain, the age-old processes used by previous generations. While these processes arguably distinguish the products and add value to them, this commitment also implies that foodstuffs with PDO protection cannot evolve in terms of product characteristics or manufacturing processes. Innovation, arguably at the heart of economic progress, is impossible.

Balaam and Veseth assert that "it mattered little to liberals, who produced the goods, where, how, or under what circumstances as long as individuals were free to buy and sell them on open markets" (2001, 112). Gilpin echoes this when he says that "neoclassical economists believe that the territorial distribution of economic activities is of little consequence as long as every economy is behaving according to the law of comparative advantage" (2001, 104–5). He goes on to note that not everyone shares this view, as PDO policies demonstrate. Says Gilpin, "the question of which countries produce what—potato chips or computer chips—is of utmost importance to groups, nations, and regions around the world." This is most certainly true for producers of PDO and PGI products.

In this chapter, I reinforce the point made by others in this volume—albeit from a slightly different perspective—that economic nationalism and liberalization need not be construed as mutually exclusive categories. Andrei Tsygankov, Rawi Abdelal, Derek Hall, and Eric Helleiner, for example, show that governments may actually pursue liberalization to achieve nationalist goals. I make the related claim that governments that pursue policies of economic nationalism do not, on principle, oppose liberalization. Governments that advocate liberalization may *simultaneously* implement economic nationalist policies *in some sectors*. European governments that resist GMOs and protect PDOs and PGIs are also among the most trade-dependent nations and the most active in advancing trade liberalization at the multilateral level. Recognizing that economic nationalism need not signal a slide into autarky—but rather represents one strategy that governments embrace to provide for the security, autonomy, and identity of the nation—may dissolve many of the negative connotations associated with a conventional definition of economic nationalism. This should especially be true when examples of economic nationalism do not display the features of protectionism with which it has traditionally, and erroneously, been associated.

I have also argued that this new era of globalization is inviting innovation in the sorts of policies governments implement to protect their national security. Many developments associated with globalization are more threatening to the cultural survival of a nation than to its legal or territorial survival. France may still appear on a map, but there is a worry that France's imagined community, represented through shared understandings, values, traditions, and practices, will be so changed as to be unrecognizable. Many tools that societies have used to distinguish themselves and to assert national identity are rendered ineffective by contemporary developments. Yet distinguishing the nation and promoting collective identity are still goals of governments, even in a period of accelerated economic integration. Governments, therefore, mobilize less traditional means, demonstrating that the form economic nationalism takes is largely contingent on the historical context.

Economic nationalists like Friedrich List and Alexander Hamilton lacked faith in the market alone to provide for the well-being of the nation. They, therefore, advocated enlisting economic policies in the service of national goals. A similar lack of faith is present in those who advocate the policies I have described above. Economic policies that regulate the movement of genetically modified organisms, as well as PDO and PGI products, provide contemporary examples of how concerns over national identity and security are still intimately intertwined with economic policies and processes.

9

Country before Money?

Economic Globalization and National Identity in New Zealand

Jacqui True

Globalization is often viewed as a threat to the nation-state and a force for the homogenization of national identities and cultures. Sooner or later, critics say, all of us will be wearing Gap jeans, every coffee shop in town will be a Starbucks, and McDonald's will be the only place left to dine out. Recent protests against the actions of the World Trade Organization, the World Bank, and the International Monetary Fund claimed that global integration threatens local diversity. Yet claims of this sort run up against strong assertions of national identity and cultural distinctiveness by states, citizens, and corporations. As states compete for global capital, we see intense efforts to play up the distinctiveness of local characteristics and competitive advantages. Louis Pauly argues that the logic of markets embraces globalism while the logic of politics remains deeply marked by nationalism (2000, 120). Yet far from being contradictory, these logics can serve to reinforce each other (True 2003; Pickel and True 2002).

A study of the New Zealand case leads us to rethink how nationalism shapes globalization, and how globalization in turn impels local actors to take advantage of—and indeed reinforce—their distinctiveness in the world. Intriguingly, these processes reveal that cultural representations of the state can advance national economic interests (albeit often the particular interests of one group within the nation) while advancing global economic integration. This suggests that some of the debates between advocates and critics of globalization have diverted our attention from the ongoing, theoretically important tension between global and local forces.

New Zealand is a particularly fascinating case of the dynamics between economic nationalism and economic globalization given its recent history of radical neoliberal economic change. Until the 1970s New Zealand was primarily an agricultural producer, and 70 percent of its exports were sold to Britain. After Britain joined the European common market in 1971, New

Zealand suffered a significant export setback and was forced to explore new markets and to expand its production beyond the agricultural sector. The government called for export diversification from meat, wool, and dairy to other land-based exports and urban manufacturing. In the 1970s the government offered huge tax breaks to offset development costs, and export incentives to promote new industries such as natural gas, aluminum manufacturing, and horticulture (see Crocombe et al. 1991). By the 1980s the New Zealand economy was in dire straits with high inflation, major foreign debt, and financial speculation that led to a forced devaluation of the New Zealand dollar. New political forces in the Labour Party, persuaded by the merits of the market mechanism, came to power in 1984 with an agenda to transform the protectionist welfare state overnight. Market-based reforms were rapidly instituted in the mid to late 1980s both in the private sector and in the central government sector. State subsidies were removed, trade tariffs were reduced, state assets were privatized, and austerity policies were imposed on core public services.

Today, the political economy of New Zealand has been radically transformed by more than fifteen years of policy change (see Boston et al. 1996). At the same time, the global economy has become increasingly integrated and has contributed to the restructuring of the New Zealand economy. For instance, due to the expansion of the service sector worldwide and the greatly lowered cost of travel, tourism is now second to the dairy industry as the biggest export earner, followed by export of educational services and meat. Government involvement in the promotion of the national export economy is one of its most important roles. Increasingly, the capacity of government to manage domestic political constituencies and to provide services to citizens rests on the success of the government initiatives in the global economic realm (see Miller 2003).

In this chapter, I discuss three examples of the interplay between economic globalization and national identity in New Zealand. The first is the creation of Brand New Zealand and efforts to play up New Zealand's national distinctiveness in the quest for global competitive advantage and economic development. Such efforts have reinvigorated nationalism and national identity as well as attracted foreign tourism and investment.

The second example is the transformation of the Chinese gooseberry into the kiwifruit that New Zealand has marketed throughout the world. The kiwifruit is considered to be one of New Zealand's greatest export successes, and crucial to its success has been an export marketing campaign that capitalizes on national motifs and a single-desk producer board that manages interactions between producers, exporters, and the competitive global market. Both the Brand New Zealand and kiwifruit cases illustrate mutually reinforcing processes of contemporary economic nationalism and economic globalization (see Helleiner 2002).

The third example explores the America's Cup yachting race, specifically New Zealand's 2003 campaign to defend the Cup from the challenges of foreign syndicates owned by billionaire businessmen. On the face of it, this is a story of an underdog nation-state pitted against global corporate wealth in a cultural (sporting) struggle that has big material payoffs for the winner. When analyzed more closely, however, New Zealand's defense of the Cup is much less a story of local nationalism prevailing over global capital than one of elites manipulating people's loyalty in order to further their own interests in the global economy. Seen from this perspective, nationalism is not only compatible with liberal capitalism; it can serve as an agent in its expansion, most especially in opening societies and sectors previously isolated from global market forces.

These examples suggest that both the economic and the political relations that accompany globalization are complex and subtle, more so than even the most vocal critics of globalization have claimed. New Zealand's national identity has always been rooted in a narrative of economic progress, of the triumph of pioneering individuals against nature. In the current context, this national narrative is reinvented to serve the ends of global competition.

Changing Identities: The Nation-State Becomes the Brand-State

Economic nationalism and economic globalization are not opposing forces but integrally related, often mutually reinforcing ideologies and processes. In his article "The Rise of the Brand State," Peter Van Hamm (2001) argues that states, cities, and regions now have to market themselves professionally through aggressive sales techniques to attract investment and business. In this quest to attract capital, the public relations expert Wally Olins writes that "nations increasingly emphasise nationality" even though global companies increasingly ignore it (1999, 1). "Nations increasingly use business-speak—growth targets, education targets, health targets; global companies increasingly emphasise 'soft' issues, their value to society and their benevolent influence. The relationship between companies and countries is getting closer. They compete, they overlap, they swap places."

Global interconnectedness facilitated by the revolution in media over the past two decades has made each state more aware of itself—of its image, reputation, and attitude as seen in other parts of the world. This situation presents new opportunities for states to leverage their national stock. The nation-state plays up its distinctive history, geography, and gender and ethnic motifs and in so doing (re)invents a sense of national identity in order to carve out a strategic niche and competitive advantage in the global economy.

In the global market, intense competition occurs over product differentiation as well as price. Consumer demand is increasingly complex and sophisticated. In her book *No Logo*, Naomi Klein registers this change in the capitalist economy. Whereas once goods and services were distinguished by their material use value, now they are distinguished by their symbolic value. In contemporary capitalism, the product is the brand, and the brand is the product. Klein gives the classic example of the Absolut vodka marketing campaign: The actual "product disappears and its brand [is] nothing but a blank-bottle-shaped space that [can] be filled with whatever content a particular audience most want[s] from its brand" (Klein 1999, 17). It is more a feeling, an emotional resonance, than anything tangible. Apply that same formula to nation-states and you have nation-state (R), the "brand-state." Image and reputation are an essential part of the nation-state's competitive advantage in the global political economy: a nation-state's image and the successful transference of this image to its exports are just as important as what the country actually produces and sells. Countries represent themselves to global consumers and investors, acting like contestants a beauty contest. Here gendered and ethnic motifs become important collateral in a nation-state's brand equity. Think of the allure of Singapore Airlines' servile "Singapore girl" and the rugged Australian he-man "Crocodile Dundee," who put their countries on the tourist map. In the case of New Zealand, a "pure," clean, green brand has recently been fashioned to distinguish the country and its exports on the global market (see Campbell-Hunt et al. 2001; Eagles 2002; *New Zealand Business* 2002/3).

New Zealand: Clean, Green, and GE Free?

The image of New Zealand as clean and green has been promoted to gain a competitive edge in trade and tourism. The New Zealand Ministry of the Environment recently commissioned a report on the overseas image of New Zealand and found that this image is worth about NZ$530 million annually to the tourism sector and NZ$938 million to the economy as a whole.[1] Linking New Zealand products to New Zealand's apparently clean and green environment has had considerable payoffs for export revenues.

The producers of everything from food and wine to fashion, films, boat building, and biotechnology seek to distinguish their products on global markets by playing on New Zealand's environmental reputation, if not its actual environmental record. This image is served up for foreign audiences, but it also bolsters New Zealanders' own national identity. And it commodifies the land for commercial gain while masking environmental problems

---

1. Fonterra, New Zealand's largest company estimates that the value of "clean and green" to each dairy farmer is between NZ$18,000 and NZ$49,000 per annum (Elworthy 2002).

(see Bell 2002; Hughes 1993; Buhr and Bartlett 1993). Most New Zealanders believe in the image, just as tourists do. They see New Zealand as a land "little affected by industrial pollution, overpopulation, traffic congestion, noise, urban decay. It is a country associated with national parks, scenic beauty, wilderness areas, beautiful deserted beaches, green pastures and a friendly population" (Hughes 1993, 4). To continually reconfirm their own sense of identity and security in the nation, they need tourists to describe their country as beautiful.

Not taken in by the nation branding, the journal *New Scientist* ran an article in 1993 titled "New Zealand's Poisoned Paradise," in which images of New Zealand as an "untouched" paradise are juxtaposed to photographs of land contaminated by hazardous chemicals (Hughes 1993). This undermining of the country's environmental image, so important to the country's economic success, upset New Zealand politicians.

To avoid such embarrassment, New Zealand producers have been forced to live up to their "environmental quality" branding at home (see Oram 2001; www.new-zealand.com/nzway.html). For example, New Zealand winegrowers are encouraged to introduce environmentally sound practices so that they fulfill the logo "New Zealand wine—riches of a clean, green land" when they market their product overseas. No other wine-growing region or country has developed such an environmental scorecard, and there are reported to be European buyers who will reward this effort (*New Zealand Herald* 2003a, A12).

Likewise, the Sustainability Council, formed by five prominent New Zealanders, has sought to extend the moratorium on genetic modification and engineering (GM/GE), which expired in October 2003, in order to make good on New Zealand's image overseas.[2] They believe that New Zealand butter, lamb, and fruit would lose their premium place in the market overnight if the country adopted genetically engineered agriculture. "If New Zealand adopted GM it would run the risk of becoming an undifferentiated producer of low value bulk agricultural products alongside the US, Argentina, Canada and increasingly China" (Elworthy 2002, 8). Moreover, they claim that New Zealand producers could obtain higher returns from food exports if they market themselves as "GE-free." According to the Sustainability Council, 71 percent of European consumers say they would not touch GE food, and in Britain all the major supermarket chains refuse to sell genetically modified food. In Asia, the Japanese, Koreans, and Taiwanese have similarly shown themselves to be reluctant to buy GM food (Neill 2003). In an increasingly GE world, the catchphrase "clean, green,

2. The founding members of the Sustainability Council are Sir Peter Elworthy (a former president of New Zealand Federated Farmers), Annabel Langbein (an author of cookbooks and a media personality), Dame Susan Devoy (a world squash champion), Sam Neill (a world-famous actor), and Professor Garth Cooper (an academic).

and GM-free" could create a distinctive market niche for New Zealand food products and boost the sales of any industry linking its products to the brand. In this way, economic globalization has provided the momentum for national self-consciousness about environmental sustainability and, indeed, a renewed sense of national identity based on environmental reputation. In turn, this local environmental awareness is expected to have payoffs on the global market.

One Hundred Percent Pure New Zealand

In the 1990s New Zealand tourism doubled its revenues from NZ$1.9 billion to NZ$4 billion. Since 1999, visitor numbers have increased more than 25 percent; in Australia, by contrast, visitor numbers increased just 8.1 percent over the same period. In 2002 the country's tourism revenues amounted to NZ$5.9 billion (Gaynor 2003). The tourism sector is now second to the dairy industry in export earnings. This impressive growth can be attributed to the creation of a global marketing brand for New Zealand.

Tourism New Zealand, the government agency responsible for motivating international travelers to visit New Zealand, launched "100% Pure New Zealand" in 1999. This promotional strategy followed on the heels of re-branding efforts in other countries (such as Great Britain's "From Rule Britannia to Cool Britannia") also seeking to reenergize their economic base with foreign capital. The "100% Pure" brand is the first New Zealand global marketing campaign that uses consistent messages and imagery in all markets, "offering visitors a single, compelling reason to visit New Zealand." It seeks to capitalize on New Zealand's reputation as an untouched paradise and, lately, as a safe haven from terrorism. It "paints a picture of remarkable people, unique culture and invigorating adventure visitors will experience within New Zealand's landscape."[3] This brand plays on people's fantasies of escaping their stressed-out lives and concrete cities. It promises a truly authentic experience, an untouched playground. A question arises, however: How "untouched" is New Zealand when more than two million tourists a year trample the same ground?

Anthropologist Jonathan Friedman distinguishes *weak* globalization, where the local assimilates the global, from *strong* globalization, which involves the homogenization of local contexts (1995, 201–2). He sees tourist marketing campaigns, such as the "100% Pure New Zealand" campaign as a form of weak globalization. Such campaigns aim to capture market share by accentuating local novelty and representing it to the gaze of the global tourist. Strong globalization is indicated by the creation of tourist venues in different local settings that reflect a standardized, predictable global prod-

---

3. See the official New Zealand Tourism website, www.purenz.com.

Figure 9.1. 100% Pure campaign. Courtesy of Tourism New Zealand.

uct, such as Club Meds in banana republics. Clearly, Tourism New Zealand would like to win tourist dollars on New Zealand's own terms, presenting a unique product to the global market. Indeed, Tourism New Zealand wants not more tourists but *wealthier* tourists who are prepared to pay a premium for authenticity. Of course, the authenticity of the New Zealand experience is questionable when it is deliberately crafted with an eye to the tourism dollar.

Brand New Zealand—Winning the World from the Edge?

After Tourism New Zealand initiated the "100% Pure" campaign, the New Zealand government embarked on an overall branding effort to build an identity for New Zealand as a place of knowledge and prosperity that will earn it a more prominent, competitive place in the global economy. In February 2002 Helen Clark, the Prime Minister, outlined the government's "framework for growing an innovative New Zealand." She stated that "government will work with the private sector to develop a consistent brand image of New Zealand across our industry sectors. As well as being seen as clean and green, we need to be more widely perceived as smart and innovative." While the "clean and green" slogan captures the "untouched" physical beauty of New Zealand, it says nothing about the human capital of New Zealanders in a globally competitive environment.

To play up the knowledge capital of New Zealanders, Brian Sweeney, head of public relations firm Sweeney Vesty, has created a website, www.nzedge.com, showcasing New Zealand people, creativity, business, and sport. Sweeney suggests that the concept of "the edge" is a metaphor for life in New Zealand. His view is that change, adventure, and growth happen at the edge of any system, not in the middle. Located on the "edge of the world," New Zealanders can create change and exploit difference to their advantage. But first they have to learn how to "get it in front of people abroad, people who will pay the full international price" for quality products and services. Singled out for criticism are New Zealand vintners who fail to charge top prices for their sauvignon blanc, even though demand far outstrips supply, and the New Zealand film industry, which allowed United States producers to capture much of the commercial value of the *Lord of the Rings* trilogy, filmed and directed in New Zealand.

Nzedge.com promotes New Zealand in a way that forces locals to rethink their identity, stories, achievement, and place in the world. Its principal target is the global community of New Zealanders linked not by their geographic residence but their "imagined community" (Anderson 1983). Brands, like nations, evoke an emotional response. Nzedge.com seeks to create an inclusive, nonterritorial national identity that can ultimately be projected globally. In the words of web author Paul Ward, "embracing global

Figure 9.2. 100% Pure Middle Earth. Courtesy of Tourism New Zealand.

citizenship risks threatening local identity, but at nzedge.com we believe in the ties of fraternity that bind together New Zealanders, on and off-island." According to Ward, one-quarter of New Zealand's population lives overseas and one in twenty young New Zealanders will leave the country permanently, lured by better opportunities in the global labor market. This sizable expatriate population, once seen as only a loss, is now viewed as potentially working for the nation's competitive advantage.

The website nzedge.com documents the potentially valuable contribution of the "Kiwi diaspora" to New Zealand. Other efforts have also been made to encourage a sense of nationalism among Kiwi expatriates who are well placed in the global knowledge economy. For instance, David Teece, a Berkeley professor of economics, and Stephen Tindall, owner of The Warehouse, New Zealand's equivalent to Wal-Mart, have set up a database of expatriate New Zealanders working in Silicon Valley and other science and technology hubs in California with the aim of leveraging their talent and skills for New Zealand's national economic development.

Prime Minister or PR Anchor?

The New Zealand Labour-led coalition government has been very active in promoting a new brand identity to allow New Zealand to project itself externally. Peter Van Hamm argues that "to do their jobs well in the future, politicians will have to train themselves in brand asset management" (2001, 3). Their tasks, he says, will include "finding a brand niche for their state, engaging in competitive marketing, assuring consumer satisfaction and most of all creating brand loyalty. Brand states will compete with superbrands, EU, CNN, Microsoft. . . . In this crowded arena, states that lack relevant brand equity will not survive." Indeed, small states like New Zealand would have to work extra hard to be seen and heard in such an arena or face extinction as a peripheral island economy irrelevant to the global market. Certainly New Zealand's Prime Minister, Helen Clark, seems to have taken the cue.

In 2002 Clark canceled her parliamentary duties for two weeks to make a documentary for the American Discovery channel titled "The Royal Tour." Then she headed to the United States, not to meet with the U.S. President or any other governmental officials, but to promote New Zealand as a safe, exotic destination. (U.S. tourism to New Zealand has increased between 10 and 20 percent each month since September 11, 2001). The Prime Minister appeared on radio and television programs, including NBC's popular *Today Show*, extolling the pleasures to be had on a New Zealand tour (Matthews 2002). All in all, Clark clocked up eighteen television interviews and numerous radio interviews, reaching a far larger audience (and potentially more lucrative market) than her constituency back home. The prime minister flew home on Air New Zealand, now branded as "the official airline to

Middle Earth" after the success of the *Lord of the Rings* trilogy. She enjoyed her time in the limelight and defended her decision to promote the country abroad. However, her colleagues in Parliament were not so enamored with her absence. Although they had yet to see the program, they viewed the trip as a frivolous waste of taxpayer money. Increasingly, the New Zealand prime minister and government walk a fine line between infusing a diverse, multicultural, and highly mobile population with a sense of national identity and promoting a national brand to potential investors and tourists, from whom New Zealand needs the capital to fund national economic and social development.

The Global Success of Kiwifruit

The case of the kiwifruit illustrates the possibilities for nations to manage their national identity successfully while seeking out competitive advantage in global markets. It was a New Zealand schoolteacher, Isabel Fraser, who brought the first seeds of what was then called the Chinese gooseberry to New Zealand after a visit to mission schools in China a hundred years ago. The firm Turners & Growers, in the Bay of Plenty region of New Zealand, suggested the new name "kiwifruit" in the early 1950s. This did much to boost the growth of kiwifruit export markets. "The Americans couldn't stand anything Chinese and the name kiwifruit was distinctive and catchy" (Smith 2003). The first export was made in 1952, but volumes remained small until the late 1960s, increasing to almost one hundred thousand trays by 1969. Today the brand of Zespri kiwifruit stands for quality and taste consistency and is closely tied to the New Zealand brand and its environmental reputation as a clean and green place.[4]

New Zealanders developed a new way of managing kiwifruit vines to maximize quantity and growth. A government-led kiwifruit authority, set up in 1978 with funding from growers and exporters, coordinated the growing and helped with the marketing of the fruit. In 1989, a single Kiwifruit Producer Marketing Board was finally instated. Without such a single desk, kiwifruit growers faced a prisoner's dilemma leading to bitter competition and threatening the survival of the industry (Smith 2003). The Marketing Board was established as a statutory board with responsibility for acquiring and marketing all New Zealand export-grade kiwifruit (except to Australia). It allowed for the standardization of kiwifruit packaging early in its development, using a *New Zealand* rather than a company brand.

---

4. The "KiwiGreen" program applies to all export-grade New Zealand kiwifruit grown to strict environmental and ethical standards (in addition to the organic kiwifruit grown to international Biogro standards).

In the late 1990s Zespri International was established to manage the commercial marketing and selling of kiwifruit separate from the statutory authority. Owned by more than 2,500 owner-producers, Zespri is the biggest marketer of kiwifruit in the world and, true to the name, New Zealand is still the biggest exporter of kiwifruit. New Zealand has 30 percent of global market share and sells to over sixty countries.[5]

To appreciate how successful the kiwifruit has become as a New Zealand industry, consider that just four major fruits and nuts were successfully domesticated in the twentieth century. The United States was responsible for three: avocados, macadamia nuts, and blueberries. New Zealand, a country the size of Colorado, got the fourth, kiwifruit, and was responsible for globally commercializing the fruit. Government policy was crucial in the development of the New Zealand kiwifruit industry and its global marketing success. The New Zealand government funded a kiwifruit research unit jointly with exporters. The Department of Scientific and Industrial Research and the Ministry of Agriculture worked jointly with growers and exporters to produce many innovations over the years in the plant itself and the technology used to sort, store, and pack kiwifruit. The introduction of Gold kiwifruit in the late 1990s is the most significant result of their research program to date.

The Kiwifruit Marketing Board has promoted its product by associating it with New Zealand's clean environment, arguing that this environment provides a sustainable advantage. But focusing too heavily on the country of origin often leads to problems of supply in poor growing seasons. International buyers also increasingly demand a constant year-round supply. Thus, in the 1990s the kiwifruit marketing board had to look beyond New Zealand to develop a global brand and increase its global market share (Beverland n.d.). Zespri International moved to year-round, worldwide marketing through tight joint-venture partnerships with Chilean and Italian growers. Yet it has continued to tie its kiwifruit brand imagery solely to New Zealand. This has been achieved by reengineering the global brand from a focus on where the kiwifruit is produced—in clean, green New Zealand—to how it is produced—in an environmentally and ethically sustainable process evocative of the New Zealand way. Zespri claims to produce a premium, great-tasting product that is produced under a sustainable, world-class quality control system. Thus, national identity and place is still integral to the global marketing of New Zealand kiwifruit.

5. Lately, China's kiwifruit crop has trebled, and by 2006 it will be the world's top producer, although not the top exporter (see Collins 2003).

Loyalty to Nation: The America's Cup Challenge

Economic globalization does not herald the end of the nation-state, nationalism, or national identities. Jan Aart Scholte observes that close contact with "foreigners" through global networks often heightens the sense of national distinctiveness. Indeed, "global spectacles like the Olympics and the World Cup thrive on nationalist fervour" (Scholte 2000, 163). The America's Cup yacht race is yet another spectacle where global competition ignites nationalism and national identity. More than a sporting event among nations, the America's Cup has always been a contest involving technology, design, and innovation. Ever since New Zealand won the Cup in 1995, New Zealanders have portrayed the challenge series as a contest between a small, relatively insignificant nation of modest means and footloose corporate syndicates with twice the budget but none of the national passion. Thus "Kiwi" patriotism is pitted against the purchasing power of some of the world's wealthiest men.

The 1851 founding document of the America's Cup, "The Deed of Gift," requires "friendly competition among nations." In the America's Cup challenge of 2003, however, only the defender, Team New Zealand, represented a nation-state and was funded by public donations and a national set of corporate sponsors organized as a trust. New Zealand and Australia are the only non-American teams to win the Cup in more than a century of challenges. The national myth has been that, with an abundance of coastal waters, all New Zealanders can partake in sailing from a young age, regardless of social class and upbringing. In contrast, the six teams that competed to challenge Team New Zealand in 2003 were each backed by billionaires who had derived their wealth from the profits of their multinational enterprises. They included Ernesto Bertarelli of Swiss-based Alinghi, Larry Ellison of San Francisco-based Oracle/BMW, and Craig McCaw and Paul Allen of Seattle's OneWorld.

The Alinghi challenger Ernesto Bertarelli's private campaign, in particular, served as a counterpoint to the national campaign of Team New Zealand.[6] (Alinghi won the Louis Vuitton Cup in late 2002 and the right to challenge Team New Zealand in early 2003.) Many of the foreign challengers hired away the very New Zealand sailors, builders, and analysts who had worked together as part of Team New Zealand to successfully defend the Cup in 2000. But the mass Kiwi exodus was sparked when Bertarelli recruited the winning Team New Zealand skipper, Russell Coutts, as his skipper for the 2003 challenge. Coutts, a New Zealander, was an Olympic yachting champion and the recipient of an imperial honour for his service

6. As a representative of one of the family of five Team New Zealand corporate sponsors said, "Team NZ is a national effort rather than a commercial syndicate" (quoted in Bingham and Gardiner 2003).

to New Zealand. He accepted a US$5 million offer to become the Alinghi skipper, taking with him Team New Zealand's strategist, Brad Butterworth, and a number of other sailors. Thus, despite its history as a race among nations, one-third of the sailors on the water in the Louis Vuitton semifinals of the America's Cup challenge were actually New Zealanders and former members of Team New Zealand. In order to compete for foreign syndicates, these Kiwi sailors had to live in and own a residence in the respective countries of their syndicates: the United States, Switzerland, Italy, the United Kingdom, and France.[7]

The spectacle of their former Cup-defending heroes selling out to the highest bidder on the global market provoked fellow New Zealanders into a wave of overt nationalism and a demonizing of the "traitors." The name "Loyal campaign" was coined for New Zealand's effort to support Team New Zealand and give it the hometown edge (ASB Bank 2003). A television advertisement showcasing the campaign featured a black-and-white lineup of prominent New Zealanders standing along the New Zealand coastline, arms linked, hands on the heart (as in the American pledge of allegiance). This visual was accompanied by the Team New Zealand theme song, "Loyal," a popular hit from the 1980s composed and sung by local artist Dave Dobbyn. The subtext of the song was spoken softly—but left no doubt about its intent. On the Team New Zealand advertisement, the nationalist message was stripped of all grace notes: "They've come from all four corners to have a go at what's ours. It's their billions against our team of 3.9 million. Team New Zealand—we're with you all of the way."[8]

The darker side of the Loyal campaign was a private venture in support of Team New Zealand that emerged in the run-up to the 2003 America's Cup challenge. It was called the Blackheart campaign, and its slogan was "Country before money." Founded by an advertising executive, Dave Walden, and several prominent New Zealanders who described themselves as "staunch and true" patriots, Blackheart took aim at Coutts and the other sailors who defected from Team New Zealand (Taylor 2002). They did not want to see the country lose the Cup to a foreign syndicate, nor did they want to lose the billions of dollars that every defense of the Cup was claimed to generate for the local economy.[9] "When it comes to New Zealand I believe

7. Ernesto Bertarelli, owner of the Alinghi syndicate, has made public his intention to simplify nationality rules for future teams competing for the America's Cup. This would turn the race from a competition among nations into a professional sport with an advantage to those syndicates with the most money (see *New Zealand Herald* 2003b).

8. The "3.9 millions" refers to the population of New Zealand in 2001. See the video clip of the loyal campaign at www.xtra.co.msn.co.nz/teamnewzealand/0,9104,00.html.

9. Although difficult to calculate, the defense of the 2000 America's Cup is said to have created 8,000 full-time jobs, generated NZ$640 million in additional spending, and boosted the national economy by almost 1 percent (www.Blackheart.com).

Figure 9.3. Loyal. The official
Team New Zealand campaign.
Courtesy of Team New Zealand.

we have always seen this as a national team. That's why it's not called Team
Steinlager or Team Lotto [the sponsors]. That's why it's got government
money. There's a difference" (quoted in Chapple 2003).

In an appeal to nationalist pride, Blackheart—*black* is the country's sports
color, and *heart* stands for heartfelt emotion—posted anti-Alinghi billboards
around Auckland. One read: "Coutts and Co.: Swiss Bankers since 2000."
Another quipped: "High on a hill lives a lonely boatman—yodelei, yodelei,
yodelei-e-e." Blackheart immediately gained extensive media coverage. Its
newsletter reveled in the mythmaking: "The newspapers are publishing
more articles about Team New Zealand's ability to take on the world and win
with limited funds. Yes! Our message is getting through. Success with less is
by no means a recent phenomenon—this country deserves its reputation
for ingenuity. It dates back to the nineteenth century and earlier. Lord
Rutherford explained it perfectly. 'We haven't got the money, so we think
instead.'"[10]

Even the sports pages of the *New York Times* reported that "dozens of black-
shirted Kiwis emblazoned with only the national emblem, a silver fern, and
the word Loyal cheered wildly for the boats belonging to Coutts' rivals"
(Wise 2003). Within a period of three months Blackheart became the
fastest-growing brand in New Zealand: 50 percent of the people had heard
of it, and 30 percent recognized its logo (Chapple 2003). This is the stuff of
banal nationalism: forging a national identity by mobilizing the public

10. Blackheart email newsletter to subscribers, February 5, 2003. Lord Rutherford was the
New Zealand scientist who first split the atom (thus preparing the way for the development
of nuclear fission) in the 1930s.

against an enemy or traitor of the nation (Billig 1995).[11] But in the context of this well-financed boat race, one is reminded of the observation, attributed to Samuel Johnson, that "patriotism is the last refuge of the scoundrel."

Those behind the Blackheart campaign stood to lose more from New Zealand's loss of the America's Cup than the vast majority of New Zealanders. Many of its ringleaders had property investments in or near Viaduct Harbour, a venue especially developed for the Cup race. The harbor, a magnet for tourists, is where these investors gather to catch foreign capital. In other words, the very foreigners that were the target of this nationalistic campaign were crucial to the ongoing wealth accumulation of the most vocal patriots, who also happened to be multimillionaires. As

Figure 9.4. "Country before Money." Courtesy of Blackheart.

a local journalist observed when these "patriots" began their campaign, "The car park at the launch [of Blackheart] resembled a flash European car sales yard with its abundance of Audis, Mercedes and BMWs (colour of choice: Black)" (Taylor 2002).

Economic nationalism may not be at odds with economic globalization. In New Zealand, market liberalization has in fact made the nationalist campaign possible. The view of the Blackhearts and the Loyal patriots is that New Zealand can have national economic development only if it attracts foreign capital (Hendery 2003a, 2003b). The America's Cup yacht race is a perfect opportunity for New Zealand to showcase itself to global investors. It facilitates the branding of New Zealand in the global limelight. The notion is that benevolent capitalists who come to Auckland for the Cup defense will help fund New Zealand's move up the OECD economic wealth ranks (cf. Wade 2001). A few days before the Cup challenge the New Zealand government hosted an "investment regatta" for super-yacht owners and other rich foreigners. The content of nationalist ideology being propounded in this case is not the usual protectionism. On the contrary, this form of economic nationalism looks to the world to bolster the local economy.

At the deepest level both the Loyal and the Blackheart campaigns are

---

11. The nationalist crusade turned more sinister than banal when in the month before the Cup challenge the Alinghi syndicate said it had received anonymous letters threatening the children and family of team members (Ash and Gower 2003).

based on a fundamental contradiction. Undeniably, Team New Zealand's winning the America's Cup in 1995 generated a huge boon for New Zealand (see Eagles 2003). There are several obvious reasons. It got New Zealand's name out there as a great sporting nation, and it underscored the country's technological edge, which had spin-offs in the national knowledge economy. On a personal note, New Zealanders loved to have foreigners come to visit and to admire their country. They wanted them to keep coming. But most of all, they wished that they would come just to admire the Cup, spend their money, and go away.

Of course, the nature of the event brings another dynamic to bear. The foreigners are, in fact, intensely interested in visiting New Zealand because they want to take away an asset that New Zealanders cherish and that many regard as the nation's ticket to future economic well-being (read: "The foreigners come with their billions to have a go at what's ours"). They hate the foreigners for that; they especially hate the power of the global capitalists who have lured Kiwi sailors away and in so doing, threatened New Zealand's monopoly of the Cup. Yet the economic nationalism of the Blackheart and Loyal campaigns was vital because it bolstered the willingness of the average citizen and the government to keep pumping money into Team New Zealand. Without this financial and emotional outpouring, the local team would have been left high and dry long before the race started. Following New Zealand's loss of the America's Cup in 2003, the New Zealand government again contributed more than $5 million to assist Team New Zealand retain key sailors for the next America's Cup race to be held overseas. Many citizens condemned this use of public funds to support an essentially private and elitist sport. The government begged to differ. It saw the America's Cup as a relatively cheap and potentially lucrative way of promoting New Zealand to international tourists and corporate investors.

In conventional economic nationalist accounts, globalization presents many threats to small, relatively unprotected nations like New Zealand that are highly dependent on foreign export earnings and foreign capital. These threats include domestic vulnerability to global economic cycles, instability engendered by global financial speculation on the local currency, outflow of capital as former state-owned enterprises are privatized and taken over by multinational corporations, difficulty in competing for distant global markets, departure of skilled professionals or knowledge workers seeking higher wages, and failure of local firms because of cheaper imports. Despite these threats, globalization has opened spaces for new forms of state agency and new representations of national identity. In the case of New Zealand it has forced a "rebranding" of identity to distinguish local products and talent in competitive global markets: "clean and green," "100% Pure New Zealand," "New Zealand Edge." Indeed, globalization rewards efforts to showcase the nation and differentiate it. New Zealand kiwifruit has been so successful on international markets because of the innovation of New Zealand producers, but also because of its association with New Zealand's wholesome environmental reputation in the marketing of "Kiwi."

In a competitive environment, governments as well as exporters seek to re-create and play up their national brand to attract and keep foreign investment for local development. New Zealand's 2003 defense of the America's Cup was presented as a national struggle to win a world sporting event. But here banal nationalism and economic nationalism met head on. Loyalty to Team New Zealand was inextricable from loyalty to the economic nation, since staging the event and retaining the Cup was expected to produce major economic spin-offs in New Zealand.

Economic nationalism is not the antithesis of globalization. To the contrary, nationalism and globalization may serve the very same material ends. Efforts to reinvent New Zealand's national identity emerged not as a form of resistance or opposition to the power of global capital but instead as a way to capture the attention of powerful investors. However, this version of economic nationalism faces a serious contradiction. Foreign capital generated by a branding campaign may undermine the very national identity that first attracted it. For example, tourism and foreign investment compromise the sustainability of New Zealand's clean, green, and GE-free brand because they seek to exploit and profit from nonrenewable national resources. At the level of practical politics, it is troubling that those who protest globalization have done little to point out these contradictions and politicize them. While critics of globalization focus their activism on international institutions, global summits, and multinational "brand bullies," the politics of globalization at the national and local levels has very often been neglected. To stay relevant, activists need to contest—or some might say "culture-jam" (Klein 1999)—the brands of nation-states, just as they have done for corporations. In this age of globalization, the nation-state is an increasingly important site for political action.

Conclusion: The Meaning and Contemporary Significance of Economic Nationalism

Eric Helleiner

This volume is designed to contribute to current debates about the meaning and significance of economic nationalism in this age of globalization. What have we learned? This volume makes three central contributions to these debates. First, it sharpens the meaning of economic nationalism by defining it according to its nationalist content, rather than as a variant of realism or a "protectionist" ideology. The most significant implication of this understanding of economic nationalism is that the term can be associated with a wide variety of policies, including economic liberal ones. Second, the volume challenges the conventional view that economic nationalism is an outdated ideology. As the various chapters highlight, nationalism and national identities continue to influence economic policies and processes in very significant ways; indeed, many chapters suggest that economic globalization and economic nationalism are mutually reinforcing. Finally, the volume contributes to recent critiques of "rationalist" political economy by highlighting the significant role that ideational factors play in economic policy. With its focus on the economic significance of national identities and nationalism, the volume develops a constructivist approach to the study of international political economy (IPE) that explores the interrelationship between identities and interests, and the different ways in which identities can be linked causally to policy outcomes.

The Meaning of Economic Nationalism: "Bringing the Nation Back In"

Although "economic nationalism" is widely discussed in debates about the global economy, the contributors to this volume show how the term has of-

I am grateful to Peter Katzenstein, Andreas Pickel, and Derek Hall for their helpful comments.

ten been used in a confusing manner by both scholars and popular writers. Some prominent IPE scholarship uses the phrase as a synonym for the doctrines of realism and mercantilism (see especially Gilpin 1987). But as Rawi Abdelal points out in his chapter, the problem with this definition is that "there is no nationalism in it." Realism and mercantilism, after all, are "statist" ideologies centrally concerned with questions of state power and interests rather than national identities. In Abdelal's words, "Nationalism is an expression of a constructed social identity. Statism is an expression of an autonomous state with interests distinct from society. The equation of the two approaches and concepts, therefore, is an analytical mistake: nationalism is not equivalent to statism; economic nationalism is not equivalent to mercantilism; and thus a Nationalist perspective on IPE, if it is to take nationalism seriously as a causal variable, cannot be equivalent to the Realist perspective."

In other literature, economic nationalism is used differently: as a phrase to describe a wide variety of policies that challenge liberal economics, ranging from tariffs and quotas to restrictions on foreign investment and state subsidies for domestic industry. I have noted elsewhere how this use of the term dates back to the interwar years when liberal economists began to try to discredit policies they did not like with this label (Helleiner 2002). Since that time, liberal economists have been among the most frequent users of the term in this way (e.g., Heilperin 1960; Johnson 1967; Hieronymi 1980). As a number of contributors to this volume note, the problem with this definition of economic nationalism is that the *nationalist* content of economic nationalism is once again neglected. The various antiliberal policies commonly described as "economic nationalism" are not necessarily motivated by nationalist thought.

In an effort to sharpen the analytical concept of economic nationalism, the contributors to this volume build on recent literature that is trying to "bring the nation back in" to its definition (Abdelal 2001; Crane 1998, 1999; Shulman 2000; Pickel 2003; Helleiner 2002). They argue that economic nationalism is best seen as a facet of national identity, rather than a variant of realism or a "protectionist" ideology. From this perspective, the study of economic nationalism involves examining how national identities and nationalism shape economic policies and processes. Interestingly, this research agenda is one that has been quite neglected in recent literature on both nationalism and international political economy, a neglect that this volume seeks to address.

This approach to the study of economic nationalism may seem new, but it is not. It was the approach endorsed by Friedrich List, a thinker widely recognized as the most important "economic nationalist" of the nineteenth century. List is best remembered today for his forceful critique of free trade and his advocacy of "infant industry" protectionism in poorer countries. But

List himself emphasized that his approach to political economy should not be defined in these policy terms. Instead, he made it clear that "the distinguishing characteristic" of his approach to political economy was "nationality" rather than advocacy of tariffs. His central goal was to critique economic liberals for seeing "individuals as mere producers and consumers, not as citizens of states or members of nations" (List [1841] 1904, 141). He thought economic liberals suffered from a "boundless cosmopolitanism" and "dead materialism" that prevented them from recognizing the economic significance of nations. When describing the core of his ideology, List preferred to stress this nationalist ontology rather than his policy prescriptions: "On the nature of nationality, as the intermediate interest between those of individualism and of entire humanity, my whole structure is based" (xliii; see also Levi-Faur 1997a, 1997b; Szporluk 1988).

With this focus on nationality, List understood economic nationalism in much the same way as the contributors to this volume (a point that a number of them note). But if economic nationalism is defined in this way, we are left with the question of what its policy content is. Put another way, what kinds of economic policies are generally associated with nationalism? The answer, we have seen, is more complicated than conventional understandings of economic nationalism suggest. Although nationalism encourages nonliberal policies in some contexts, it embraces liberal policies in others. This inconsistency suggests that it is impossible to say anything definitive about the policy content of economic nationalism. The reason, as the contributors to this volume suggest, is that the specific content of national identities and nationalism vary enormously, as do the contexts in which nationalists find themselves.

To be sure, nationalists share core values such as a commitment to national sovereignty, a belief in the "horizontal comradeship" of the nation's members, and the like (e.g., Anderson 1983). These values may, in turn, influence economic policy in some general ways that can be identified. Abdelal, for example, usefully suggests in his chapter that nationalism influences economic policy through four general mechanisms: it gives the economy social purpose; it encourages economic sacrifice to achieve social goals; it lengthens the time horizons of the community; and it specifies a direction for policy away from a nation's "other." But as Abdelal notes, these mechanisms still do not help us address the question of how nationalism and national identities influence the specific content of economic policy. The reason is simple: in his words, "national purposes vary . . . and so must economic nationalisms."

We have encountered some cases where the policy content of economic nationalism is similar to that predicted by more conventional understandings of economic nationalism. Meredith Woo-Cumings, for example, explains how economic nationalism played a central role in prompting

Northeast Asian countries to pursue state-led rapid industrialization strategies. In these cases, the policy content of economic nationalism followed List's prescriptions for poorer countries (see also Woo-Cumings 1999). Another example of "conventional" economic nationalist policy comes from Patricia Goff's analysis of how concerns about "cultural sovereignty" have encouraged selective agricultural protectionism in Europe. Maya Eichler and Abdelal also both describe how Ukrainian economic nationalism was associated with a preference for a degree of economic autonomy, particularly from Russia.

At the same time, a number of the chapters highlight cases where nationalism has encouraged the adoption of free trade and other liberal economic policies. Klaus Müller's discussion of economic policy in the postwar Federal Republic of Germany, for example, shows how support for economic liberalism often was associated with national identity and pride because of the distinct circumstances of that country. Derek Hall provides another example in his analysis of Japanese economic liberalization during the 1990s. A conventional analysis would portray this policy trend as a rejection of "economic nationalism," but Hall notes how the liberalizers have often been driven by various nationalist objectives, including guaranteeing the nation's survival and competitiveness in the new global economy and responding positively to the demands of its important ally, the United States. One further case comes from my discussion of Quebec nationalists' support for North American monetary union. This support has puzzled those who see NAMU as a liberal project that is antithetical to the idea of economic nationalism, but I show how it does in fact have strong nationalist roots. NAMU could not only ease the path to national independence for Quebec and reduce its dependence on the rest of Canada, but also protect the nation from powerful global financial markets and even perhaps promote national competitiveness.

This kind of "liberal economic nationalism" has been particularly prominent in the countries of the former Soviet Union. Both Andrei Tsygankov and Eichler highlight how many Russian policymakers in the early Yeltsin administration embraced the "neoliberal" shock therapy advocated by the IMF because these policies were identified with their particular conception of Russia's national identity as a "Western nation" in the post-Soviet era. Similarly, Abdelal shows how Lithuanian nationalists backed their country's integration into the liberal global economy because of their desire to both reduce Russian influence and see Lithuania assume a "European" identity.

A more unusual and specific case of "liberal economic nationalism" is provided by Goff's discussion of European efforts to promote "protected designations of origin" (PDOs) as a form of trade-related intellectual property rights (TRIPs). TRIPs are usually associated with the trade liberalization agenda of the Uruguay Round of international trade talks; many liberals (though not all) argued at the time that a strengthening of TRIPs would foster technological innovation by protecting patent rights worldwide more effectively. But the strengthening of PDOs is being promoted by nationalists whose goal is the preservation of tradition. Indeed, it is rather ironic—from a liberal standpoint—that the PDO designation can be earned only when producers agree not to alter traditional methods of production.

What is interesting about each of these cases is that they challenge the conventional view that economic nationalism is always a "protectionist" ideology backing nonliberal economic policies. In these instances, nationalists in fact find themselves working alongside economic liberals in supporting policies of economic liberalization or the strengthening of liberal international trade and monetary regimes. The identification of this kind of "liberal economic nationalism" is hardly novel. In his analysis of Britain's free trade "empire" in the nineteenth century, List made exactly the same observation. While he saw "infant industry" protectionism as the most appropriate nationalist policy for agricultural countries such as Germany and the United States, he recognized that Britain's economic nationalism at the time took the form of an endorsement of free trade. Many British policymakers supported free trade, he pointed out, not because it would benefit the economic welfare of humanity, as David Ricardo argued, but because it would give their country "a world-manufacturing monopoly" that would bolster British wealth and international power. As he put it, their support for international free trade was "one of the most extraordinary of first-rate political manouevres that have ever been played upon the credulity of the world" (quoted in Semmel 1993, 66, 65).

If nationalists often back liberal economic policies, their motivations for doing so are quite distinct from those of liberals. Hall usefully identifies three liberal motivations for liberal economic policies: cosmopolitan utilitarian objectives, a commitment to maximize individual freedom, and the goals of self-interested economic actors. What then are the nationalist motivations? In addition to the "free-trade imperialism" of a dominant economic power, we can identify several other examples from the various cases cited above. In some instances, we have seen how nationalists may back liberal economic policies because they bolster national growth and competitiveness, especially in the context of the rapidly changing contemporary global economy (see also Reich 1991). In other cases, support for liberal policies derives from a specific national identity, such as the "pro-Western/European" identity held by some nationalists in the former Soviet Union (see the chapters by Abdelal, Eichler, and Tsygankov). As we saw in the cases of the Quebec and Lithuanian nationalists, support for liberal trade and monetary regimes can be driven by the goal of reducing the economic influence of the nation's "other" in a regional context.

In sum, if economic nationalism is understood as a facet of national identity, as the contributors to this volume suggest, its policy content is best seen as ambiguous.

Economic nationalism may interact with liberal economic policies in mutually reinforcing ways in some contexts, while encouraging the opposite kind of economic policy in others. Tsygankov summarizes this ambiguity well when he describes economic nationalism as "aliberal." There is, in other words, no definitive single answer to the question of economic nationalism's policy content. Instead, the goal of research should be to explore the diverse and complex influences that nationalism and national identities have on economic policy and processes. This ambiguity is a product partly of the fact that the specific content of national identities—and their relationship to the economy—is so variable across time and space. As George Crane puts it (1998, 74), "We should expect specific policy prescriptions of economic nationalists to vary with representations of the economic nation." The ambiguity also reflects the diverse contexts within the global system in which nationalists find themselves, a point List made forcefully in his analysis of the divergent needs of agricultural versus industrial countries. Woo-Cumings, for example, highlights how the international security context prompted postwar South Korea and Taiwanese policymakers to see the economy in a particular way. Similarly, a number of the chapters argue that "liberal economic nationalism" has been fostered by the new globalized economy and unique political circumstances of the post–Cold War world.

If economic nationalism can be associated with very diverse economic policies, does this mean that economic nationalism is too vague a term to be useful? Is everything economic nationalism? No. Although its *policy content* can be "everything," economic nationalism remains defined by its nationalism; that is, it is associated with core nationalist values such as a commitment to national sovereignty. "Economic nationalism" is, thus, not nearly as large a concept as "economic identity" or "economic culture." It is associated only with *national* identities.

Is Economic Nationalism Outdated?

The goal of this volume has been to reassess not just the meaning of economic nationalism but also its contemporary significance. The chapters present a challenge to the common argument that economic nationalism is an outdated ideology in this age of economic globalization. This conventional wisdom usually draws on the view popularized by liberal economists earlier in the twentieth century that economic nationalism is best seen as an ideology that endorses a variety of nonliberal policies. The triumph of liberal economic policies in this globalized era, the argument goes, is proof that economic nationalism is a defeated force. But if economic nationalism is understood in the broader way suggested above, this conventional view is less convincing. From our perspective, as long as nationalism and national identities endure, so too will various forms of economic nationalism.

One form may be the conventional kind of "economic nationalism" that liberal economists criticize. Woo-Cumings's chapter, for example, highlights how nationalism continues to encourage "developmental state" policies across much of the East Asian region. Other chapters highlight how the enduring strength of national identities and nationalism are encouraging new and innovative forms of state intervention in markets that are more compatible with the new liberal global economy. Goff's discussion of PDOs provides perhaps the most interesting example. And still other chapters highlight how policies promoting liberalization and integration within the global economy themselves often reflect nationalist values and sentiments, as I have just discussed.

In these ways, the volume shows that economic nationalism remains alive and well in today's global economy. Particularly important is the fact that the chapters call attention to the diverse ways in which nationalism acts as a source of economic policy in the contemporary era. The contrast between the experiences of East Asian and ex-Soviet countries discussed in the first two parts of the book provides a good example. Some analysts who are familiar with the successful East Asian state-led industrialization experience have bemoaned the embrace of neoliberal economic policies by ex–Eastern bloc countries after the fall of communism. They have criticized policymakers in these countries for embracing neoliberal ideology and implored them to study the Northeast Asian experience in order to recognize the pitfalls of embracing free-market development strategies. They have in fact noted that ex–Eastern bloc countries are particularly well positioned to adopt the kind of "developmental state" strategies of Korea and Taiwan because they share similar conditions such as high levels of education and income equality (Amsden, Kochanowicz, and Taylor 1994; Amsden 2001). This advice is understandable, but it rests on an analysis that draws too sharp a contrast between the ideational sources of economic policy in the two regions. We have seen how "shock therapy" was not always embraced by postcommunist policymakers because of an enthusiasm for neoliberal ideology. It often reflected the influence of a different ideology—nationalism—that also has inspired East Asian policymakers. In these instances, what is significant in explaining the policy choices in the two regions is less the difference in ideology than the specific content of national identities and the context in which nationalists find themselves.

In addition to calling attention to the enduring influence of economic nationalism, some chapters go further to argue that economic nationalism and globalization may even be mutually reinforcing. We have already identified one example: when economic nationalism leads to support for liberal economic policies, it may bolster the economic globalization trend. But the causal link in this mutually reinforcing relationship can also flow in the other direction.

For example, Goff shows how economic globalization can generate a heightened concern for the protection of national culture and tradition, a concern that may lead to demands for market intervention by the state, as in the case of European measures to ban imports of genetically modified organisms (GMO). Jacqui True's analysis of "nation branding" provides another case where economic globalization can strengthen economic nationalism. She highlights how countries such as New Zealand are increasingly playing up their national economic distinctiveness as part of a strategy to develop a competitive niche in the new global economy. This new kind of economic nationalism is designed not just to project a certain image of the nation to foreigners for the purpose of bolstering exports, tourism, and foreign investment. It is also aimed at the nation's citizens themselves, particularly those living abroad (the "Kiwi diaspora") whom the government hopes to lure home. In this way, globalization is prompting domestic constituencies to explore and reinforce nationalist claims about the economic distinctiveness of their respective countries.

Globalization may also be encouraging policymakers to appeal to national economic solidarity as a tool to facilitate their country's rapid economic adjustments to changing world market conditions. Both Abdelal and Woo-Cumings note how nationalism is often used to mobilize support for economic policies involving economic sacrifice. Hall also identifies this phenomenon in Japan, where politicians sought to build support for liberalization—over the opposition of sectoral groups—by portraying it as a great national project. His example is particularly interesting since liberal economists have often defined economic nationalism as a "rent-seeking" ideology. In this instance, however, it is used as a tool to overcome rent-seeking behavior. In a similar way, Tsygankov notes how national identities can help facilitate liberal adjustments to the imperatives of the global economy.

It is important not to overstate the case that economic nationalism and globalization are mutually reinforcing. The European ban on GMO imports, after all, works against the globalization trend by interfering with the free flow of goods across borders. True also cautions that the very tourism and foreign investment that is attracted by New Zealand's distinctive "national brand" can ultimately erode that very basis of New Zealand's national distinctiveness. Hall also describes how Japanese liberalizers believe that their country's national identity will become a barrier to further liberalization and internationalization. Still, despite these caveats, each of these cases demonstrates that globalization and economic nationalism are less mutually exclusive than conventional wisdom suggests.

One final question raised by the chapters in this volume needs to be addressed: if economic nationalism remains an important force in today's global economy, *how* important is it in explaining economic policy choices and economic processes? Here the consensus among the contributors breaks down. The differences in opinion largely stem from their varying perspectives about the relative weight that should be assigned to the explanatory power of this "ideational" factor.

Some chapters ascribe very considerable explanatory power to economic nationalism. In explaining the economic policy choices of ex-Soviet governments, Abdelal, for example, explicitly compares his "nationalist" approach to more institutionalist or strictly rationalist and materialist analyses, and he concludes that "national identities" are a more powerful explanatory variable than factors that these other analytical approaches examine. Goff, too, argues that European legislation against GMOs cannot be explained with reference to specific material interests; instead it is largely driven by concerns about identities. Similarly, Woo-Cumings strongly endorses Hirschman's argument that ideas—in this case, nationalism—are the central binding agent in economic development and have a key autonomous explanatory power.

Taking a somewhat different view are True and Eichler. Both portray economic nationalism in more instrumentalist terms as a force that serves particular material interests. True suggests that economic nationalism is often used to benefit the material interests of specific private capitalist groups, and that its content reflects this purpose. Eichler makes a similar case in the Ukrainian context, arguing that competing interpretations of national identities are tools that various state and social actors use to legitimize the policy preferences they favor for materialist reasons. For her, national identities are less the basis of explanation than something requiring explanation themselves.

The other chapters adopt a perspective that falls somewhere in between these two positions. The authors of these chapters argue that national identities and nationalism have an autonomous explanatory role, but they are also keen to examine how these identities are contested and how their content is determined by political struggles between competing material interests. Tsygankov's chapter is perhaps the most self-conscious in outlining this middle-ground position. Thus, while all the contributors to this volume agree that economic nationalism is not outdated, they differ on how significant it is in driving developments within today's global economy.

Ideational Analysis and International Political Economy

This disagreement brings us to the third and final contribution of this volume to existing literature. Over the past decade, political scientists have shown new interest in the explanatory role of ideologies, beliefs, and identities. This trend has reflected a reaction against "rationalist" or "interest-based" approaches that analyze politics by assuming actors are guided by materialist, interest-maximizing behavior. With its emphasis on the role played by nationalism and national identities in economic policy, this volume reinforces these recent critiques of "rationalist" political economy. But in what specific ways do the chapters in this volume contribute to current literature about the significance of ideational factors in political analysis?

Bringing Constructivism into International Political Economy

The ideational literature is diverse in several respects. To begin with, different authors focus on different types of "ideas". Albert Yee (1996) usefully suggests that these types can be differentiated according to their level of generality. At a fairly specific level, some ideational analysis examines the influence of specific policy programs or policy paradigms. Others focus on more general ideologies or philosophies. And at the deepest or most general level is analysis that concentrates on the significance of culture and identities.

This volume is obviously in the last category. This is, in fact, the first way in which this volume contributes to existing literature. Most other recent ideational writing in political economy has focused on the role of economic ideologies. For example, John Ruggie's article (1982) about the significance of "social purpose" in U.S. and British foreign economic policymaking at the time of Bretton Woods examines the role of "embedded liberal" ideology. Similarly, Kathryn Sikkink's 1991 work on the significance of ideas in economic policymaking in Argentina and Brazil focuses on "developmentalist" ideology. In her article about the role of ideas in international political economy, Ngaire Woods (1995) also concentrates on the economic theories rather than deeper identities or culture. A similar approach has been taken by other important "ideational" writing in political economy, such as that by Mark Blyth (1997, 2002), Kathleen McNamara (1998), Peter Hall (1989), and the "epistemic community" literature (Haas 1992).

One partial exception has been the work of neo-Gramscian scholars such as Stephen Gill (2003) and Robert Cox (2003). Although these scholars have focused most of their attention on the role of neoliberal ideology in economic policies and processes, they have also called attention to deeper ideational factors such as the economic significance of the spread of Western market rationality, "consumer culture," and civilizational values. Still missing from this analysis, however, has been a focus on the issue that concerns this volume: the role of national identities and nationalism in IPE.

Work on this latter topic has been sparse to date, with the notable exceptions of the recent work of many of the contributors to this volume.[1] In

---

1. For this work, see references throughout the volume. See also the work of Crane (1998, 1999) and Shulman (2000). Some might argue that some of the literature focusing on the

adopting this focus, the chapters of this book embrace the notion that ideas can be examined as intersubjective identities shared by large groups of people. With this approach and the focus on identities, this volume is clearly working within the emerging school of analysis known as constructivism (as some contributors emphasize). Much of the early prominent constructivist analysis concerned international security issues. Scholars such as Peter Katzenstein (1996a, 1996b) highlighted how distinctive national identities shaped perceptions of a state's security interests. More recently, other constructivist writings have examined the significance of identities and other intersubjective meanings in policy areas such as international human rights, science policy, and the laws of war (Finnemore 1993; Klotz 1995; Price 1997).

As Katzenstein, Robert Keohane, and Stephen Krasner point out (1998, 673–75), constructivist analysis has so far had a less significant impact on the study of international political economy. One reason, they suggest, is that the field has not experienced the kind of challenge that the end of the Cold War posed to traditional security studies. Equally important has been the power of rationalist approaches in a field whose subject is, after all, material life. Whatever the cause, the project of bringing constructivism into IPE has been taken up by few scholars. This volume begins to correct this imbalance.

The Relationship between Ideas and Interests

If the goal of ideational analysis is to challenge rationalist interest-based approaches to the study of politics, the question immediately arises: what is the relationship between ideas and interests? One answer to this question is provided by Judith Goldstein and Keohane in their 1993 edited book *Ideas and Foreign Policy*. In their view, ideas do not shape agents' interests. Instead, they are important because they can influence interest-maximizing agents' behavior in contexts of strategic interaction or imperfect information by providing a "road map" or a "focal point" for collective action. According to this formulation, ideas and interests act as competing variables in the explanation of policy outcomes. Martha Finnemore and Sikkink call this approach "weak cognitivism" because it assumes that interests are fixed and exogenously determined (2001, 402). This assumption is one that leaves Goldstein and Keohane's analysis still rooted partially within a rationalist camp.

An alternative approach moves beyond this rationalist assumption by ar-

influence of economic ideologies has addressed the role of nationalism. But it has usually done so by highlighting an ideology of "economic nationalism" that is defined according to its policy preferences of tariffs, restrictions on foreign investment, etc. In other words, it has adopted an approach to the study of economic nationalism that is devoid of *nationalist* content, an approach that this volume criticizes.

guing that ideas are important because they can *transform* interests. Instead of seeing interests and ideas as separate and competing explanatory variables, this approach sees them as intricately interconnected. Blyth summarizes this approach well, arguing that interests are "ideationally bound" because the content of interests is inevitably linked to a set of ideas or beliefs that an actor has about what is desirable and how the world works. In his words, "agents cannot have interests without reference to their ideas about their interests" (Blyth 2002, 34, 270). This approach challenges rationalist assumptions that actors' preferences can be inferred simply by examining their class or sectoral position within the economy or a state's position of power within the interstate system. Instead, an examination of preferences requires an analysis of the self-understanding of the actor.

From a constructivist standpoint, the most important ideational factors influencing that self-understanding will be widely shared intersubjective beliefs or identities (Finnemore and Sikkink 2001). In this context, it follows that an agent's interests are best seen as "social constructs" heavily influenced by the agent's social context (Blyth 2002, 270–71; Sikkink 1991; Woods 1995; Yee 1996). But this social context is not seen as static. Instead, it is assumed to be constantly contested and remade in response to political struggles and changing conditions. Indeed, a central research agenda for constructivists is to understand the political construction of social identities. In other words, this approach holds a dynamic view in which agents and structures are mutually constituted (e.g., Finnemore and Sikkink 2001)

All the contributors to this volume embrace this general constructivist approach, but they do not all take up the task of explaining the construction of national identities as a central goal. Abdelal, for example, acknowledges that national identities are socially constructed and contested, but he does not attempt in his chapter to analyze the source of these identities. Instead, he takes national identities as given and examines their impact.

Those contributors who do analyze the social construction of national identities adopt quite different approaches. Some highlight the role played by specific domestic agents in promoting a particular conception of national identity that may serve their material interests. This is the approach of Eichler and True, each of whom is inclined to see dominant economic elites as playing the central role in shaping national identities. From this perspective, constructions of identities largely reflect and reify existing relations of power. As noted earlier, this type of approach—labeled "critical constructivism" by Finnemore and Sikkink (2001)—tends to ascribe less autonomous explanatory power to identities than other constructivist writing.

Other contributors recognize the role played by "political entrepreneurs" of this kind, but they are also inclined to see national identities as influenced by institutional and external contexts. The significance of the external context receives particular attention from a number of the contributors, but

their analysis departs from that of much of the existing constructivist literature. Within that literature, scholars have devoted considerable attention to
the role of international norms or "world culture" in transforming identities (Finnemore 1996; Finnemore and Sikkink 1998; Meyer et al. 1997).
The contributors to this volume, however, focus on other external factors
that influence the construction of national identities.

One such factor is economic globalization. As noted in the previous section, some authors highlight the role of globalization in transforming the
content of nationalist identities and promoting new kinds of economic nationalism. The international security context is also significant for some contributors. The Cold War plays a central role in Woo-Cumings's analysis of the
formation and content of national identities in East Asian countries. Tsygankov also notes how the changing international security context in the
post–Cold War world played a role in shaping different conceptions of Russian national identity.

Several chapters also highlight the importance of the regional external
context in influencing national identities. Both Goff and Müller point to the
importance of growing regional integration for national identities in Europe. Tsygankov also highlights the role of Russia's relations with Eurasia in
influencing changing conceptions of its national identity during the 1990s.
Hall calls attention to the importance of the U.S.-Japanese relationship in
altering conceptions of Japan's economic nationalism. My chapter shows
how Quebec's relationship with the rest of Canada and its changing economic place in North America have played a central role in influencing the
content of economic nationalism in Quebec.

Causal Links between Ideas and Policy Outcomes

Within existing "ideational" scholarship, a final issue that has generated considerable debate concerns the precise nature of the causal link between
ideas and policy outcomes. Several leading scholars have noted that a central weakness of the emerging ideational literature is its failure to specify this
causal link (Yee 1996; Ruggie 1998; Finnemore and Sikkink 2001). Ideas
influence state policymaking, but *how*?

The question is a difficult one to answer partly for methodological reasons. Ideas can have a causal impact through intersubjective meanings and
symbolic discourses that are hard to analyze empirically. Analysts working in
a constructivist tradition are thus usually committed to interpretative modes
of analysis (e.g., Yee 1996; Finnemore and Sikkink 2001). In some cases, this
analysis adopts a postmodern or deconstructive stance. The contributors to
this volume, however, are all working in a framework that is committed to
the task of developing positive knowledge claims.

The most general causal mechanism that is outlined in this constructivist
literature is the one just discussed: ideas influence policy outcomes by

changing or shaping behavior and preferences. But as Yee (1996) points out, analysts must then be clear in specifying whose behavior and preferences are being changed or shaped. Is it those of policymakers, organizations, broader social groups, or society as a whole? Since constructivist analysis does not make an ontological claim about the nature of agents or social structures, this question can be answered in many different ways by scholars working within a constructivist framework.

Such diversity is apparent in this volume. At the most general level, the volume makes the claim that nationalism and national identities influence policy outcomes by shaping behavior and preferences. In some chapters, the behavior and preferences are primarily those of policymakers. Tsygankov, for example, highlights how conceptions of geoeconomic national identity influence the conception of national economic interest held by state policymakers. Hall adopts a similar approach in his examination of Japanese policy, although he includes an analysis of how policymakers' perceptions of the national identity of Japanese society can also influence their behavior.

At the other end of the spectrum is Woo-Cumings's analysis, which describes how nationalism influences the behavior of domestic society as a whole in Taiwan and South Korea. A particular brand of nationalism was, in her words, "deeply internalized" among the population of these two countries. Goff adopts a similar approach in explaining French resistance to GMOs, as does Müller in his discussion of German monetary nationalism.

Other chapters fall between these two approaches and examine how nationalism and national identities shape the behavior of several different kinds of groups at the same time. Abdelal highlights how national identities influence the behavior of specific societal groups who are particularly committed to a nationalist project, but he also argues that the success of their project depends on the extent to which it resonated in the domestic society as a whole. My analysis of Quebec's monetary politics adopts a similar approach, and it in fact highlights the interrelationship between the shaping of preferences at different levels. I argue that nationalist policymakers' support for monetary union was strongly influenced by their recognition of the ambivalent support for the nationalist goal of Quebec sovereignty among the Quebec population as a whole (and hence the lack of a strong willingness among the population to undergo economic sacrifice for nationalist reasons). With their strategic goal of influencing swing voters, they embraced a different set of policy preferences from many nationalist social groups despite sharing the same nationalist project.

Yee (1996) also emphasizes that scholars need to distinguish the stage of the policy process at which ideas have their most significant impact. Most of the chapters in this volume focus on the impact of ideas on the process of policymaking. But some authors also observe how ideas can have an important impact on policy outcomes through their role in policy implementation. One example is the argument stated above that nationalism can help to mobilize support for the implementation of policies requiring economic sacrifice. Another is Eichler's case that nationalism and national identities are significant because they influence people's preferences in ways that legitimate the policy projects of elite groups. Hall's analysis of how Japanese liberalizers fear their country's national identity will block liberalization also invokes the significance of ideas at the stage of policy implementation. In these ways, this volume once again highlights several diverse causal links between ideas and policy outcomes.

What then have we learned? First, the contributors to this volume have made a strong case that economic nationalism should not be seen as a synonym for realism or as a doctrine defined by its support for nonliberal policies. Instead, they suggest that the study of economic nationalism is better understood as the study of the diverse and complex influences of nationalism and national identities on economic policies and processes. Like nationalism itself, however, economic nationalism is what Woo-Cumings refers to as an "empty" or "vacant" ideology whose policy content is ambiguous and must be filled in by specific temporal and spatial contexts.

Second, the chapters suggest that reports of the death of economic nationalism are greatly exaggerated. Although the contributors to this volume may not agree on the relative explanatory power of economic nationalism, they are united in emphasizing that economic nationalism remains a significant force in this current age. Each chapter shows how, far from becoming obsolete, nationalism and national identities continue to influence economic policy choices and processes within the new globalized economy. Indeed, we have seen that globalization and economic nationalism, far from being inherently opposed forces, can even be mutually reinforcing.

More generally, this volume reinforces the importance of recent critiques of "rationalist" political analysis by underscoring the significant role that ideational factors play in economic policy. Most ideational analysis in IPE to date has focused on the significance of economic ideologies or theories. This volume, however, presents one of the first book-length analyses of the significance of deeper national identities within IPE. In so doing, the contributors adopt a constructivist approach to the study of IPE that explores the mutual interrelationship between identities and interests and identifies ways in which identities can be linked causally to policy outcomes.

These three conclusions have been drawn from the specific case studies presented here. Will they be relevant to other temporal and spatial contexts? This question can be answered only by further research. The study of how nationalism and national identities influences economic life in this era of globalization is certainly deserving of great attention. We hope this volume helps to generate interest in the subject.

References

Abdelal, Rawi. 2001. *National Purpose in the World Economy: Post-Soviet States in Comparative Perspective*. Ithaca, N.Y.: Cornell University Press.

——. 2002. "Memories of Nations and States: Institutional History and National Identity in Post-Soviet Eurasia." *Nationalities Papers* 30 (3): 459–84.

Abelshauser, Werner. 1983. *Wirtschaftsgeschichte der Bundesrepublik Deutschland 1945–1980*. Frankfurt a. M.: Suhrkamp.

——. 1991. "Die ordnungspolitische Epochengeschichte der Weltwirtschaftskrise in Deutschland. Ein Beitrag zur Entstehungsgeschichte der SozialenMarktwirtschaft." In *Ordnungspolitische Weichenstellungen nach dem Zweiten Weltkrieg*, edited by Dietmar Petzina, 11–29. Berlin: Dunker and Humboldt.

Alesina, A., and R. Barro. 2001. "One Country, One Currency?" In *Currency Unions*, edited by Alesina and Barro. Stanford: Hoover Institution.

Alexandrova, Olga. 1994. "Rußland als Faktor ukrainischer Sicherheitsvorstellungen." *Außenpolitik* 1:69–78.

Alexandrova, Olga, and Heinz Timmermann. 1997. "Integration und Desintegration in den Beziehungen Rußland—Belarus'—GUS." *Osteuropa* 47 (10/11): 1022–52.

Alker, Hayward R., Tahir Amin, Thomas Biersteker, and Takashi Inoguchi. 1998. "How Should We Theorize Contemporary Macro-Encounters: In Terms of Superstates, World Orders, or Civilizations?" Paper presented at the Third Pan-European International Relations Conference, SGIR-ISA, Vienna, September.

Amaya, Naohiro. 1994. *Eichi kokkaron* (Argument for a wise country). Tokyo: PHP Kenkyūjo.

Amsden, Alice. 1989. *Asia's Next Giant*. Oxford: Oxford University Press.

——. 2001. *The Rise of "the Rest": Challenges to the West from Late-Industrializing Economies*. New York: Oxford University Press.

Amsden, Alice, Jacek Kochanowicz, and Lance Taylor. 1994. *The Market Meets Its Match: Restructuring the Economies of Eastern Europe*. Cambridge: Harvard University Press.

Anderson, Benedict. 1983. *Imagined Communities: Reflections on the Origin and Spread of Nationalism*. London: Verso.

235

Anderson, Hugh. 1978. "Dollar Tailspins on Quebec Talk of Own Currency." *Globe and Mail,* May 18.

Anderson, Jeffrey. 1999. *German Unification and the Union of Europe: The Domestic Politics of Integration Policy.* Cambridge: Cambridge University Press.

Anderson, Perry. 1974. *Lineages of the Absolutist State.* New York: New Left Books.

Appel, Hilary. 2000. "The Ideological Determinants of Liberal Economic Reform: The Case of Privatization." *World Politics* 52 (4): 520–49.

Appel, Hilary, and John Gould. 2000. "Identity Politics and Economic Reform: Examining Industry-State Relations in the Czech and Slovak Republics." *Europe-Asia Studies* 52 (1): 111–31.

Arel, Dominique. 1995. "Ukraine: The Temptation of the Nationalizing State." In *Political Culture and Civil Society in Russia and the New States of Eurasia,* edited by Vladimir Tismaneanu. Armonk, N.Y.: M. E. Sharpe.

Aron, Leon. 1994. "The Emergent Priorities of Russian Foreign Policy." In *The Emergence of Russian Foreign Policy,* edited by Aron and Kenneth M. Jensen, 17–34. Washington, D.C.: United States Institute of Peace Press.

———. 1998. "The Foreign Policy Doctrine of Postcommunist Russia and Its Domestic Context." In *The New Russian Foreign Policy,* edited by Michael Mandelbaum, 23–63. New York: Council on Foreign Relations.

ASB Bank. 2003. "Loyal Momentum Builds as Challenge Approaches." Press release, January 20.

Ash, Julie, and Patrick Gower. 2003. "Hate Campaign Threatens Alinghi's Crew's Children." *New Zealand Weekend Herald,* January 4–5.

Ash, Timothy Garton. 1994. "Journey to the Post-Communist East." *New York Review of Books,* June 23.

Atkinson, Lloyd. 1991. "A Comment." In *Two Nations, One Money,* edited by D. Laidler and W. Robson. Toronto: C. D. Howe.

Badie, Bertrand. 2000. *The Imported State: The Westernization of the Political Order.* Stanford: Stanford University Press.

Balaam, David N., and Michael Veseth. 2001. *Introduction to International Political Economy.* 2nd ed. Upper Saddle River, N.J.: Prentice Hall.

Balkhausen, Dieter. 1992. *Gutes Geld und schlechte Politik.* Düsseldorf: Econ.

Bank of Lithuania. 1997. *Monetary Policy Program of the Bank of Lithuania for 1997–99.* Vilnius: Bank of Lithuania.

Bates, Stephen. 1999. "Tougher EU Controls Mean Moratorium on GM Crops." *Guardian,* June 26, 8.

Baur, Johannes. 1999. "Russische Außen- und Sicherheitspolitik: Entwicklungen und Tendenzen." *Osteuropa* 49 (3): 241–55.

Beine, Michael, and Serge Coulombe. 2003. "Regional Perspectives on Dollarization in Canada." *Journal of Regional Science* 43 (3): 541–70.

Beissinger, Mark. 1996. "How Nationalisms Spread: Eastern Europe Adrift in the Tides and Cycles of Nationalist Contention." *Social Research* 63 (1): 97–147.

———. 1998. "Nationalisms That Bark and Nationalisms That Bite." In *The State of the Nation,* edited by John A. Hall. Cambridge: Cambridge University Press.

———. 2002. *Nationalist Mobilization and the Collapse of the Soviet State.* Cambridge: Cambridge University Press.

Bélanger-Campeau Commission. 1991. *The Report of the Commission on the Political and Constitutional Future of Quebec.* Quebec: Government of Quebec.

Bell, Claudia. 2002. "Sustaining the Green Myth." Paper presented at the University of Auckland Sustainability Lecture Series, August.

Bell, Daniel. 1997. "A Communitarian Critique of Authoritarianism." *Political Theory* 25 (1): 6–32.

Bendix, Reinhard. 1977. *Nation-Building and Citizenship*. 2nd ed. Berkeley: University of California Press.

———. 1978. *Kings or People: Power and the Mandate to Rule*. Berkeley: University of California Press.

Berezovski, Boris. 1998. "SNG: Ot razvala k sotrudnichestvu. Kakoiye sodruzhestvo nam nuzhno i real'no?" *Nezavisimaya gazeta,* November 13.

Berger, S., and R. Dore, eds. 1996. *National Diversity and Global Capitalism*. Ithaca, N.Y.: Cornell University Press.

Bernhard, William. 1998. "A Political Explanation of Variations in Central Bank Independence." *American Political Science Review* 92 (2): 311–27.

Beverland, Michael. n.d. "Relationship Marketing in Agribusiness: Evidence from Six New Zealand Case Studies." Photocopy, Department of Marketing, Monash University, Melbourne.

Beyme, Klaus V. 1977. *Sozialismus oder Wohlfahrtsstaat?* Munich: Pieper.

Billig, Michael. 1995. *Banal Nationalism*. London: Sage.

Bilyi, Oleh, and Yevhen Bystrytsky. 1996. "State-Building in Ukraine: Ways of Legitimation." *Politychna Dumka* 7:122–33.

Bingham, Eugene, and James Gardiner. 2003. "Heroes and Villains." *New Zealand Weekend Herald,* January 25–26.

Blasi, Joseph R., Maya Kroumova, and Douglas Kruse. 1997. *Kremlin Capitalism: Privatizing the Russian Economy*. Ithaca, N.Y.: Cornell University Press.

Bloc Québécois. 2002. "Orientations of the Bloc Québécois." www.bloc.org/web/electoral/frameenglish.htm.

Blum, Doug. 2000. "Russia's New Caspian Policy." Program on New Approaches to Russian Security, memo no. 162. http://www.fas.harvard.edu/~ponars.

Blyth, Mark. 1997. "Any More Bright Ideas? The Ideational Turn of Comparative Political Economy." *Comparative Politics* 29 (2): 229–50.

Blyth, Mark. 2002. *Great Transformations: Economic Ideas and Institutional Change in the Twentieth Century*. Cambridge: Cambridge University Press.

Bobkov, V. A., N. V. Kuznetsov, and V. P. Osmolovsky. 1997. *Politicheskie Partii Belarusi* (Political parties of Belarus), 3–98. Minsk: BGEU.

Bofinger, Peter, Stephan Collignon, and Ernst Moritz. 1993. *Währungsunion oder Währungschaos? Was kommt nach der D-Mark*. Wiesbaden: Gabler.

Bofinger, Peter, Carsten Heffeker, and Kai Carsten. 1998. *Stabilitätskultur in Europa*. Stuttgart: Deutscher Sparkassen Verlag.

Bojcun, Marko. 2001. "Civilisation: A New Debate about Ukraine's Identity." Working paper, Ukraine Centre, University of North London. www.unl.ac.uk/ukraine-centre/wpusc-e.shtml.

Bonfante, Jordan. 1998. "A German Requiem." *Time* (Europe), July 6.

Bönker, Frank, Klaus Müller, and Andreas Pickel, eds. 2002. *Postcommunist Transformation and the Social Sciences: Cross-Disciplinary Approaches*. Boulder: Rowman and Littlefield.

Boston, Jonathan, John Martin, June Pallot, and Pat Welch. 1996. *Public Management: The New Zealand Model*. Oxford: Oxford University Press.

Bourassa, Robert. 1980. *L'unité monétaire et l'unité politique sont indissociable.* Montreal: Parti Libéral du Quebec.

Bové, José, and François Dufour. Interview by Gilles Luneau. In *The World Is Not for Sale.* New York: Verso.

Boyer, Robert, and Daniel Drache, eds. 1996. *States against Markets: The Limits of Globalization.* New York: Routledge.

Boyle, Elizabeth Hegel. 2000. "Is Law the Rule? Using Political Frames to Explain Cross-National Variation in Legal Activity." *Social Forces* 78 (4): 1195–226.

Brubaker, Rogers. 1996. *Nationalism Reframed.* Cambridge: Cambridge University Press.

Bruno, Michael, and William Easterly. 1998. "Inflation Crisis and Long-Run Growth." *Journal of Monetary Economics* 41 (1): 3–26.

Brzezinski, Zbigniew. 1989. *The Grand Failure.* New York: Charles Scribner's Sons.

Buchanan, Patrick J. 1998. *The Great Betrayal: How American Sovereignty and Social Justice Are Being Sacrificed to the Gods of the Global Economy.* New York: Little, Brown.

Bueckert, Dennis. 2000. "Quebec Could Acquire Terrific Negotiating Leverage with Ottawa over Sovereignty by Threatening to Adopt the U.S. Dollar as Its Currency, Says Former Quebec Premier Jacques Parizeau." Canadian Press newswire, January 29.

Bugrova, Irina, and Svetlana Naumova. 1996. "Parliamentary Elections and Foreign Policy Orientation of Belarus." *Vector* 1 (1): 4–9.

Bührs, Ton, and R. Bartlett. 1993. *Environmental Policy in New Zealand: The Politics of Clean and Green.* Oxford: Oxford University Press.

Bunce, Valerie. 1999. *Subversive Institutions.* Cambridge: Cambridge University Press.

Bunge, Mario. 1999. *The Sociology-Philosophy Connection.* New York: Transaction.

Burant, Stephen R. 1995. "Foreign Policy and National Identity: A Comparison of Ukraine and Belarus." *Europe-Asia Studies* 47 (7): 1125–44.

Burawoy, Michael. 2001. "Neoclassical Sociology: From the End of Communism to the End of Classes." *American Journal of Sociology* 106 (4): 1099–120.

Burawoy, Michael, and Katherine Verdery. 1999. "Introduction." In *Uncertain Transition: Ethnographies of Change in the Postsocialist World,* edited by Burawoy and Verdery, 1–17. Lanham, Md.: Rowman and Littlefield.

Burda, Michael C., and Jennifer Hunt. 2001. "From Unification to Economic Reintegration." *Brookings Papers on Economic Activity* 2:1–92.

Buszynski, Leszek. 1996. *Russian Foreign Policy after the Cold War.* Westport, Conn.: Praeger.

Cadot, Olivier, Akiko Suwa-Eisenmann, and Daniel Traça. 2001 "Trade-Related Issues in the Regulation of Genetically Modified Organisms." Paper prepared for workshop on European and American Perspectives on Regulating Genetically Engineered Food, INSEAD, Paris, June.

Calgary Herald. 1991. "Parizeau Scoffs at the Idea of Losing Dual Citizenship." December 12.

Calhoun, Craig. 1997. *Nationalism.* Minneapolis: University of Minnesota Press.

Campbell-Hunt, Colin, James Brocklesby, Sylvie Chetty, Lawrie Corbett, Sally Davenport, Deborah Jones, and Pat Walsh. 2001. *World Famous in New Zealand: How New Zealand's Leading Firms Became World-Class Competitors.* Auckland: Auckland University Press.

Canada. House of Commons. 1999. *Debates.* March 15. Web version. http://www.parl

.gc.ca/36/1/parlbus/chambus/house/debates/196_1999-03-15/HAN196-E
.htm#LINK38

Carlin, Wendy 1996. "West German Growth and Institutions." In *Economic Growth in Europe since 1945,* edited by Nicholas Crafts and Gianni Toniolo, 455–96. Cambridge: Cambridge University Press.

Carr, E. H. 1945. *Nationalism and After.* London: Macmillan.

Chapple, Irene. 2003. "Advertising Year in Review: Sails Pitch the Big News," *New Zealand Herald,* January 3.

Chervonnaia, Svetlana. 1993. *Grazhdanskie dvizheniia v Litve* (Civic Movements in Lithuania). Moscow: TsIMO.

Chua, Amy L. 1998. "Markets, Democracy, and Ethnicity: Toward a New Paradigm for Law and Development." *Yale Law Journal* 108:1–105.

Clough, Ralph. 1978. *Island China.* Cambridge: Harvard University Press.

Cohen, Roger. 1999. "Fearful over the Future, Europe Seizes on Food." *New York Times,* August 29.

Collins, Simon. 2003. "Chinese Blow a Gooseberry." *New Zealand Weekend Herald,* October 18–19, A11.

Commission of the European Union. 2002a. "Questions and Answers on the Regulation of GMOs in the EU." EU Institutions Press Releases Series, memo 02/160, Brussels, July 1. Website of the European Commission. http://europa .eu.int/comm/research/biosociety/pdf/memo_gmos_qa.pdf

——. 2002b. "Proposal for a Council Regulation Amending the Annex to Commission Regulation (EC) No. 1107/96 with regard to the name 'Feta.'" COM. 2002. 314 final, Brussels, June 14. http://europa.eu.int/eur-lex/en/com/ reg/en_register_0305.html.

Cook, Ian, Philip Crang, and Mark Thorpe. 1999 "Eating into Britishness: Multicultural Imaginaries and the Identity Politics of Food." In *Practising Identities: Power and Resistance,* edited by Sasha Roseneil and Julie Seymour. New York: St. Martin's.

Corcoran, Terence. 1991. "Bank of Canada Reform Gathers Steam." *Globe and Mail,* June 15.

Cornellier, Manon. 1995. *The Bloc.* Translated by Robert Chodos, Simon Warren, and Wanda Taylor. Toronto: James Lorimer.

Council for Foreign and Defense Policy. 2000. *Strategiya dlya Rossiyi: Povestka dlya prezidenta—2000.* Moscow: Sovyet povneshnei i oboronnoi politike. www.svop .edu.

Courchene, Thomas, and Marc-Antoine Laberge. 2000. "The Future of the Canadian Currency Union: NAFTA and Quebec Independence." In *Regional Aspects of Monetary Policy in Europe,* edited by Jurgen von Hagen and Christopher Waller. Boston: Kluwer Academic.

Cox, Robert. 2003. *The Political Economy of a Plural World.* London: Routledge.

Cox, Terry. 1996. *From Perestroika to Privatisation.* Aldershot: Avebury.

Crane, George T. 1998. "Economic Nationalism: Bringing the Nation Back." *Millennium* 27 (1): 55–75.

——. 1999. "Imagining the Economic Nation: Globalisation in China." *New Political Economy* 4:215–32.

Crocombe, Graham T., Michael J. Enright, Michael E. Porter, with Tony Caughey. 1991. *Upgrading New Zealand's Competitive Advantage.* Auckland: Oxford University Press.

Crowley, Stephen. 1995. "Between Class and Nation: Worker Politics in the New Ukraine," *Communist and Post-Communist Studies* 28 (1): 43–69.

Cumings, Bruce. 1981. *The Origins of the Korean War,* vol. 1. Princeton, N.J.: Princeton University Press.

Czarnitzki, Dirk. 2003. "Extent and Evolution of the Productivity Gap in Eastern Germany." Working paper, Centre for European Economic Research, Mannheim.

Daignault, Richard. 1978. "Common Money Unlikely." *Montreal Star,* May 19.

Dalos, György. 1993. "Die Arroganz des Bollwerks. Wie die DDR ihre Bruderländer Kujonierte." *Kursbuch* 111:157–62.

D'Anieri, Paul. 1997a. "Nationalism and International Politics: Identity and Sovereignty in the Russian-Ukrainian Conflict." *Nationalism and Ethnic Politics* 3 (2): 1–28.

——. 1997b. "Dilemmas of Interdependence: Autonomy, Prosperity, and Sovereignty in Ukraine's Russia Policy." *Problems of Post-Communism* 44 (1): 16–26.

——. 1999. *Economic Interdependence in Ukrainian-Russian Relations.* Albany: State University of New York Press.

D'Anieri, Paul J., Robert Kravchuk, and Taras Kuzio. 1999. *Politics and Society in Ukraine.* Boulder: Westview.

Dawisha, Karen. 1997. "Constructing and Deconstructing Empire in the Post-Soviet Space." In *The End of Empire?* edited by Karen Dawisha and Bruce Parrott. Armonk, N.Y.: M. E. Sharpe.

Dawisha, Karen, and Bruce Parrott. 1994. *Russia and the New States of Eurasia.* Cambridge: Cambridge University Press.

De Bary, William. 1998. *Asian Values and Human Rights.* Cambridge: Harvard University Press.

Deutsche Bundesbank. 1997. "Die Entwicklung der Staatsverschuldung seit der deutschen Vereinigung." *Monatsbericht,* March, 17–32.

——. 2003a. "Die Entwicklung der öffentlichen Finanzen in Deutschland nach der Qualifikation für die Europäische Währungsunion." *Monatsbericht,* March, 25–34.

——. 2003b. "Zur Währungsverfassung nach dem Entwurf einer Verfassung für die Europäischen Union." *Monatsbericht,* November, 67–71.

Ditchburn, Jennifer. 1998. "Bloc Mulls Over Possibility of U.S. Dollar as Common Currency." Canadian Press newswire, December 9.

DIW. 1997. "Vereinigungsfolgen belasten Sozialversicherung, in Deutsches Institut für Wirtschaftsforschung." *Wochenbericht* 64 (40): 725–29.

Dodds, Klaus. 2000. *Geopolitics in a Changing World.* New York: Prentice Hall.

Dominion of Canada. 1934. House of Commons. *Debates.* 17th Parliament, 5th Session. Ottawa: J. O. Patenaude.

——. 1936. House of Commons. *Debates.* 18th Parliament, 1st Session. Ottawa: J. O. Patenaude.

Donaldson, Robert, and Joseph L. Nogee. 1998. *The Foreign Policy of Russia: Changing Systems, Enduring Interests.* Armonk, N.Y.: M. E. Sharpe.

Dore, Ronald P. 1999. "Japan's Reform Debate: Patriotic Concern or Class Interest? Or Both?" *Journal of Japanese Studies* 25:65–89.

——. 2000. *Stock Market Capitalism—Welfare Capitalism: Japan and Germany versus the Anglo-Saxons.* New York: Oxford University Press.

Doremus, Paul N., William Keller, Louis W. Pauly, and Simon Reich. 1999. *The Myth of the Global Corporation.* Princeton, N.J.: Princeton University Press.

Dostaler, Gilles. 1980. *Socialisme et indépendence.* Montreal: Boreal Express.

Drover, Glenn, and K. K. Leung. 2001. "Nationalism and Trade Liberalization in Quebec and Taiwan." *Pacific Affairs* 74:205–24.

Dymond, William A., and Michael M. Hart. 2000. "Post-Modern Trade Policy: Reflections on the Challenges to Multilateral Trade Negotiations after Seattle." Working paper, Center for International Studies, University of Southern California, February.

Dyson, Kenneth. 1999. "The Franco-German Relationship and Economic and Monetary Union: Using Europe to 'Bind Leviathan.'" *West European Politics* 22 (1): 25–44.

Eagles, Jim. 2002. "Success Overseas Born of Doing It the NZ Way," *New Zealand Weekend Herald,* September 28–29, C5.

———. 2003. "Cup a Showcase for Our Talents," *New Zealand Herald,* January 15, C1.

ECB (European Central Bank). 2003. "The Outcome of the ECB's Evaluation of Its Monetary Policy Strategy." *Monthly Bulletin,* June, 79–92.

Eggert, Konstantin. 1992. "Rossiia v roli Evraziiskogo zhandarma? Predsedatel' parlamentskogo komiteta razrabotal svoiu kontseptsiiu vneshnei politiki," *Izvestiia,* August 7.

Elias, Norbert. 1978. *The Civilizing Process.* New York: Urizen.

———. 1996. *The Germans: Power Struggles and the Development of Habitus in the Nineteenth and Twentieth Centuries.* New York: Columbia University Press.

Elworthy, Peter. 2002. Press release of speech launching the Sustainability Council of New Zealand. July 3.

Emminger, Otmar. 1986. *D-Mark, Dollar, Währungskrisen.* Stuttgart: DVA.

Erhard, Ludwig. 1953. "Die Deutsche Wirtschaftspolitik im Blickfeld Europäischer Politik." In *Wirtschaft ohne Wunder,* edited by Albert Hunold, 128–35. Erlenbach-Zürich: Rentsch.

Eucken, Walter. 1952. *Grundsätze der Wirtschaftspolitik.* Tübingen: Mohr.

Evangelista, Matthew. 1996a. "Stalin's Revenge: Institutional Barriers to Internationalization in the Soviet Union." In *Internationalization and Domestic Politics,* edited by Helen Keohane and Robert Milner. Cambridge: Cambridge University Press.

———. 1996b. "From Each according to Its Abilities: Competing Theoretical Approaches to the Post-Soviet Energy Sector." In *The Sources of Russian Foreign Policy after the Cold War,* edited by Celeste Wallander. Boulder: Westview.

Finnemore, Martha. 1993. "International Organizations as Teachers of Norms: The United Nations Educational, Scientific, and Cultural Organization and Science Policy." *International Organization* 47:565–97.

———. 1996. "Norms, Culture and World Politics: Insights from Sociology's Institutionalism." *International Organization* 50:325–47.

Finnemore, Martha, and K. Sikkink. 1998. "International Norm Dynamics and Political Change." *International Organization* 52:887–917.

———. 2001. "Taking Stock: The Constructivist Research Program in International Relations and Comparative Politics." *Annual Review of Political Science* 4:391–416.

Fischler, Franz. 2002. "Quality Matters: A New Focus for Agricultural Policy." Speech to the European Food Summit, Brussels, April 12.

Flaherty, Patrick. 1991. "Perestroika and the Neo-Liberal Project." In *Communist Regimes: The Aftermath. Socialist Register 1991,* edited by Ralph Miliband and Leo Panitch, 128–68. London: Merlin.

Ford, Peter. 2001. "Pâté, Bonhomie, and a Slap at Engineered Food." *Christian Science Monitor,* August 31.

Fortin, Bernard. 1978. *Les avantages et les coûts des différentes options monétaires d'une petite économie ouverte: un cadre analytique.* Montreal: Édition Official du Quebec.

Frank, Dana. 1999. *Buy American: The Untold Story of Economic Nationalism.* Boston: Beacon.

Fraser, Graham. 1980. "PQ Skirts Currency Reality." *Montreal Gazette,* February 12.

——. 1984. *P.Q.: René Lévesque and the Parti Québécois in Power.* Toronto: Macmillan.

Freeman, Alan, and Patrick Grady. 1995. *Dividing the House: Planning for the Canada without Quebec.* Toronto: HarperCollins.

Frieden, Jeffrey, and Ronald Rogowski. 1996. "The Impact of the International Economy on National Politics: An Analytical Overview." In *Internationalization and Domestic Politics,* edited by Helen Milner and Robert Keohane, 25–47. Cambridge: Cambridge University Press.

Friedman, Jonathan. 1995. "Global System, Globalization and the Parameters of Modernity." In *Global Modernities,* edited by Mike Featherstone, Scott Lash, and Roland Robertson. London: Sage.

Friedman, Thomas L. 1999. *The Lexus and the Olive Tree.* New York: Farrar, Straus and Giroux.

Fukuyama, Francis. 1989. "The End of History?" *National Interest* 16:3–16.

Furman, Dmitri. 1992. "Rossiyskiye demokrati i raspad soyuza." *Vek XX i mir* 1:10–19.

Furman, Dmitri, and Oleg Bukhovets. 1996. "Belorusskoe samosoznanie i belorusskaia politika" (Belorussian self-awareness and Belorussian politics). *Svobodnaia mysl'* 1:57–75.

Gallagher, Mary. 2002. "'Reform and Openness': Why China's Economic Reforms Have Delayed Democracy." *World Politics* 54:338–72.

Garrett, Geoffrey. 1998. *Partisan Politics in the Global Economy.* Cambridge: Cambridge University Press.

Gaynor, Brian. 2003. "Tourists Flocking to Hot Destination." *New Zealand Weekend Herald,* February 8–9, C2.

Gefter, Mikhail. 1991. *Iz tekh i etikh let.* Moscow: Progress.

Gellner, Ernest. 1983. *Nations and Nationalism.* Ithaca, N.Y.: Cornell University Press.

German economists. 1994. "EC Currency Union—An Acid Test for Europe, 1992 Manifesto Signed by Sixty German Economists." In *30 Years of European Monetary Integration from the Werner Plan to EMU,* edited by Alfred Steinherr. New York: Longman.

Gerschenkron, Alexander. 1962. *Economic Backwardness in Historical Perspective.* Cambridge: Harvard University Press.

Gibbens, Robert. 1978. "Bourassa Attacks PQ Dollar Plan." *Montreal Star,* May 17.

——. 1994. "Quebec Dollar Uproar." *Financial Post* (Toronto), July 30.

Gibney, Frank. 1998. "Introduction." In *Unlocking the Bureaucrat's Kingdom: Deregulation and the Japanese Economy,* edited by F. Gibney. Washington, D.C.: Brookings Institution.

Gill, Stephen. 2003. *Power and Resistance in the New World Order.* New York: Palgrave MacMillan.

Gilpin, Robert. 1987. *The Political Economy of International Relations.* Princeton, N.J.: Princeton University Press.

———. 2001. *Global Political Economy.* Princeton, N.J.: Princeton University Press.

Girnius, Saulius. 1997. "Back in Europe, to Stay." *Transitions* 3 (6): 7–10.

Globe and Mail. 1978. "Customs Union Only Need for Quebec, Parizeau Says." July 17.

———. 1979. "The White Paper on Quebec's Referendum." November 2.

———. 1992. "Sovereign Quebec Would Use Canadian Dollar, Parizeau Insists." February 22.

———. 1998. "Bloc Wants Talks on U.S. Dollar." December 10.

Godin, Iuri. 2000. "Dilemma Rossiyi v postsovietskom prostranstve." *Nezavisimaya gazeta,* December 27.

Goff, Patricia. 2000. "Invisible Borders: Economic Liberalization and National Identity." *International Studies Quarterly* 44:533–62.

———. 2002. "Trading Culture: Identity and Culture Industry Trade Policy in the U.S., Canada, and the EU." In *Constructivism and Comparative Politics: Theoretical Issues and Case Studies,* edited by Daniel Green. Armonk, N.Y.: M. E. Sharpe.

Golay, Frank H., Ralph Anspach, M. Ruth Pfanner, and Eliezer B. Ayal. 1969. *Underdevelopment and Economic Nationalism in Southeast Asia.* Ithaca, N.Y.: Cornell University Press.

Gold, Tom. 1986. *State and Society in the Taiwan Miracle.* Armonk, N.Y.: M. E. Sharpe.

Goldstein, Judith, and Robert Keohane, eds. 1993. *Ideas and Foreign Policy: Beliefs, Institutions and Political Change.* Ithaca, N.Y.: Cornell University Press.

Gorbachev, Mikhail. 1995. *Avgust 1991: Moya pozitsiya.* Moscow: Novosti.

Goricheva, L. 1997. "On the Integrity of the National Economy." *Russian Social Science Review* 38 (3): 3–25.

Götz, Roland. 2001. "Zehn Jahre Wirtschaftstransformation in Rußland—und der Westen." *Osteuropa* 11 (12): 1286–1304.

Graham, Clyde. 1994. "Independent Quebec use of Canadian dollar would be nuts—Martin." *Halifax Chronicle Herald,* December 22.

Granovetter, Mark, and Richard Swedberg, eds. 1992. *The Sociology of Economic Life.* Boulder: Westview.

Greenfeld, Liah. 1995. "The Worth of Nations: Some Economic Implications of Nationalism." *Critical Review* 10 (3): 555–84.

———. 2001a. *The Spirit of Capitalism: Nationalism and Economic Growth.* Cambridge: Harvard University Press.

———. 2001b. "Etymology, Definitions, Types." In *Encyclopedia of Nationalism,* 1:251–65. New York: Academic Press.

Greiffenhagen, Martin. 1997. *Politische Legitimität in Deutschland.* Gütersloh: Bertelsmann.

Grieco, Joseph M. 1997. "Realist International Theory and the Study of World Politics." In *New Thinking in International Relations Theory,* edited by Michael W. Doyle and G. John Ikenberry. Boulder: Westview.

Grimes, William W. 2000. "Internationalization as Insulation: Dilemmas of the Yen." *Japanese Economy* 28:46–75.

———. 2003. "Internationalization of the Yen and the New Politics of Monetary Insulation." In *Monetary Orders: Ambiguous Economics, Ubiquitous Politics,* edited by Jonathan Kirshner, 172–94. Ithaca, N.Y.: Cornell University Press.

Güllner, Manfred. 1998. "Die Deutschen und der Euro." In *Der Kampf um den Euro,* edited by Hans-Ulrich Jörges, 134–39. Hamburg: Hoffman und Campe.

Haas, Ernst. 1997. *The Rise and Decline of Nationalism.* Ithaca, N.Y.: Cornell University Press.

Haas, Peter. 1992. "Introduction: Epistemic Communities and International Policy Coordination." *International Organization* 46:1–35.

Habermas, Jürgen. 1989. "Die Stunde der Nationalen Empfindung." In *Die nachholende Revolution,* 157–66. 1990. Frankfurt a. M.: Suhrkamp.

——. 1998. *Die postnationale Konstellation.* Frankfurt a. M.: Suhrkamp.

Hadekel, Peter. 1978. "A Dollar for Quebec?" *Winnipeg Free Press,* May 27.

Haggard, Stephan. 1990. *Pathways from the Periphery.* Ithaca, N.Y.: Cornell University Press.

Hall, Ivan P. 1998. *Cartels of the Mind: Japan's Intellectual Closed Shop.* New York: W. W. Norton.

Hall, Peter, ed. 1989. *The Political Power of Economic Ideas: Keynesianism across Nations.* Princeton, N.J.: Princeton University Press.

Hall, Peter, and Robert J. Franzese. 1998. "Mixed Signals: Central Bank Independence, Coordinated Wage Bargaining, and European Monetary Union." *International Organization* 52:505–35.

Hall, Peter A., and David Soskice. 2001. *Varieties of Capitalism.* Oxford: Oxford University Press.

Hankel, Wilhelm. 1972. *Währungspolitik.* Stuttgart: Kohlhammer.

Hankel, Wilhelm, et al. 1998. *Die Euro-Klage.* Hamburg: Rowohlt.

Harlen, Christine Margerum. 1999. "A Reappraisal of Classical Economic Nationalism and Economic Liberalism." *International Studies Quarterly* 43:733–44.

Hartcher, Peter. 1998. *The Ministry: How Japan's Most Powerful Institution Endangers World Markets.* Boston: Harvard Business School Press.

Haselbach, Dieter. 1991. *Autoritärer Liberalismus und Soziale Marktwirtschaft.* Baden-Baden: Nomos.

Hauner, Milan. 1990. *What Is Asia to Us? Russia's Asian Heartland Yesterday and Today.* Boston: Unwin Hyman.

Hayes, Carlton J. H. 1928. "Nationalism as a Religion." In *Essays on Nationalism.* New York: Macmillan.

——. 1931. *The Historical Evolution of Modern Nationalism.* New York: Richard R. Smith.

Hefner, Robert W. 1998. *Market Cultures: Society and Morality in the New Asian Capitalisms.* Boulder: Westview.

Heilemann, Ulrich, and Reimuth Jochimson. 1993. "Christmas in July? The Political Economy of German Unification Reconsidered." *Brookings Occasional Papers.* Washington, D.C.: Brookings Institution.

Heilperin, Michael. 1960. *Studies in Economic Nationalism.* Geneva: Publications de L'Institut Universitaire de Hautes Etudes Internationales.

Held, David, and Anthony McGrew, eds. 2000. *The Global Transformations Reader.* Cambridge: Polity.

Helleiner, Eric. 1994. *States and the Reemergence of Global Finance: From Bretton Woods to the 1990s.* Ithaca, N.Y.: Cornell University Press.

——. 2002. "Economic Nationalism as a Challenge to Neoliberalism? Lessons from the 19th Century." *International Studies Quarterly* 46:307–29.

——. 2003a. "Dollarization Diplomacy: U.S. Policy Comes Full Circle?" *Review of International Political Economy* 10:406–29.

——. 2003b. "The Strange Politics of Canada's NAMU Debate." *Studies in Political Economy* 71/2:67–99.

——. 2003c. *The Making of National Money: Territorial Currencies in Historical Perspective.* Ithaca, N.Y.: Cornell University Press.

Henderson, Jeffrey. 1999. "Uneven Crises: Institutional Foundations of East Asian Economic Turmoil." *Economy and Society* 28:327–68.

Hendery, Simon. 2003a. "Wealthy Visitors Expected to Bring Their Wallets," *New Zealand Herald,* January 24.

——. 2003b. "Super-rich Visitors Sample New Zealand's Finest," *Weekend New Zealand Herald,* February 15–16, C1.

Hentschel, Volker. 1996. *Ludwig Erhard.* Berlin: Ullstein.

Herr, Hansjoerg. 1991. "Der Merkantilismus der Bundesrepublik in der Weltwirtschaft." In *Marktwirtschaft und politische Regulierung,* edited by Klaus Voy. Marburg: Metropolis.

Hieronymi, Otto. 1980. *The New Economic Nationalism.* Greenwood.

Hintze, Otto. 1975. *The Historical Essays of Otto Hintze,* edited by Felix Gilbert. Oxford: Oxford University Press.

Hirschman, Albert O. 1958. *The Strategy of Economic Development.* New Haven, Conn.: Yale University Press.

——. 1968. "The Political Economy of Import Substitution Industrialization in Latin America." *Quarterly Journal of Economics* 82:1–32.

——. 1986. *Rival Views of Market Society.* New York: Viking.

Hoffmann, Lutz. 1993. *Warten auf den Aufschwung.* Transfer-Verlag: Regensburg

Hofstede, Geert. 1980. *Culture's Consequences: International Differences in Work-Related Values.* Newbury Park, Calif.: Sage.

——. 1991. *Cultures and Organizations: Software of the Mind* London: McGraw-Hill.

——. 1999. "Problems Remain, But Theories Will Change: The Universal and the Specific in 21st-Century Global Management." *Organizational Dynamics* 28 (1): 34–44.

Hollerman, Leon. 1998. "Whither Deregulation? An Epilogue to Japan's Industrial Policy." In *Unlocking the Bureaucrat's Kingdom: Deregulation and the Japanese Economy,* edited by Frank Gibney. Washington, D.C.: Brookings Institution Press.

Hollingsworth, J. Rogers, and R. Boyer, eds. 1997. *Contemporary Capitalism: The Embeddedness of Institutions.* Cambridge: Cambridge University Press.

Hornblower, Margot, and Hannah Beech. 1999. "Never Mind the Riots. The Real Threat to the WTO's Free-Trade Agenda Lies in Discord among Member Nations." *Time,* December 13.

Hudson, Valerie, ed. 1996. *Culture and Foreign Policy.* Boulder: Lynne Rienner.

Hughes, Christopher. 1997. "Globalization and Nationalism: Squaring the Circle in Chinese International Relations Theory." *Millennium* 26 (1): 103–24.

Hughes, Helen Rigg. 1993. "New Zealand's Clean Green Image—Fact or Fiction?" Thomas Cawthron Memorial Lecture No. 52, Wellington, November.

Huntington, Samuel. 1968. *Political Order in Changing Societies.* New Haven, Conn.: Yale University Press.

Hutchison, Terence W. 1979. "Notes on the Effects of Economic Ideas on Policy: The Example of the German Social Market Economy." *Journal of Institutional and Theoretical Economics* 135:426–41.

Ikenberry, G. John. 1986. "The Irony of State Strength: Comparative Responses to the Oil Shocks in the 1970s." *International Organization* 40:105–37.

IMF (International Monetary Fund). 2003. *World Economic Outlook.* Washington, D.C.: International Monetary Fund.

International Institute of Strategic Studies. 1994. *The Military Balance, 1994–95.* London: Brassey's.

Issing, Otmar. 1995. "Ethics and Morals in Central Banking—Do They Exist, Do They Matter?" In *Auszüge aus Presseartikeln,* vol. 80, edited by Deutsche Bundesbank, 10–15. Frankfurt: Deutsche Bundesbank.

Itagaki, Yoichi. 1971. "The North-South Problem and Economic Nationalism." *Developing Economies* 9 (2): 111–32.

Itō, Takatoshi. 1992. *Shōhisha jūshi no keizaigaku: kisei kanwa wa naze hitsuyō ka* (Economics as if consumers mattered: Why is deregulation necessary?). Tokyo: Nihon Keizai Shinbunsha.

Itoh, Mayumi. 2000. *Globalization of Japan: Japanese Sakoku Mentality and U.S. Efforts to Open Japan.* New York: St. Martin's.

Iverson, Torben, Jonas Pontusson, and David Soskice, eds. 2000. *Unions, Employers, and Central Banks.* Cambridge: Cambridge University Press.

Iwabuchi, Koichi. 2002. *Recentering Globalization: Popular Culture and Japanese Transnationalism.* Durham, N.C.: Duke University Press.

Jepperson, Ronald L., Alexander Wendt, and Peter J. Katzenstein. 1996. "Norms, Identity, and Culture in National Security." In *The Culture of National Security,* edited by Peter J. Katzenstein. New York: Columbia University Press.

Jessop, Bob. 1999. "Narrating the Future of the National State: Remarks on Remapping Regulation and Reinventing Governance." In *State/Culture: State-Formation after the Cultural Turn,* edited by George Steinmetz. Ithaca, N.Y.: Cornell University Press.

Johnson, Chalmers. 1982. *MITI and the Japanese Miracle.* Stanford: Stanford University Press.

——. 1995. *Japan, Who Governs?* New York: W. W. Norton.

——. 1999. "The Developmental State: Odyssey of a Concept." In *The Developmental State,* edited by Meredith Woo-Cumings. Ithaca, N.Y.: Cornell University Press.

Johnson, Harry. [1965] 1994. "Economic Nationalism in New States." In *Nationalism,* edited by John Hutchinson and Anthony D. Smith. Oxford: Oxford University Press, 236–40.

——, ed. 1967. *Economic Nationalism in Old and New States.* Chicago: University of Chicago Press.

Jurgatiene, Kornelija, and Ole Waever. 1996. "Lithuania." In *European Integration and National Adaptations,* edited by Hans Mouritzen, Ole Wæver, and Hakan Wiberg. Commack, N.Y.: Nova Science.

Kasaiyev, Alan. 2001. "Sovyet Bezopasnosti Rossiyi reshil zakrit' SNG." *Nezavisimaya gazeta,* February 7.

Katzenstein, Peter J. 1985. *Small States in World Markets.* Ithaca, N.Y.: Cornell University Press.

——. 1996a. *Cultural Norms and National Security: Police and Military in Postwar Japan.* Ithaca, N.Y.: Cornell University Press.

——, ed. 1996b. *The Culture of National Security Norms and Identity in World Politics.* New York: Columbia University Press.

Katzenstein, Peter, R. Keohane, and S. Krasner. 1998. "International Organization and the Study of World Politics." *International Organization* 52:645–85.

Kawabata, Yasao. 2002. "'Sutajiamu no nekkyō no hazama kara,' dai ikkai: 'Nihon to Nihonjin' ni totte no Wārudo Kappu" (From the wild, packed stadium, part 1: What the World Cup means for Japan and the Japanese). http://www.sportsnavi.com/column/article/ZZZUR2HFZ1D.html.

Keidanren. 1992. "Jiyū–tōmei–kōsei na shijō keizai o mezashite: kisei kanwa no tame no teigen" (Toward a liberal, transparent, fair market economy: a proposal for regulatory loosening). Tokyo: Keidanren.

Kirshner, Jonathan. 1999. "The Political Economy of Realism." In *Unipolar Politics: Realism and State Strategies after the Cold War,* edited by Ethan Kapstein and Michael Mastanduno. New York: Columbia University Press.

Klein, Naomi. 1999. *No Logo: Taking Aim at the Brand Bullies.* New York: Picador.

Klodt, Hans. 2000. "Industrial Policy and the East German Productivity Puzzle." *German Economic Review* 1 (3): 315–33.

Klotz, Audie. 1995. *Norms in International Relations: The Struggle against Apartheid.* Ithaca, N.Y.: Cornell University Press.

Klyachko, Tatyana, and Valeri Solovei. 1995. "Neozhydannye liki Yegora Gaidara." *Novoye vremya* 11:14–16, 12:46–49.

Kobrinskaya, Irina. 1997. "Pragmaticheski liberalizm vo vneshnei politike." *Otkritaia politika* 7–8:27–31.

Kochetov, Ernst G. 1999. *Geoekonomika.* Moscow: BEK.

Kortunov, Andrei. 1995. "Russia, the Near Abroad, and the West." In *The New Russia: Troubled Transformation,* edited by Gail Lapidus. Boulder: Westview Press.

Kotz, David, with Fred Weir. 1997. *Revolution from Above: The Demise of the Soviet System.* New York: Routledge.

Kouzmin, Alexander. 1997. "From Phobias to Ideological Prescription: Toward Multiple Models in Transformation Management for Socialist Economies in Transition." *Administration and Society* 29 (2): 139–88.

Kozyrev, Andrei. 1994. "Don't Threaten Us." *New York Times,* March 18.

Krastev, Nikola. 2002. Russia: "Moscow Impresses but Also Worries Oil Investors." *RFE/RL,* April 4, http://www.rfel.org/nca/features/2002/03/29032002095845.asp.

Krauss, Melvyn B. 1978. *The New Protectionism: The Welfare State and International Trade.* New York: New York University Press.

Krugman, Paul. 1996. "Making Sense of the Competitiveness Debate." *Oxford Review of Economic Policy* 13 (3): 17–25.

Kubicek, Paul. 1996a. "Dynamics of Contemporary Ukrainian Nationalism: From Empire-Breaking to State-Building." *Canadian Review of Studies in Nationalism* 23:39–50.

———. 1996b. "Variations on a Corporatist Theme: Interest Associations in Post-Soviet Ukraine and Russia." *Europe-Asia Studies* 48:27–46.

———. 1999. "Ukrainian Interest Groups, Corporatism, and Economic Reform." In *State and Institution Building in Ukraine,* edited by Taras Kuzio, Robert S. Kravchuk, and Paul D'Anieri. New York: St. Martin's.

Kuchma, Leonid. 1995. Interview. *Osteuropa* 45 (8): A486–89. Reprinted from *Ogonek,* March 5–10.

Kusano, Atsushi. 1999. "Deregulation in Japan and the Role of Naiatsu." *Social Science Japan Journal* 2:65–84.

Kuzio, Taras. 1996. "National Identity in Independent Ukraine: An Identity in Transition." *Nationalism and Ethnic Politics* 2 (4): 582–609.

——. 1997. *Ukraine under Kuchma: Political Reform, Economic Transformation and Security Policy in Independent Ukraine.* New York: St. Martin's.

——. 1998a. "The Domestic Sources of Ukrainian Security Policy." *Journal of Strategic Studies* 21 (4): 18–49.

——. 1998b. *Ukraine: State and Nation Building.* London: Routledge.

Kyvelidis, Ioannis. 2000. "State Isomorphism in the Post-Socialist Transition." *European Integration Online Papers* 4 (2). http://eiop.or.at/eiop/texte/2000-002a.htm.

Laidler, David and William Robson. 1991. *Two Nations, One Money.* Toronto: C. D. Howe Institute.

Lamont, Michele. 1995. "National Identity and National Boundary Patterns in France and The United States." *French Historical Studies* 19 (2): 349–65.

Lamont, Michele, and Laurent Thevenot, eds. 2000. *Rethinking Comparative Cultural Sociology: Repertoires of Evaluation in France and the United States.* Cambridge: Cambridge University Press.

Lane, David. 1999. "The Transformation of State Socialism in Russia: From 'Chaotic' Economy to State-Led Cooperative Capitalism." Paper presented at the American Association for the Advancement of Slavic Studies, St. Louis, Mo., November.

Lasswell, Harold. 1997. *Essays on the Garrison State.* New Brunswick, N.J.: Transaction.

Lee, Kuan Yew. 1998. *The Singapore Story: Memoirs of Lee Kuan Yew.* Singapore: Simon and Schuster.

Leheny, David. 2003. *The Rules of Play: National Identity and the Shaping of Japanese Leisure.* Ithaca, N.Y.: Cornell University Press.

Lemco, Jonathan. 1994. *Turmoil in the Peaceable Kingdom.* Toronto: University of Toronto Press.

Leslie, Peter. 1979. "Equal to Equal: Economic Association and the Canadian Common Market." Discussion Paper 6, Institute of Intergovernmental Relations, Queens University, Kingston, Ont.

Lévesque, René. 1968. *An Option for Quebec.* Toronto: McClelland and Stewart.

——. 1979. *My Quebec.* Translated by Gaynor Fitzpatrick. Toronto: Methuen.

Levi-Faur, David. 1997a. "Economic Nationalism: From Friedrich List to Robert Reich." *Review of International Studies* 23:359–70.

——. 1997b. "Friedrich List and the Political Economy of the Nation-State." *Review of International Political Economy* 4 (1): 154–78.

Lewis, K. 1999. "Trying to Explain the Home Bias in Equities and Consumption." *Journal of Economic Literature* 37 (June 1999): 571–608.

Lewis, Reese Phillip. 1993. *The Origins of Taiwan's Trade and Industrial Policies.* Ph.D. diss., Columbia University.

Lincoln, Edward. 1998. "Deregulation in Japan and the United States: A Study in Contrasts." In *Unlocking the Bureaucrat's Kingdom: Deregulation and the Japanese Economy,* edited by Frank Gibney. Washington, D.C.: Brookings Institution.

——. 2001. *Arthritic Japan: The Slow Pace of Economic Reform.* Washington, D.C.: Brookings Institution.

Linz, Juan J., and Alfred Stepan. 1996. *Problems of Democratic Transition and Consolidation.* Baltimore: Johns Hopkins University Press.

Lisée, Jean-François. 1994. *The Trickster: Robert Bourassa and Quebecers, 1990–1992*. Abridged and translated by Robert Chodos, Simon Horn, and Wanda Tayor. Toronto: Lames Lorimer.

List, Friedrich. [1837] 1983. *The Natural System of Political Economy*. Totowa, N.J.: Frank Cass.

——. [1841] 1904. *The National System of Political Economy*. Translated by S. Lloyd. London: Longmans, Green.

——. [1841] 1966. *The National System of Political Economy*. New York: Augustus M. Kelley.

Lithuania. Government. 1997. *Action Program of the Government of the Republic of Lithuania for 1997–2000*. Vilnius: Government of Lithuania.

Lithuania. Ministry of Foreign Affairs. 1997. *Lithuania's Foreign Policy*. Vilnius: Ministry of Foreign Affairs of Lithuania.

Lockwood, William. 1968. *The Economic Development of Japan*. Princeton, N.J.: Princeton University Press.

Lofgren, Joan. 1997. "A Different Kind of Union." *Transitions* 4 (6): 47–52.

Lozowy, Ivan. 1994. *The Popular Movement of Ukraine Rukh 1994: Statehood, Democracy, Reforms*. Kiev: International Relations Secretariat, Popular Movement of Ukraine Rukh.

MacDonald, Don. 1991. "Parizeau Keen on Canadian Dollar." *Vancouver Sun,* May 28.

Macdonald, Roderick, and Huw Thomas, eds. 1997. *Nationality and Planning in Scotland and Wales*. Cardiff: University of Wales Press.

Mackie, Richard. 1995. "Use of Canadian Dollar Wouldn't Make Sense, Leader Says." *Globe and Mail,* August 3.

Maddison, Angus. 2001. *The World Economy*. Paris: Organization for Economic Cooperation and Development.

Maes, Ivo. 2002. "On the Origins of the Franco-German EMU Controversies." *National Bank of Belgium Working Papers no. 43* (July).

Mahant, Edelgart. 2003. "Evolving Institutions as Frameworks or Prison Bars: The European Union from Rome to Maastricht." Paper presented at the International Studies Association, Budapest.

Malcolm, Neil, and Alex Pravda. 1996. "Introduction." In *Internal Factors in Russian Foreign Policy,* edited by Neil Malcolm, Alex Pravda, Roy Allison, and Margot Light, 1–32. Oxford: Oxford University Press.

Mansfield, Edward D., and Helen V. Milner, eds. 1997. *The Political Economy of Regionalism*. New York: Columbia University Press.

Marceau, Richard. 1999. "A Quebec Perspective on a North American Currency." *Canadian Parliamentary Review* 22 (2): 2–4.

Markus, Ustina. 1996a. "Belarus, Ukraine Take Opposite Views." *Transition* 2 (23): 20–22.

——. 1996b. "Imperial Understretch: Belarus's Union with Russia." *Current History* 95 (603): 335–39.

Marples, David R. 1999. *Belarus: A Denationalized Nation*. Amsterdam: Harwood.

Marsh, David. 1992. *The Bank That Rules Europe*. London: Heineman.

Matthews, Philip. 2002. "I'm Helen, Fly Me." *Listener,* January 11, 16–20.

Mayall, James. 1990. *Nationalism and International Society*. Cambridge: Cambridge University Press.

McAdams, A. James. 1997. "Germany after Unification: Normal at Last?" *World Politics* 49:282–308.

McConnell, David L. 2000. *Importing Diversity: Inside Japan's Jet Program.* Berkeley: University of California Press.

McCrone, David. 1998. *The Sociology of Nationalism.* London: Routledge.

McFaul, Michael. 1999. "The Political Economy of Social Policy Reform in Russia: Ideas, Insititutions, and Interests." In *Left Parties and Social Policy in Postcommunist Europe,* edited by Linda J. Cook, Mitchell A. Orenstein, and Marilyn Rueschemeyer, 207–34. Boulder: Westview.

McKenna, Barrie, and Alan Freeman. 1995. "Parizeau Admits to War Chest." *Globe and Mail,* November 3.

McNamara, Kathleen. 1998. *The Currency of Ideas.* Ithaca, N.Y.: Cornell University Press.

McRoberts, Kenneth. 1988. *Quebec: Social Change and Political Crisis.* 3rd ed. Toronto: McClelland and Stewart.

Melville, Andrei. 2002. "The Achievement of Domestic Consensus on Russian Foreign Policy?" Paper presented at the 43rd annual convention of the International Studies Association, New Orleans.

Meyer, John, John Boli, George M. Thomas, and Francisco O. Ramirez. 1997. "World Society and the Nation-State." *American Journal of Sociology* 103 (1): 144–81.

Michalopoulos, Constantine, and David G. Tarr. 1992. *Trade and Payments Arrangements for the States of the Former USSR.* Washington, D.C.: World Bank.

Migranian, Andranik. 1994. "Rossiia i blizhneye zarubezhiye." *Nezavisimaya gazeta,* January 12.

Miller, David. 1995. *On Nationality.* Oxford: Clarendon.

Miller, Raymond, ed. 2003. *New Zealand Government and Politics.* 3rd ed. Melbourne: Oxford University Press.

Mitscherlich, Alexander, and Margarete Mitscherlich. [1967] 1990. *Die Unfähigkeit zu trauern,* Leipzig: Reclam.

Miyamoto, Masao. 1995. *Straitjacket Society: An Insider's Irreverent View of Bureaucratic Japan.* Tokyo: Kodansha International.

———. 1998. "Deregulating Japan's Soul." In *Unlocking the Bureaucrat's Kingdom: Deregulation and the Japanese Economy,* edited by Frank Gibney. Washington, D.C.: Brookings Institution.

Molchanov, Mikhail A. 2000. "Post-Communist Nationalism as a Power Resource: A Russia-Ukraine Comparison." *Nationalities Papers* 28 (2): 263–88.

Montreal Gazette. 1999a. "The Buck Stops Here." *Montreal Gazette,* January 30.

———. 1999b. "To Use U.S. dollar." *Montreal Gazette,* March 16.

Moore, Barrington. 1967. *Social Origins of Dictatorship and Democracy.* Boston: Beacon Press.

Morgan, James. 1992. "Germany's Magic Debt Mountain." *Financial Times,* October 31/November 1.

Mosca, Jenny. 2000. "The Battle between the Cheeses." *Tulane Journal of International and Comparative Law* 8 (Spring): 559–99.

Müller, Klaus. 1995. Der osteuropäische Wandel und die deutsch-deutsche Transformation." In *Chancen und Risiken der industriellen Restrukturierung in Ostdeutschland,* edited by Rudi Schmidt and Burkart Lutz, 1–42. Berlin: Akademie.

Nagano, Yoshinobu. 2002. *Koizumi Jun'ichirō to Hara Takashi: kōzō kaikaku o rekishi ni manabu* (Koizumi Junichiro and Hara Takashi: Lessons from history about structural reform). Tokyo: Chūō Kōron Shinsha.

Nakatani, Iwao. 1997. "A Design for Transforming the Japanese Economy." *Journal of Japanese Studies* 23:399–417.

Neill, Sam. 2003. "In the Field of GE Food We're Being Sold a Pup." *New Zealand Herald*, January 3.

Neklessa, A. I. 1997. "Postsovremennyi mir v novoi sisteme koordinat." *Vostok* 2:2–25.

Nekrasas, Evaldas. 1998. "Is Lithuania a Northern or Central European Country?" *Lithuanian Foreign Policy Review* 1:19–45.

Neufeld, Mark, and Sandra Whitworth. 1997. "Imag(in)ing Canadian Foreign Policy." In *Understanding Canada*, edited by Wallace Clement, 197–214. Montreal and Kingston: McGill-Queen's University Press.

Neumann, Iver B. 1996. *Russia and the Idea of Europe: A Study in Identity and International Relations*. London: Routledge.

New Zealand Business. 2002/3. Special issue, "One Hundred Top New Zealand Exporters." December/January.

New Zealand Herald. 2003a. "Clean, Green and from NZ." January 21.

——. 2003b. "Alinghi to Make Changes to America's Cup." January 21.

NFPA (American National Food Processors Association). 2001. Letter, dated December 17, 2001, from NFPA to the U.S. Department of Commerce in response to Notice and Request for Comments on the Annual National Trade Estimate Report on Foreign Trade Barriers 66, *Federal Register* 60237, December 3.

Nicholson, Martin. 2001. "Putin's Russia: Slowing the Pendulum without Stopping the Clock." *International Affairs* 77 (3): 867–84.

Norman, E. H. 1975. *Origins of the Modern Japanese State*. New York: Pantheon.

Nystrom, Lorne. 1999. "Common Currency." Mimeograph of Member of Parliament, New Democratic Party. Ottawa.

OECD (Organization for Economic Cooperation and Development). 1999. *EMU: Facts, Challenges and Policies*. Paris: OECD.

OECD (Organization for Economic Cooperation and Development). 2000. *EMU: One Year On*. Paris: OECD.

Offe, Claus. 1996. *Varieties of Transition: The East European and East German Experience*. Cambridge: Polity.

Olcott, Martha Brill, Anders Aslund, and Sherman W. Garnett. 1999. *Getting It Wrong: Regional Cooperation and the Commonwealth of Independent States*. Washington, D.C.: Carnegie Endowment for International Peace.

Olins, Wally. 1999. *Trading Identities: Why Countries and Companies Are Taking on Each Other's Roles*. London: Foreign Policy Center.

Olson, Mancur. 1987. "Economic Nationalism and Economic Progress." *World Economy* 10 (3): 241–64.

Oram, Rod. 2001. "Brand New Zealand." *Unlimited Magazine*, December 1. www.sharechat.co.nz/features/unlimited/article.php/e348f217.

Ó Tuathail, Gearóid. 1996. *Critical Geopolitics: The Politics of Writing Global Space*. Minneapolis: University of Minnesota Press.

Ó Tuathail, Gearóid, and Simon Dalby, eds. 1998. *Rethinking Geopolitics*. London: Routledge.

Otunbayeva, Roza. 1991. "V preddveriyi novogo miroporyadka." *Mezhdunarodnaya zhizn'* 3:183–91.

Overturf, Stephen F. 1997. *Money and European Union*. New York: St. Martin's.

Panitch, Leo, and Colin Leys, eds. 2001. *Working Classes, Global Realities. Socialist Register 2001*. London: Merlin.

Pankov, Vladimir. 1996. "Ökonomisch-politische Beziehungen zwischen Rußland und der Ukraine." *Österreichische Militärische Zeitschrift* 34 (5): 539–46.

Parboni, R. 1981. *The Dollar and Its Rivals.* London: Verso.

Parizeau, Jacques. 1999. "Globalization and the National Interests: The Adventure of Liberalization." In *Out of Control, Canada in an Unstable Financial World,* edited by Brian MacLean. Ottawa: Canadian Center for Policy Alternatives.

Park, Chung Hee. 1979. *Korea Reborn: A Model for Development.* Englewood Cliffs, N.J.: Prentice Hall.

Parsons, Talcott. [1942] 1966. "Democracy and Social Structure in Pre-Nazi Germany." In *Essays in Sociological Theory,* rev. ed. New York: Free Press.

Parti Québécois. 1972. *Quand nous serons vraiment chez nous.* Montreal: Parti Québécois.

Parti Québécois, National Executive Council. [1993] 1994. *Quebec in a New World.* Translated by Robert Chodos. Toronto: James Lorimer.

Paschenko, Vitali Ya. 2000. *Ideologiya Yevraziystva.* Moscow: MGU.

Pauly, Louis. 2000. "Capital Mobility and the New Global Order." In *Political Economy in a Changing Global Order,* 2nd ed., edited by Geoffrey Underhill and Richard Stubbs, 119–28. Oxford: Oxford University Press.

Peacock, Alan, and Hans Willgerodt, eds. 1989a. *German Neo-Liberals and the Social Market Economy.* London: Macmillan.

——. 1989b: *Germany's Social Market Economy.* London: Macmillan.

Pentland, Charles. 1977. "Association after Sovereignty?" In *Must Canada Fail?,* edited by Richard Simeon. Montreal: McGill-Queens University Press.

Peregudov, Sergei 1994. "Organizovannyye interesy i rossiyskoye gosudarstvo." *Polis* 5:64–75.

Petro, Nicolai N. 1995. *The Rebirth of Russian Democracy: An Interpretation of Political Culture.* Cambridge: Harvard University Press.

Pettman, Jan Jindy. 1998. "Nationalism and After." *Review of International Studies* 24:49–64.

Pfaff, William. 1991. Redefining World Power. *Foreign Affairs* 70 (1): 36–48.

Pharr, Susan. 2000. "Officials' Misconduct and Public Distrust: Japan and the Trilateral Democracies." In *Disaffected Democracies: What's Troubling the Trilateral Countries?* edited by Susan Pharr and Robert Putnam. Princeton, N.J.: Princeton University Press.

Phillips, Andrew. 1980. "Economists Scoff at PQ Energy, Monetary Proposals." *Montreal Gazette,* April 22.

Picard, Andre. 1995. "P.Q. Plans Owned Currency, Johnson Says." *Globe and Mail,* February 16.

Pickel, Andreas. 2003. "Explaining, and Explaining with Economic Nationalism." *Nations and Nationalism* 9 (1): 105–27.

Pickel, Andreas, and Jacqui True. 1999. "Global Forces, Transnational Linkages and Local Actors: Towards a New Political Economy of Post-Socialist Transformation." Paper presented at the American Association for the Advancement of Slavic Studies, St. Louis, Mo.

——. 2002. "Global, Transnational and National Change Mechanisms: Bridging International and Comparative Approaches to Post-Communist Transformation." In *Postcommunist Transformation and the Social Sciences: Cross-Disciplinary Approaches,* edited by F. Bönker, K. Müller, and A. Pickel. Boulder: Rowman and Littlefield.

Pleines, Heiko. 1998. "Die Regionen der Ukraine." *Osteuropa* 48 (4): 365–72.

Plyais, Iakov. 1993. Soiuzniki, partneri, sosedi: zigzagi vneshnei politiki Rossii. *Nezavisimaia gazeta*, July 16.

——. 1995. *Rossiia i mir na poroge XXI veka: aktual' nye problemy sovremennoi Rossii.* Moscow: Izdatel'stva Moskovskogo gosudarstvennogo universiteta kommertsii.

Posen, Adam. 1993. "Why Central Bank Independence Does Not Cause Low Inflation: There Is No Institutional Fix for Politics." In *Finance and the International Economy*, vol. 7, edited by Richard O'Brian, 40–65. Oxford: Oxford University Press.

——. 1997. "Lessons from the Bundesbank on the Occasion of Its 40th Birthday." In *Auszüge aus Presseartikeln* 58, edited by Deutsche Bundesbank, 10–19. Frankfurt: Deutsche Bundesbank.

——. 2003. "Is Germany Turning Japanese?" Washington, D.C.: IIE. Mimeograph.

Postsovremenni mir: novaya sistema koordinat. 1998. "Forum." *Vostok* 1:5–47.

Pravda, Alex, and Neil Malcolm. 1996. "Conclusion." In *Internal Factors in Russian Foreign Policy*, edited by Neil Malcolm, Alex Pravda, Roy Allison, and Margot Light, 286–309. Oxford: Oxford University Press.

Price, R. 1997. *The Chemical Weapons Taboo.* Ithaca, N.Y.: Cornell University Press.

Prizel, Ilya. 1997. "Ukraine between Proto-Democracy and "Soft" Authoritarianism." In *Democratic Changes and Authoritarian Reactions in Russia, Ukraine, and Moldova*, edited by Karen Dawisha and Bruce Parrott, 330–69. Cambridge: Cambridge University Press.

——. 1998. *National Identity and Foreign Policy: Nationalism and Leadership in Poland, Russia, and Ukraine.* Cambridge: Cambridge University Press.

Pushkov, Aleksei. 1998. "Znat', kuda stuchat'sia." *Mezhdunarodniya zhizn'* 1:20–23.

Putin, Vladimir. 1999. Russia at the Turn of the Millennium. http://www .government.gov.ru/government/minister/article-vvp1.html.

——. 2000. "Rossiya: noviye vostochniye perspektivi." *Nezavisimaya gazeta*, October 1.

Radice, Hugo. 2000. "Responses to Globalisation: A Critique of Progressive Nationalism." *New Political Economy* 5 (1): 5–14.

Raz, Aviad E. 1999. *Riding the Black Ship: Japan and Tokyo Disneyland.* Cambridge: Harvard University Asia Center.

Reich, Robert. 1991. *The Work of Nations.* New York: Alfred Knopf.

Richter, James. 1996. "Russian Foreign Policy and the Politics of National Identity." In *The Sources of Russian Foreign Policy after the Cold War*, edited by Celeste A. Wallander, 69–93. Boulder: Westview.

Ritschl, Albrecht O. 1996. "An Exercise in Futility: East German Economic Growth and Decline, 1945–98." In *Economic Growth in Europe since 1945*, edited by Nicolas Crafts and Gianni Toniolo, 498–540. Cambridge: Cambridge University Press.

Robson, William. 1995. *Change for a Buck? The Canadian Dollar after Quebec Secession*, C. D. Howe Institute Commentary 68. Toronto: C. D. Howe Institute.

Roche, Michel. 1996. "The G-7 and 'Market Reform' in Russia: 'Shock Therapy' against Democracy." In *The Former "State Socialist" World: Views from the Left*, edited by David Mandel, 122–36. London: Black Rose.

Rogov, Sergei. 1998. *Yevrasiyskaya strategiya dlya Rossiyi.* Moscow: Institute SshA i Kanadi.

Rontoyanni, Clelia. 2001. "'In Europe with Russia' or 'In Europe without Russia'?

Belarus and Ukraine Face Globalisation." Paper presented at the ECPR Standing Group on International Relations Conference, University of Kent, U.K.

Rose, Richard. 2001. "How Floating Parties Frustrate Democratic Accountability: A Supply-Side View of Russia's Elections." In *Contemporary Russian Politics,* edited by Archie Brown, 215–23. Oxford: Oxford University Press.

Röpke, Wilhelm. 1961. "Die Laufbahn der Sozialen Marktwirtschaft." In *Wirtschaft, Gesellschaft und Kultur,* edited by Franz Greiß and Fritz Meyer, 3–9. Berlin: Dunker and Humblodt.

Ruggie, John. 1982. "International Regimes, Transactions and Change: Embedded Liberalism in the Postwar Economic Order." *International Organization* 36:379–415.

——. 1998. "What Makes the World Hang Together? Neo-Utilitarianism and the Social Constructivist Challenge." *International Organization* 52:855–85.

Rukh. [1989] 1990. *The Popular Movement for Restructuring Rukh: Program and Charter.* Baltimore: Smoloskyp.

Rupert, Mark. 2000. *Ideologies of Globalization: Contending Visions of a New World Order.* London: Routledge.

Rüstow, Alexander. 1957. "Die geschichtliche Bedeutung der sozialen Marktwirtschaft, in Beckenrath." In *Wirtschaftsfragen der freien Welt,* edited by Erwin von Beckerath, Fritz W. Meyer, and Alfred Müller-Armack, 73–77. Frankfurt a. M.: Knapp.

Rutland, Peter. 1994. "Privatisation in Russia: One Step Forward, Two Steps Back?" *Europe-Asia Studies* 45 (7): 1109–31.

——. 2003. "The Spirit of Capitalism." Review of *The Spirit of Capitalism,* by Liah Greenfeld. *History and Theory* 42 (1): 116–26.

Said, Edward. 1993. *Culture and Imperialism.* New York: Knopf.

Sajudis. 1989. *Obshchaia programma Litovskogo dvizheniia za perestroiku* (Overall program of the Lithuanian movement for perestroika). Vilnius: Mintis.

Sakakibara, Eisuke. 1998. "Reform, Japanese-Style." In *Unlocking the Bureaucrat's Kingdom: Deregulation and the Japanese Economy,* edited by Frank Gibney, 79–88. Washington, D.C.: Brookings Institution.

Sakharov, Andrei D. 1990. *Trevoga i nadezhda.* Moscow: Progress.

Sakwa, Richard, and Mark Webber. 1999. "The Commonwealth of Independent States, 1991–1998: Stagnation and Survival." *Europe-Asia Studies* 51 (3): 379–415.

Samuels, Richard. 2003. *Machiavelli's Children: Leaders and Their Legacies in Italy and Japan.* Ithaca, N.Y.: Cornell University Press.

Samuels, Richard, and Eric Heginbotham. 1998. "Mercantile Realism and Japanese Foreign Policy." *International Security* 22:171–203.

Sandblom, Lisa Oladotter. 2000. *Genetically Modified Organisms (GMOs): A Transatlantic Trade Dispute.* Masters thesis, Monterey Institute of International Studies.

Saunders, John. 1980. "Sharing the Dollar: Who Calls the Tune?" *Montreal Gazette,* April 12.

Schelsky, Helmuth. 1954. "Der Realitätsverlust der modernen Gesellschaft." In *Auf der Suche nach der Wirklichkeit,* 392–414. Stuttgart: Diederichs.

Schlesinger, Hans. 1991. "The Road to European Economic and Monetary Union." *Intereconomics* 26 (4): 151–58.

Schmidt, Helmut. 1997. "Aufgeschoben ist Aufgehoben." *Die Zeit,* June 13.

Schmidt, Manfred G. 1999. "Grundzüge der Sozialpolitik in der DDR." In *Die*

Endzeit der DDR-Wirtschaft, edited by Eberhard Kuhrt et al., 273–319. Opladen: Leske and Budrich.

Schmitt, Carl. 1976. *The Concept of the Political.* New Brunswick, N.J.: Rutgers University Press.

Scholte, Jan Aart. 2000. *Globalization: A Critical Introduction.* Basingstoke: Palgrave.

Schoppa, Leonard. 1997. *Bargaining with Japan: What American Pressure Can and Cannot Do.* New York: Columbia University Press.

Schorlemer, Friedrich. 1998. "Der Fetisch D-Mark." In *Der Kampf um den Euro,* edited by Hans-Ulrich Jörges, 331–36. Hamburg: Hoffman und Campe.

Schröder, Hans-Henning. 1999. "El'tsin and the Oligarchs: The Role of Financial Groups in Russian Politics between 1993 and July 1998." *Europe-Asia Studies* 51 (6): 957–88.

Schroeder, Klaus. 1998. *Der SED-Staat.* Munich: Hanser.

Schumpeter, Joseph A. 1954. *History of Economic Analysis.* New York: Oxford University Press.

———. 1970. *Das Wesen des Geldes.* Göttingen: Vandenhoek.

Schürer, Gerhard, et al. 1989. "Analyse der ökonomischen Lage der DDR mit Schlußfolgerungen." *Deutschland Archiv* 25 (10): 1112–20.

Scott, Sarah. 1991. "Quebec Would Keep Dollar for Role in Central Bank: Landry." *Montreal Gazette,* January 15.

Semmel, B. 1993. *The Liberal Ideal and the Demons of Empire.* Baltimore: Johns Hopkins University Press.

Senn, Alfred Erich. 1995. "Post-Soviet Political Leadership in Lithuania." In *Patterns of Post-Soviet Leadership,* edited by Timothy J. Colton and Robert C. Tucker. Boulder: Westview.

Shakhnazarov, Georgi. 2001. *S vozhdyami i bez nikh.* Moscow: Vagrius.

Shishkov, Yu. V., ed. 1997. *Blizhneie i dal' neie zarubezhie v geoekonomicheskoi strategii Rossii.* Moscow: IMEMO.

Shmelev, Boris. 1998. "Integratsiya na postsovetskom prostranstve: mifi i real' nost'." *Vlast'* 5:74–76.

Shonfield, Andrew. 1965. *Modern Capitalism.* Oxford: Oxford University Press.

Shortt, Adam. 1964. "History of Canadian Metallic Currency." In *Money and Banking in Canada,* edited by E. P. Neufeld. Toronto: McClelland and Stewart.

———. 1986. *History of Canadian Currency and Banking, 1600–1880.* Toronto: Canadian Bankers Association.

Shulman, Stephen. 2000. "Nationalist Sources of International Economic Integration." *International Studies Quarterly* 44 (3): 365–90.

Sikkink, Kathryn. 1991. *Ideas and Institutions: Developmentalism in Brazil and Argentina.* Ithaca, N.Y.: Cornell University Press.

Silverman, Bertram, and Murray Yanowitch. 1997. *New Rich, New Poor, New Russia: Winners and Losers on the Russian Road to Capitalism.* Armonk, N.Y.: M. E. Sharpe.

Simonia, Nodari. 2001. "Economic Interests and Political Power in Post-Soviet Russia." In *Contemporary Russian Politics,* edited by Archie Brown, 269–88. Oxford: Oxford University Press.

Sinn, Hans Werner. 1996. "Der Euro kostet Deutschland bis zu 90 Milliarden DM." *Frankfurter Allgemeine Zeitung,* June 5.

Skidelsky, Robert. 1995. *The Road from Serfdom.* New York: Penguin.

Smith, Eric Owen. 1994. *The German Economy.* London: Routledge.

Smith, Graeme. 2001. "Dump Loonie, Landry Says." *Globe and Mail,* November 27.

Smith, Rosalie. 2003. "Kiwifruit—the Spark Which Became an Industry." *Orchardist*, no. 3.

Sorge, Arndt. 1999. "Organizing Societal Space within Globalization: Bringing Society Back In." Working paper. Cologne: Max-Planck Institute for the Study of Societies.

Spencer, Philip, and Howard Wollman. 1998. "Good and Bad Nationalisms: A Critique of Dualism." *Journal of Political Ideologies* 3 (3): 255–74.

Spero, Joan E., and Jeffrey A. Hart. 1997. *The Politics of International Economic Relations.* 5th ed. New York: St. Martin's.

Spruyt, Hendrik. 1997. "The Prospects for Neo-Imperial and Nonimperial Outcomes in the Former Soviet Space." In *The End of Empire? The Transformation of the USSR in Comparative Perspective,* edited by Karen Dawisha and Bruce Parrott. Armonk, N.Y.: M. E. Sharpe.

Stallings, Barbara, ed. 1995. *Global Change, Regional Response: The New International Context of Development.* Cambridge: Cambridge University Press.

Starbatty, Joachim. 1997. "Soziale Marktwirtschaft als Forschungsgegenstand." In *Soziale Marktwirtschaft als Weichenstellung. Festschrift zum Hundertsten Geburtstag von Ludwig Erhard,* 63–98. Bonn: ST Verlag.

Steele, Jonathan. 1994. *Eternal Russia: Yeltsin, Gorbachev, and the Mirage of Democracy.* Cambridge: Harvard University Press.

Steinmetz, George, ed. 1999. *State/Culture: State-Formation after the Cultural Turn.* Ithaca, N.Y.: Cornell University Press.

Stiglitz, Joseph. 1998. "Central Banking in a Democratic Society." *De Economist* 146 (2): 199–226.

Streeck, Wolfgang. 1992. *Social Institutions and Economic Performance: Studies of Industrial Relations in Advanced Capitalist Economies.* Thousand Oaks, Calif.: Sage.

Streeck, Wolfgang. 1997. "German Capitalism: Does It Exist? Can It Survive?" *New Political Economy* 2 (2): 237–56.

———. 1999. "Competitive Solidarity: Rethinking the 'European Social Model.'" Working Paper 99/8. Cologne: Max-Planck-Institut für Gesellschaftsforschung.

Streeck, Wolfgang, and Colin Crouch. 1997. *Political Economy of Modern Capitalism: Mapping Convergence and Diversity.* London: Sage.

Strekal, Oleg. 1996. "Ukrainische Neutralität: Eine Politik ohne Zukunft?" *Europäische Sicherheit* 5:49–51.

Subtelny, Orest. 1995. "Russocentrism, Regionalism, and the Political Culture of Ukraine." *Political Culture and Civil Society in Russia and the New States of Eurasia,* edited by Vladimir Tismaneanu. Armonk, N.Y.: M. E. Sharpe.

SVR (Sachverständigenrat zur Begutachtung der gesamtwirtschaftlichen Entwicklung). 1990. *Auf dem Wege zur wirtschaftlichen Einheit Deutschlands.* Stuttgart: Metzler and Poeschel.

———. 2003. *Jahresgutachten 2003.* Stuttgart: Metzler & Poeschel

Szeleny, Anna. 1999. "Old Political Rationalities and New Democracies: Compromise and Confrontation in Hungary and Poland." *World Politics* 51:484–519.

Szporluk, Roman. 1988. *Communism and Nationalism: Karl Marx versus Friedrich List.* New York: Oxford University Press.

Tamir, Yael. 1993. *Liberal Nationalism.* Princeton: Princeton University Press.

Tarrow, Sidney. 1994. *Power in Movement.* Cambridge: Cambridge University Press.

Taylor, Peter. 1989. *Political Geography: World-Economy, Nation-State, and Locality.* 2nd ed. London: Longman Group.

Taylor, Phil. 2002. "Who Does Dave Walden Think He Is?" *Sunday Star Times,* September 22, C1–2.

Tett, Gillian. 2003. *Saving the Sun: A Wall Street Gamble to Rescue Japan from Its Trillion-Dollar Meltdown.* New York: HarperBusiness.

Thurow, Lester. 2000. "Globalization: The Product of a Knowledge-Based Economy." *Annals of the American Academy of Political and Social Science,* no. 570:19–31.

Tikhomirov, Vladimir. 2000. *The Political Economy of Post-Soviet Russia.* New York: St. Martin's.

Tilly, Charles. 1998. "Social Movements and (All Sorts of) Other Political Interactions—Local, National, and International—Including Identities." *Theory and Society* 27:453–80.

——. 1999. "Epilogue: Now Where?" In *State/Culture: State-Formation after the Cultural Turn,* edited by George Steinmetz, 407–19. Ithaca, N.Y.: Cornell University Press.

Tolz, Vera. 2001. *Russia: Inventing the Nation.* London: Arnold; New York: Oxford University Press.

Toulin, Alan, and Joel-Denis Bellavance. 2001. "Bank Aims to Cosy Up to Quebec: Crow Hurt Image." *Financial Post,* March 27.

Trittin, Jürgen. 1998. "Gegen DM-Chauvinismus und Deregulierung eine gemeinsame europäische Währung." In *Der Kampf um den Euro,* edited by Hans-Ulrich Jörges, 354–58. Hamburg: Hoffman und Campe.

True, Jacqui. 2003. *Gender, Globalization and Postsocialism: The Czech Republic after Communism.* New York: Columbia University Press.

TsIMO. 1991. *Grazhdanskie dvizheniia v Belorussii: dokumenty i materialy, 1986–1991* (Civic movements in Belorussia: documents and materials, 1986–1991). Moscow: TsIMO.

Tsygankov, Andrei P. 1998. "Hard-Line Eurasianism and Russian Contending Geopolitical Perspectives." *East European Quarterly* 32:315–34.

——. 2001. *Pathways after Empire: National Identity and Foreign Economic Policy in the Post-Soviet World.* Lanham, Md.: Rowman and Littlefield.

——. 2003. "Mastering Space in Eurasia: Russian Geopolitical Thinking after the Soviet Break-Up." *Communist and Post-Communist Studies* 35:101–27.

Urban, Michael, and Vladimir Gel'man. 1997. "The Development of Political Parties in Russia." In *Democratic Changes and Authoritarian Reactions in Russia, Ukraine, Belarus, and Moldova,* edited by Karen Dawisha and Bruce Parrot, 175–219. Cambridge: Cambridge University Press.

U.S. Permanent Mission to the Chairman of the Dispute Settlement Body, World Trade Organization. 2003. "European Communities—Protection of Trademarks and Geographical Indications for Agricultural Products and Foodstuffs: Request for the Establishment of a Panel by the United States." WT/DS174/20. http://www.wto.org/english/tratop_e/dispu_e/dispu_subjects_index_e.htm#bkmk53.

Vancouver Sun. 1977. "Separate Currency Eyed." July 25.

——. 1995. "Ottawa 'Can't Prevent' Use of Canadian Dollar." September 19.

Van Hamm, Peter. 2001. "The Rise of the Brand State: The Postmodern Politics of Image and Reputation." *Foreign Affairs* 80:2–6.

Van Wolferen, Karel. 1989. *The Enigma of Japanese Power.* New York: Knopf.

Van Zon, Hans. 1998. "The Mismanaged Integration of Zaporizhzhya with the World Economy: Implications for Regional Development in Peripheral Regions." *Regional Studies* 32 (7): 607–18.

———. 2000. *The Political Economy of Independent Ukraine.* New York: St. Martin's.

Vartiainen, Juhana. 1999. "The State and Structural Change: What Can Be Learned from the Successful Late Industrializers?" In *The Developmental State,* edited by Meredith Woo-Cumings. Ithaca, N.Y.: Cornell University Press.

Verdery, Katherine. 1996. "Whither 'Nation' and 'Nationalism'?" In *Mapping the Nation,* edited by Gopal Balakrishnan, 226–34. London: Verso.

Vilpisaukas, Romunas. 1997. "Trade between Lithuania and the European Union." In *Lithuania's Integration into the European Union,* edited by Klaudijus Maniokas and Gediminas Vitkus. Vilnius: European Integration Studies Center.

Vlastos, Stephen, ed. 1997. *Mirror of Modernity: Invented Traditions of Modern Japan.* Berkeley and Los Angeles: University of California Press.

Vogel, Steven. 1996. *Freer Markets, More Rules.* Ithaca, N.Y.: Cornell University Press.

———. 1999a. "Can Japan Disengage? Winners and Losers in Japan's Political Economy, and the Ties That Bind Them." *Social Science Japan Journal* 2:3–21.

———. 1999b. "When Interests Are Not Preferences: The Cautionary Tale of Japanese Consumers." *Comparative Politics* 31:187–207.

Wade, Robert. 1990. *Governing the Market.* Princeton, N.J.: Princeton University Press.

———. 1996a. "Globalization and Its Limits: Reports of the Death of the National Economy Are Greatly Exaggerated." In *National Diversity and Global Capitalism,* edited by S. Berger and R. Dore, 60–88. Ithaca, N.Y.: Cornell University Press.

———. 1996b. "Japan, the World Bank, and the Art of Paradigm Management: The East Asian Miracle in Political Perspective." *New Left Review,* no. 217:3–36.

———. 2001. "Economic Growth and the Role of Government: Or How to Stop New Zealand with Falling out of the OECD." Paper presented to the Catching the Knowledge Wave conference, Auckland.

Waever, Ole. 1995. "Identity, Integration, and Security: Solving the Sovereignty Puzzle in EU Studies," *Journal of International Affairs* 48 (2): 389–431.

Walt, Stephen M. 1987. *The Origins of Alliances.* Ithaca, N.Y.: Cornell University Press.

Waltz, Kenneth N. 1979. *Theory of International Politics.* New York: McGraw-Hill.

Weatherbe, Steve. 1997. "Thinking the Unthinkable: Gordon Wilson and Gibson Pondered the Separation of Quebec, and BC." *British Columbia Report* 8 (51): 8.

Webber, Mark. 1997. *CIS Integration Trends: Russia and the Former Soviet South.* London: Royal Institute of International Affairs.

Weiss, Linda. 1998. *The Myth of the Powerless State.* Ithaca, N.Y.: Cornell University Press.

———. 1999. "State Power and the Asian Crisis." *New Political Economy* 4:317–42.

Welteke, Ernst. 2003. "Renaissance der Ordnungspolitik?" In *Auszüge aus Presseartikeln 29,* edited by Deutsche Bundesbank, 3–6. Frankfurt: Deutsche Bundesbank.

Wilson, Andrew. 1997. *Ukrainian Nationalism in the 1990s.* Cambridge: Cambridge University Press.

———. 2000. *The Ukrainians: Unexpected Nation.* New Haven, Conn.: Yale University Press.

Wise, Mike. 2003. "New Zealand Cries Betrayal." With Warren St. John. *New York Times,* January 10.

Wittfogel, Karl August. 1957. *Oriental Despotism.* New Haven, Conn.: Yale University Press.

Wittkowsky, Andreas. 1996. "Politische Eliten der Ukraine im Umbruch: Reformen und die Strukturierung von Interessengruppen." *Osteuropa* 46 (4): 364–80.

——. 1998. "Nationalstaatsbildung in der Ukraine: Die Politische Ökonomie eines 'Historischen Kompromisses.'" *Osteuropa* 48 (6): 576–94.

——. 2001. "Regional, Sectoral, and State Actors in Ukraine: The Struggle against Hard Budget Constraints." In *Explaining Post-Soviet Patchworks: The Political Economy of Regions, Regimes and Republics,* edited by Klaus Segbers, 3:246–64. Aldershot: Ashgate.

Wolczuk, Kataryna. 2001. "History, Europe and the 'National Idea': The 'Official' Narrative of National Identity in Ukraine." *Nationalities Papers* 28 (4): 671–94.

Woo, Jung-en. 1991. *Race to the Swift: State and Finance in Korean Industrialization.* New York: Columbia University Press.

Woo-Cumings, Meredith. 1995. "Developmental Bureaucracy in Comparative Perspective." In *The Japanese Civil Service and Economic Development,* edited by Hyung-Ki Kim, Michio Muramatsu, T. J. Pempel, and Kozo Yamamura. New York: Clarendon.

——. 1999. "Introduction: Chalmers Johnson and the Politics of Nationalism and Development." In *The Developmental State,* edited by Woo-Cumings. Ithaca, N.Y.: Cornell University Press.

Woodruff, David M. 2000. "Rules for Followers: Institutional Theory and the New Politics of Economic Backwardness in Russia." *Politics and Society* 28 (4): 437–82.

Woods, Ngaire. 1995. "Economic Ideas and International Relations: Beyond Rational Neglect." *International Studies Quarterly* 39:161–80.

World Bank. 1992. *Statistical Handbook: States of the Former Soviet Union.* Washington, D.C.: World Bank.

——. 2002. *Transition: The First Ten Years.* Washington, D.C.: World Bank.

Yakunin, Vladimir. 2001. "Zavtra nachinaiyetsia segodnia. Geopoliticheskiye aspekti tranzitnogo potentsiala Rossiyi." *Nezavisimaia gazeta,* June 5.

Yamaguchi, Jirō. 2001. *Nihon seiji: saisei no jōken* (Japan's politics: conditions for recovery). Tokyo: Iwanami Shinsho.

Yashiro, Naohiro. 2000. "Shakaiteki kisei wa naze hitsuyō ka" (Why is social regulation necessary?). In *Shakaiteki kisei no keizai bunseki* (Economic analysis of social regulation), edited by N. Yashiro. Tokyo: Nihon Keizai Shinbunsha.

——, ed., 1999. *Shijō jūshi no kyōiku kaikaku* (Educational reform that emphasizes the market). Tokyo: Nihon Keizai Shinbunsha.

Yee, Albert. 1996. "The Causal Effects of Ideas on Policies." *International Organization* 50:69–108.

Zagorskii, Andrei. 1993. "Rossiia i Evropa: vmeste ili vroz?" In *Rossiia pered Evropeiskim vyzovom,* edited by Andrei Zagorskii and Michael Lukas, 41–74. Moscow: Mezhdunarodnye Otnosheniia—Institut po issledovaniiu problem Vostok-Zapad.

——. 1994. *SNG: Ot dezintegratsiyi k reintegratsiyi?* Moscow: MGIMO.

Zagorskii, Andrei, Anatoli Zlobin, Sergei Solodovnik, and Mark Khrustalev. 1992. *Posle raspada SSSR: Rossiya v novom mire.* Moscow: MGIMO.

Zaprudnik, Jan, and Michael Urban. 1997. "Belarus: From Statehood to Empire?" In *New States, New Politics: Building the Post-Soviet Nations,* edited by Ian Bremmer and Ray Taras. Cambridge: Cambridge University Press.

Zatulin, Konstantin. 2000. "'Vot kto mister Putin,' ili muchtel'noiye rasstavaniye s Yeltsinim i yego epokhoi." *Nezavisimaya gazeta,* September 27.

Zlenko, Anatolii M. 1993. "Vneshniaia politika Ukrainy: printsipy formirovaniia i problemy realizatsii." *Mezhdunarodnaia zhizn'* 12:5–12.

Zweig, Konrad. 1980. *The Origins of the German Market Economy.* London: Adam Smith Institute.

Zysman, John. 1996. "The Myth of a 'Global' Economy: Enduring National Foundations and Emerging Regional Realities." *New Political Economy* 1 (2): 157–85.

Index

Abdelal, Rawi, 72–73, 122, 130, 165, 201, 221–24, 227–28, 231, 233
Accountability, 91
Action Démocratique du Québec, 169
Adamishin, Anatolin, 64n.51
Adenauer, Konrad, 153
Agenda 2010 (Germany), 159
Agreement on Trade-Related Aspects of Intellectual Property Rights (TRIPS), 195, 197–98, 200, 223–24
Agriculture, 183, 189, 191–92, 202–3, 206
sustainable, 190
Aid, 105–8, 144
agencies, 106
military, 106
Air New Zealand, 211
Akayev, Askar, 62n.42
Allen, Paul, 214
Ambartsumov, Yevgenii, 79n.14
America's Cup Yacht Race, 204, 214–15, 217–19
American National Food Processors Association (NFPA), 198–99
Amsden, Alice, 118
Anderson, Benedict, 93
Anderson, Perry, 93
Anticommunism, 92, 105, 110–11, 114
Appel, Hilary, 73–74
Appellation d'origine controlée laws, 198
Argentina, 148n.2, 170, 189, 193, 206, 229
Armenia, 28
Asian financial crisis (1997), 91, 115, 119, 175
Asian values, 92, 112–15
Australia, 207, 212, 214
Austria, 116, 153, 193

Authoritarianism, 112–13
Azerbaijan, 28

Balaam, David, 185
Baltic States, 47. *See also* Estonia; Latvia; Lithuania
Bank of Canada, 167, 169, 172, 175–76, 178
Bank of Montreal, 178
Bank of Quebec, 169n.2
Banque de France, 161
Baran, Paul, 94
Beissinger, Mark, 25
Bélanger-Campeau Commission, 168, 169n.1
Belarus, 14, 22–23, 28–42, 54
Belarusian Popular Front, 34n.23, 35, 40
Benelux countries, 153
Berezovski, Boris, 64, 79n.16
Berlin Wall, 154
Bertarelli, Ernesto, 214, 215n.7
Biotechnology, 189, 205. *See also* Genetically Modified Organisms
Bismarck, 155
Blackheart, 215–18
Bloc Quebecois, 169–70, 175
Blyth, Mark, 229, 231
Bouchard, Lucien, 169–70
Bourassa, Robert, 166–68, 172, 178
Bové, José, 190–91
Brand New Zealand, 203
Brand-state, 205
Branding. *See* Nation: branding
Brazauskas, Algirdas, 36
Brazil, 148n.2, 229
Bretton Woods system, 149, 152

261

Cornell Studies in Political Economy

A series edited by

PETER J. KATZENSTEIN